THOMAS TRAHERNE

POEMS, CENTURIES
AND THREE
THANKSGIVINGS

Oxford University Press, Ely House, London W. 1

GLASGOW   NEW YORK   TORONTO   MELBOURNE   WELLINGTON
CAPE TOWN   SALISBURY   IBADAN   NAIROBI   LUSAKA   ADDIS ABABA
BOMBAY   CALCUTTA   MADRAS   KARACHI   LAHORE   DACCA
KUALA LUMPUR   HONG KONG

THOMAS TRAHERNE

POEMS, CENTURIES
AND THREE
THANKSGIVINGS

EDITED BY
ANNE RIDLER

LONDON
OXFORD UNIVERSITY PRESS
NEW YORK   TORONTO
1966

THOMAS TRAHERNE
Born 1637
Died 1674

The Oxford Standard Authors edition of the Poems, Centuries
and Three Thanksgivings *was first published in 1966*

Introduction and Selection
© *Oxford University Press 1966*

CONTENTS

CONTENTS

ABBREVIATIONS

C   *Centuries of Meditations* (Bodleian MS. Eng. th. e. 50)
D   Dobell Folio (Bodleian MS. Eng. poet. c. 42)
F   *Poems of Felicity* (British Museum MS. Burney 392)
M   H. M. Margoliouth: *Thomas Traherne: Centuries, Poems, and Thanksgivings*, 1958, 2 vols.
T   Thomas Traherne
PT   Philip Traherne
TLS *Times Literary Supplement*
†   Indicates that the word is explained in the Glossary

INTRODUCTION

I. LIFE

When I came into the Country, and being seated among silent Trees, had all my Time in mine own Hands, I resolved to Spend it all, whatever it cost me, in Search of Happiness, and to Satiat that burning Thirst which Nature had Enkindled, in me from my Youth. In which I was so resolut, that I chose rather to live upon 10 pounds a yeer, and to go in Lether Clothes, and feed upon Bread and Water, so that I might hav all my time clearly to my self: then to keep many thousands per Annums in an Estate of Life where my Time would be Devoured in Care and Labor. (*Centuries*, III. 46.)

THESE few lines give the essentials of Traherne's life, provided that we understand what he means by happiness: 'of all our Desires the Strongest is to be Good to others'. But although his writings, especially the third *Century*, tell us much about his character, the sources for his history are meagre. They are set out in the late Dr. Margoliouth's introduction to his edition of Traherne,[1] and the following summary is based upon this and upon the Life by Miss G. I. Wade.[2]

Traherne was born in 1637, the son of a shoemaker who was also called Thomas. His father worked in Hereford, and came originally from the neighbouring village of Lugwardine; he seems to have been poor (C III, 16), and to have died while Thomas and his brother Philip were small. The boys were probably brought up by their uncle Philip Traherne, a well-to-do innkeeper who was twice Mayor of Hereford.

In 1652–3 Traherne came up to Brasenose College, Oxford, in 1656 he took his B.A., and in 1660 he was ordained deacon and priest. Under the Commonwealth he had been appointed to the benefice of Credenhill, a sparsely populated parish some five miles from Hereford, but he did not take up residence there until 1661, when he was again appointed, with different sponsors. In that year he was made M.A. by decree. At Credenhill Traherne was spiritual adviser to a lively and pious lady named Susanna Hopton, *née*

[1] *Centuries, Poems, and Thanksgivings*, edited by H. M. Margoliouth, Clarendon Press, 1958.
[2] *Thomas Traherne, A Critical Biography*, by Gladys I. Wade, Princeton University Press, 1944.

Harvey, living at Kington, fifteen miles away. She had become a Roman Catholic under the Commonwealth, but returned to the Anglican Church after the Restoration.[1] For her, or for her circle, the *Centuries* were written, and it was she who caused the *Thanksgivings* to be published, anonymously, in 1699.[2] Other manuscripts which remained in her possession and were published under her name after her death must in fact be ascribed to Traherne, as Miss Wade has shown.

Traherne left Credenhill in 1669, when he took his B.D. (as did his brother also, a month later) and became chaplain to Sir Orlando Bridgeman, Lord Keeper of the Great Seal. He held this post, living either in London or at Sir Orlando's seat at Teddington, until his death in 1674. Records show that he continued to be nominally Rector of Credenhill until he died, and that he served as 'minister' at Teddington, where he was buried.

We have a contemporary description of him, printed in the Preface to the first edition of his *Thanksgivings*, and possibly written by Susanna Hopton.

He was a man of a cheerful and sprightly Temper, free from any thing of the sourness or formality, by which some great pretenders of Piety rather disparage and misrepresent true Religion, than recommend it; and therefore was very affable and pleasant in his Conversation, ready to do all good Offices to his Friends, and Charitable to the Poor almost beyond his ability.

He was, it seems, so 'wonderfully transported with the Love of God to Mankind', and with the study of Felicity, 'that those that would converse with him, were forced to endure some discourse upon these subjects, whether they had any sense of Religion, or not'.

A newly discovered manuscript of 'Select Meditations' adds an interesting self-criticism by Traherne himself. I quote from an article in the *Times Literary Supplement*[3] by Dr. James M. Osborn, the owner of the manuscript.

Profound Inspection, Reservation and Silence; are my Desires. O that I could attain them: Too much openness and proneness to speak are

---

[1] Wade, op. cit., p. 81.

[2] *A Serious and Pathetical Contemplation of the Mercies of God, in several most Devout and Sublime Thanksgivings for the same.* Published by the Reverend Doctor Hicks, At the request of a Friend of the Authors.

[3] 'A new Traherne MS', 8.10.64.

my Diseas . . . Speaking too much and too Long in the Best Things . . .
Here I am Censured for speaking in the singular number, and saying
I . . . Felicity is a Bird of paradice so strang, that it is Impossible to flie
among men without Loseing some feathers were she not Immortal.

2. WRITINGS

In his lifetime Traherne published only *Roman Forgeries*, a work
which, as Margoliouth says, was very likely offered as 'the seven-
teenth-century equivalent of the modern B.D. thesis'. One other
work, *Christian Ethicks*, he had prepared for publication just before
he died, and it was printed in 1675. This book is more avowedly in-
structive than the *Centuries*, but just as characteristic of its author:
Traherne as ethical teacher shows no narrow preoccupation with
morals, but seeks, as his Preface declares, 'to excite (men's) Desire,
to encourage them to Travel, to comfort them in the Journey, and
so at last to lead them to true Felicity, both here and hereafter'.[1]

Apart from these works, Traherne was so little concerned to leave
his name to posterity that none of his manuscripts is signed, and
this persistent anonymity meant that his writings were either lost,
or given to the world with their authorship wrongly ascribed. We
owe the discovery of his poems and meditations, after more than
200 years of oblivion, to a chance purchase of the manuscripts for
a few pence by W. T. Brooke in 1896, and to the skill and persistence
of Bertram Dobell, who, dissatisfied with A. B. Grosart's ascription
of the poems to Henry Vaughan, ferreted out the identity of Tra-
herne.[2] The full story of his remarkable literary detective-work
is given in Dobell's edition of the poems in modernized spelling,
published in 1903, and another chapter was added when in 1910
Sir Idris Bell published a collection of poems bearing Traherne's
name, which he had discovered in the British Museum while he
was looking for something else.[3] The manuscript had lain there
unnoticed since 1818, when it had been acquired among the

[1] An edition in modernized spelling with an introduction by Margaret Bottrall is pub-
lished by the Faith Press, using Traherne's sub-title, *The Way to Blessedness*.

[2] The first clue was found in the rhymed passages of the *Thanksgivings*, in which Dobell
recognized the author of the manuscript poems. Although the book had no name on the
title-page, the Preface stated that its author had been chaplain to Sir Orlando Bridgeman.
Antony à Wood's *Athenae Oxonienses* identified this chaplain as Thomas Traherne, author
of *Roman Forgeries* and *Christian Ethicks*, and in *Christian Ethicks* are to be found the lines
beginning 'As in a Clock', which also occur, in a slightly different form, in C III. 21.

[3] *Poems of Felicity*, ed. H. I. Bell, Clarendon Press.

Burney MSS. It is in the handwriting of Thomas's brother Philip, who had evidently prepared it for publication, using most, though not all, of the poems in the Dobell MS., and drawing also on another manuscript book, which has not yet been discovered.[1] He evidently intended that there should be a second collection, for this manuscript is inscribed 'Vol I'. Philip made many alterations in the text of his brother's poems, and greatly to their detriment, as Margoliouth has shown.

Two more manuscript books, containing among much other material a few original poems, were acquired by Dobell, and in 1964 the latest chapter has been added to this surprising story, with the discovery of a manuscript in Traherne's handwriting containing 376 meditations, said to be similar to, though not identical with, the ones we already know.[2]

The present edition, with its notes, is based on Margoliouth's two volumes, but the text has been recollated with the manuscripts, and the arrangement of the poems is somewhat different. Margoliouth included both versions of the twenty-two poems which appear in the British Museum manuscript as well as in Dobell, because he wished to show the extent to which Philip had meddled with the text. I have merely printed all the poems from the Dobell manuscript (D), in the author's corrected version except where otherwise stated, followed by those poems from the Museum manuscript (F) which are not found in D. It should thus be easy for the reader to distinguish the poems which we know to be wholly Traherne's, from those which have been altered by his brother, though for a full textual analysis the Margoliouth edition is needed.

Traherne's spelling and punctuation are eccentric, and there are grounds for thinking that his special idiosyncrasy in omitting the final *e* in certain words is due to the influence of his brother. But after some hesitation I decided that more was to be gained than lost by reproducing the original. It does after all bring us into contact with the author himself, and the oddities are not such as to make the work difficult to read. Traherne's use of capitals often gives a particular emphasis to his sentences; moreover, the seventeenth-century spelling should put us on our guard against giving modern meanings to certain words whose sense has changed.

---

[1] The evidence, which is complicated, will be found fully set out in M. For the facts known about Philip, who died in 1723, see H. I. Bell, op. cit., pp. ix et seq.

[2] See Osborn, op. cit.

After the poems from D and F, there follow the verse passages from *Christian Ethicks*, and in an Appendix I have given some prose extracts to show their context.

Next are six poems from *Hexameron*, or *Meditations on the Six Days of Creation*, a book published in 1717 and ascribed to Susanna Hopton. Miss Wade[1] has shown conclusively that the prose is in fact by Traherne, and though the poems, which must be early work, are not at all characteristic of him, there is no ground for excluding them, once the prose is admitted to be his.

The final group of poems comes from two Traherne notebooks acquired by the Bodleian from Bertram Dobell's son, a full account of which will be found in Margoliouth's Introduction. The first (Bodleian MS. Eng. th. e. 51) he called 'The Church's Year Book', as it is a collection of meditations suitable for the chief feasts, some of which are copied from other authors. The three poems are translations.

The second notebook (Lat. misc. f. 45) evidently belonged to Philip, but contains material in Traherne's hand. Some of the poems are signed, contrary to his usual practice, with the initials T. T., and it seemed to me probable that only these could be accepted as his own, apart from the brief translation from Seneca, which he would not have initialled as original work. With the help of Miss Margaret Crum of the Bodleian Library I identified four of the pieces which Margoliouth included in his edition as being by Francis Quarles,[2] and while this book was going through the press Miss Crum found the 'Serious Night-Meditation' (p. 209 in Margoliouth, ii)[3] in a book by William Austin of Lincoln's Inn, *Devotionis Augustiniae Flamma*, posthumously published in 1635. Traherne seems to have written out the lines from memory, to judge by the changes which he made: they form part of a beautiful 118-line Meditation on *Job* xvii. 13. Traherne's own poetry does not, as far as I can judge, owe anything to Austin, but his early couplets show the influence of Quarles, and in the lines beginning

---

[1] Op. cit., pp. 153 et seq.

[2] 'As fragrant Mirrhe', which looks like a complete poem, is in fact made up of two unconnected stanzas from *Sions Sonets*: III. 2, and IX. 1. The two couplets, 'Whate'er I have' and 'Oh how injurious' are also from *Sions Sonets*: III. 1 and VII. 7. The quatrain 'To bee a Monarch' is from *Hadassa, or The History of Queene Esther*, Med. prima, 9-12.

[3] The full heading is 'A Serious and a Curious night-Meditation', and the final three lines, which are presumably the 'Curious' Meditation, are from a different source, not yet identified.

'As in a Clocke' there is a direct echo of Quarles's *Job Militant*, Meditatio Secunda, where we find:

> As in a Clocke, one motion doth conuay
> And carry divers wheels a severall Way:
> Yet all together, by the great wheel's force
> Direct the Hand unto his proper course . . .

The *Centuries* are here printed from the manuscript in the Bodleian Library (Eng. th. e. 50); the principles followed in transcription are set out on p. 165.

The discovery, mentioned above, of a fresh collection of Traherne's 'Meditations' has thrown into the melting-pot all theories about their genesis and composition. The introductory quatrain to the published *Centuries*, offering them to 'the friend of my best friend', has been taken to refer to Susanna Hopton, the 'best friend' being God; and Margoliouth concluded that the meditations would have been written for her when Traherne was no longer able to converse with her—that is, after he had left Credenhill for London. In support of this theory Margoliouth could point to C I. 80, which begins 'My excellent friend' and asks 'Cannot we see and Lov one another at 100 Miles Distance?' Against this one may argue that '100 Miles Distance' could also refer to the distance (roughly) between Oxford and Kington, and could have been written at one of the periods when Traherne was resident there for work on his *Roman Forgeries*.[1] Margoliouth also adduced the retrospective tone of certain autobiographical passages as argument for a late date; but he showed that the *Centuries* could not have been Traherne's last work, cut short by death, as Miss Wade opined, because it has a version of a poem, 'The Approach', which is clearly earlier than that copied out in D.

The newly discovered *Centuries* appear to contain much of the same material, and also to be addressed to a woman (Dr. Osborn quotes 'Know lady of our Happiness in being Redeemed', I. 93). In an Appendix to his book *The Paradise Within*,[2] Dr. Louis Martz discusses the new discovery, and points out that the title 'Select Meditations' implies that there may have been yet another and larger body of meditations, some of which survive in the published *Centuries*. Both he and Dr. Osborn think that the new meditations

---

[1] M. i. 90.
[2] Yale University Press, 1964.

are probably earlier work than those we know. The factual evidence for this seems slight; the stylistic evidence is probably stronger; but if it is so, it disposes of Margoliouth's theory that Traherne omitted the heading in the first of the published *Centuries* because he did not decide so to group his meditations until he had already written a hundred of them. For the new manuscript contains the *Century* heading from the start, that is, No. 82, for unhappily the first forty-three leaves are missing. It ends at No. 468.

Dr. Osborn thinks that both the collections may have been addressed to Susanna Hopton, but on the face of it this seems improbable, as the material is so similar. However, we must wait to be enlightened by the publication of his discovery, and perhaps yet more manuscripts may be found.

Traherne's *Thanksgivings* really have a place with his poems, for their rhythms are closer to poetry than prose, and passages of the English Psalms are woven into the text. Their ecstatic praise of the flesh recalls to me Smart's *Rejoice in the Lamb*, though there is no resemblance in the actual style. I could include only three out of the nine, two of which contain verse in regular metre; the text is that of the 1699 edition.

Traherne is a master of the Affirmative Way, which pursues perfection through delight in the created world. Every emphasis in his writings is on inclusive love, and one has only to read the *Centuries* alongside other religious writings of his time—for instance the *Discourses* of the Cambridge Platonist John Smith, with whom he is sometimes compared—to see how unusual he was in his lack of emphasis on sin. The affirmations of the *Centuries* may seem to diverge from the central theme of mysticism, as expressed by St. John of the Cross, that the soul must free itself from the love of created beings, for Traherne boldly says 'Never was any thing in this World loved too much'.[1] 'But,' he continues, 'many Things hav been loved in a fals Way: and all in too short a Measure.' 'In a fals Way': this should save us from misunderstanding him, for his conception of love is as orthodox as Aquinas's 'Love is simply the willing of good'. All the great passages on Love in the second *Century* elaborate on this: 'We never Enjoy our selvs but when we are the Joy of others . . . thus we see the Seeds of Eternity Sparkling in our Natures.' But Traherne also knows the ecstatic vision of the convert:

[1] C II. 66.

B

he saw his fellow men as Bunyan described them in *Grace Abounding*,[1] shining, 'like people that carried the Broad Seal of Heaven about them'.

The *Centuries* are not easy to read consecutively, because of what Dr. Martz has called their 'massive repetitions'.[2] But there is, as he has shown, a purpose in this method, which seeks to lead us on by repetition of the known to what is unknown; and he has traced its ancestry to the *Confessions* and *De Trinitate* of St. Augustine, and has shown moreover that the plan of the *Centuries* does conform in some part to the pattern of the mystical treatise, as exemplified in the work of St. Bonaventura.

Traherne wrote prose with an instinctive rhythmical sense which he lacked as a poet. Few of his poems reach a complete formal perfection; and the fact that he never repeated a stanza–pattern meant that he never became entirely at ease with any. Yet he has an honourable place in the line of poets, from Dante to Edwin Muir, who have held and renewed the vision of childhood; and his special gift, in verse as well as in prose, is to illuminate the abstract by the sensuous image.

> My Soul doth there long Thoughts extend;
>   No End
> Doth find, or Being comprehend:
>   Yet somwhat sees that is
>   The obscure shady Face
>   Of endless Space . . .

[1] Para. 74.
[2] See op. cit., pp. 44 et seq.

PRINTED IN GREAT BRITAIN
AT THE UNIVERSITY PRESS, OXFORD
BY VIVIAN RIDLER
PRINTER TO THE UNIVERSITY

THE POEMS

With poems from D, the principle followed has been to use T's own corrected version in most places, and to give it in the footnotes when not used. His deleted versions are not noted, except where necessary to explain a difference between M's text and mine. For a full list of variants, M's edition must be consulted.

With poems from F, the version first written down by Philip can generally be presumed to be Traherne's; the notes record the few places where this version has not been used.

The Author to the Critical Peruser [1]

The naked Truth in many faces shewn,
Whose inward Beauties very few hav known,
A Simple Light, transparent Words, a Strain
That lowly creeps, yet maketh Mountains plain,
Brings down the highest Mysteries to sense   5
And keeps them there; that is Our Excellence:
At that we aim; to th' end thy Soul might see
With open Eys thy Great *Felicity*,
Its Objects view, and trace the glorious Way
Wherby thou may'st thy Highest Bliss enjoy.   10

No curling Metaphors that gild the Sence,
Nor Pictures here, nor painted Eloquence;
No florid Streams of Superficial Gems,
But real Crowns and Thrones and Diadems!
That Gold on Gold should hiding shining ly   15
May well be reckon'd baser Heraldry.

An easy Stile drawn from a native vein,
A clearer Stream than that which Poets feign,
Whose bottom may, how deep so'ere, be seen,
Is that which I think fit to win Esteem: 20
Els we could speak *Zamzummim* words, and tell
A Tale in tongues that sound like *Babel-Hell*;
In Meteors speak, in blazing Prodigies,
Things that amaze, but will not make us wise.

On Shining Banks we could nigh *Tagus* walk;   25
In flow'ry Meads of rich *Pactolus* talk;
Bring in the *Druids*, and the *Sybills* view;
See what the Rites are which the *Indians* do;
Derive† along the channel of our Quill
The Streams that flow from high *Parnassus* hill;   30
Ransack all Nature's Rooms, and add the things
Which *Persian* Courts enrich; to make Us Kings:

[1] This poem is found only in PT's MS. M thinks that the title may be his.
21. *Zamzummim*: a race of giants, cf. Deut. 2²⁰.

To make us Kings indeed! Not verbal Ones,
But reall Kings, exalted unto Thrones;
35   And more than Golden Thrones! 'Tis this I do,
Letting Poëtick Strains and Shadows go.

    I cannot imitat their vulgar Sence
Who Cloaths admire, not the Man they fence
Against the Cold; and while they wonder at
40   His Rings, his precious Stones, his Gold and Plate;
The middle piece, his Body and his Mind,
They over-look; no Beauty in them find:
God's Works they slight, their *own* they magnify,
His they contemn, or careless pass them by;

45   Their woven Silks and wel-made Suits they prize,
Valu their Gems, but not their useful Eys:
Their precious Hands, their Tongues and Lips divine,
Their polisht Flesh where whitest Lillies join
With blushing Roses and with saphire Veins,
50   The Bones, the Joints, and that which els remains
Within that curious Fabrick, *Life* and Strength,
I'th' wel-cómpacted bredth and depth and length
Of various Limbs, that living Engins be
Of glorious worth; God's Work they will not see:
55   Nor yet the *Soul*, in whose concealed Face,
Which comprehendeth all unbounded Space,
GOD may be seen; tho she can understand
The Length of Ages and the Tracts of Land
That from the *Zodiac* do extended ly
60   Unto the *Poles*, and view *Eternity*.

Ev'n thus do idle Fancies, Toys, and Words,
(Like gilded Scabbards hiding rusty Swords)
Take vulgar Souls; who gaze on rich Attire
But God's diviner Works do ne'r admire.

                                                   T. T.

46–48. As first written in MS, except that *join* is M's conjecture. It would have been a true rhyme with *Divine*.

65. Philip imitated Thomas's own signature-initials, and added four further lines, signed with his own initials.

The Salutation

1

These little Limmes,
These Eys and Hands which here I find,
These rosie Cheeks wherwith my Life begins,
  Where have ye been,? Behind
What Curtain were ye from me hid so long!
Where was? in what Abyss, my Speaking Tongue?

2

When silent I,
So many thousand thousand yeers,
Beneath the Dust did in a Chaos lie,
  How could I Smiles or Tears,
Or Lips or Hands or Eys or Ears perceiv?
Welcom ye Treasures which I now receiv.

3

I that so long
Was Nothing from Eternitie,
Did little think such Joys as Ear or Tongue,
  To Celebrat or See:
Such Sounds to hear, such Hands to feel, such Feet,
Beneath the Skies, on such a Ground to meet.

4

New Burnisht Joys!
Which yellow Gold and Pearl excell!
Such Sacred Treasures are the Lims in Boys,
  In which a Soul doth Dwell;
Their Organized Joynts, and Azure Veins
More Wealth include, then all the World contains.

5

From Dust I rise,
And out of Nothing now awake,
These Brighter Regions which salute mine Eys,
A Gift from GOD I take.
The Earth, the Seas, the Light, the Day, the Skies,
The Sun and Stars are mine; if those I prize.

6

Long time before
I in my Mothers Womb was born,
A GOD preparing did this Glorious Store,
The World for me adorne.
Into this Eden so Divine and fair,
So Wide and Bright, I com his Son and Heir.

7

A Stranger here
Strange Things doth meet, Strange Glories See;
Strange Treasures lodg'd in this fair World appear,
Strange all, and New to me.
But that they mine should be, who nothing was,
That Strangest is of all, yet brought to pass.

Wonder

I

How like an Angel came I down!
How Bright are all Things here!
When first among his Works I did appear
O how their GLORY me did Crown?
The World resembled his *Eternitie*,
In which my Soul did Walk;
And evry Thing that I did see,
Did with me talk.

2

The Skies in their Magnificence,
    The Lively, Lovely Air;   10
Oh how Divine, how soft, how Sweet, how fair!
    The Stars did entertain my Sence,
And all the Works of GOD so Bright and pure,
        So Rich and Great did seem,
        As if they ever must endure,   15
            In my Esteem.

3

    A Native Health and Innocence
        Within my Bones did grow,
And while my GOD did all his Glories shew,
    I felt a Vigour in my Sence   20
That was all SPIRIT. I within did flow
        With Seas of Life, like Wine;
    I nothing in the World did know,
        But 'twas Divine.

4

    Harsh ragged Objects were conceald,   25
        Oppressions Tears and Cries,
Sins, Griefs, Complaints, Dissentions, Weeping Eys,
    Were hid: and only Things reveald,
Which Heav'nly Spirits, and the Angels prize.
        The State of Innocence   30
    And Bliss, not Trades and Poverties,
        Did fill my Sence.

5

    The Streets were pavd with Golden Stones,
        The Boys and Girles were mine,
Oh how did all their Lovly faces shine!   35
    The Sons of Men were Holy Ones.
Joy, Beauty, Welfare did appear to me,
        And evry Thing which here I found,
    While like an Angel I did see,
            Adornd the Ground.   40

6

Rich Diamond and Pearl and Gold
In evry Place was seen;
Rare Splendors, Yellow, Blew, Red, White and Green,
Mine Eys did evrywhere behold,
45   Great Wonders clothd with Glory did appear,
Amazement was my Bliss.
That and my Wealth was evry where:
No Joy to this!

7

Cursd and Devisd Proprieties,†
50   With Envy, Avarice
And Fraud, those Feinds that Spoyl even Paradice,
Fled from the Splendor of mine Eys.
And so did Hedges, Ditches, Limits, Bounds,
I dreamd not ought of those,
55   But wanderd over all mens Grounds,
And found Repose.

8

Proprieties themselvs were mine,
And Hedges Ornaments;
Walls, Boxes, Coffers, and their rich Contents
60   Did not Divide my Joys, but shine.
Clothes, Ribbans, Jewels, Laces, I esteemd
My Joys by others worn;
For me they all to wear them seemd
When I was born.

Eden

I

A learned and a Happy Ignorance
Divided me,
From all the Vanitie,
From all the Sloth Care Pain and Sorrow that advance,
5   The madness and the Miserie
Of Men. No Error, no Distraction I
Saw soil the Earth, or overcloud the Skie.

2

. I knew not that there was a Serpents Sting, *I*
     Whose Poyson shed *2*
     On Men, did overspread *2*   10
The World: nor did I Dream of such a Thing *4*
     As Sin; in which Mankind lay Dead. *2*
They all were Brisk and Living Wights to me, *3*
Yea Pure, and full of Immortalitie. *3*

3

Joy, Pleasure, Beauty, Kindness, Glory, Lov,   15
     Sleep, Day, Life, Light,
     Peace, Melody, my Sight,
My Ears and Heart did fill, and freely mov.
     All that I saw did me Delight.
The *Universe* was then a World of Treasure,   20
To me an Universal World of Pleasure.

4

Unwelcom Penitence was then unknown,
     Vain Costly Toys,
     Swearing and Roaring Boys,
Shops, Markets, Taverns, Coaches were unshewn;   25
     So all things were that Drownd my Joys.
No Briers choakt up my Path, nor hid the face
Of Bliss and Beauty, nor Ecclypst the Place.

5

Only what Adam in his first Estate,
     Did I behold;   30
     Hard Silver and Drie Gold
As yet lay under Ground; my Blessed Fate
     Was more acquainted with the Old
And Innocent Delights, which he did see
In his Original Simplicitie.   35

13. *Wights*, spelt 'Weights' in MS.
27. *Briers*, corr. to 'Thorns'.

6

Those Things which first his Eden did adorn,
My Infancy
Did crown. Simplicitie
Was my Protection when I first was born.
40   Mine Eys those Treasures first did see,
Which God first made. The first Effects of Lov
My first Enjoyments upon Earth did prov;

7

And were so Great, and so Divine, so Pure,
So fair and Sweet,
45   So True; when I did meet
Them here at first, they did my Soul allure,
And drew away my Infant feet
Quite from the Works of Men; that I might see
The Glorious Wonders of the DEITIE.

Innocence

1

But that which most I Wonder at, which most
I did esteem my Bliss, which most I Boast,
And ever shall Enjoy, is that within
I felt no Stain, nor Spot of Sin.

5   No Darkness then did overshade,
But all within was Pure and Bright,
No Guilt did Crush, nor fear invade
But all my Soul was full of Light.

A Joyfull Sence and Puritie
10   Is all I can remember.
The very Night to me was Bright,
Twas Summer in December.

2

A Serious Meditation did employ
My Soul within, which taken up with Joy
15   Did seem no Outward thing to note, but flie
All Objects that do feed the Eye.

While it those very Objects did   *
Admire, and prize, and prais, and love, 2
Which in their Glory most are hid, 1
Which Presence only doth remove. 2   20

Their Constant Daily Presence I *
    Rejoycing at, did see;   2
And that which takes them from the Ey *
Of others, offerd them to me. 2

3

No inward Inclination did I feel   *   25
To Avarice or Pride: My Soul did kneel *
In Admiration all the Day. No Lust, nor Strife, 2
    Polluted then my Infant Life.   2

No Fraud nor Anger in me movd *
No Malice Jealousie or Spite; 2   30
All that I saw I truly lovd. *
Contentment only and Delight 2

Were in my Soul. O Heav'n! what Bliss *
    Did I enjoy and feel! 2
What Powerfull Delight did this *   35
Inspire! for this I daily Kneel. 2

4

Whether it be that Nature is so pure, *
And Custom only vicious; or that sure *
God did by Miracle the Guilt remov, 2
    And make my Soul to feel his Lov, 2   40

So Early: Or that 'twas one Day, *
Wher in this Happiness I found; 2
Whose Strength and Brightness so do Ray, *
That still it seemeth to Surround. 2

What ere it is, it is a Light   *   45
    So Endless unto me 2
That I a World of true Delight *
Did then and to this Day do see. 2

5

That Prospect was the Gate of Heav'n, that Day
50   The anchient Light of Eden did convey
Into my Soul: I was an Adam there,
    A little Adam in a Sphere

Of Joys! O there my Ravisht Sence
Was entertaind in Paradice,
55   And had a Sight of Innocence.
All was beyond all Bound and Price.

An Antepast† of Heaven sure!
    I on the Earth did reign.
Within, without me, all was pure.
60   I must becom a Child again.

The Preparative

I

My Body being Dead, my Lims unknown;
    Before I skild to prize
    Those living Stars mine Eys,
Before my Tongue or Cheeks were to me shewn,
    Before I knew my Hands were mine,
Or that my Sinews did my Members joyn,
    When neither Nostril, Foot, nor Ear,
As yet was seen, or felt, or did appear;
    I was within
10   A House I knew not, newly clothd with Skin.

2

Then was my Soul my only All to me,
    A Living Endless Ey,
    Far wider then the Skie
Whose Power, whose Act, whose Essence was to see.
15   I was an Inward *Sphere of Light*,
Or an Interminable Orb of *Sight*,

13. *Far wider then*, corr. to 'Just bounded with', but cf. *Thoughts*, III. 43.

An Endless and a Living Day, *4*
A *vital Sun* that round about did *ray 4*
     All Life and Sence,
A Naked Simple Pure *Intelligence.*   20

       3
I then no Thirst nor Hunger did conceiv, *take into on for min / the mind*
     No dull Necessity,
     No Want was Known to me;
Without Disturbance then I did receiv
     The fair Ideas of all Things,   25
And had the Hony even without the Stings.
     A Meditating Inward Ey
Gazing at Quiet did within me lie,
       And evry Thing
Delighted me that was their Heavnly King.   30

       4
For *Sight* inherits Beauty, *Hearing* Sounds,
     The *Nostril* Sweet Perfumes,
     All *Tastes* have hidden Rooms
Within the *Tongue*; and *Feeling Feeling* Wounds
     With Pleasure and Delight, but I   35
Forgot the rest, and was all Sight, or Ey.
     Unbodied and Devoid of Care,
Just as in Heavn the Holy Angels are.
       For Simple Sence
Is Lord of all Created Excellence.   40

       5
Be'ing thus prepard for all Felicity,
     Not prepossest with Dross,
     Nor stifly glued to gross
And dull Materials that might ruine me,
     Not fetterd by an Iron Fate   45
With vain Affections in my Earthy State
     To any thing that might Seduce
My Sence, or els bereave it of its use
       I was as free
As if there were nor Sin, nor Miserie.   50

     48. *els bereave it of,* corr. from 'misemploy it from'.

6

Pure Empty Powers that did nothing loath,
    Did like the fairest Glass,
    Or Spotless polisht Brass,
Themselvs soon in their Objects Image cloath.
55   Divine Impressions when they came,
Did quickly enter and my Soul inflame.
    Tis not the Object, but the Light
That maketh Heaven; Tis a Purer Sight.
      Felicitie
60 Appears to none but them that purely see.

7

A Disentangled and a Naked Sence
    A Mind thats unpossest,
    A Disengaged Brest,
An Empty and a Quick Intelligence
65   Acquainted with the Golden Mean,
An Even Spirit Pure and Serene,
    Is that where Beauty, Excellence,
And Pleasure keep their Court of Residence.
      My Soul retire,
70 Get free, and so thou shalt even all Admire.

The Instruction

1

Spue out thy filth, thy flesh abjure;
Let not Contingents† thee defile.
For Transients only are impure,
And Aery things thy soul beguil.

2

5 Unfelt, unseen let those things be
Which to thy Spirit were unknown,
When to thy Blessed Infancy
The World, thy Self, thy God was shewn.

3. *only are*: i.e. 'are merely'.   4. *thy soul*, corr. from 'alone'.

3

All that is Great and Stable stood
Before thy Purer Eys at first: 10
All that in Visibles is Good
Or pure, or fair, or unaccurst.

4

Whatever els thou now dost see
In Custom, Action, or Desire,
Tis but a Part of Miserie   15
In which all Men on Earth conspire.

The Vision

1

Flight is but the Preparative: The Sight
    Is Deep and Infinit;
Ah me! tis all the Glory, Love, Light, Space,
    Joy Beauty and Varietie
That doth adorn the Godheads Dwelling Place   5
    Tis all that Ey can see.
Even Trades them selvs seen in Celestial Light,
    And Cares and Sins and Woes are Bright.

2

Order the Beauty even of Beauty is,
    It is the Rule of Bliss,   10
The very Life and Form and Caus of Pleasure;
    Which if we do not understand,
Ten thousand Heaps of vain confused Treasure
    Will but oppress the Land.
In Blessedness it self we that shall miss   15
    Being Blind which is the Caus of Bliss.

3

For then behold the World as thine, and well
    Upon the Object Dwell.

The Instruction: 16. *on Earth*, corr. to 'at once'.
The Vision: 18. corr. to 'Note that where thou dost Dwell'.

See all the Beauty of the Spacious Case,†
　　Lift up thy pleasd and ravisht Eys,
Admire the Glory of the Heavnly place,
　　And all its Blessings prize.
That Sight well seen thy Spirit shall prepare,
The first makes all the other Rare.

4

Mens Woes shall be but foyls unto thy Bliss,
　　Thou once Enjoying this:
Trades shall adorn and Beautify the Earth,
　　Their Ignorance shall make thee Bright,
Were not their Griefs Democritus his Mirth?
　　Their Faults shall keep thee right.
All shall be thine, becaus they all Conspire,
　　To feed and make thy Glory higher.

5

To see a Glorious Fountain† and an End
　　To see all Creatures tend
To thy Advancement, and so sweetly close
　　In thy Repose: To see them shine
In Use in Worth in Service, and even Foes
　　Among the rest made thine.
To see all these unite at once in Thee
　　Is to behold Felicitie.

6

To see the *Fountain* is a Blessed Thing.
　　It is to see the King
Of Glory face to face: But yet the End,
　　The Glorious Wondrous End is more;
And yet the fountain there we Comprehend,
　　The Spring we there adore.
For in the End the Fountain best is Shewn,
As by Effects the Caus is Known.

29. *Democritus*, known as 'the laughing philosopher' because of his cheerfulness in adversity, *ca.* 640 B.C.

7

From One, to One, in one to see *All Things*
    To see the King of Kings   50
At once in two; to see his Endless Treasures
    Made all mine own, my self the End
Of all his Labors! Tis the Life of Pleasures!
    To see my self His friend!
Who all things finds conjoynd in Him alone,   55
    Sees and Enjoys the Holy one.

The Rapture

1

    Sweet Infancy!
O fire of Heaven! O Sacred Light!
    How Fair and Bright!
    How Great am I,
Whom all the World doth magnifie!   5

2

    O Heavenly Joy!
O Great and Sacred Blessedness,
    Which I possess!
    So great a Joy
Who did into my Armes convey!   10

3

    From GOD abov
Being sent, the Heavens me enflame,
    To prais his Name.
    The Stars do move!
The Burning Sun doth shew his Love.   15

4

    O how Divine
Am I! To all this Sacred Wealth,
    This Life and Health,
    Who raisd? Who mine
Did make the same? What Hand Divine!   20

The Vision: 55. *Him*: i.e. himself (the capital H is misleading).
The Rapture: 14. i.e. 'move me to praise'.

The Improvment

1

Tis more to recollect,† then make. The one
Is but an Accident without the other.
We cannot think the World to be the Throne,
Of God, unless his *Wisdom* shine as Brother
    Unto his *Power*, in the Fabrick, so
    That we the one may in the other know.

2

His *Goodness* also must in both appear,
And all the *Children* of his *Lov* be found,
In the Creation of the *Starry* Sphere,
And in the Forming of the *fruitfull* Ground;
    Before we can that *Happiness* descrie,
    Which is the Daughter of the *DEITIE*.

3

His *Wisdom* Shines in Spreading forth the Skie,
His *Power's* Great in Ordering the Sun,
His *Goodness* very Marvellous and High
Appears, in evry Work his Hand hath done.
    And all his Works in their varietie,
    Even scattered abroad *delight* the Eye.

4

But neither Goodness, Wisdom, Power, nor Love,
Nor Happiness it self in things could be,
Did not they all *in one fair Order* move,
And joyntly by their Service End in *me*.
    Had he not made an *Ey* to be the Sphere
    Of all Things, none of these would e're appear.

5

His Wisdom, Goodness, Power, as they unite
All things in one, that they may be the *Treasures*
Of one *Enjoy'r*, shine in the utmost Height
They can attain; and are most Glorious *Pleasures*,
    When all the Univers conjoynd in one,
    Exalts a Creature, as if that alone.

6

To bring the Moisture of far distant Seas
Into a *point*, to make them present here,
In *virtu*, not in *Bulk*; one man to pleas
With all the *Powers* of the Highest Sphere,
 From East, from West, from North and South, to bring 35
 The pleasing *Influence* of evry thing;

7

Is far more *Great* then to Creat them there
Where now they stand; His *Wisdom* more doth shine
In that, his *Might* and *Goodness* more appear,
In recollecting; He is more *Divine*   40
 In making evry Thing a Gift to one
 Then in the Parts of all his Spacious *Throne*.

8

Herein we see *a Marvellous Designe*,
And apprehending Clearly the *Great Skill*
Of that Great *Architect*, whose Lov doth shine   45
In all his Works, we find his *Life* and *Will*.
 For *lively Counsels* do the *Godhead* shew,
 And these his *Lov and Goodness* make us know.

9

By *Wise Contrivance* he doth all things *guid*,
And so dispose them, that while they unite,   50
For Man he Endless Pleasures doth *Provide*,
And shews that *Happiness* is his *Delight*,
 His Creatures Happiness as well as His:
 For that in Truth he seeks, and thats *his Bliss*.

10

O Rapture! Wonder! Extasie! Delight!   55
How Great must then his *Glory* be, how Great
Our *Blessedness*! How vast and Infinit
Our *Pleasure*, how Transcendent, how compleat,
 If we the *Goodness* of our God possess,
 And all *His Joy* be in *our Blessedness*!   60

POEMS

11

Almighty Power when it is employd
For one, that he with *Glory* might be Crownd;
Eternal Wisdom when it is Enjoyd
By one, whom all its Pleasures do surround,
    Produce a Creature, that must, all his Days,
    Return the Sacrifice of *Endless Prais*.

12

But Oh! the vigor of mine Infant Sence
Drives me too far: I had not yet the Eye
The Apprehension, or Intelligence
Of Things so very Great Divine and High.
    But all things were *Eternal* unto me,
    And *mine*, and *Pleasing* which mine Ey did see.

13

That was enough at first: Eternitie,
Infinity, and Lov were Silent Joys;
Power, Wisdom, Goodness and Felicitie;
All these which now our Care and Sin destroys,
    By Instinct *virtualy*† were well discernd,
    And by their *Representatives* were learnd.

14

As Spunges gather Moisture from the Earth
(Which seemeth Drie,) in which they buried are;
As Air infecteth Salt; so at my Birth
All these were unperceivd, yet did appear:
    Not by Reflexion, and Distinctly known,
    But, by their Efficacy, all mine own.

The Approach[1]

1

That Childish Thoughts such Joys inspire,
Doth make my Wonder and his Glory Higher;
    His Bounty, and my Wealth more Great,
It shews his Kingdom and his Work Compleat:
        In which there is not any Thing   5
Not meet to be the Joy of Cherubim.

2

He in our Childhood with us walks,
And with our Thoughts Mysteriously he talks;
    He often visiteth our Minds,
But cold Acceptance in us ever finds: 10
        We send him often grievd away;
Els would he shew us all his Kingdoms Joy.

3

O Lord I wonder at thy Love,
Which did my Infancy so Early move:
    But more at that which did forbear,   15
And move so long, tho Sleighted many a yeer:
        But most of all, at last that Thou
Thyself shouldst me convert I scarce know how.

4

Thy Gracious Motions oft in vain
Assaulted me: My Heart did Hard remain   20
    Long time: I sent my God away,
Grievd much that he could not impart his Joy.
        I careless was, nor did regard
The End for which he all these Thoughts prepard.

5

But now with New and Open Eys,   25
I see beneath as if above the Skies;

[1] i.e. God's approach. This poem is also found not only in F but in C III. 4. M argues conclusively that the D version is later than that of the *Centuries*, which cannot therefore have been T's last work.

And as I Backward look again,
See all his Thoughts and mine most Clear and Plain.
    He did Approach, he me did Woo
30 I wonder that my God this thing would doe.

6

From Nothing taken first I was,
What Wondrous Things his Glory brought to pass!
    Now in this World I him behold,
And me enveloped in more then Gold;
35   In deep Abysses of Delights,
In present Hidden Precious Benefits.

7

Those Thoughts his Goodness long before
Prepard as Precious and Celestial Store,
    With curious Art in me inlaid,
40 That Childhood might it self alone be said,
    My Tutor, Teacher, Guid to be,
Instructed then even by the Deitie.

Dumnesse

Sure Man was born to Meditat on Things,
And to Contemplat the Eternal Springs
Of God and Nature, Glory, Bliss and Pleasure;
That Life and Love might be his Heavnly Treasure:
5   And therfore Speechless made at first, that he
Might in himself profoundly Busied be:
And not vent out, before he hath t'ane in
Those Antidots that guard his Soul from Sin.
    Wise Nature made him Deaf too, that he might
10 Not be disturbd, while he doth take Delight
In inward Things, nor be depravd with Tongues,
Nor Injurd by the Errors and the Wrongs
That *Mortal Words* convey. For Sin and Death
Are most infused by accursed Breath,
15 That flowing from Corrupted Intrails, bear
Those hidden Plagues that Souls alone may fear.

   This, my Dear friends, this was my Blessed Case;
For nothing spoke to me but the fair Face
Of Heav'n and Earth, before my self could speak,
I *then my Bliss did, when my Silence, break.*   20
My Non-Intelligence of Human Words
Ten thousand Pleasures unto me affords;
For while I knew not what they to me said,
Before their Souls were into mine conveyd,
Before that Living Vehicle of Wind   25
Could breath into me their infected Mind
Before my Thoughts were levend with theirs, before
There any Mixture was; the Holy Door,
Or Gate of Souls was closd, and mine being One
With in it self to me alone was Known.   30
Then did I dwell within a World of Light,
Distinct and Seperat from all Mens Sight,
Where I did feel strange Thoughts, and Secrets see
That were, or seemd, only reveald to Me,
There I saw all the World Enjoyd by one;   35
There I was in the World my Self alone;
No Business Serious seemd but one; No Work
But one was found; and that did in me lurk.
   D'ye ask me What? It was with Cleerer Eys
To see all Creatures full of Deities;   40
Especialy Ones self: And to Admire
The Satisfaction of all True Desire:
Twas to be Pleasd with all that God hath done;
Twas to Enjoy *even All* beneath the Sun:
Twas with a Steddy and immediat Sence   45
To feel and measure all the Excellence
Of Things: Twas to inherit Endless Treasure,
And to be fild with Everlasting Pleasure:
To reign in Silence, and to Sing alone
To see, love, Covet, hav, Enjoy and Prais, in one: 50
To Prize and to be ravishd: to be true,
Sincere and Single in a Blessed View
Of all his Gifts. Thus was I pent within
A Fort, Impregnable to any Sin:

33. *Secrets*, corr. to 'such Things'.

55 Till the Avenues being Open laid,
Whole Legions Enterd, and the Forts Betrayd.
Before which time a Pulpit in my Mind,
A Temple, and a Teacher I did find,
With a large Text to comment on. No Ear,
60 But Eys them selvs were all the Hearers there.
And evry Stone, and Evry Star a Tongue,
And evry Gale of Wind a Curious Song.
The Heavens were an Orakle, and spake
Divinity: The Earth did undertake
65 The office of a Priest; And I being Dum
(Nothing besides was dum;) All things did com
With Voices and Instructions; but when I
Had gaind a Tongue, their Power began to die.
Mine Ears let other Noises in, not theirs;
70 A Nois Disturbing all my Songs and Prayers.
My foes puld down the Temple to the Ground,
They my Adoring Soul did deeply Wound,
And casting that into a Swoon, destroyd
The Oracle, and all I there enjoyd.
75 And having once inspird me with a Sence
Of forrein Vanities, they march out thence
In Troops that Cover and despoyl my Coasts,
Being the Invisible, most Hurtfull Hosts.
        Yet the first Words mine Infancy did hear,
80 The Things which in my Dumness did appear,
Preventing† all the rest, got such a root
Within my Heart, and stick so close unto't
It may be Trampld on, but still will grow;
And Nutriment to *Soyl* it self will owe.
85 *The first Impressions are Immortal all*:
And let mine Enemies hoop, Cry, roar, Call,
Yet these will whisper if I will but hear,
And penetrat the Heart, if not the Ear.

Silence

A quiet Silent Person may possess
All that is Great or High in Blessedness.
The Inward Work is the Supreme: for all
The other were occasiond by the Fall.
A man, that seemeth Idle to the view   5
Of others, may the Greatest Business do.
Those Acts which Adam in his Innocence
Performed, carry all the Excellence.
These outward Busy Acts he knew not, were
But meaner Matters, of a lower Sphere.   10
Building of Churches, giving to the Poor,
In Dust and Ashes lying on the floor,
Administring of Justice, Preaching Peace,
Ploughing and Toyling for a forc't Increas,
With visiting the Sick, or Governing   15
The rude and Ignorant: This was a thing
As then unknown. For neither Ignorance
Nor Poverty, nor Sickness did advance
Their Banner in the World, till Sin came in:
These therfore were occasiond all by Sin.   20
The first and only Work he had to do,
Was in himself to feel his Bliss, to view
His Sacred Treasures, to admire, rejoyce
Sing Praises with a Sweet and Heavnly voice,
See, Prize, Give Thanks within, and Love   25
Which is the High and only Work, above
Them all. And this at first was mine; These were
My Exercises of the Highest Sphere.
To see, Approve, take Pleasure, and rejoyce,
Within, is better than an Empty Voice: 30
No Melody in Words can Equal that;
The Sweetest Organ, Lute, or Harp is flat,
And Dull, compard thereto. And O that Still
I might Admire my Fathers Lov and Skill!
This is to Honor, Worship and Adore,   35
This is to lov Him: nay it is far more.

10. corr. from 'Things of a second or a lower Sphere'.

It is to Enjoy Him, and to Imitate
The Life and Glory of his High Estate.
Tis to receiv with Holy Reverence,
To understand his Gifts, and with a Sence
Of Pure Devotion, and Humilitie,
To prize his Works, his Lov to Magnify.
O happy Ignorance of other Things,
Which made me present with the King of kings!
And like Him too! All Spirit, Life and Power,
All Lov and Joy, in his Eternal Bower.
A World of Innocence as then was mine,
In which the Joys of Paradice did shine
And while I was not here I was in Heaven,
Not resting one, but evry Day in Seven.
For ever Minding with a lively Sence,
The Univers in all its Excellence.
No other Thoughts did intervene, to Cloy,
Divert, extinguish, or Ecclyps my Joy.
No other Customs, New-found Wants, or Dreams
Invented here polluted my pure Streams.
No Aloes or Dregs, no Wormwood Star
Was seen to fall into the Sea from far.
No rotten Soul, did like an Apple, near
My Soul approach. There's no Contagion here.
An unperceived Donor gave all Pleasures,
There nothing was but I, and all my Treasures.
In that fair World one only was the Friend,
One Golden Stream, one Spring, one only End.
There only one did Sacrifice and Sing
To only one Eternal Heavenly King.
The Union was so Strait between them two,
That all was eithers which my Soul could view.
His Gifts, and my Possessions, both our Treasures;
He mine, and I the Ocean of his Pleasures.
He was an Ocean of Delights from Whom
The Living Springs and Golden Streams did com:
My Bosom was an Ocean into which
They all did run. And me they did enrich.

47. *as then*: i.e. like Adam's world.
57. *Wormwood Star*: Lucifer?

A vast and Infinit Capacitie,   75
Did make my Bosom like the Deitie,
In Whose Mysterious and Celestial Mind
All Ages and all Worlds together shind.
Who tho he nothing said did always reign,
And in Himself Eternitie contain.   80
The World was more in me, then I in it.
The King of Glory in my Soul did sit.
And to Himself in me he always gave,
All that he takes Delight to see me have.
For so my Spirit was an Endless Sphere,   85
Like God himself, and Heaven and Earth was there.

My Spirit

1

My Naked Simple Life was I.
    That Act so Strongly Shind
Upon the Earth, the Sea, the Skie,
It was the Substance of My Mind.
    The Sence it self was I.   5
I felt no Dross nor Matter in my Soul,
No Brims nor Borders, such as in a Bowl
We see, My Essence was Capacitie.
    That felt all Things,
      The Thought that Springs   10
Therfrom's it self. It hath no other Wings
To Spread abroad, nor Eys to see,
    Nor Hands Distinct to feel,
      Nor Knees to Kneel:
But being Simple like the Deitie   15
    In its own Centre is a Sphere
Not shut up here, but evry Where.

2

It Acts not from a Centre to
    Its Object as remote,
But present is, when it doth view,   20
Being with the Being it doth note.
    Whatever it doth do,

4. *It*, corr. from 'That'.

It doth not by another Engine work,
But by it self; which in the Act doth lurk.
25   Its Essence is Transformd into a true
              And perfect Act.
              And so Exact
Hath God appeard in this Mysterious Fact,
    That tis all Ey, all Act, all Sight,
30   And what it pleas can be,
            Not only see,
Or do; for tis more Voluble† then Light:
    Which can put on ten thousand Forms,
    Being clothd with what it self adorns.

3

35   This made me present evermore
        With whatso ere I saw.
    An Object, if it were before
    My Ey, was by Dame Natures Law,
        Within my Soul. Her Store
40 Was all at once within me; all her Treasures
Were my Immediat and Internal Pleasures,
Substantial Joys, which did inform my Mind.
        With all she wrought,
        My Soul was fraught,
45 And evry Object in my Soul a Thought
    Begot, or was; I could not tell,
        Whether the Things did there
          Themselvs appear,
Which in my Spirit *truly* seemd to dwell;
50   Or whether my conforming† Mind
Were not even all that therin shind.

4

    But yet of this I was most sure,
        That at the utmost Length,
    (so Worthy was it to endure)
55   My Soul could best Express its Strength.
    It was so Quick and Pure,

---

45. *Soul*, corr. to 'Heart'.   51. *even . . . therin*, corr. from 'alone even all that'.
56. corr. from 'It was Indivisible, and so Pure', which was a foot too long. M prefers the original, because of the concept of indivisibility, but this is retained in line 92.

That all my Mind was wholy Evry where
What ere it saw, twas ever wholy there;
The Sun ten thousand Legions off, was nigh:
   The utmost Star,   60
   Tho seen from far,
Was present in the Apple of my Eye.
  There was my Sight, my Life, my Sence,
   My Substance and my Mind
    My Spirit Shind   65
Even there, not by a Transeunt† Influence.
  The Act was Immanent, yet there.
  The Thing remote, yet felt even here.

5

   O Joy! O Wonder, and Delight!
    O Sacred Mysterie!
   My Soul a Spirit infinit!   70
   An Image of the Deitie!
    A pure Substantiall Light!
That Being Greatest which doth Nothing seem!
Why, twas my All, I nothing did esteem   75
But that alone. A Strange Mysterious Sphere!
   A Deep Abyss
   That sees and is
The only Proper Place or Bower of Bliss.
  To its Creator tis so near   80
   In Lov and Excellence
   In Life and Sence,
In Greatness Worth and Nature; And so Dear;
  In it, without Hyperbole,
  The Son and friend of God we see.   85

6

  A Strange Extended Orb of Joy,
   Proceeding from within,
  Which did on evry side convey
  It self, and being nigh of Kin
   To God did evry Way   90

75. I have borrowed the first comma from Philip's version, for clarity.

Dilate it self even in an Instant, and
Like an Indivisible Centre Stand
At once Surrounding all Eternitie.
          Twas not a Sphere
          Yet did appear
One infinit. Twas somwhat evry where.
          And tho it had a Power to see
          Far more, yet still it shind
          And was a Mind
Exerted† for it saw Infinitie
          Twas not a Sphere, but twas a Power
          Invisible, and yet a Bower.

                    7

          O Wondrous Self! O Sphere of Light,
              O Sphere of Joy most fair;
          O Act, O Power infinit;
          O Subtile, and unbounded Air!
              O Living Orb of Sight!
Thou which within me art, yet Me! Thou Ey,
And Temple of his Whole Infinitie!
O what a World art Thou! a World within!
              All Things appear,
              All Objects are
Alive in thee! Supersubstancial, Rare,
          Abov them selvs, and nigh of Kin
              To those pure Things we find
              In his Great Mind
Who made the World! tho now Ecclypsd by Sin.
          There they are Usefull and Divine,
          Exalted there they ought to Shine.

The Apprehension [1]

I

If this I did not evry moment see,
    And if my Thoughts did stray
    At any time, or idly play,
    And fix on other Objects, yet
      This Apprehension set   5
        In me
Was all my whole felicitie.

Fullnesse [2]

I

    That Light, that Sight, that Thought,
    Which in my Soul at first He wrought,
Is sure the only Act to which I may
      Assent to Day:
    The Mirror of an Endless Life,   5
    The Shadow of a Virgin Wife,
A Spiritual World Standing within,
    An Univers enclosd in Skin.
My Power exerted, or my Perfect Being,
If not Enjoying, yet an Act of Seeing.   10
      My Bliss
      Consists in this,
      My Duty too
      In this I view.
    It is a Fountain or a Spring,   15
    Refreshing me in evry thing.
From whence those living Streams I do derive,
By which my Thirsty Soul is kept alive.

[1] Evidently a fragment of a discarded longer poem, which T placed here as a kind of postscript to *My Spirit*.

[2] The number 1 suggests that another stanza originally followed, but M instances *Contentment* (p. 146) as another example of the single long stanza.

D

The Centre and the Sphere
20   Of my Delights are here.
It is my Davids Tower,
Where all my Armor lies,
The Fountain of my Power,
My Bliss, my Sacrifice:
25   A little Spark,
That shining in the Dark,
Makes, and encourages my Soul to rise.
The Root of Hope, the Golden Chain,
Whose End is, as the Poets feign,
30   Fastned to the very Throne
Of Jove.
It is a Stone,
On which I sit,
An Endless Benefit,
35   That being made my Regal Throne,
Doth prove
An oracle of his Eternal Love.

Nature

That Custom is a Second Nature, we
Most Plainly find by Natures Purity.
For Nature teacheth Nothing but the Truth.
I'me Sure mine did in my Virgin Youth.
5   The very Day my Spirit did inspire,
The Worlds fair Beauty set my Soul on fire.
My Senses were Informers to my Heart,
The Conduits of his Glory Power and Art.
His Greatness Wisdom Goodness I did see,
10   His Glorious Lov, and his Eternitie,
Almost as soon as Born: and evry Sence
Was in me like to som Intelligence.
I was by Nature prone and apt to love
All Light and Beauty, both in Heaven above,

32. *a Stone*: M thinks this a reference to the Stone of Scone, on which Charles II was crowned, 23 Apr. 1661.

And Earth beneath, prone even to Admire,   15
Adore and Prais as well as to Desire.
My Inclinations raisd me up on high,
And guided me to all Infinitie.
A Secret self I had enclosd within,
That was not bounded with my Clothes or Skin,   20
Or terminated with my Sight, the Sphere
Of which was bounded with the Heavens here:
But that did rather, like the Subtile Light,
Securd from rough and raging Storms by Night,
Break through the Lanthorns sides, and freely ray   25
Dispersing and Dilating evry Way:
Whose Steddy Beams too Subtile for the Wind,
Are such, that we their Bounds can scarcely find.
It did encompass, and possess rare Things,
But yet felt more, and on its Angels Wings
Pierc'd through the Skies immediatly, and sought   30
For all that could beyond all Worlds be thought.
It did not move, nor one way go, but stood,
And by Dilating of it self, all Good
It strove to see, as if twere present there,   35
Even while it present stood conversing here:
And more suggested then I could discern,
Or ever since by any Means could learn.
Vast unaffected Wonderfull Desires,
Like Inward, Nativ, uncausd, hidden fires,   40
Sprang up with Expectations very strange,
Which into New Desires did quickly change.
For all I saw beyond the Azure Round,
Was Endless Darkness with no Beauty crownd.
Why Beauty should not there, as well as here,   45
Why Goodness should not likewise there appear,
Why Treasures and Delights should bounded be,
Since there is such a Wide Infinitie;
These were the Doubts and Troubles of my Soul,
By which I do perceiv without Controll,   50

32. *beyond all Worlds*: corr. from 'even any where'.
49. *These were the*, corr. from 'Were the sad Doubts'.
   50. *without Controll*: this could mean 'I freely perceive', or that the 'Joys' of l. 51 are
'without control'—unbounded.

A World of Endless Joys by Nature made,
That needs must flourish ever, never fade.
A Wide Magnificent and Spacious Skie,
So rich tis Worthy of the Deitie,
Clouds here and there like Winged Charets flying,
Flowers ever flourishing, yet always Dying,
A Day of Glory where I all things see,
As twere enrichd with Beams of Light for me,
And drownd in Glorious Rays of purer Light,
Succeeded with a Black, yet Glorious Night,
Stars Sweetly Shedding to my pleased Sence,
On all things their Nocturnal Influence,
With Secret Rooms in Times and Ages more
Past and to com enlarging my great Store,
These all in Order present unto Me
My Happy Eys did in a Moment see
With Wonders there-too, to my Soul unknown,
Till they by Men and Reading first were shewn.
All which were made that I might ever be
With som Great Workman, som Great Deitie.
But yet there were new Rooms, and Spaces more,
Beyond all these, Wide Regions ore and ore,
And into them my pent-up-Soul like fire
Did break, Surmounting all I here admire.
The Spaces fild were like a Cabinet
Of Joys before me most Distinctly set:
The Empty, like to large and Vacant Room
For Fancy to enlarge in, and presume
A Space for more, removd, but yet adorning
These neer at hand, that pleasd me evry Morning.
Here I was seated to behold New Things,
In the fair fabrick of the King of Kings.
All, all was mine. The fountain tho not Known,
Yet that there must be one was plainly shewn.
Which fountain of Delights must needs be Lov
As all the Goodness of the things did prov.
It shines upon me from the highest Skies,
And all its Creatures for my sake doth prize,
Of whose Enjoyment I am made the End.
While how the same is so I comprehend.

55
60
65
70
75
80
85
90

69. *All which were made*, corr. from 'Yet all prepard'.
72. *Wide*, corr. to 'New'.   73. *And into them*, corr. to 'Into all which'.

Ease

1

How easily doth Nature teach the Soul,
How irresistible is her Infusion!
There's Nothing found that can her force controll,
But Sin. How Weak and feeble's all Delusion!

2

Things fals are forcd, and most Elaborate,   5
Things pure and true are Obvious unto Sence;
The first Impressions, in our Earthly State,
Are made by Things most Great in Excellence.

3

How easy is it to believ the Skie
Is Wide and Great and fair? How soon may we   10
Be made to know the Sun is Bright and High,
And very Glorious, when its Beams we see?

4

That all the Earth is one continued Globe,
And that all Men theron are Living Treasures,
That fields and Meadows are a Glorious Robe,   15
Adorning it with Sweet and Heavenly Pleasures;

5

That all we see is ours, and evry One
Possessor of the Whole; that evry Man
Is like a God Incarnat on the Throne,
Even like the first for whom the World began;   20

6

Whom all are taught to honor serv and lov,
Becaus he is Belovd of God unknown;
And therfore is on Earth it self above
All others, that his Wisdom might be shewn:

7

25   That all may Happy be, Each one most Blest,
Both in Himself and others; all most High,
While all by each, and each by all possest,
Are intermutual Joys, beneath the Skie.

8

This shows a Wise Contrivance, and discovers
30   Som Great Creator Sitting on the Throne,
That so disposeth things for all his Lovers,
That evry one might reign like GOD alone.

Speed

1

The Liquid Pearl in Springs,
The usefull and the Precious Things
Are in a Moment Known.
Their very Glory does reveal their Worth,
5   (And that doth set their Glory forth;)
As soon as I was Born, they all were Shewn.

2

True Living Wealth did flow,
In Chrystall Streams below
My feet, and trilling down
10   In Pure, Transparent, Soft, Sweet, Melting Pleasures,
Like Precious and Diffusive Treasures,
At once my Body fed, and Soul did Crown.

3

I was as High and Great,
As Kings are in their Seat.
All other Things were mine.
15   The World my House, the Creatures were my Goods,
Fields, Mountains, Valleys, Woods,
Floods, Cities, Churches, Men, for me did shine.

4

Great, Lofty, Endless, Stable,
Various and Innumerable,   20
Bright usefull fair Divine,
Immovable and Sweet the Treasures were,
The Sacred Objects did appear
Most rich and Beautifull, as well as mine.

5

New all! New Burnisht Joys;   25
Tho now by other Toys
Ecclypst: New all and mine.
Great Truth so Sacred seemd for this to me,
Becaus the Things which I did see
Were such, my State I knew to be Divine.   30

6

Nor did the Angels faces,
The Glories, and the Graces,
The Beauty Peace and Joy
Of Heaven it self, more Sweetness yeeld to me.
Til filthy Sin did all destroy,   35
These were the Offspring of the Deitie.

The Designe[1]

I

When first Eternity Stoopd down to Nought,
And in the Earth its Likeness sought,
When first it out of Nothing framd the Skies,
And formd the Moon and Sun
That we might see what it had don,   5
It was so Wise,
That it did prize
Things truly Greatest Brightest fairest, Best.
All which it made, and left the rest.

[1] In F this is entitled *The Choice*.

2

10   Then did it take such Care about the Truth,
Its Daughter, that even in her Youth,
Her face might Shine upon us, and be known,
That by a better fate,
It other Toys might Antedate,
15   As soon as shewn;
And be our own,
While we were hers; And that a Virgin Love
Her best Inheritance might prove.

3

Thoughts undefiled, Simple, Naked, Pure;
20   Thoughts Worthy ever to endure,
Our first and Disengaged thoughts it lovs,
And therfore made the Truth,
In Infancy and Tender Youth,
So Obvious to
25   Our Easy view
That it doth prepossess our Soul, and proves
The Caus of what it all Ways moves.

4

By Merit and Desire it doth allure;
For Truth is so Divine and Pure,
30   So Rich and Acceptable, being seen,
(Not parted, but in Whole)
That it doth Draw and force the Soul,
As the Great Queen
Of Bliss, between
35   Whom and the Soul, no one Pretender ought
Thrust in, to Captivat a Thought.

5

Hence did Eternity contrive to make
The Truth so fair for all our Sake

That being Truth, and Fair and Easy too,
  While it on all doth Shine,   40
  We might by it becom Divine
    Being led to Woo
    The Thing we view,
And as chast Virgins Early with it joyn,
  That with it we might likewise Shine. 45

6

Eternity doth give the richest Things
  To evry Man, and makes all Kings.
The Best and Richest Things it doth convey
    To all, and evry one.
  It raised me unto a Throne!   50
    Which I enjoy,
    In such a Way,
That Truth her Daughter is my chiefest Bride,
  Her Daughter Truth's my chiefest Pride.

7

All mine! And seen so Easily! How Great, how Blest! 55
  How soon am I of all possest!
My Infancie no Sooner Opes its Eys,
    But Straight the Spacious Earth
    Abounds with Joy Peace Glory Mirth
    And being Wise,   60
    The very Skies,
And Stars do mine becom; being all possest
  Even in that Way that is the Best.

---

53. *chiefest*: perhaps a slip in T's transcription, as M points out. Philip changed it to 'only'.

The Person

1

Ye Sacred Lims,
A richer Blazon I will lay
    On you, then first I found:
That like Celestial Kings,
Ye might with Ornaments of Joy
    Be always Crownd.
A Deep Vermilion on a Red,
On that a Scarlet I will lay,
    With Gold Ile Crown your Head,
    Which like the Sun shall Ray.
With Robes of Glory and Delight
    Ile make you Bright.
Mistake me not, I do not mean to bring
    New Robes, but to Display the Thing:
Nor Paint, nor Cloath, nor Crown, nor add a Ray,
But Glorify by taking all away.

2

The Naked Things
Are most Sublime, and Brightest shew,
    When they alone are seen:
    Mens Hands then Angels Wings
Are truer Wealth even here below:
    For those but seem.
Their Worth they then do best reveal,
When we all Metaphores remove,
    For Metaphores conceal,
    And only Vapours prove.
They best are Blazond when we see
    The Anatomie,
Survey the Skin, cut up the Flesh, the Veins
    Unfold: The Glory there remains.
The Muscles, Fibres, Arteries and Bones
Are better far then Crowns and precious Stones.

3

Shall I not then
Delight in these most Sacred Treasures
    Which my Great Father gave, 35
    Far more then other Men
Delight in Gold? Since these are Pleasures,
    That make us Brave!
Far Braver then the Pearl and Gold
That glitter on a Ladies Neck! 40
    The Rubies we behold,
    The Diamonds that Deck
The Hands of Queens, compard unto
    The Hands we view;
The Softer Lillies, and the Roses are 45
    Less Ornaments to those that Wear
The same, then are the Hands, and Lips, and Eys
Of those who those fals Ornaments so prize.

4

Let Veritie
Be thy Delight: let me Esteem 50
    True Wealth far more then Toys:
    Let Sacred Riches be,
While falser Treasures only seem,
    My real Joys.
For Golden Chains and Bracelets are 55
But Gilded Manicles, wherby
    Old Satan doth ensnare,
    Allure, Bewitch the Ey.
Thy Gifts O God alone Ile prize,
    My Tongue, my Eys, 60
My Cheeks, my Lips, my Ears, my Hands, my Feet,
    Their Harmony is far more Sweet;
Their Beauty true. And these in all my Ways
Shall Themes becom, and Organs of thy Praise.

The Estate

1

But shall my Soul no Wealth possess,
    No Outward Riches have?
Shall Hands and Eys alone express
    Thy Bounty? Which the Grave
5   Shall strait devour. Shall I becom
With in my self a Living Tomb
Of Useless Wonders? Shall the fair and brave
And great Endowments of my Soul lie Waste,
Which ought to be a fountain, and a Womb
10   Of Praises unto Thee?
Shall there no Outward Objects be,
    For these to see and Taste?
Not so, my God, for Outward Joys and Pleasures
Are even the Things for which my Lims are Treasures.

2

15   My Palate ought to be a Stone
    To trie thy Joys upon:
And evry Member ought to be
    A Tongue, to Sing to Thee.
There's not an Ey thats framd by Thee,
20   But ought thy Life and Lov, to see.
Nor is there, Lord, upon mine Head an Ear,
But that the Musick of thy Works should hear.
Each Toe, each Finger framed by thy Skill,
        Ought Oyntments to Distill.
25   Ambrosia, Nectar, Wine should flow
    From evry Joynt I owe,
Or Things more Rich; while all mine Inward Powers
Are Blessed, Joyfull, and Eternal Bowers.

3

They ought, my God, to be the Pipes,
30   And Conduits of thy Prais.
Mens Bodies were not made for Stripes,
    Nor any thing but Joys.

They were not made to be alone:
But made to be the very Throne
Of Blessedness, to be like Suns, whose Raies, 35
Dispersed, Scatter many thousand Ways.
They Drink in Nectars, and Disburs again
        In Purer Beams, those Streams,
Those Nectars which are causd by Joys.
        And as the spacious Main 40
Doth all the Rivers, which it Drinks, return,
Thy Love receivd doth make the Soul to burn.

4

Elixars richer are then Dross,
        And Ends are more Divine
Then Causes are: Material loss 45
        Materials (tho they Shine
Like Gold and Silver) are, compard
To what thy Spirit doth regard,
Thy Soul desire, thy Lov embrace, thy Mind
Esteem, thy Nature most Illustrious find. 50
These are the Things wher with we God reward.
        Our Love he more doth prize:
Our Gratitude is in his Eys,
        Far richer then the Skies.
And those Affections which we do return, 55
Are like the Lov which in Himself doth burn.

5

We plough the very Skies, as well
        As Earth, the Spacious Seas
Are ours; the Stars all Gems excell.
        The Air was made to pleas 60
The Souls of Men: Devouring fire
Doth feed and Quicken Mans Desire.
The Sun it self doth in its Glory Shine,
And Gold and Silver out of very Mire,
And Pearls and Rubies out of Earth refine, 65
        While Herbs and Flowers aspire
To touch and make our feet Divine.
        How Glorious is Mans Fate
The Laws of God, the Works he did Create,
His Ancient Ways, are His, and my Estate. 70

The Enquirie

1

Men may delighted be with Springs,
        While Trees and Herbs their Senses pleas,
And taste even living Nectar in the Seas:
                May think their Members things
5 Of Earthly Worth at least, if not Divine,
And Sing becaus the Earth for them doth Shine.

2

        But can the Angels take Delight,
                To see such Faces here beneath?
Or can Perfumes indeed from Dunghils breath?
10   Or is the World a Sight
Worthy of them? Then may we Mortals be
Surrounded with Eternal Claritie.

3

        Even Holy Angels may com down
                To walk on Earth, and see Delights,
15 That feed and pleas, even here, their Appetites.
                Our Joys may make a Crown
For them. And in his Tabernacle Men may be
Like Palmes we mingled with the Cherubs see.

4

        Mens Sences are indeed the Gems,
20   Their Praises the most Sweet Perfumes,
Their Eys the Thrones, their Hearts the Heavnly Rooms,
                Their Souls the Diadems,
Their Tongues the Organs which they lov to hear,
Their Cheeks and faces like to theirs appear.

5

25   The Wonders which our God hath done,
                The Glories of his Attributes,
Like dangling Apples or like Golden Fruits,
                Angelick Joys become.
His Wisdom Shines, on Earth his Lov doth flow,
30 Like Myrrh or Incense even here below.

6

And shall not we such Joys possess,
Which God for Man did chiefly make?
The Angels hav them only for our sake!
And yet they all confess
His Glory here on Earth to be Divine,
And that his GODHEAD in his Works doth shine.

35

The Circulation[1]

1

As fair Ideas† from the Skie,
Or Images of Things,
Unto a Spotless Mirror flie,
On unperceived Wings;
And lodging there affect the Sence,
As if at first they came from thence;
While being there, they richly Beautifie
The Place they fill, and yet communicat
Themselvs, reflecting to the Seers Ey,
Just such is our Estate.
No Prais can we return again,
No Glory in our selvs possess,
But what derived from without we gain,
From all the Mysteries of Blessedness.

5

10

2

No Man breaths out more vital Air,
Then he before suckt in.
Those Joys and Praises must repair
To us, which tis a Sin
To bury, in a Senceless Tomb.
An Earthly Wight must be the Heir
Of all those Joys, the Holy Angels Prize,
He must a King, before a Priest becom,

15

20

[1] This poem and the succeeding ones up to p. 77 are found only in D.
20. Wight spelt 'Weight' in MS.

And Gifts receiv, or ever Sacrifice.
    Tis Blindness Makes us Dumb.
25   Had we but those Celestial Eys,
    Wherby we could behold the Sum
Of all his Bounties, *we should overflow*
With Praises, did we but their Causes Know.

3

    All Things to Circulations owe
30   Themselvs; by which alone
They do exist: They cannot shew
    A Sigh, a Word, a Groan,
A Colour, or a Glimps of Light,
The Sparcle of a Precious Stone,
35 A virtue, or a Smell; a lovly Sight,
A Fruit, a Beam, an Influence, a Tear;
But they anothers Livery must Wear:
    And borrow Matter first,
Before they can communicat.
40   Whatever's empty is accurst:
And this doth shew that we must some Estate
Possess, or never can communicate.

4

    A Spunge drinks in that Water, which
        Is afterwards *exprest.*
45   A Liberal hand must first be rich:
        Who blesseth must be Blest.
The Thirsty Earth drinks in the Rain,
    The Trees suck Moysture at their Roots,
Before the one can Lavish Herbs again,
50 Before the other can afford us Fruits.
No Tenant can rais Corn, or pay his Rent,
        Nor can even hav a Lord,
    That has no Land. No Spring can vent,
    No vessel any Wine afford
55 Wherin no Liquor's put. No Empty Purs,
Can Pounds or Talents of it self disburs.

23. *Sacrifice*: verb.

5

Flame that Ejects its Golden Beams,
Sups up the Grosser Air;
To Seas, that pour out their Streams
In Springs, those Streams repair; 60
Receivd Ideas make even Dreams.
No Fancy painteth foule or fair
But by the Ministry of Inward Light,
That in the Spirits Cherisheth its Sight.
The Moon returneth Light, and som men say 65
The very Sun no Ray
Nor Influence could hav, did it
No forrein Aids, no food admit.
The Earth no Exhalations would afford,
Were not its Spirits by the Sun restord. 70

6

All things do first receiv, that giv.
Only tis GOD above,
That from, and in himself doth live,
Whose All sufficient Love
Without Original can flow 75
And all the Joys and Glories shew
Which Mortal Man can take Delight to know.
He is the Primitive Eternal Spring
The Endless Ocean of each Glorious Thing.
The Soul a Vessel is 80
A Spacious Bosom to Contain
All the fair Treasures of his Bliss
Which run like Rivers from, into the Main,
And all it doth receiv returns again.

E

Amendment

I

That all things should be mine;
This makes his Bounty most Divine.
But that they all more Rich should be,
And far more Brightly shine,
          As usd by Me:
It ravisheth my Soul to see the End,
To which this Work so Wonderfull doth tend.

2

That we should make the Skies
More Glorious far before thine Eys,
Then Thou didst make them, and even Thee
Far more thy Works to prize,
          As usd they be,
Then as they're made; is a Stupendious Work,
Wherin thy Wisdom Mightily doth lurk.

3

Thy Greatness, and thy Love,
Thy Power, in this, my Joy doth move,
Thy Goodness and Felicitie,
          In this Exprest abov
          All Praise, I see:
While thy Great Godhead over all doth reign,
And such an End in such a sort attain.

4

What Bound may we Assign
O God to any Work of thine!
Their Endlessness discovers Thee
          In all to be Divine;
          A DEITIE,
That wilt for evermore Exceed the End
Of all that Creatures Wit can comprehend.

5

Am I a Glorious Spring
Of Joys and Riches to my King?   30
Are Men made Gods! And may they see
So Wonderfull a Thing
As GOD in me!
And is my Soul a Mirror that must Shine
Even like the Sun, and be far more Divine?   35

6

Thy Soul, O GOD, doth prize
The Seas, the Earth, our Souls, the Skies,
As we return the same to Thee;
They more delight thine Eys,
And sweeter be,   40
As unto Thee we Offer up the same,
Then as to us, from Thee at first they came.

7

O how doth Sacred Lov
His Gifts refine, Exalt, Improve!
Our Love to Creatures makes them be   45
In thine Esteem above
Themselvs to Thee!
O here his Goodness evermore admire
He made our Souls to make his Creatures Higher.

The Demonstration

I

The Highest Things are Easiest to be shewn,
And only capable of being *Known*.
A Miste involvs the Ey,
While in the Middle it doth lie;
And till the Ends of Things are seen,   5
The Way's uncertain that doth stand between.

2. *only capable*: i.e. 'alone are capable'.

As in the Air we see the Clouds
   Like Winding Sheets, or Shrouds;
Which tho they nearer are obscure
The Sun, which Higher far, is far more Pure.

2

Its very Brightness makes it neer the Ey,
Tho many thousand Leagues beyond the Skie.
   Its Beams by violence
  Invade, and ravish distant Sence.
  Only Extremes and Hights are Known;
No Certainty, where no Perfection's shewn.
   Extremities of Blessedness
    Compell us to confess
  A GOD indeed. Whose Excellence,
In all his Works, must needs exceed all Sence.

3

And for this Caus Incredibles alone
May be by Demonstration to us shewn.
    Those Things that are most Bright
   Sun-like appear in their own Light.
   And Nothing's truly seen that's Mean:
Be it a Sand, an Acorn, or a Bean,
    It must be clothd with Endless Glory,
    Before its perfect Story
  (Be the Spirit ne're so Clear)
Can in its Causes and its Ends appear.

4

What can be more Incredible then this,
Where may we find a more profound Abyss?
   What Heavnly Height can be
  Transcendent to this Summitie!
   What more Desirable Object can
Be offerd to the Soul of Hungering Man!
   His Gifts as they to us com down
    Are infinit, and crown

The Soul with Strange Fruitions; yet
Returning from us they more value get.   40

5

And what then this can be more Plain and Clear
What Truth then this more Evident appear!
          The GODHEAD cannot prize
          The Sun at all, nor yet the Skies,
          Or Air, or Earth, or Trees, or Seas,   45
Or Stars, unless the Soul of Man they pleas.
          He neither sees with Humane Eys
              Nor needs Himself Seas Skies
          Or Earth, or any thing: He draws
No Breath, nor Eats or Drinks by Natures Laws.   50

6

The Joy and Pleasure which his Soul doth take
In all his Works, is for his Creatures sake.
          So Great a Certainty
          We in this Holy Doctrine see
          That there could be no Worth at all   55
In any Thing Material Great or Small
          Were not som Creature more Alive,
              Whence it might Worth Derive.
          GOD is the Spring whence Things came forth
Souls are the fountains of their Real Worth.   60

7

The Joy and Pleasure which his Soul doth take
In all his Works is for his Creatures sake
          Yet doth he take Delight
          Thats altogether Infinite
          In them even as they from him com   65
For such his Lov and Goodness is, the Sum
          Of all his Happiness doth seem,
              At least in his Esteem,
          In that Delight and Joy to lie
Which is his Blessed Creatures Melodie.   70

57. *more*: other (creature).

8

In them he sees, and feels, and Smels, and Lives,
In them Affected is to whom he gives:
    In them ten thousand Ways,
    He all his Works again enjoys,
75   All things from Him to Him proceed
By them; Are His in them: As if indeed
His Godhead did it self exceed.
    To them He all Conveys;
    Nay even Himself: He is the End
80 To whom in them Himself, and All things tend.

The Anticipation

1

My Contemplation Dazles in the End†
    Of all I comprehend.
    And soars abov all Heights,
Diving into the Depths of all Delights.
5   Can He becom the End,
    To whom all Creatures tend?
Who is the Father of all Infinites!
Then may He Benefit receiv from Things,
And be *not Parent only* of all Springs.

2

10 The End doth Want the Means, and is the Caus,
    Whose Sake, by Natures Laws,
    Is that for which they are.
Such Sands, such Dangerous Rocks we must beware
    From all Eternitie
    A Perfect Deitie
15 Most Great and Blessed he doth still appear.
His Essence Perfect was in all its Features
He ever Blessed in his Joys and Creatures.

3

From Everlasting he these Joys did Need,
  And all these Joys proceed   20
  From Him Eternaly.
From Everlasting His felicitie
  Compleat and Perfect was:
  Whose Bosom is the Glass,
Wherin we all Things Everlasting See.   25
His Name is NOW, his Nature is forever.
None Can his Creatures from their Maker Sever.

4

The End in Him from Everlasting is
  The Fountain of all Bliss.
  From Everlasting it   30
Efficient was, and Influence did Emit,
  That caused all. Before
  The World, we do Adore
This Glorious End. Becaus all Benefit
From it proceeds. Both are the very same.   35
The End and Fountain differ but in Name.

5

That so the End should be the very Spring,
  Of evry Glorious Thing;
  And that which seemeth Last,
The Fountain and the Caus; attaind so fast,   40
  That it was first; and movd
  The Efficient, who so lovd
All Worlds and made them for the sake of this
It shews the End Compleat before, and is
A Perfect Token of his Perfect Bliss.   45

6

The End Compleat, the Means must needs be so.
  By which we plainly Know,
  From all Eternitie,
The Means wherby God is, must perfect be.

50   God is Himself the Means,
            Wherby he doth exist:
    And as the Sun by Shining's clothd with Beams,
    So from Himself to All His Glory Streams,
    Who is a Sun, yet what Himself doth list.

                        7

55 His Endless Wants and His Enjoyments be
            From all Eternitie,
            Immutable in Him:
    They are His Joys before the Cherubim.
            His Wants appreciat all,
60   And being infinit,
    Permit no Being to be Mean or Small
    That He enjoys, or is before his Sight.
    His Satisfactions do His Wants Delight.

                        8

    Wants are the Fountains of Felicitie
65   No Joy could ever be
            Were there no Want. No Bliss
    No Sweetness Perfect were it not for this.
            Want is the Greatest Pleasure
            Becaus it makes all Treasure.
70 O what a Wonderfull Profound Abyss
    Is God! In whom Eternal Wants and Treasures
    Are more Delightfull caus they both are Pleasures.

                        9

    He infinitly wanteth all his Joys;
            (No Want the Soul ore cloys.)
75   And all those Wanted Pleasures
    He infinitly Hath. What Endless Measures,
            What Heights and Depths may we
            In his Felicitie
    Conceiv! Whose very Wants are Endles Pleasures.
80 His Life in Wants and Joys is infinit.
    And both are felt as His Supreme Delight.

58. corr. (for metrical reasons) from 'And such, they are the Glory of the Cherubim',
which suggests that 'before' here means 'in the presence of'.

10

He's not like us; Possession doth not Cloy,
    Nor Sence of Want Destroy.
      Both always are together:
No force can either from the other Sever.   85
      Yet theres a Space between
      Thats Endless. Both are seen
Distinctly still, and both are seen for ever.
As soon as ere he wanteth all his Bliss,
His Bliss, tho Everlasting, in Him is.   90

11

His Essence is all Act: He did, that He
    All Act might always be.
      His Nature burns like fire;
His Goodness infinitly doth desire,
      To be by all possest;   95
      His Love makes others Blest.
It is the Glory of his High Estate,
And that which I for ever more Admire,
He is an Act that doth Communicate.

12

From all to all Eternity He is   100
    That Act: An Act of Bliss:
      Wherin all Bliss to all,
That will receiv the same, or on him call,
      Is freely given: from Whence
      Tis Easy even to Sence,   105
To apprehend That all Receivers are
In Him, all Gifts, all Joys, all Eys, even all
At once, that ever will, or shall appear.

13

He is the Means of them, they not of Him.
    The Holy Cherubim   110
      Souls Angels from him came
Who is a Glorious Bright and Living Flame,
      That on all things doth shine,
      And makes their Face Divine.

115 And Holy, Holy, Holy, is his Name.
     He is the Means both of Himself and all,
     Whom we the Fountain Means and End do call.

14

     In whom as in the Fountain all things are,
              In whom all things appear
120   As in the Means, and End
     From whom they all proceed, to whom they tend.
              By whom they are made ours
              Whose Souls are Spacious Bowers
     Of all like His. Who ought to have a Sence
125 Of all our Wants, of all His Excellence,
     That while we all, we Him might comprehend.

The Recovery

1

         To see us but receiv, is such a Sight
         As makes his Treasures infinit!
         Becaus His Goodness doth possess
     In us, His own, and our own Blessedness.
5   Yea more, His Love doth take Delight
         To make our Glory Infinite
              Our Blessedness to see
              Is even to the Deitie
     A Beatifick Vision! He attains
10   His Ends while we enjoy. In us He reigns.

2

         For God enjoyd is all his End.
         Himself he then doth Comprehend.
         When He is Blessed, Magnified,
     Extold, Exalted, Praisd and Glorified
15   Honord, Esteemd, Belovd, Enjoyd,
         Admired, Sanctified, Obeyd,
              That is receivd. For He
              Doth place his Whole Felicitie
     In that, who is despised and defied
20   Undeified almost if once denied.

3

In all his Works, in all his Ways,
We must his Glory see and Prais;
And since our Pleasure is the End,
We must his Goodness and his Lov attend.
    If we despise his Glorious Works,   25
    Such Sin and Mischief in it lurks,
        That they are all made vain
        And this is even Endless Pain
To him that sees it. Whose Diviner Grief
Is hereupon (Ah me!) without relief.   30

4

We pleas his Goodness that receiv:
Refusers Him of all bereav.
As Bride grooms Know full well that Build
A Palace for their Bride. It will not yeeld
    Any Delight to him at all   35
    If She for whom He made the Hall
        Refuse to dwell in it
        Or plainly Scorn the Benefit.
Her Act that's Wo'ed, yeelds more delight and Pleasure
If she receivs, Then all that Pile of Treasure.   40

5

But we have Hands and Lips and Eys
And Hearts and Souls can Sacrifice.
And Souls themselvs are made in vain
If we our Evil Stubbornness retain.
    Affections, Praises, are the Things   45
    For which he gave us all these Springs,
        They are the very fruits
        Of all these Trees and Roots
The Fruits and Ends of all his Great Endeavors,
Which he abolisheth whoever Severs.   50

6

Tis not alone a Lively Sence
A clear and Quick Intelligence

A free, Profound, and full Esteem:
Tho these Elixars all and Ends to[o] seem
55 But Gratitude, Thanksgiving, Prais,
A Heart returnd for all these Joys,
These are the Things admird,
These are the Things by Him desird.
These are the Nectar and the Quintessence
60 The Cream and Flower that most affect his Sence.

7

The voluntary Act wherby
These are repaid, is in his Ey
More Precious then the very Skie.
All Gold and Silver is but Empty Dross
65 Rubies and Saphires are but Loss
The very Sun and Stars and Seas
Far less his Spirit pleas.
One Voluntary Act of Love
Far more Delightfull to his Soul doth prove
70 And is abov all these as far as Love.

Another

1

He seeks for ours as we do seek for his.
Nay O my Soul, ours is far more His Bliss
Then his is ours; at least it so doth seem
Both in his own and our Esteem.

2

5 His Earnest Lov, his Infinit Desires,
His Living, Endless, and Devouring fires,
Do rage in Thirst, and fervently require
A lov, tis Strange it should desire.

3

We cold and Careless are, and scarcely think
10 Upon the Glorious Spring wherat we Drink.
Did he not lov us, we could be content.
We Wretches are Indifferent!

4

He prizes our Lov with infinit Esteem.
And seeks it so that it doth almost seem
Even all his Blessedness. His Lov doth prize   15
    It as the only Sacrifice.

5

Tis Death my Soul to be Indifferent,
Set forth thy self unto thy whole Extent,
And all the Glory of his Passion prize,
    Who for Thee livs, who for Thee Dies.   20

6

His Goodness made thy Lov so Great a Pleasure,
His Goodness made thy Soul so Great a Treasure
To Thee and Him: that thou mightst both inherit
    Prize it according to its Merit.

7

There is no Goodness nor Desert in Thee,   25
For which thy Lov so Coveted should be,
His Goodness is the fountain of thy Worth
    O liv to lov and set it forth.

8

Thou Nothing givst to Him, he gav all Things,
To Thee, and made Thee like the King of Kings.   30
His Lov the fountain is of Heaven and Earth
    The Caus of all thy Joy and Mirth.

9

Thy Lov is Nothing but it self, and yet
So infinit is his, that he doth set
A value infinit upon it. Oh!   35
    This, canst thou Careless be, and Know!

10

Let that same Goodness, which is infinit,
Esteems thy Lov with Infinit Delight,
Tho less then His, Tho Nothing, always be
    An Object Infinit to Thee.   40

11

And as it is the Caus of all Esteem,
Of all the Worth which in thy Lov doth seem,
So let it be the Caus of all thy Pleasure
    Causing its Being and its Measure.

Love

1

    O Nectar! O Delicious Stream!
O ravishing and only Pleasure! Where
      Shall such another Theme
Inspire my Tongue with Joys, or pleas mine Ear!
      Abridgement† of Delights!
        And Queen of Sights!
O Mine of Rarities! O Kingdom Wide!
O more! O Caus of all! O Glorious Bride!
      O God! O Bride of God! O King!
      O Soul and Crown of evry Thing!

2

    Did not I covet to behold
Som Endless Monarch, that did always live
      In Palaces of Gold
Willing all Kingdoms Realms and Crowns to give
      Unto my Soul! Whose Lov
        A Spring might prov
Of Endless Glories, Honors, friendships, Pleasures,
Joys, Praises, Beauties and Celestial Treasures!
      Lo, now I see there's such a King,
      The fountain Head of evry Thing!

3

    Did my Ambition ever Dream
Of such a Lord, of such a Love! Did I
      Expect so Sweet a Stream
As this at any time! Could any Ey

       Believ it? Why all Power   25
           Is used here
 Joys down from Heaven on my Head to shower
 And Jove beyond the Fiction doth appear
    Once more in Golden Rain to come.
    To Danae's Pleasing Fruitfull Womb.   30

             4

   His Ganimede! His Life! His Joy!
 Or he comes down to me, or takes me up
     That I might be his Boy,
 And fill, and taste, and give, and Drink the Cup.
    But these (tho great) are all   35
      Too short and small,
 Too Weak and feeble Pictures to Express
 The true Mysterious Depths of Blessedness.
    I am his Image, and his Friend.
    His Son, Bride, Glory, Temple, End.   40

Thoughts. I[1]

             I

   Ye brisk Divine and Living Things,
 Ye great Exemplars, and ye Heavenly Springs,
     Which I within me see;
      Ye Machines Great,
    Which in my Spirit God did Seat,   5
    Ye Engines of Felicitie;
    Ye Wondrous Fabricks of his Hands,
 Who all possesseth that he understands;
    That ye are pent within my Brest,
    Yet rove at large from East to West,   10
 And are Invisible, yet Infinite;
 Is my Transcendent, and my Best Delight.

[1] The numbering of the *Thoughts* poems was added by Philip. M notes that in D they are 'arranged to alternate with other poems, two outer pairs with abstract titles . . . and a middle poem without a title but, in effect, an ecstatic "Thoughts" poem'.

2

By you I do the Joys possess
Of Yesterdays-yet-present Blessedness;
15   As in a Mirror Clear,
            Old Objects I
Far distant do even now descrie
Which by your help are present here.
Ye are your selvs the very Pleasures.
20 The Sweetest, last, and most Substantial Treasures.
        The Offsprings and Effects of Bliss
        By whose Return my Glory is
Renewd, and represented to my View:
O ye Delights, most Pure, Divine, and True!

3

25   Ye Thoughts and Apprehensions are
The Heavenly Streams which fill the Soul with rare
            Transcendent Perfect Pleasures.
                At any time,
            As if ye still were in your Prime,
30   Ye Open all his Heavenly Treasures.
        His Joys accessible are found
To you, and those Things enter which Surround
        The Soul. Ye Living Things within!
        Where had all Joy and Glory been
35 Had ye not made the Soul those Things to Know.
Which Seated in it make the fairest Shew?

4

I know not by what Secret Power
Ye flourish so: but ye within your Bower,
            More Beautifull do seem,
40   And better Meat
        Ye daily yeeld my Soul to eat,
        Then even the Objects I esteem
Without my Soul. What were the Skie,
What were the Sun, or Stars, did ye not lie
45   In me! and represent them there
        Where els they never could appear!

Yea What were Bliss without such Thoughts to me,
What were my Life, what were the Deitie?

5

O ye *Conceptions* of Delight!
Ye that *inform* my Soul with Life and Sight! 50
    Ye Representatives, and Springs
      Of inward Pleasure!
Ye Joys! Ye Ends of Outward Treasure!
Ye Inward, and ye Living Things!
    The Thought, or Joy Conceived is 55
The inward Fabrick of my Standing Bliss.
    It is the Substance of my Mind
    Transformd, and with its Objects lind.
The Quintessence, Elixar, Spirit, Cream.
Tis Strange that Things unseen should be Supreme. 60

6

    The Ey's confind, the Body's pent
In narrow Room: Lims are of small Extent.
      But Thoughts are always free.
      And as they're best,
    So can they even in the Brest, 65
    Rove ore the World with Libertie:
    Can Enter Ages, Present be
In any Kingdom, into Bosoms see.
    Thoughts, Thoughts can come to Things, and view,
    What Bodies cant approach unto. 70
They know no Bar, Denial, Limit, Wall:
But have a Liberty to look on all.

7

    Like Bees they flie from Flower to Flower,
Appear in Evry Closet, Temple, Bower;
      And suck the Sweet from thence, 75
      No Ey can see:
    As Tasters to the Deitie.
Incredible's their Excellence.

F

For ever-more they will be seen
80   Nor ever moulder into less Esteem.
They ever shew an Equal face,
And are Immortal in their place.
Ten thousand Ages hence they are as Strong,
Ten thousand Ages hence they are as Yong.

Blisse[1]

1

All Blisse
Consists in this,
To do as Adam did:
And not to know those Superficial Toys
5   Which in the Garden once were hid.
Those little new Invented Things.
Cups, Saddles Crowns are Childish Joys.
So Ribbans are and Rings.
Which all our Happiness destroys.

2

10   Nor God
In his Abode
Nor Saints nor little Boys
Nor Angels made them, only foolish Men,
Grown mad with Custom on those Toys
15   Which more increas their Wants do dote.
And when they Older are do then
Those Bables chiefly note
With Greedier Eys, more Boys tho Men.

---

[1] Two stanzas of a longer poem, *The Apostacy* (lines 37–54) which appear with many changes in Philip's MS, see p. 87.

Thoughts. II

1

A Delicate and Tender Thought
The Quintessence is found of all he Wrought.
   It is the fruit of all his Works,
      Which we conceive,
      Bring forth, and Give,   5
Yea and in which the Greater Value lurks.
   It is the fine and Curious Flower,
Which we return, and offer evry hour:
     So Tender in our Paradice
      That in a Trice   10
   It withers strait, and fades away,
If we but ceas its Beautie to display.

2

   Why Things so Precious, should be made
So Prone, so Easy, and so Apt to fade
     It is not easy to declare.   15
      But God would have
      His Creatures Brave†
And that too by their own Continual Care.
    He gave them Power evry Hour,
Both to Erect, and to Maintain a Tower,   20
     Which he far more in us doth Prize
      Then all the Skies.
    That we might offer it to Him,
And in our Souls be like the Seraphim.

3

   That Temple David did intend,   25
Was but a Thought, and yet it did transcend
    King Solomons. A Thought we know
      Is that for which
      God doth Enrich
With Joys even Heaven above, and Earth below.   30
    For that all Objects might be seen
He made the Orient† Azure and the Green:

That we might in his Works delight.
And that the Sight
35   Of those his Treasures might Enflame
The Soul with Love to him, he made the same.

4

This Sight which is the Glorious End
Of all his Works, and which doth comprehend
Eternity, and Time, and Space,
40   Is far more dear,
And far more near
To him, then all his Glorious Dwelling Place.
It is a Spiritual World within.
A Living World, and nearer far of Kin
45   To God, then that which first he made.
While that doth fade
This therfore ever shall Endure,
Within the Soul as more Divine and Pure.

¶

1

Ye hidden Nectars, which my GOD doth drink,
Ye Heavenly Streams, ye Beams Divine,
On which the Angels think,
How Quick, how Strongly do ye shine!
5   Ye Images of Joy that in me Dwell,
Ye Sweet Mysterious Shades
That do all Substances Excell,
Whose Glory Never fades;
Ye Skies, ye Seas, ye Stars, or things more fair,
10   O ever, ever unto me repair.

2

Ye Pleasant Thoughts! O how that Sun Divine
Appears to Day which I did see
So Sweetly then to Shine.
Even in my very Infancy!

Ye rich Ideas which within me live   15
     Ye Living Pictures here
Ye Spirits that do bring and Give
     All Joys; when ye appear,
Even Heavn it self, and God, and all in You,
Come down on Earth, and pleas my Blessed View.   20

3

I never Glorious Great and Rich am found,
     Am never ravished with Joy,
       Till ye my Soul Surround,
     Till ye my Blessedness display.
No Soul but Stone, No Man but Clay am I,   25
     No flesh, but Dust; till ye
     Delight, invade to move my Ey,
       And do replenish me.
My Sweet Informers and my Living Treasures
My Great Companions, and my only Pleasures!   30

4

O what Incredible Delights, What Fires,
     What Appetites, what Joys do ye
       Occasion, what Desires,
     What Heavenly Praises! While we see
What evry Seraphim above admires!   35
     · Your Jubilee and Trade
     Ye are so Strangely, and Divinely made,
       Shall never, never fade.
Ye ravish all my Soul, Of you I twice
Will speak. For in the Dark y'are Paradice.   40

Thoughts. III

Thoughts are the Angels which we send abroad,
To visit all the Parts of Gods Abode.
Thoughts are the Things wherin we all confess
The Quintessence of Sin and Holiness
Is laid. All Wisdom in a Thought doth Shine,   5
By Thoughts alone the Soul is made Divine.

Thoughts are the Springs of all our Actions here
On Earth, tho they them selvs do not appear.
They are the Springs of Beauty, Order, Peace,
10   The Cities Gallantries, the feilds Increas.
Rule, Government and Kingdoms flow from them,
And so doth all the New Jerusalem.
At least the Glory, Splendor and Delight,
For tis by Thoughts that even she is Bright.
15   Thoughts are the Things wherwith even God is Crownd,
And as the Soul without thems useless found,
So are all other Creatures too. A Thought .
Is even the very Cream of all he wrought.
All Holy fear, and Love, and Reverence,
20   With Honor, Joy and Prais, as well as Sence,
Are hidden in our Thoughts. Thoughts are the Things
That us affect: The Hony and the Stings
Of all that is, are Seated in a Thought,
Even while it seemeth weak, and next to Nought.
25   The Matter of all Pleasure, Virtue, Worth,
Grief, Anger, Hate, Revenge, which Words set forth,
Are Thoughts alone. Thoughts are the highest Things,
The very Offspring of the King of Kings.
Thoughts are a kind of Strange Celestial Creature,
30   That when they're Good, they're such in evry Feature,
They bear the Image of their father's face,
And Beautifie even all his Dwelling Place:
So Nimble and Volatile, unconfind,
Illimited, to which no Form's assignd,
35   So Changeable, Capacious, Easy, free,
That what it self doth pleas a Thought may be.
From Nothing to Infinitie it turns,
Even in a Moment: Now like fire it burns,
Now's frozen Ice: Now shapes the Glorious Sun,
40   Now Darkness in a Moment doth become,
Now all at once: Now crowded in a sand,
Now fils the Hemisphere, and sees a Land:
Now on a Suddain's Wider then the Skie,
And now runs Parile† with the Deitie.
45   Tis such, that it may all or Nothing be.
And's made so Active Voluble† and Free

Becaus tis Capable of all thats Good,
And is the End of all when understood.
A Thought can Clothe it self with all the Treasures
Of GOD, and be the Greatest of his Pleasures. 50
It all his Laws, and Glorious Works, and Ways,
And Attributs, and Counsels; all his Praise
It can conceiv, and Imitate, and give:
It is the only Being that doth live.
Tis Capable of all Perfection here, 55
Of all his Love and Joy and Glory there.
It is the only Beauty that doth Shine,
Most Great, Transcendent, Heavnly and Divine.
The very Best or Worst of Things it is,
The Basis of all Misery or Bliss. 60
Its Measures and Capacities are such,
Their utmost Measure we can never touch.
For Ornament on Ornament may still
Be laid; Beauty on Beauty, Skill on Skill,
Strength Still on Strength, and Life it self on Life. 65
Tis Queen of all things, and its Makers Wife.
The Best of Thoughts is yet a thing unknown,
But when tis Perfect it is like his Own:
Intelligible, Endless, yet a Sphere
Substantial too: In which all Things appear. 70
All Worlds, all Excellences, Sences, Graces,
Joys, Pleasures, Creatures, and the Angels Faces.
It shall be Married ever unto all:
And all Embrace, tho now it seemeth Small.
A Thought my Soul may Omnipresent be. 75
For all it toucheth which a Thought can see.
Oh that Mysterious Being! Thoughts are Things,
Which rightly used make his Creatures Kings.

63. *For*, corr. to 'Here', but the original makes the sense clearer.

Desire

1

For giving me Desire,
An Eager Thirst, a burning Ardent fire,
A virgin Infant Flame,
A Love with which into the World I came,
5   An Inward Hidden Heavenly Love,
Which in my Soul did Work and move,
And ever ever me Enflame,
With restlesse longing Heavenly Avarice,
That never could be satisfied,
10 That did incessantly a Paradice
Unknown suggest, and som thing undescried
Discern, and bear me to it; be
Thy Name for ever praisd by me.

2

My Parchd and Witherd Bones
15 Burnt up did seem: My Soul was full of Groans:
My Thoughts Extensions† were:
Like Paces Reaches Steps they did appear:
They somwhat hotly did persue,
Knew that they had not all their due;
20 Nor ever quiet were:
But made my flesh like Hungry Thirsty Ground,
My Heart a deep profound Abyss,
And evry Joy and Pleasure but a Wound,
So long as I my Blessedness did miss.
25 O Happiness! A Famine burns,
And all my Life to Anguish turns!

3

Where are the Silent Streams,
The Living Waters, and the Glorious Beams,
The Sweet Reviving Bowers,
30 The Shady Groves, the Sweet and Curious Flowers,

14-15. corr. from 'Parched my Witherd Bones And Eys did seem'.
17. corr. from 'Like Steps and Paces they did still appear'.

The Springs and Trees, the Heavenly Days,
The Flowry Meads, the Glorious Rayes,
    The Gold and Silver Towers?
Alass, all these are poor and Empty Things,
    Trees Waters Days and Shining Beams   35
Fruits, Flowers, Bowers, Shady Groves and Springs,
No Joy will yeeld, no more then Silent Streams.
    These are but Dead Material Toys,
    And cannot make my Heavenly Joys.

4

        O Love! ye Amities,   40
And Friendships, that appear abov the Skies!
        Ye Feasts, and Living Pleasures!
Ye Senses, Honors, and Imperial Treasures!
        Ye Bridal Joys! Ye High Delights;
        That satisfy all Appetites!   45
        Ye Sweet Affections, and
Ye high Respects! What ever Joys there be
        In Triumphs, Whatsoever stand
In Amicable Sweet Societie
Whatever Pleasures are at his right Hand   50
        Ye must, before I am Divine,
        In full Proprietie† be mine.

5

        This Soaring Sacred Thirst,
Ambassador of Bliss, approached first,
        Making a Place in me,   55
That made me apt to Prize, and Taste, and See,
        For not the Objects, but the Sence
        Of Things, doth Bliss to Souls dispence,
        And make it Lord like Thee.
Sence, feeling, Taste, Complacency† and Sight,   60
        These are the true and real Joys,
The Living Flowing Inward Melting, Bright
And Heavenly Pleasures; all the rest are Toys:
        All which are founded in Desire,
        As Light in Flame, and Heat in fire.   65

Thoughts. IV[1]

In thy Presence there is fulness
of Joy, and at thy right hand there
are Pleasures for ever more.

Thoughts are the Wings on which the Soul doth flie,
The Messengers which soar abov the Skie,
Elijahs firey Charet, that conveys
The Soul, even here, to those Eternal Joys.
5   Thoughts are the privileged Posts that Soar
Unto his Throne, and there appear before
Our selvs approach. These may at any time
Abov the Clouds, abov the Stars may clime.
The Soul is present by a Thought; and sees
10   The New Jerusalem, the Palaces,
The Thrones and feasts, the Regions of the Skie,
The Joys and Treasures of the DEITIE.
His Wisdom makes all things so Bright and pure,
That they are Worthy ever to endure.
15   His Glorious Works his Laws and Counsels are,
When seen, all like himself, beyond compare.
All Ages with his Love and Glory Shine,
As they are his all Kingdoms are Divine.
Whole Hosts of Angels at his Throne attend,
20   And joyfull Praises from his Saints ascend.
Thousands of thousands Kneel before his face
And all his Benefits with Joy embrace.
His Goodness makes all Creatures for his Pleasure,
And makes itself his Creatures chiefest Treasure.
25   Almighty Power doth it self employ
In all its Works to make it self the Joy
Of all his Hosts, and to compleat the Bliss
Which Omnipresent and Eternal is.
His Omnipresence is an Endless Sphere,
30   Wherin all Worlds as his Delights appear.

---

[1] The heading in D is simply '—IV' in PT's handwriting; T's own heading is the free
quotation from Psalm xvi.
   5. *privileged Posts*: Letters to the King or officers of State had free carriage.

His Bounty is the Spring of all Delight,
Our Blessedness, like his, is infinit.
His Glory Endless is and doth Surround
And fill all Worlds, without or End or Bound.
What hinders then, but we in heav'n may be   35
Even here on Earth did we but rightly see?
As Mountains, Charets, Horsemen all on fire,
To guard Elisha did of old conspire,
Which yet his Servant could not see, being blind,
Ourselvs environd with his Joys we find.   40
Eternity it self is that true Light,
That doth enclose us being infinite.
The very Seas do overflow and Swim
With Precious Nectars as they flow from him.
The Stable Earth which we beneath behold,   45
Is far more precious then if made of Gold.
Fowls Fishes Beasts, Trees Herbs and precious flowers,
Seeds Spices Gums and Aromatick Bowers,
Wherwith we are enclos'd and servd, each day
By his Appointment do their Tributes pay,   50
And offer up themselvs as Gifts of Love,
Bestowd on Saints, proceeding from above.
Could we but justly, wisely, truly prize
These Blessings, we should be above the Skies,
And Praises sing with pleasant Heart and Voice,   55
Adoring with the Angels should rejoyce.
The fertile Clouds give Rain, the Purer Air,
Is Warm and Wholsom, Soft and Bright and fair.
The Stars are Wonders which his Wisdom names,
The Glorious Sun the Knowing Soul enflames.   60
The very Heavens in their Sacred Worth,
At once serv us, and set his Glory forth.
Their Influences touch the Gratefull Sence,
They pleas the Ey with their Magnificence.
While in his Temple all his Saints do sing,   65
And for his Bounty prais their Heavenly King.
All these are in his Omnipresence still
As Living Waters from his Throne they trill.
As Tokens of his Lov they all flow down,
Their Beauty Use and Worth the Soul do Crown.   70

Men are like Cherubims on either hand,
Whose flaming Love by his Divine Command,
Is made a Sacrifice to ours; which Streams
Throughout all Worlds, and fills them all with Beams.
75   We drink our fill, and take their Beauty in,
While Jesus Blood refines the Soul from Sin.
His Grievous Cross is a Supreme Delight,
And of all Heavenly ones the greatest Sight.
His Throne is neer, tis just before our face,
80   And all Eternitie his Dwelling place.
His Dwelling place is full of Joys and Pleasures,
His Throne a fountain of Eternal Treasures.
His Omnipresence is all Sight and Love,
Which whoso sees, he ever dwells above.
85   With soft Embraces it doth Clasp the Soul,
And Watchfully all Enemies controul.
It enters in, and doth a Temple find,
Or make a Living one within the Mind.
That while Gods Omnipresence in us lies,
90   His Treasures might be all before our Eys:
For Minds and Souls intent upon them here,
Do with the Seraphims abov appear:
And are like Spheres of Bliss, by Lov and Sight,
By Joy, Thanksgiving, Prais, made infinite.
95   O give me Grace to see thy face, and be
A constant Mirror of Eternitie.
Let my pure Soul, transformed to a Thought,
Attend upon thy Throne, and as it ought
Spend all its Time in feeding on thy Lov,
100   And never from thy Sacred presence mov.
So shall my Conversation ever be
In Heaven, and I O Lord my GOD with Thee!

Goodnesse

I

The Bliss of other Men is my Delight:
    (When once my Principles are right:)
    And evry Soul which mine doth see
        A Treasurie.
The Face of GOD is Goodness unto all,   5
And while he Thousands to his Throne doth call,
    While Millions bathe in Pleasures,
    And do behold his Treasures
        The Joys of all
        On mine do fall   10
And even my Infinitie doth seem
A Drop without them of a mean Esteem.

2

The Light which on ten thousand faces Shines
    The Beams which crown ten thousand Vines
    With Glory and Delight, appear   15
        As if they were,
Reflected only from them all for me,
That I a Greater Beauty there might see.
    Thus Stars do Beautifie
    The Azure Canopie   20
        Gilded with Rayes
        Ten thousand Ways
They serv me, while the Sun that on them shines
Adorns those Stars, and crowns those Bleeding Vines.

3

Where Goodness is within, the Soul doth reign.   25
    Goodness the only Sovereign!
    Goodness delights alone to see
        Felicitie.
And while the Image of his Goodness lives
In me, whatever he to any gives   30

20. *Azure*, corr. for metrical reasons from 'Lofty Azure'.

Is my Delight and Ends
In me in all my Friends
For Goodness is
The Spring of Bliss
35   And tis the End of all it gives away
And all it gives it ever doth enjoy.

4

His Goodness! Lord, it is his Highest Glory!
The very Grace of all his Story!
What other thing can me delight
40   But the Blest Sight
Of his Eternal Goodness? While his Love
His Burning Lov the Bliss of all doth prove
While it beyond the Ends
Of Heaven and Earth extends
45   And Multiplies
Above the Skies
His Glory Love and Goodness in my Sight,
Is for my Joy therby more infinite.

5

The Soft and Swelling Grapes that on their Vines
50   Receiv the Lively Warmth that Shines
Upon them, ripen there for me:
Or Drink they be
Or Meat. The Stars salute my pleased Sence
With a Derivd and borrowed Influence
55   But better Vines do Grow
Far Better Wines do flow
Above, and while
The Sun doth Smile
Upon the Lillies there, and all things warme
60   Their pleasant Odors do my Spirit charm.

6

Their rich Affections do like precious Seas
Of Nectar and Ambrosia pleas.
Their Eys are Stars, or more Divine:
And Brighter Shine

48. *Joy therby*, corr. to 'Pleasure made'.   61. *do*, corr. to 'me'.

Their Lips are soft and Swelling Grapes, their Tongues   65
A Quire of Blessed and Harmonious Songs.
    Their Bosoms fraught with Love
    Are Heavens all Heavens above
And being Images of GOD, they are
The Highest Joys his Goodness did prepare.   70

An Infant-Ey[1]

A simple Light from all Contagion free,
A Beam that's purely Spiritual, an Ey
That's altogether Virgin, Things doth see
    Ev'n like unto the Deity:
That is, it shineth in an hevenly Sence,   5
And round about (unmov'd) its Light dispence.

The visiv† Rays are Beams of Light indeed,
Refined, subtil, piercing, quick and pure;
And as they do the sprightly Winds exceed,
    Are worthy longer to endure: 10
They far out-shoot the Reach of Grosser Air,
Which with such Excellence may not compare.

But being once debas'd, they soon becom
Less activ than they were before; and then
After distracting Objects out they run,   15
    Which make us wretched Men.
A simple Infant's Ey is such a Treasure
That when 'tis lost, w' enjoy no reall Pleasure.

O that my Sight had ever simple been!
And never faln into a grosser state!   20
Then might I evry Object still have seen
    (As now I see a golden Plate)
In such an hev'nly Light, as to descry
In it, or by it, my Felicity.

---

[1] This opens the section of poems or versions found only in Philip Traherne's MS. In D he wrote 'An Infant-Ey. p. 1' after the poem *Innocence*, so that, as M says, it must have been the first poem of the missing MS book. (See Introd. p. xiv.)

25 As easily might soar aloft as mov .
On Earth; and things remote as well as nigh
My Joys should be; and could discern the Lov
    Of God in my Tranquility.
But Streams are heavy which the Winds can blow;
30 Whose grosser body must needs move below.

The *East* was once my Joy; and so the Skies
And Stars at first I thought; the West was mine:
Then Praises from the Mountains did arise
    As well as Vapors: Evry Vine
35 Did bear me Fruit; the Fields my Gardens were;
My larger Store-house all the Hemisphere.

But Wantonness and Avarice got in
And spoil'd my Wealth; (I never can complain
Enough, till I am purged from my Sin
40   And made an Infant once again:)
So that my feeble and disabled Sense
Reacht only Near Things with its Influence.

A House, a Woman's Hand, a piece of Gold,
A Feast, a costly Suit, a beauteous Skin
45 That vy'd with Ivory, I did behold;
    And all my Pleasure was in Sin:
Who had at first with simple Infant-Eys
Beheld as mine ev'n all Eternities.

O dy! dy unto all that draws thine Ey
50 From its first Objects: let not fading Pleasures
Infect thy Mind; but see thou carefully
    Bid them adieu. Return: Thy Treasures
Abide thee still, and in their places stand
Inviting yet, and waiting thy Command.

The Return

To Infancy, O Lord, again I com,
    That I my Manhood may improv:
    My early Tutor is the Womb;
        I still my Cradle lov.
    'Tis strange that I should Wisest be,   5
    When least I could an Error see.

Till I gain strength against Temptation, I
    Perceiv it safest to abide
    An Infant still; and therfore fly
        (A lowly State may hide   10
    A man from Danger) to the Womb,
    That I may yet New-born becom.

My God, thy Bounty then did ravish me!
    Before I learned to be poor,
    I always did thy Riches see,   15
        And thankfully adore:
    Thy Glory and thy Goodness were
    My sweet Companions all the Year.

News[1]

    News from a forein Country came,
As if my Treasures and my Joys lay there;
    So much it did my Heart enflame,
'Twas wont to call my Soul into mine Ear;
        Which thither went to meet   5
            Th' approaching Sweet,
        And on the Threshold stood
        To entertain the secret Good;
            It hover'd there
        As if 'twould leav mine Ear,   10

[1] For T's version of this poem see p. 276. Comparison shows the changes made by Philip.
In half a dozen places in F he has copied down the *Centuries* version before making his own
alteration.

And was so eager to embrace
Th' expected Tidings, as they came,
That it could change its dwelling-place
  To meet the voice of Fame.

15 As if new Tidings were the Things
Which did comprise my wished unknown Treasure,
  Or els did bear them on their wings,
With so much Joy they came, with so much Pleasure,
    My Soul stood at the Gate
20   To recreäte
    It self with Bliss, and woo
Its speedier Approach; a fuller view
        It fain would take,
    Yet Journeys back would make
25 Unto my Heart, as if 'twould fain
Go out to meet, yet stay within,
Fitting a place to entertain
    And bring the Tidings in.

What Sacred Instinct did inspire
30 My Soul in Childhood with an hope so strong?
What secret Force mov'd my Desire
T' expect my Joys beyond the Seas, so yong?
        Felicity I knew
        Was out of view;
35   And being left alone,
    I thought all Happiness was gon
        From Earth: for this
    I long'd-for absent Bliss,
Deeming that sure beyond the Seas,
40 Or els in somthing near at hand
Which I knew not, since nought did pleas
    I knew, my Bliss did stand.

But little did the Infant dream
That all the Treasures of the World were by,
45 And that himself was so the Cream
And Crown of all which round about did ly.
    Yet thus it was! The Gem,
        The Diadem,

The Ring enclosing all
That stood upon this Earthen Ball; 50
The hev'nly Ey,
Much wider than the Sky,
Wherin they All included were;
The Lov, the Soul, that was the King
Made to possess them, did appear 55
A very little Thing.

Felicity

Prompted to seek my Bliss abov the Skies,
How often did I lift mine Eys
Beyond the Spheres!
Dame Nature told me there was endless Space
Within my Soul; I spy'd its very face: 5
Sure it not for nought appears.
What is there which a Man may see
Beyond the Spheres?
FELICITY.

There in the Mind of God, that Sphere of Lov, 10
(In nature, hight, extent, abov
All other Spheres,)
A Man may see Himself, the World, the Bride
Of God *His Church*, which as they there are ey'd
Strangely exalted each appears: 15
His Mind is higher than the Space
Above the Spheres,
Surmounts all Place.

No empty Space; it is all full of Sight,
All Soul and Life, an Ey most bright, 20
All Light and Lov;
Which doth at once all things possess and giv,
Heven and Earth, with All that therin liv;
It rests at quiet, and doth mov;
Eternal is, yet Time includes; 25
A Scene abov
All Interludes.

Adam

God made Man upright at the first;
Man made himself by Sin accurst:
Sin is a Deviation from the Way
Of God: 'Tis that wherin a Man doth stray
5   From the first Path wherin he was to walk,
From the first Truth he was to talk.

His Talk was to be all of Prais,
Thanksgiving, Rapture, Holy-days;
For nothing els did with his State agree:
10   Being full of Wonder and Felicity,
He was in thankful sort to meditate
Upon the Throne in which he sate.

No Gold, nor Trade, nor Silver there,
Nor Cloaths, nor Coin, nor Houses were,
15   No gaudy Coaches, Feasts, or Palaces,
Nor vain Inventions newly made to pleas;
But Native Truth, and Virgin-Purity,
An uncorrupt Simplicity.

His faithful Heart, his Hands, and Eys
20   He lifted up unto the Skies;
The Earth he wondring kneel'd upon; the Air,
He was surrounded with; the Trees, the fair
And fruitful Fields, his needful Treasures were;
And nothing els he wanted there.

25   The World its self was his next Theme,
Wherof himself was made Supream:
He had an Angel's Ey to see the Price†
Of evry Creature; that made Paradise:
He had a Tongue, yea more, a Cherub's Sense
30   To feel its Worth and Excellence.

Encompass'd with the Fruits of Lov,
He crowned was with Heven abov,
Supported with the Foot-stool of God's Throne,
A Globe more rich than Gold or precious Stone,

The fertil Ground of Pleasure and Delight,   35
  Encircled in a Sphere of Light.

The Sense of what He did possess
  Fill'd him with Joy and Thankfulness;
He was transported even here on Earth,
As if he then in Heven had his Birth: 40
The truth is, Heven did the Man surround,
  The Earth being in the middle found.

The World

When *Adam* first did from his Dust arise,
    He did not see,
    Nor could there be
  A greater Joy before his Eys:
  The Sun as bright for me doth shine;   5
    The Spheres abov
    Do shew his Lov,
  While they to kiss the Earth incline,
  The Stars as great a Service do;
    The Moon as much I view   10
As *Adam* did, and all God's Works divine
    Are Glorious still, and Mine.

Sin spoil'd them; but my Savior's precious Blood
    Sprinkled I see
    On them to be,   15
  Making them all both safe and good:
  With greater Rapture I admire
    That I from Hell
    Redeem'd, do dwell
  On Earth as yet; and here a Fire   20
  Not scorching but refreshing glows,
    And living Water flows,
Which *Dives* more than Silver doth desire,
    Of Crystals far the best.

25   What shal I render unto thee, my God,
                    For teaching me
                    The Wealth to see
              Which doth enrich thy Great Abode?
              My virgin-thoughts in Childhood were
30   Full of Content,
                    And innocent,
              Without disturbance, free and clear,
              Ev'n like the Streams of Crystal Springs,
                  Where all the curious things
35   Do from the bottom of the Well appear
                When no filth or mud is there.

        For so when first I in the Summer-fields
                    Saw golden Corn
                    The Earth adorn,
40   (This day that Sight its Pleasure yields)
              No Rubies could more take mine Ey;
                    Nor Pearls of price,
                    By man's Device
              Set in enamel'd Gold most curiously,
45   More costly seem to me,
                  How rich so'er they be
        By men esteem'd; nor could these more be mine
                That on my finger shine.

        The Skies abov so sweetly then did smile,
50   Their Curtains spread
                    Abov my Head
              And with its hight mine Ey beguile;
              So lovly did the distant Green
                    That fring'd the field
55   Appear, and yield
              Such pleasant Prospects to be seen
              From neighb'ring Hills; no precious Stone,
                  Or Crown, or Royal Throne,
        Which do bedeck the Richest Indian Lord,
60   Could such Delight afford.

44-45. As first written by Philip, therefore probably T's own version, though metrically
wrong.

The Sun, that gilded all the bordering Woods,
      Shone from the Sky
        To beautify
My Earthly and my Hevenly Goods;
Exalted in his Throne on high,   65
      He shed his Beams
        In golden Streams
That did illustrat† all the Sky;
Those Floods of Light, his nimble Rays,
      Did fill the glitt'ring Ways,   70
While that unsufferable piercing Ey
      The Ground did glorify.

The choicest Colors, Yellow, Green, and Blew
      Did on this Court
        In comly sort   75
A mixt variety bestrew;
Like Gold with Emeralds between;
      As if my God
        From his Abode
By these intended to be seen.   80
And so He was: I Him descry'd
·   In 's Works, the surest Guide
Dame Nature yields; His Lov, His Life doth there
      For evermore appear.

No House nor Holder in this World did I   85
      Observ to be:
        What I did see
Seem'd all *Mine Own*; wherin did ly
A Mine, a Garden, of Delights;
      Pearls were but Stones;   90
        And great King's Thrones,
Compared with such Benefits,
But empty Chairs; a Crown, a Toy
      Scarce apt to pleas a Boy.
All other are but petty trifling Shews,   95
      To that which God bestows.

69. *his nimble Rays* corr. from 'which he displays'.

A Royal Crown, inlaid with precious Stones,
Did less surprize
The Infant Eys
100   Of many other little Ones,
Than the great Beauties of this Frame,
Made for my sake,
Mine Eys did take,
Which I Divine, and *Mine*, do name.
105   Surprizing Joys beyond all Price
Compos'd a Paradise,
Which did my Soul to lov my God enflame,
And ever will the same.

The Apostacy

One Star
Is better far
Than many Precious Stones:
One Sun, which is abov in Glory seen,
5   Is worth ten thousand Golden Thrones:
A juicy Herb, or Spire of Grass,
In useful Virtu, native Green,
An Em'rald doth surpass;
Hath in't more Valu, tho less seen.

10   No Wars,
Nor mortal Jars,
Nor bloody Feuds, nor Coin,
Nor Griefs which they occasion, saw I then;
Nor wicked Thievs which this purloin:
15   I had no Thoughts that were impure;
Esteeming both Women and Men
God's Work, I was secure,
And reckon'd Peace my choicest Gem.

As *Eve*
20   I did believ
My self in *Eden* set,
Affecting neither Gold, nor Ermin'd Crowns,
Nor ought els that I need forget;

No Mud did foul my limpid Streams,
No Mist eclypst my Sun with frowns;   25
   Set off with hev'nly Beams,
My Joys were Meadows, Fields, and Towns.

      Those things
    Which *Cherubins*
  Did not at first behold   30
Among God's Works, which *Adam* did not see;
  As Robes, and Stones enchas'd in Gold,
  Rich Cabinets, and such like fine
  Inventions; could not ravish me:
    I thought not Bowls of Wine   35
Needful for my Felicity.

      All Bliss
    Consists in this,
  'To do as *Adam* did;
And not to know those superficial Joys   40
  Which were from him in *Eden* hid:
  Those little new-invented Things,
  Fine Lace and Silks, such Childish Toys
    As Ribbans are and Rings,
  Or worldly Pelf that Us destroys.   45

      For God,
    Both Great and Good,
  The Seeds of Melancholy
Creäted not: but only foolish Men,
  Grown mad with customary Folly   50
  Which doth increase their Wants, so dote
  As when they elder grow they then
    Such Baubles chiefly note;
  More Fools at Twenty Years than Ten.

      But I,   55
    I knew not why,
  Did learn among them too
At length; and when I once with blemisht Eys
  Began their Pence and Toys to view,

37-54. cf. *Blisse*, among the D poems, p. 64. The alterations seem on the MS evidence
to be due to Philip.

60 Drown'd in their Customs, I became
A Stranger to the Shining Skies,
  Lost as a dying Flame;
And Hobby-horses brought to prize.

   The Sun
65   And Moon forgon,
  As if unmade, appear
No more to me; to God and Heven dead
I was, as tho they never were:
Upon som useless gaudy Book,
70 When what I knew of God was fled,
   The Child being taught to look,
His Soul was quickly murthered.

   O fine!
  O most divine!
75 O brave! they cry'd; and shew'd
Som Tinsel thing whose Glittering did amaze,
And to their Cries its beauty ow'd;
Thus I on Riches, by degrees,
Of a new Stamp did learn to gaze;
80   While all the World for these
I lost: my Joy turn'd to a Blaze.

Solitude

  How desolate!
Ah! how forlorn, how sadly did I stand
  When in the field my woful State
  I felt! Not all the Land,
5   Not all the Skies,
  Tho Heven shin'd before mine Eys,
Could Comfort yield in any Field to me,
Nor could my Mind Contentment find or see.

  Remov'd from Town,
10 From People, Churches, Feasts, and Holidays,
  The Sword of State, the Mayor's Gown,
  And all the Neighb'ring Boys;

As if no Kings
On Earth there were, or living Things,
The silent Skies salute mine Eys, the Seas   15
My Soul surround; no Rest I found, or Eas.

My roving Mind
Search'd evry Corner of the spacious Earth,
From Sky to Sky, if it could find,
(But found not) any Mirth: 20
Not all the Coasts,
Nor all the great and glorious Hosts,
In Hev'n or Earth, did Comfort me afford;
I pin'd for hunger at a plenteous Board.

I do believ,   25
The Ev'ning being shady and obscure,
The very Silence did me griev,
And Sorrow more procure:
A secret Want
Did make me think my Fortune scant.   30
I was so blind, I could not find my Health,
No Joy mine Ey could there espy, nor Wealth.

Nor could I ghess
What kind of thing I long'd for: But that I
Did somwhat lack of Blessedness,   35
Beside the Earth and Sky,
I plainly found;
It griev'd me much, I felt a Wound
Perplex me sore; yet what my Store should be
I did not know, nothing would shew to me.   40

Ye sullen Things!
Ye dumb, ye silent Creatures, and unkind!
How can I call you Pleasant Springs
Unless ye eas my Mind!
Will ye not speak   45
What 'tis I want, nor Silence break?
O pity me, and let me see som Joy:
Som Kindness shew to me, altho a Boy.

47. *and . . . som*, corr. from 'at least point out my'.

They silent stood;
50   Nor Earth, nor Woods, nor Hills, nor Brooks, nor Skies,
       Would tell me where the hidden Good,
           Which I did long for, lies:
           The shady Trees,
       The Ev'ning dark, the humming Bees,
55   The chirping Birds, mute Springs and Fords, conspire,
To giv no Answer unto my Desire.

           Bells ringing I
Far off did hear, som Country Church they spake;
       The Noise re-ecchoing throu the Sky
60   My Melancholy brake;
           When't reacht mine Ear
       Som Tidings thence I hop'd to hear:
But not a Bell me News could tell, or shew
My longing Mind, where Joys to find, or know.

65   I griev'd the more,
'Caus I therby somwhat encorag'd was
       That I from those should learn my Store;
           For Churches are a place
           That nearer stand
70   Than any part of all the Land
To Hev'n; from whence som little Sense I might
To help my Mind receiv, and find som Light.

           They louder sound
Than men do talk, somthing they should disclose;
75   The empty Sound did therfore wound
           Becaus not shew Repose.
           It did revive
       To think that Men were there alive;
But had my Soul, call'd by the Toll, gon in,
80   I might have found, to eas my Wound, a Thing.

           A little Eas
Perhaps, but that might more molest my Mind;
       One flatt'ring Drop would more diseas
           My Soul with Thirst, and grind
85   My Heart with grief:
       For Peeple can yield no Relief

In publick sort when in that Court they shine,
Except they mov my Soul with Lov divine.

Th' External Rite,
Altho the face be wondrous sweet and fair, 90
Will never sate my Appetit
No more than empty Air
Yield solid Food.
Must I the best and highest Good
Seek to possess; or Blessedness in vain 95
(Tho 'tis alive in som place) strive to gain?

O! what would I
Diseased, wanting, melancholy, giv
To find what is Felicity,
The place where Bliss doth liv? 100
Those Regions fair
Which are not lodg'd in Sea nor Air,
Nor Woods, nor Fields, nor Arbour yields, nor Springs,
Nor Hev'ns shew to us below, nor Kings.

I might hav gon 105
Into the City, Market, Tavern, Street,
Yet only change my Station,
And strove in vain to meet
That Eas of Mind
Which all alone I long'd to find: 110
A common Inn doth no such thing betray,
Nor doth it walk in Peeple's Talk, or Play.

O Eden fair!
Where shall I seek the Soul of Holy Joy
Since I to find it here despair; 115
Nor in the shining Day,
Nor in the Shade,
Nor in the Field, nor in a Trade
I can it see? Felicity! O where
Shall I thee find to eas my Mind! O where! 120

101. *Those*, corr. from 'The', but 'The' might have been a slip, since the previous line begins thus.

111-12. Changes have been made in these lines, but it is impossible to restore T's original.

Poverty

As in the House I sate
Alone and desolate,
No Creature but the Fire and I,
The Chimney and the Stool, I lift mine Ey
5   Up to the Wall,
And in the silent Hall
          Saw nothing mine
But som few Cups and Dishes shine
The Table and the wooden Stools
10   Where Peeple us'd to dine:
A painted Cloth there was
Wherin som ancient Story wrought
A little entertain'd my Thought
Which Light discover'd throu the Glass.

15   I wonder'd much to see
That all my Wealth should be
Confin'd in such a little Room,
Yet hope for more I scarcely durst presume.
          It griev'd me sore
20   That such a scanty Store
          Should be my All:
For I forgat my Eas and Health,
Nor did I think of Hands or Eys,
          Nor Soul nor Body prize;
25   I neither thought the Sun,
Nor Moon, nor Stars, nor Peeple, *mine*,
Tho they did round about me shine;
And therfore was I quite undon.

Som greater things I thought
30   Must needs for me be wrought,
Which till my pleased Mind could see
I ever should lament my Poverty:
          I fain would have
          Whatever Bounty gave;
35   Nor could there be
Without, or Lov or Deity:

For, should not He be Infinit
    Whose Hand created me?
    Ten thousand absent things
Did vex my poor and absent Mind,   40
Which, till I be no longer blind,
    Let me not see the King of Kings.

    His Lov must surely be
    Rich, infinit, and free;
Nor can He be thought a God   45
Of Grace and Pow'r, that fills not his Abode,
    His Holy Court,
    In kind and liberal sort;
    Joys and Pleasures,
Plenty of Jewels, Goods, and Treasures,   50
(To enrich the Poor, cheer the forlorn)
    His Palace must adorn,
    And given all to me:
For till *His* Works *my* Wealth became,
No Lov, or Peace, did me enflame: 55
But now I have a DEITY.

Dissatisfaction

    In Cloaths confin'd, my weary Mind
        Persu'd Felicity;
    Throu ev'ry Street I ran to meet
            My Bliss:
But nothing would the same disclose to me.   5
            What is,
    O where, the place of holy Joy!
Will nothing to my Soul som Light convey!
    In ev'ry House I sought for Health,
Searcht ev'ry Cabinet to spy my Wealth,   10
        I knockt at ev'ry Door,
    Askt ev'ry Man I met for Bliss,
In ev'ry School, and Colledg, sought for this:
    But still was destitute and poor.

15   My piercing Eys unto the Skies
                 I lifted up to see;
           But no Delight my Appetit
                        Would sate;
           Nor would that Region shew Felicity:
20   My Fate
           Deny'd the same; Abov the Sky,
           Yea all the Hev'n of Hev'ns, I lift mine Ey;
           But nothing more than empty Space
           Would there discover to my Soul its face.
25   Then back dissatisfy'd
                 To Earth I came; among the Trees,
           In Taverns, Houses, Feasts, and Palaces,
                 I sought it, but was still deny'd.

                 Panting and faint, full of Complaint,
30   I it persu'd again,
                 In Diadems, and Eastern Gems,
                        In Bags
           Of Gold and Silver: But got no more Gain
                        Than Rags,
35   Or empty Air, or Vanity;
           Nor did the Temples much more signify:
                 Dirt in the Streets; in Shops† I found
           Nothing but Toil. Walls only me surround
                 Or worthless Stones or Earth;
40   Dens full of Thievs, glutted with Blood,
           Complaints and Widows Tears: no other Good
                 Could there descry, no Hev'nly Mirth.

                 Mens Customs here but vile appear;
                 The Oaths of Roaring Boys,
45   Their Gold that shines, their sparkling Wines,
                        Their Lies,
           Their gawdy Trifles, are mistaken Joys:
                        To prize
           Such Toys I loath'd. My Thirst did burn;
50   But where, O whither should my Spirit turn!
                 Their Games, their Bowls, their cheating Dice,
           Did not compleat, but spoil, my Paradise.

On things that gather Rust,
Or modish Cloaths, they fix their minds,
Meer outward Shew their Fancy blinds,   55
Their Eys b'ing all put out with Dust.

Sure none of these, sensless as Trees,
Can shew me tru Repose.
Philosophy! canst thou descry
My Bliss?   60
Will Books or Sages it to me disclose?
I miss
Of this in all: They tell me Pleasure,
Or earthly Honor, or a fading Treasure,
Will never with it furnish me.   65
But then, Where is? What is, Felicity?
Here all Men are in doubt,
And unresolv'd, they cannot speak
What 'tis; and all or most that Silence break
Discover Nothing but their Throat.   70

Weary of all that since the Fall
Mine Eys on Earth can find,
I for a Book from Heven look,
Since here
No Tidings will salute or eas my Mind: 75
Mine Ear,
My Ey, my Hand, my Soul, doth long
For som fair Book fill'd with Eternal Song.
O *that*! my Soul: for *that* I burn:
That is the Thing for which my Heart did yern.   80
Diviner Counsels there;
The Joys of God, the Angels Songs,
The secret Causes which employ their Tongues,
Will surely pleas when they appear.

What Sacred Ways! What hev'nly Joys!   85
Which Mortals do not see?
What hidden Springs! What glorious Things
Abov!
What kind of Life among them led may be
In Lov!   90

H

What Causes of Delight they have!
What pleasing joyous Objects God them gave!
This mightily I long'd to know;
Oh, that som Angel these would to me shew!
95   How full, divine, and pure,
Their Bliss may be, including All
Things visible or invisible, which shall
To Everlasting firm endure.

O this! In this I hop'd for Bliss;
100   Of this I dreamt by Night:
For this by Day I gasping lay;
                    Mine Eys
For this did fail: For this, my great Delight
                    The Skies
105   Became, in hopes they would disclose
My Sacred Joys, and my desir'd Repose.
Oh! that som Angel would bring down
The same to me; That Book should be my Crown.
I breathe, I long, I seek:
110   Fain would I find, but still deny'd,
I sought in ev'ry Library and Creek†
Until *the Bible* me supply'd.

The Bible

That! That! There I was told
That I *the Son of God* was made,
His Image. O Divine! And that fine Gold,
With all the Joys that here do fade,
5   Are but a Toy, compared to the Bliss
Which Hev'nly, God-like, and Eternal is.

That We on earth are Kings;
And, tho we're cloath'd with mortal Skin,
Are Inward Cherubins; hav Angels Wings;
10   Affections, Thoughts, and Minds within,
Can soar throu all the Coasts of Hev'n and Earth;
And shall be sated with Celestial Mirth.

Completely satisfied

Christendom

When first mine Infant-Ear
Of *Christendom* did hear,
I much admired what kind of Place or Thing
It was of which the Folk did talk:
What Coast, what Region, what therin   5
Did mov, or might be seen to walk.
My great Desire
Like ardent fire
Did long to know what Things did ly behind
That *Mystic Name*, to which mine Ey was blind.   10

Som Depth it did conceal,
Which, till it did reveal
Its self to me, no Quiet, Peace, or Rest,
Could I by any Means attain;
My earnest Thoughts did me molest   15
Till som one should the thing explain:
I thought it was
A Glorious Place,
Where Souls might dwell in all Delight and Bliss;
So thought, yet fear'd lest I the Truth might miss: 20

Among ten thousand things,
Gold, Silver, Cherub's Wings,
Pearls, Rubies, Diamonds, a Church with Spires,
Masks, Stages, Games and Plays,
That then might suit my yong Desires,   25
Fine Feathers, Farthings, Holidays,
Cards, Musick, Dice,
So much in price;
A *City* did before mine Eys present
Its self, wherin there reigned sweet Content.   30

A Town beyond the Seas,
Whose Prospect much did pleas,
And to my Soul so sweetly raise Delight
As if a long expected Joy,
Shut up in that transforming Sight,   35
Would into me its Self convey;

And Blessedness
I there possess,
As if that City stood on reall Ground,
And all the Profit mine which there was found.

Whatever Force me led,
My Spirit sweetly fed
On these Conceits; That 'twas a City strange,
Wherin I saw no gallant Inns,
No Markets, Shops or Old Exchange,
No Childish Trifles, useless Things;
No Wall, nor Bounds
That Town surrounds;
But as if all its Streets ev'n endless were;
Without or Gate or Wall it did appear.

Things Native sweetly grew,
Which there mine Ey did view,
Plain, simple, cheap, on either side the Street,
Which was exceeding fair and wide;
Sweet Mansions there mine Eys did meet;
Green Trees the shaded Doors did hide:
My chiefest Joys
Were Girls and Boys
That in those Streets still up and down did play,
Which crown'd the Town with constant Holiday.

A sprightly pleasant Time,
(Ev'n Summer in its prime),
Did gild the Trees, the Houses, Children, Skies,
And made the City all divine;
It ravished my wondring Eys
To see the Sun so brightly shine:
The Heat and Light
Seem'd in my sight
With such a dazling Lustre shed on them,
As made me think 'twas th' *New Jerusalem*.

Beneath the lofty Trees
I saw, of all Degrees,

Folk calmly sitting in their doors; while som
Did standing with them kindly talk,
Som smile, som sing, or what was don   75
Observ, while others by did walk;
      They view'd the Boys
      And Girls, their Joys,
The Streets adorning with their Angel-faces,
Themselvs diverting in those pleasant Places.   80

      The Streets like Lanes did seem,
      Not pav'd with Stones, but green,
Which with red Clay did partly mixt appear;
      'Twas Holy Ground of great Esteem;
      The Springs choice Liveries did wear   85
      Of verdant Grass that grew between
       The purling Streams,
       Which golden Beams
Of Light did varnish, coming from the Sun,
By which to distant Realms was Service don.   90

      In fresh and cooler Rooms
      Retir'd they dine: Perfumes
They wanted not, having the pleasant Shade
      And Peace to bless their House within,
      By sprinkled Waters cooler made,   95
      For those incarnat Cherubin.
       This happy Place,
       With all the Grace
The Joy and Beauty which did it beseem,
Did ravish me and highten my Esteem.   100

      That here to rais Desire
      All Objects do conspire,
Peeple in Years, and Yong enough to play,
      Their Streets of Houses, common Peace,
      In one continued Holy day   105
      Whose gladsom Mirth shall never cease:
       Since these becom
       My *Christendom*,
What learn I more than that *Jerusalem*
Is *mine*, as 'tis *my Maker's*, choicest Gem.   110

95. *By*, corr. from 'While', which does not fit the syntax.

Before I was aware
Truth did to me appear,
And represented to my Virgin-Eys
Th' unthought of Joys and Treasures
115   Wherin my Bliss and Glory lies;
My God's Delight, (which givs me Measure)
His Turtle Dov,
Is Peace and Lov
In Towns: for holy Children, Maids, and Men
120   Make up the King of Glory's Diadem.

On Christmas-Day

Shall Dumpish Melancholy spoil my Joys
While Angels sing
And Mortals ring
My Lord and Savior's Prais!
5   Awake from Sloth, for that alone destroys,
'Tis Sin defiles, 'tis Sloth puts out thy Joys.
See how they run from place to place,
And seek for Ornaments of Grace;
Their Houses deckt with sprightly Green,
10   In Winter makes a Summer seen;
They Bays and Holly bring
As if 'twere Spring!

Shake off thy Sloth, my drouzy Soul, awake;
With Angels sing
Unto thy King,
15   And pleasant Musick make;
Thy Lute, thy Harp, or els thy Heart-strings take,
And with thy Musick let thy Sense awake.
See how each one the other calls
20   To fix his Ivy on the walls,
Transplanted there it seems to grow
As if it rooted were below:
Thus He, who is thy King,
Makes Winter, Spring.

25   Shall Houses clad in Summer-Liveries
His Praises sing
And laud thy King,
And wilt not thou arise?

Forsake thy Bed, and grow (my Soul) more wise,
Attire thy self in cheerful Liveries: 30
     Let pleasant Branches still be seen
     Adorning thee, both quick and green;
     And, which with Glory better suits,
     Be laden all the Year with Fruits;
        Inserted into Him,   35
        For ever spring.

'Tis He that Life and Spirit doth infuse:
      . Let ev'ry thing
       The Praises sing
     Of *Christ* the King of Jews;   40
Who makes things green, and with a Spring infuse
A Season which to see it doth not use:
     Old Winter's Frost and hoary hair,
     With Garland's crowned, Bays doth wear;
     The nipping Frost of Wrath b'ing gon,   45
     To Him the Manger made a Throne,
        Du Praises let us sing,
        Winter and Spring.

See how, their Bodies clad with finer Cloaths,
       They now begin   50
       His Prais to sing
     Who purchas'd their Repose:
Wherby their inward Joy they do disclose;
Their Dress alludes to better Works than those:
     His gayer Weeds and finer Band,   55
     New Suit and Hat, into his hand
     The Plow-man takes; his neatest Shoos,
     And warmer Glovs, he means to use:
        And shall not I, my King,
        Thy Praises sing?   60

See how their Breath doth smoak, and how they haste
       His Prais to sing
       With Cherubim;
      They scarce a Break-fast taste;
But throu the Streets, lest precious Time should waste,   65
When Service doth begin, to Church they haste.
     And shall not I, Lord, com to Thee,
     The Beauty of thy Temple see?

Thy Name with Joy I will confess,
70 Clad in my Savior's Righteousness;
'Mong all thy Servants sing
To Thee my King.

'Twas thou that gav'st us Caus for fine Attires;
Ev'n thou, O King,
75 As in the Spring,
Dost warm us with thy fires
Of Lov: Thy Blood hath bought us new Desires;
Thy Righteousness doth cloath with new Attires.
Made fresh and fine let me appear
80 This Day divine, to close the Year;
Among the rest let me be seen
A living Branch and always green,
Think it a pleasant thing
Thy Prais to sing.

85 At break of Day, O how the Bells did ring?
To thee, my King,
The Bells did ring;
To thee the Angels sing:
Thy Goodness did produce this other Spring,
90 For this it is they make the Bells to ring:
The sounding Bells do throu the Air
Proclaim thy Welcom far and near;
While I alone with Thee inherit
All these Joys, beyond my Merit.
95 Who would not always sing
To such a King?

I all these Joys, abov my Merit, see
By Thee, my King,
To whom I sing,
100 Entire convey'd to me.
My Treasure, Lord, thou mak'st thy Peeple be
That I with pleasure might thy Servants see.
Ev'n in their rude external ways
They do set forth my Savior's Prais,

---

82. corr. from 'A Branch of the tru Vine', which M thinks may have been an experiment of Philip's.

And minister a Light to me;   105
While I by them do hear to Thee
 Praises, my Lord and King,
  Whole Churches ring.

Hark how remoter Parishes do sound!
  Far off they ring   110
  For thee, my King,
 Ev'n round about the Town:
The Churches scatter'd over all the Ground
Serv for thy Prais, who art with Glory crown'd.
 This City is an Engin great   115
 That makes my Pleasure more compleat;
 The Sword, the Mace, the Magistrate,
 To honor Thee attend in State;
  The whole Assembly sings;
  The Minster rings.   120

Bells

I

Hark! hark, my Soul! the Bells do ring,
 And with a louder voice
Call many Families to sing
His publick Praises, and rejoice:
Their shriller Sound doth wound the Air,   5
Their grosser Strokes affect the Ear,
 That we might thither all repair
 And more Divine ones hear.
  If Lifeless Earth
  Can make such Mirth,   10
What then shall Souls abov the starry Sphere!

Bells are but Clay that men refine
 And rais from duller Ore;
Yet now, as if they were divine,
They call whole Cities to adore;   15
Exalted into Steeples they
Disperse their Sound, and from on high
Chime-in our Souls; they ev'ry way

Speak to us throu the Sky:
20   Their iron Tongues
Do utter Songs,
And shall our stony Hearts make no Reply!

From darker Mines and earthy Caves
At last let Souls awake,
25   And rousing from obscurer Graves
From lifeless Bells example take;
Lifted abov all earthly Cares,
Let them (like these) rais'd up on high,
Forsaking all the baser Wares
30   Of dull Mortality,
His Praises sing,
Tunably ring,
In a less Distance from the peaceful Sky.

II

From Clay, and Mire, and Dirt, my Soul,
35   From vile and common Ore,
Thou must ascend; taught by the Toll
In what fit place thou mayst adore;
Refin'd by fire, thou shalt a Bell
Of Prais becom, in Mettal pure;
40   In Purity thou must excell,
No Soil or Grit endure.
Refin'd by Lov,
Thou still *abov*
Like them must dwell, and other Souls allure.

45   Doth not each trembling Sound I hear
Make all my Spirits dance?
Each Stroak's a Message to my Ear
That casts my Soul into a Trance
Of Joy: They're us'd to notify
50   Religious Triumphs, and proclaim
The Peace of Christianity,
In *Jesus* holy Name.
Authorities
And Victories
55   Protect, increas, enrich, adorn the same.

Kings, O my Soul, and Princes now
    Do prais His holy Name,
Their golden Crowns and Scepters bow
In Honor of my Lord: His Fame
Is gon throu-out the World, who dy'd   60
Upon the Cross for me: And He
That once was basely crucify'd
    Is own'd a Deity.
        The Higher Powers
        Hav built these Towers   65
Which here aspiring to the Sky we see.

Those Bells are of a piece, and sound,
    Whose wider mouths declare
Our Duty to us: Being round
And smooth and whole, no Splinters are   70
In them, no Cracks, nor holes, nor flaws
That may let out the Spirits thence
Too soon; *that* would harsh jarring caus
    And lose their Influence.
        We must unite   75
        If we Delight
Would yield or feel, or any Excellence.

Churches

I

Those stately Structures which on Earth I view
To GOD erected, whether Old or New;
His Sacred Temples which the World adorn,
Much more than Mines of Ore or Fields of Corn,
My Soul delight: How do they pleas mine Ey   5
When they are fill'd with Christian Family!
Upon the face of all the peepl'd Earth
There's no such sacred Joy or solemn Mirth,
To pleas and satisfy my Heart's Desire,
As that wherwith my Lord is in a Quire,   10
In holy Hymns by warbling Voices prais'd,
With Eys lift up, and joint Affections rais'd.

The Arches built (like Hev'n) wide and high
Shew his Magnificence and Majesty
Whose House it is: With so much Art and Cost
The Pile is fram'd, the curious Knobs embost,
Set off with Gold, that me it more doth pleas
Than Princes Courts or Royal Palaces;
Great Stones pil'd up by costly Labors there
Like Mountains carv'd by human Skill appear;
Where Towers, Pillars, Pinnacles, and Spires
Do all concur to match my great Desires,
Whose Joy it is to see such Structures rais'd
To th' end my God and Father should be prais'd.

II

Were there but one alone
Wherin we might approach his Throne,
One only where we should accepted be,
As in the Days of old
It was, when *Solomon* of Gold
His Temple made; we then should see
A numerous Host approaching it,
Rejoicing in the Benefit:
The Queen of *Sheba* com
With all her glorious Train,
The *Pope* from *Rome*,
The Kings beyond the Main;
The Wise men of the East from far,
As guided by a Star,
With Rev'rence would approach unto that Ground,
At that sole Altar be adoring found.

Great Lords would thither throng,
And none of them without a Song
Of Prais; Rich Merchants also would approach
From ev'ry forein Coast;
Of Ladies too a shining Host,
If not on Hors-back, in a Coach;
This Single Church would crouded be
With Men of Great and High Degree:

We Princes might behold 25
With glitt'ring Scepters there
In-laid with Gold
And precious Stones, draw near.
No Room for mean Ones there would be,
Nor place for Thee and Me: 30
An endless Troop would crouding there appear,
Bringing new Presents daily ev'ry Year.

But now we Churches have
In ev'ry Coast, which Bounty gave
Most freely to us; now they sprinkled stand 35
With so much Care and Lov,
In this rich Vale, nigh yonder Grove
That men might com in ev'ry Land
To them with greater Eas; lo, we
Those blest Abodes neglected see: 40
As if our God were worse
Becaus His Lov is more,
And doth disburse
Its self in greater Store;
Nor can object with any face 45
The Distance of the place;
Ungrateful We with slower haste do com
Unto his Temple, 'caus 'tis nearer home.

Misapprehension

Men are not wise in their Tru Interest,
Nor in the Worth of what they long possest:
They know no more what is their Own
Than they the Valu of 't have known.
They pine in Misery, 5
Complain of Poverty,
Reap not where they hav sown,
Griev for Felicity,
Blaspheme the Deity;

38. *men*, corr. from 'we', which may have been a slip.

10   And all becaus they are not blest
        With Eys to see the Worth of Things:
        For did they know their Reall Interest,
                No doubt they'd all be Kings.

        There's not a Man but covets and desires
15   A Kingdom, yea a World; nay, he aspires
                To all the Regions he can see
                Beyond the Hev'ns Infinity:
                        The World too little is
                        To be his Sphere of Bliss;
20   Eternity must be
                        The Object of his View
                        And his Possession too;
                Or els Infinity's a Dream
                That quickly fades away; He lovs
25   All Treasures; but he hates a failing Stream
                That dries up as it movs.

        Can Fancy make a Greater King than God?
        Can Man within his Soveraign's Abode
                Be dearer to himself than He
30   That is the Angels Deity?
                        Man is as wel belov'd
                        As they, if he improv'd
                        His Talent as we see
                        They do; and may as well
35   In Blessedness excell.
        But Man hath lost the ancient Way,
        That Road is gon into Decay;
        Brambles shut up the Path, and Briars tear
                Those few that pass by there.

40   They think no Realms nor Kingdoms theirs,
        No Lands nor Houses, that have other Heirs.
                But native Sense taught me more Wit,
                The World did too, I may admit:
                        As soon as I was born
                        It did my Soul adorn,
45   And was a Benefit

That round about me lay;
And yet without Delay
'Twas seated quickly in my Mind,
Its Uses also I yet find   50
Mine own: for God, that All things would impart,
Center'd it in my Heart.

The World set in Man's Heart, and yet not His!
Why, all the Compass of this great Abyss,
Th' united Service and Delight,   55
Its Beauty that attracts the Sight,
That Goodness which I find,
Doth gratify my Mind;
The common Air and Light
That shines, doth me a Pleasure   60
And surely is my Treasure:
Of it I am th' inclusive Sphere,
It doth entire in me appear
As well as I in it: It givs me Room,
Yet lies within my Womb.   65

The Odour

These Hands are Jewels to the Ey,
Like Wine, or Oil, or Hony, to the Taste:
These Feet which here I wear beneath the Sky
Are us'd, yet never waste.
My Members all do yield a sweet Perfume;   5
They minister Delight, yet not consume.

Ye living Gems, how Tru! how Near!
How Reall, Useful, Pleasant! O how Good!
How Valuable! yea, how Sweet! how Fair!
B'ing once well understood!   10
For Use ye permanent remain intire,
Sweet Scents diffus'd do gratify Desire.

Can melting Sugar sweeten Wine?
Can Light communicated keep its Name?
Can Jewels solid be, tho they do shine?   15
From Fire rise a flame?

Ye solid are, and yet do Light dispence;
Abide the same, tho yield an Influence.

      Your Uses flow while ye abide:
20   The Services which I from you receiv
Like sweet Infusions throu me daily glide
        Ev'n while they Sense deceiv,
B'ing unobserved: for *only Spirits* see
What Treasures Services and Uses be.

25   The *Services* which from you flow
Are such diffusiv Joys as know no measure;
Which shew His boundless Lov who did bestow
        These Gifts to be my Treasure.
Your Substance is the Tree on which it grows;
30 Your Uses are the Oil that from it flows.

      Thus Hony flows from Rocks of Stone;
Thus Oil from Wood; thus Cider, Milk, and Wine,
From Trees and Flesh; thus Corn from Earth; to one
        That's hev'nly and divine.
35 But He that cannot like an Angel see,
In Heven its self shall dwell in Misery.

      If first I learn not what's *Your* Price
Which are alive, and are to me so near;
How shall I all the Joys of Paradise,
40   Which are so Great and Dear,
Esteem? Gifts ev'n at distance are our Joys,
But lack of Sense the Benefit destroys.

      Liv to thy Self; thy Limbs esteem:
From Hev'n they came; with Mony can't be bought,
45 They are such Works as God himself beseem,
        May *precious* well be thought.
Contemplat then the Valu of this Treasure,
By *that* alone thou feelest all the Pleasure.

      Like Amber fair thy Fingers grow;
50 With fragrant Hony-sucks thy Head is crown'd;
Like Stars, thine Eys; thy Cheeks like Roses shew:
        All are Delights profound.
Talk with thy self; thy self enjoy and see:
At once the Mirror and the Object be.

What's Cinnamon, compar'd to thee? 55
Thy Body is than Cedars better far: ·
Those Fruits and Flowers which in Fields I see,
      With *thine*, can not compare.
Where ere thou movest, there the Scent I find
Of fragrant Myrrh and Aloes left behind. 60

    But what is Myrrh? What Cinnamon?
What Aloes, Cassia, Spices, Hony, Wine?
O sacred *Uses*! You to think upon
      Than these I more incline.
To see, taste, smell, observ; is to no End, 65
If I *the Use* of each don't apprehend.

Admiration

    Can Human Shape so taking be,
        That Angels com and sip
    Ambrosia from a Mortal Lip!
Can Cherubims descend with Joy to see
        God in his Works beneath! 5
        Can Mortals breath
        FELICITY!
    Can Bodies fill the hev'nly Rooms
    With welcom Odours and Perfumes!
Can Earth-bred Flow'rs adorn Celestial Bowers 10
Or yield such Fruits as pleas the hev'nly Powers!

    Then may the Seas with Amber flow;
        The Earth a Star appear;
    Things be divine and hevenly here.
The Tree of Life in Paradise may grow 15
        Among us now: the Sun
        Be overcom
        With Beams that shew
    More bright than his: Celestial Mirth
    May yet inhabit all this Earth. 20
It cannot be! Can Mortals be so blind?
Hav Joys so near them, which they never mind?

The Lilly and the Rosy-Train
Which, scatter'd on the ground,
25   Salute the Feet which they surround,
Grow for thy sake, O Man; that like a Chain
Or Garland they may be
To deck ev'n thee:
They all remain
30   Thy Gems; and bowing down their head
Their liquid Pearl they kindly shed
In Tears; as if they meant to wash thy Feet,
For Joy that they to serv thee are made meet.

The Sun doth smile, and looking down
From Hev'n doth blush to see
35   Himself excelled here by thee:
Yet frankly doth dispers his Beams that crown
A Creature so divine;
He lovs to shine,
Nor lets a Frown
40   Eclyps his Brow, becaus he givs
Light for the Use of one that livs
Abov himself. Lord! What is Man that he
Is thus admired like a Deity!

Right Apprehension

Giv but to things their tru Esteem,
And those which now so vile and worthless seem
Will so much fill and pleas the Mind,
That we shall there the only Riches find,
How wise was I
5   In Infancy!
I then saw in the clearest Light;
But corrupt Custom is a second Night.

Custom; that must a Trophy be
10   When Wisdom shall compleat her Victory:
For Trades, Opinions, Errors, are
False Lights, but yet receiv'd to set off Ware
More false: We're sold
For worthless Gold.

Diana was a Goddess made   15
That Silver-Smiths might have the better Trade.

But giv to Things their tru Esteem,
And then what's magnify'd most vile will seem:
What commonly's despis'd, will be
The truest and the greatest Rarity.   20
        What Men should prize
        They all despise;
The best Enjoiments are abus'd;
The Only Wealth by Madmen is refus'd.

A Globe of Earth is better far   25
Than if it were a Globe of Gold: A Star
    Much brighter than a precious Stone:
The Sun more Glorious than a Costly Throne;
        His warming Beam,
        A living Stream   30
Of liquid Pearl, that from a Spring
Waters the Earth, is a most precious thing.

What Newness once suggested to,
Now clearer Reason doth improv, my View:
    By Novelty my Soul was taught   35
At first; but now Reality my Thought
        Inspires: And I
        With clarity
Both ways instructed am; by Sense
Experience, Reason, and Intelligence.   40

A Globe of Gold must Barren be,
Untill'd and Useless: We should neither see
    Trees, Flowers, Grass, or Corn
Such a Metalline Massy Globe adorn:
        As Splendor blinds,   45
        So Hardness binds;
    No Fruitfulness it can produce;
A Golden World can't be of any Use.

Ah me! This World is more divine:
The Wisdom of a God in this doth shine.   50

What ails Mankind to be so cross?†
The Useful Earth they count vile Dirt and Dross:
And neither prize
Its Qualities,
55   Nor Donor's Lov. I fain would know
How or why Men God's Goodness disallow.

The Earth's rare ductile Soil,
Which duly yields unto the Plow-man's Toil,
Its fertile Nature, givs Offence;
60   And its Improvment by the Influence
Of Hev'n; For, these
Do not well pleas,
Becaus they do upbraid Mens hardned Hearts,
And each of them an Evidence imparts

65   Against the Owner; whose Design
It is that Nothing be reputed fine,
Nor held for any Excellence,
Of which he hath not in himself the Sense.
He too well knows
70   That no Fruit grows
In his Obduratness, nor yields
Obedience to the Hevens like the Fields:

But being, like his loved Gold,
Stiff, barren, hard impenetrable; tho told
75   He should be otherwise: He is
Uncapable of any hev'nly Bliss.
His Gold and he
Do well agree;
For he's a formal† Hypocrite,
80   Like *that* Unfruitful, yet on th' outside bright.

Ah! Happy Infant! Wealthy Heir!
How blessed did the Hev'n and Earth appear
Before thou knew'st there was a thing
Call'd Gold! Barren of Good; of Ill the Spring
85   Beyond Compare!
Most quiet were
Those Infant-Days, when I did see
Wisdom and Wealth couch'd in Simplicity.

The Image

If I be like my God, my King,
  (Tho not a Cherubim,)
    I will not care,
  Since all my Pow'rs derived are
    From none but Him.   5
The best of Images shall I
  Comprised in Me see;
    For I can spy
  All Angels in the Deity
    Like me to ly.   10

The Evidence

His *Word* confirms the Sale:
  Those Sheets enfold my Bliss:
Eternity its self's the Pale
Wherin my tru Estate enclosed is:
  Each ancient Miracle's a Seal: 5
Apostles, Prophets, Martyrs, Patriarchs are
The Witnesses; and what their Words reveal,
  Their written Records do declare.
All may well wonder such a 'State to see
In such a solemn sort settled on me.   10

  Did not his *Word* proclaim
    My Title to th' Estate,
His *Works* themselvs affirm the same
By what they do; my Wish they antedate.
  Before I was conceiv'd, they were   15
Allotted for my great Inheritance;
As soon as I among them did appear
  They did surround me, to advance
My Interest and Lov. Each Creature says,
God made us Thine, that we might shew His Prais.   20

    The Services they do,
      Aloud proclaim them *Mine*;
    In that they are adapted to
  Supply my Wants; in which they all combine

25   To pleas and serv me, that I may
    God, Angels, Men, Fowls, Beasts, and Fish enjoy,
    Both in a natural and transcendent way;
        And to my Soul the Sense convey
    Of Wisdom, Goodness, Power, and Lov Divine,
30   Which made them *all*, and made them to be *mine*.

Shadows in the Water

    In unexperienc'd Infancy
    Many a sweet Mistake doth ly:
    Mistake tho false, intending† tru;
    A *Seeming* somwhat more than *View*;
5   That doth instruct the Mind
        In Things that ly behind,
    And many Secrets to us show
    Which afterwards we com to know.

    Thus did I by the Water's brink
10   Another World beneath me think;
    And while the lofty spacious Skies
    Reversed there abus'd† mine Eys,
        I fancy'd other Feet
        Came mine to touch and meet;
15   As by som Puddle I did play
    Another World within it lay.

    Beneath the Water Peeple drown'd.
    Yet with another Hev'n crown'd,
    In spacious Regions seem'd to go
20   Freely moving to and fro:
        In bright and open Space
        I saw their very face;
    Eys, Hands, and Feet they had like mine;
    Another Sun did with them shine.

25   'Twas strange that Peeple there should walk,
    And yet I could not hear them talk:
    That throu a little watry Chink,
    Which one dry Ox or Horse might drink,

We other Worlds should see,
Yet not admitted be;   30
And other Confines there behold
Of Light and Darkness, Heat and Cold.

I call'd them oft, but call'd in vain;
No Speeches we could entertain:
Yet did I there expect to find   35
Som other World, to pleas my Mind.
    I plainly saw by these
    A new *Antipodes*,
Whom, tho they were so plainly seen,
A Film kept off that stood between.   40

By walking Men's reversed Feet
I chanc'd another World to meet;
Tho it did not to View exceed
A Phantasm, 'tis a World indeed,
    Where Skies beneath us shine,   45
    And Earth by Art divine
Another face presents below,
Where Peeple's feet against Ours go.

Within the Regions of the Air,
Compass'd about with Hev'ns fair,   50
Great Tracts of Land there may be found
Enricht with Fields and fertil Ground;
    Where many num'rous Hosts,
    In those far distant Coasts,
For other great and glorious Ends,   55
Inhabit, my yet unknown Friends.

O ye that stand upon the Brink,
Whom I so near me, throu the Chink,
With Wonder see: What Faces there,
Whose Feet, whose Bodies, do ye wear?   60
    I my Companions see
    In You, another Me.
They seemed Others, but are We;
Our second Selvs those Shadows be.

65   Look how far off those lower Skies
    Extend themselvs! scarce with mine Eys
    I can them reach. O ye my Friends,
    What *Secret* borders on those Ends?
       Are lofty Hevens hurl'd
70   'Bout your inferior World?
    Are ye the Representatives
    Of other Peopl's distant Lives?

    Of all the Play-mates which I knew
    That here I do the Image view
75   In other Selvs; what can it mean?
    But that below the purling Stream
       Som unknown Joys there be
       Laid up in Store for me;
    To which I shall, when that thin Skin
80   Is broken, be admitted in.

On Leaping over the Moon

    I saw new Worlds beneath the Water ly,
      New Peeple; and another Sky,
        And Sun, which seen by Day
        Might things more clear display.
5   Just such another
        Of late my Brother
    Did in his Travel see, and saw by Night
      A much more strange and wondrous Sight:
    Nor could the World exhibit such another,
10   So Great a Sight, but in a Brother.

    Adventure strange! No such in Story we
      New or old, tru or feigned, see.
        On Earth he seem'd to mov
        Yet Heven went abov;
15   Up in the Skies
        His Body flies

3. *And*, corr. from 'Another'. M conjectures that T's lines ran: 'Another Sun by Day Did things more clear display'.

In open, visible, yet Magick, sort:
    As he along the Way did sport
Like Icarus over the Flood he soars
    Without the help of Wings or Oars.   20

As he went tripping o'r the King's high-way,
    A little pearly River lay
        O'r which, without a Wing
        Or Oar, he dar'd to swim,
            Swim throu the Air   25
            On Body fair;
He would not use nor trust *Icarian* Wings
    Lest they should prov deceitful things;
For had he faln, it had been wondrous high,
    Not from, but from abov, the Sky: 30

He might hav dropt throu that thin Element
    Into a fathomless Descent;
        Unto the nether Sky
        That did beneath him ly,
            And there might tell   35
            What Wonders dwell
On Earth abov. Yet bold he briskly runs
    And soon the Danger overcoms;
Who, as he leapt, with Joy related soon
    How *happy he* o'r-leapt the Moon.   40

What wondrous things upon the Earth are don
    Beneath, and yet abov, the Sun?
        Deeds all appear again
        In higher Spheres; remain
            In Clouds as yet: 45
            But there they get
Another Light, and in another way
    Themselvs to us *abov* display.
The Skies themselvs this earthly Globe surround;
    W'are even here within them found.   50

On hev'nly Ground within the Skies we walk,
    And in this middle Center talk:

Did we but wisely mov,
On Earth in Hev'n abov,
We then should be
Exalted high
55
Abov the Sky: from whence whoever falls,
Through a long dismall Precipice,
Sinks to the deep Abyss where *Satan* crawls
Where horrid Death and Despair lies.
60

As much as others thought themselvs to ly
Beneath the Moon, so much more high
Himself he thought to fly
Above the starry Sky,
As *that* he spy'd
65
Below the Tide.
Thus did he yield me in the shady Night
A wondrous and instructiv Light,
Which taught me that under our Feet there is
As o'r our Heads, a Place of Bliss.
70

¶

To the same purpos; he, not long before
Brought home from Nurse, going to the door
To do som little thing
He must not do within,
With Wonder cries,
5
As in the Skies
He saw the Moon, *O yonder is the Moon*
Newly com after me to Town,
That shin'd at Lugwardin but yesternight,
Where I enjoy'd the self-same Light.
10

As if it had ev'n twenty thousand faces,
It shines at once in many places;
To all the Earth so wide
God doth the Stars divide

2. *going*, corr. from 'went', which M prefers, but it will not do in the context of PT's version.

With so much Art   15
The Moon impart,
They serve us all; serv wholy ev'ry One
As if they served him alone.
While evry single Person hath such Store,
'Tis want of Sense that makes us poor.   20

Sight

Mine Infant-Ey
Abov the Sky
Discerning endless Space,
Did make me see
Two *Sights* in me,   5
Three Eys adorn'd my Face:
Two Luminaries in my Flesh
Did me refresh;
But one did lurk within,
Beneath my Skin,   10
That was of greater Worth than both the other;
For those were Twins; but this had ne'r a Brother.

Those Eys of Sense
That did dispense
Their Beams to nat'ral things,   15
I quickly found
Of narrow Bound
To know but earthly Springs.
But *that* which throu the Hevens went
Was excellent,   20
And Endless; for the Ball
Was Spirit'all:
A visiv† Ey things visible doth see;
But with th' Invisible, Invisibles agree.

One World was not   25
(Be't ne'r forgot)
Ev'n then enough for me:
My better Sight
Was infinit,
New Regions I must see.   30

In distant Coasts new Glories I
　　　　Did long to spy:
　　　What this World did present
　　　　Could not content;
35　But, while I look'd on Outward Beauties *here*,
　Most earnestly expected Others *there*.

　　　　I know not well
　　　　What did me tell
　　　Of endless Space: but I
40　　　Did in my Mind
　　　　Som such thing find
　　　To be beyond the Sky
　That had no Bound; as certainly
　　　　As I can see
45　　　That I have Foot or Hand
　　　　To feel or Stand:
　Which I discerned by another Sight
　Than that which grac'd my Body much more bright.

　　　　I own it was
50　　　A Looking-Glass
　　　Of signal Worth; wherin,
　　　　More than mine Eys
　　　　Could see or prize,
　　　Such things as Virtues win,
55　Life, Joy, Lov, Peace, appear'd: a Light
　　　　Which to my Sight
　　　Did Objects represent
　　　　So excellent;
　That I no more without the same can see
60　Than Beasts that have no tru Felicity.

　　　　This Ey alone,
　　　（That peer hath none）
　　　Is such, that it can pry
　　　　Into the End
65　　　To which things tend,
　　And all the Depths descry
　That God and Nature do include.
　　　　By this are view'd

The very Ground and Caus
Of sacred Laws,   70
All Ages too, Thoughts, Counsels, and Designs;
So that no Light in Hev'n more clearly shines.

Walking

To *walk* abroad is, not with Eys,
But Thoughts, the Fields to see and prize;
   Els may the silent Feet,
     Like Logs of Wood,
Mov up and down, and see no Good,   5
   Nor Joy nor Glory meet.

Ev'n Carts and Wheels their place do change,
But cannot see; tho very strange
   The Glory that is by:
     Dead Puppets may   10
Mov in the bright and glorious Day,
   Yet not behold the Sky.

And are not Men than they more blind,
Who having Eys yet never find
   The Bliss in which they mov: 15
     Like Statues dead
They up and down are carried,
   Yet neither see nor lov.

To *walk* is by a Thought to go;
To mov in Spirit to and fro;   20
   To mind the Good we see;
     To taste the Sweet;
Observing all the things we meet
   How choice and rich they be.

To note the Beauty of the Day,   25
And golden Fields of Corn survey;
   Admire the pretty Flow'rs
     With their sweet Smell;
To prais their Maker, and to tell
   The Marks of His Great Pow'rs.   30

29. *prais*, corr. from 'celebrat'.

To fly abroad like activ Bees,
Among the Hedges and the Trees,
   To cull the Dew that lies
     On evry Blade,
35 From evry Blossom; till we lade
   Our *Minds*, as they their *Thighs*.

Observ those rich and glorious things,
The Rivers, Meadows, Woods, and Springs,
   The fructifying Sun;
     To note from far
40 The Rising of each Twinkling Star
   For us his Race to run.

A little Child these well perceivs,
Who, tumbling among Grass and Leaves,
   May Rich as Kings be thought,
     But there's a Sight
45 Which perfect Manhood may delight,
   To which we shall be brought.

While in those pleasant Paths we talk
'Tis *that* tow'rds which at last we walk;
   But we may by degrees
     Wisely proceed
50 Pleasures of Lov and Prais to heed,
   From viewing Herbs and Trees.

The Dialogue

Q. Why dost thou tell me that the fields are mine?
A. Becaus for thee the fields so richly shine.

Q. Am I the Heir of the Works of Men?
A. For thee they dress, for thee manure them.

5 Q. Did I my self by them intended see,
   That I the Heir of their Works should be,
   It well would pleas; But they themselvs intend:
   I therfore am not of their Works the End.

A. The reall Benefit of all their Works,
   Wherin such mighty Joy and Beauty lurks,   10
   Derives† its self to *thee*; to *thee* doth com,
   As do the Labors of the Shining Sun;
   Which doth not think on *thee* at all, my Friend,
   Yet all his Beams of Light on *thee* do tend:
   For *thee* they shine and do themselvs display;   15
   For *thee*, they do both make and gild the Day;
   For *thee* doth rise that glorious Orb of Light;
   For thee it sets, and so givs way for Night;
   That glorious Bridegroom daily shews his face,
   Adorns the World, and swiftly runs his Race,   20
   Disperseth Clouds, and raiseth Vapors too,
   Exciteth Winds, distills the Rain and Dew,
   Concocteth† Mines, and makes the liquid Seas
   Contribute Moisture to thy Plants and Trees,
   Doth quicken Beasts, revive thy vital Powers,   25
   Thrusts forth the Grass, and beautifies thy Flowers,
   By tacit Causes animats the Trees,
   As they do Thee so he doth cherish Bees,
   Digesteth Mettals, raiseth Fruit and Corn,
   Makes Rivers flow, and Mountains doth adorn: 30
   All these it doth, not by its own Design,
   But by thy God's, which is far more divine;
   Who so disposeth Things, that they may be
   In Hev'n and Earth kind Ministers to Thee:
   And tho the Men that toil for Meat, and Drink,   35
   And Cloaths, or Houses, do not on Thee think;
   Yet all their Labors by His hevenly Care
   To Thee, in Mind or Body, helpful are:
   And that God thus intends thy single Self,
   Should pleas thee more, than if to heap up Wealth   40
   For Thee, all men did work, and sweat, and bleed;
   Mean Thee alone (my Friend) in ev'ry Deed.

41. corr. from 'All men for Thee . . .'.

Dreams

'Tis strange! I saw the Skies;
I saw the Hills before mine Eys;
The Sparrow fly;
The Lands that did about me ly;
5   The reall Sun, *that* hev'nly Ey!
Can closed Eys ev'n in the darkest Night
See throu their Lids, and be inform'd with Sight?

The Peeple were to me
As tru as those by day I see;
10   As tru the Air,
The Earth as sweet, as fresh, as fair
As that which did by day repair
Unto my waking Sense! Can all the Sky,
Can all the World, within my Brain-pan ly?

15   What sacred Secret's this,
Which seems to intimat my Bliss?
What is there in
The narrow Confines of my Skin,
That is alive and feels within
20   When I am dead? Can Magnitude possess
An activ Memory, yet not be less?

May all that I can see
Awake, by Night within me be?
My Childhood knew
25   No Difference, but all was Tru,
As Reall all as what I view;
The World its Self was there. 'Twas wondrous strange,
That Hev'n and Earth should so their place exchange.

Till *that* which vulgar Sense
30   Doth falsly call Experience,
Distinguisht things:
The Ribbans, and the gaudy Wings
Of Birds, the Virtues, and the Sins,
That represented were in Dreams by night
35   As really my Senses did delight,

Or griev, as those I saw
By day: Things terrible did aw
    My Soul with Fear;
The Apparitions seem'd as near
As Things could be, and Things they were: 40
Yet were they all by Fancy in me wrought,
And all their Being founded in a Thought.

    O what a Thing is Thought!
Which seems a Dream; yea, seemeth Nought,
    Yet doth the Mind   45
Affect as much as what we find
Most near and tru! Sure Men are blind,
And can't the forcible Reality
Of things that Secret are within them see.

    Thought! Surely *Thoughts* are tru;   50
They pleas as much as *Things* can do:
    Nay Things are dead,
And in themselvs are severed
From Souls; nor can they fill the Head
Without our Thoughts. Thoughts are the Reall things   55
From whence all Joy, from whence all Sorrow springs.

The Inference

I

Well-guided *Thoughts* within possess
The Treasures of all Blessedness.
Things are indifferent; nor giv
    Joy of themselvs, nor griev.
The very Deity of God torments   5
    The male-contents
Of Hell; To th' Soul alone it provs
A welcom Object, that Him lovs.
Things tru affect not, while they are unknown:
But *Thoughts* most sensibly, when quite alone.   10

K

Thoughts are the inward Balms or Spears;
The living Joys, or Griefs and Fears;
The Light, or els the Fire; the Theme
On which we pore or dream.
15   Thoughts are alone by Men the Objects found
That heal or wound.
Things are but dead: they can't dispense
Or Joy or Grief: Thoughts! Thoughts the Sense
Affect and touch. Nay, when a Thing is near
20   It can't affect but as it doth appear.

Since then by Thoughts I only see;
Since Thought alone affecteth me;
Since these are Reall things when shewn;
And since as Things are known
25   Or thought, they pleas or kill: What Care ought I
(Since Thoughts apply
Things to my Mind) those Thoughts aright to frame,
That *Hev'nly Thoughts* me *hev'nly Things* may gain.

Ten thousand thousand Things are dead;
30   Ly round about me; yet are fled,
Are absent, lost, and from me gon;
And those few Things alone,
Or griev my Soul, or gratify my Mind,
Which I do find
35   Within. Let then the Troubles dy,
The noisom Poisons buried ly:
Ye Cares and Griefs avaunt, that breed Distress
Let only those remain which God will bless.

How many Thousands see the Sky,
40   The Sun and Moon, as well as I?
How many more that view the Seas,
Feel neither Joy nor Eas?
Those Things are dead and dry and banished.
Their Life is led
45   As if the World were yet unmade:
A Feast, fine Cloaths, or els a Trade,
Take up their Thoughts; and, like a grosser Skreen
Drawn o'r their Soul, leav better Things unseen.

But O! let me the Excellence
Of God, in all His Works, with Sense   50
Discern: Oh! let me celebrat
And feel my blest Estate:
Let all my Thoughts be fixt upon His Throne;
And Him alone
For all His gracious Gifts admire,   55
Him only with my Soul desire:
Or griev for Sin. That with du Sense, the Pleasure
I may possess of His Eternal Treasure.

II

David a Temple in his Mind conceiv'd;
And that Intention was so well receiv'd
By God, that all the Sacred Palaces
That ever were did less His Glory pleas.
If Thoughts are such; such Valuable Things;   5
Such reall Goods; such human Cherubins;
Material Delights; transcendent Objects; Ends
Of all God's Works, which most His Ey intends.
O! What are Men, who can such Things produce,
So excellent in Nature, Valu, Use?   10
Which not to Angels only grateful seem,
But God, most Wise, himself doth them esteem
Worth more than Worlds? How many thousand may
Our Hearts conceiv and offer evry Day?
Holy Affections, grateful Sentiments,   15
Good Resolutions, virtuous Intents,
Seed-plots of activ Piety; He values more
Than the Material World He made before.
By these the Blessed Virgin (and no other)
Obtain'd the Grace to be the Happy Mother   20
Of God's own Son; for, of her pious Care
To treasure up those Truths which she did hear
Concerning Christ, in thoughtful Mind, w're told;
But not that e'r with Offerings of Gold
The Temple she enricht. This understood,   25
How glorious, how divine, how great, how good

May we becom! How like the Deity
In managing our Thoughts aright! A Piety
More grateful to our God than building Walls
30   Of Churches, or the Founding Hospitalls:
Wherin He givs us an Almighty Power
To pleas Him so, that could we Worlds creäte,
Or more New visible Earths and Hev'ens make,
'Twould be far short of this; which is the Flower
35   And Cream of Strength. This we might plainly see,
But that we Rebels to our Reason be.
Shall God such sacred Might on us bestow?
And not employ't to pay the Thanks we ow?
Such grateful Offerings able be to giv;
40   Yet them annihilat,† and God's Spirit griev?
Consider that for All our Lord hath don,
All that He can receiv is this bare Sum
Of God-like Holy Thoughts: These only He
Expects from Us, our Sacrifice to be.

The City

What Structures here among God's Works appear?
      Such Wonders *Adam* ne'r did see
      In Paradise among the Trees,
         No Works of Art like these,
5   Nor Walls, nor Pinnacles, nor Houses were.
         All these for me,
      For me these Streets and Towers,
These stately Temples, and these solid Bowers,
         My Father rear'd:
10   For me I thought they thus appear'd.

The City, fill'd with Peeple, near me stood;
      A Fabrick like a Court divine,
      Of many Mansions bright and fair;
         Wherin I could repair
15   To Blessings that were Common, Great, and Good:
         Yet all did shine

As burnisht and as new
As if before none ever did them view:
    They seem'd to me
  Environ'd with Eternity.   20

As if from Everlasting they had there
  Been built, more gallant than if gilt
  With Gold, they shew'd: Nor did I know
    That they to Hands did ow
Themselvs. Immortal they did all appear   25
    Till I knew Guilt.
    As if the Publick Good
Of all the World for me had ever stood,
    They gratify'd
  Me, while the Earth they beautify'd.   30

The living Peeple that mov'd up and down,
  With ruddy Cheeks and sparkling Eys;
  The Musick in the Churches, which
    Were Angels Joys (tho Pitch
Defil'd me afterwards) did then me crown: 35
    I then did prize
    These only I did lov
As do the blessed Hosts in Heven abov:
    No other Pleasure
  Had I, nor wish'd for other Treasure.   40

The Hevens were the richly studded Case
  Which did my richer Wealth inclose;
  No little privat Cabinet
    In which my Gems to set
Did I contrive: I thought the whole Earth's face   45
    At my Dispose:
    No Confines did include
What I possest, no Limits there I view'd;
    On evry side
  All endless was which then I spy'd.   50

'Tis Art that hath the late Invention found
  Of shutting up in little Room
  Ones boundless Expectations: Men
    Have in a narrow Penn
Confin'd themselvs: Free Souls can know no Bound;   55
    But still presume

That Treasures evry where
From Everlasting Hills must still appear,
          And be to them
60   Joys in the New *Jerusalem*.

We first by Nature all things boundless see;
     Feel all illimited; and know
          No Terms or Periods: But go on
               Throughout the Endless Throne
65   Of God, to view His wide Eternity;
                    Ev'n here below
               His Omnipresence we
Do pry into, *that* Copious Treasury.
          Tho we are taught
70   To limit and to bound our Thought.

Such Treasures as are to be valu'd more
          Than those shut up in Chests and Tills,
               Which are by Citizens esteem'd,
                    To me the Peeple seem'd:
75   The City doth encreas my glorious Store,
                    Which sweetly fills
               With choice Variety
The Place wherin I see the same to be;
               And strangely is
80   A Mansion or Tower of Bliss.

Nor can the City such a Soul as mine
          Confine; nor be my only Treasure:
               I must see other Things to be
                    For my Felicity
85   Concurrent Instruments, and all combine
                    To do me Pleasure.
               And God, to gratify
This Inclination, helps me to descry
                    Beyond the Sky
90   More Wealth provided, and more high.

Insatiableness

I

No Walls confine! Can nothing hold my Mind?
Can I no Rest nor Satisfaction find?
    Must I behold Eternity
        And see
    What Things abov the Hev'ns be?   5
      Will nothing serv the Turn?
    Nor Earth, nor Seas, nor Skies?
        Till I what lies
      In Time's beginning find;
Must I till then for ever burn?   10

Not all the Crowns; not all the heaps of Gold
On Earth; not all the Tales that can be told,
    Will Satisfaction yield to me:
        Nor Tree,
    Nor Shade, nor Sun, nor *Eden*, be   15
      A Joy: Nor Gems in Gold,
      (Be't Pearl or precious Stone,)
        Nor Spring, nor Flowers,
      Answer my *Craving* Powers,
Nor any Thing that Eyes behold.   20

Till I what was before all Time descry,
The World's Beginning seems but Vanity.
    My Soul doth there long Thoughts extend;
        No End
    Doth find, or Being comprehend: 25
      Yet somwhat sees that is
      The obscure shady face
        Of endless Space,
      All Room within; where I
Expect to meet Eternal Bliss.   30

29. *All Room within*: This is obscure: it could mean that endless space is suggested by all
finite space, as M thinks; or possibly 'Room' might mean 'the dimension, or scope, of the
whole universe'.

II

This busy, vast, enquiring Soul
　　　Brooks no Controul,
　　No Limits will endure,
　Nor any Rest: It will all see,
Not Time alone, but ev'n Eternity.
　　　What is it? Endless sure.

'Tis mean Ambition to desire
　　　A single World:
　　To many I aspire,
　Tho one upon another hurl'd:
Nor will they all, if they be all confin'd,
　　　Delight my Mind.

This busy, vast, enquiring Soul
　　　Brooks no Controul:
　　'Tis hugely curious too.
　Each one of all those Worlds must be
Enricht with infinit Variety
　　　And Worth; or 'twill not do.

'Tis nor Delight nor perfect Pleasure
　　　To have a Purse
　　That hath a Bottom of its Treasure,
Since I must thence endless Expense disburse.
Sure there's a GOD (for els there's no Delight)
　　　One Infinit.

Consummation

　The Thoughts of Men appear
Freely to mov within a Sphere
　　Of endless Reach; and run,
Tho in the Soul, beyond the Sun.
The Ground on which they acted be
Is unobserv'd Infinity.

　Extended throu the Sky,
Tho here, beyond it far they fly:

Abiding in the Mind
An endless Liberty they find: 10
Throu-out all Spaces can extend,
Nor ever meet or know an End.

They, in their native Sphere,
At boundless Distances appear:
Eternity can measure;   15
Its no Beginning see with Pleasure.
Thus in the Mind an endless Space
Doth nat'rally display its face.

Wherin becaus we no
Object distinctly find or know;   20
We sundry Things invent,
That may our Fancy giv content;
See Points of Space beyond the Sky,
And in those Points see Creatures ly.

Spy Fishes in the Seas,   25
Conceit them swimming there with Eas;
The Dolphins and the Whales,
Their very Finns, their very Scales,
As there within the briny Deep
Their Tails the flowing Waters sweep.   30

Can see the very Skies,
As if the same were in our Eys;
The Sun, tho in the Night,
As if it mov'd within our Sight;
One Space beyond another still   35
Discovered; think while ye will.

Which, tho we don't descry,
(Much like by night an Idle Ey,
Not shaded with a Lid,
But in a darksom Dungeon hid)   40
At last shall in a glorious Day
Be made its Objects to display

25–27. Constellations: Pisces, Delphinus, Cetus.
37. *Which*: M thinks a stanza containing the antecedent may have been omitted. But 'which' could conceivably refer to the 'Space' of 35.

And then shall Ages be
Within its wide Eternity;
45   All Kingdoms stand,
Howe'r remote, yet nigh at hand;
The Skies, and what beyond them ly,
Exposed unto evry Ey.

Nor shall we then invent
50   Nor alter Things; but with content
All in their places see,
As doth the Glorious Deity;
Within the Scope of whose Great Mind,
We all in their tru Nature find.

Hosanna

No more shall Walls, no more shall Walls confine
That glorious Soul which in my Flesh doth shine:
No more shall Walls of Clay or Mud
          Nor Ceilings made of Wood,
5   Nor Crystal Windows, bound my Sight,
But rather shall admit Delight.
          The Skies that seem to bound
                    My Joys and Treasures,
               Of more endearing Pleasures
10   Themselvs becom a Ground:
While from the Center to the utmost Sphere
My Goods are multiplied evry where.

The Deity, the Deity to me
Doth All things giv, and make me clearly see
15   The Moon and Stars, the Air and Sun
               Into my Chamber com:
The Seas and Rivers hither flow,
Yea, here the Trees of *Eden* grow,
          The Fowls and Fishes stand,
20   Kings and their Thrones,
          As 'twere, at my Command;
          God's Wealth, His Holy Ones,
The Ages too, and Angels all conspire:
While I, that I the Center am, admire.

No more, No more shall Clouds eclyps my Treasures,   25
Nor viler Shades obscure my highest Pleasures;
      No more shall earthen Husks confine
        My Blessings which do shine
     Within the Skies, or els *abov*:
     Both Worlds one Heven made by Lov,   30
        In common happy I
          With Angels walk
        And there my Joys espy;
        With God himself I talk;
Wondring with Ravishment all Things to see   35
Such *Reall* Joys, so truly *Mine*, to be.

No more shall Trunks & Dishes be my Store,
Nor Ropes of Pearl, nor Chains of Golden Ore;
      As if such Beings yet were not,
        They all shall be forgot.   40
     No such in Eden did appear,
     No such in Heven: Heven here
        Would be, were those remov'd;
          The Sons of Men
        Liv in Jerusalem,   45
        Had they not Baubles lov'd.
These Clouds dispers'd, the Hevens clear I see.
Wealth new-invented, *mine* shall never be.

Transcendent Objects doth my God provide,
In such convenient Order all contriv'd,   50
      That All things in their proper place
        My Soul doth best embrace,
     Extends its Arms beyond the Seas,
     Abov the Hevens its self can pleas,
        With God enthron'd may reign: 55
          Like sprightly Streams
        My Thoughts on Things remain;
        Or els like vital Beams
They reach to, shine on, quicken Things, and make
Them truly Usefull; while I *All* partake.   60

For Me the World created was by Lov;
For Me the Skies, the Seas, the Sun, do mov;

The Earth for Me doth stable stand;
For Me each fruitful Land
65   For Me the very Angels God made *His*
And *my* Companions in Bliss:
His Laws command all Men
That they lov Me,
Under a Penalty
70   Severe, in case they miss:
His Laws require His Creatures all to prais
His Name, and when they do't be most my Joys.

The Review

I

Did I grow, or did I stay?
Did I prosper or decay?
When I so
From *Things* to *Thoughts* did go?
5   Did I flourish or diminish,
When I so in *Thoughts* did finish
What I had in *Things* begun;
When from God's Works to think upon
The Thoughts of Men my Soul did com?
10   The Thoughts of Men, had they been Wise,
Should more delight me than the Skies.
They mighty Creatures are
For these the Mind
Affect, afflict, do eas or grind;
15   But foolish Thoughts ensnare.

Wise ones are a sacred Treasure;
Tru ones yield Substantial Pleasure:
Compar'd to them,
I *Things* as *Shades* esteem.
20   False ones are a foolish Flourish,
(Such as Mortals chiefly nourish)
When I them to *Things* compare,
Compar'd to *Things*, they Trifles are;
Bad Thoughts do hurt, deceiv, ensnare.

A good Man's Thoughts are of such price   25
That they creäte a Paradise:
   But he that misemploys
     That Faculty,
God, Men, and Angels doth defy;
   Robs them of all their Joys.   30·

II

   My Child-hood is a Sphere
Wherin ten thousand hev'nly Joys appear:
   Those *Thoughts* it doth include,
   And those Affections, which review'd,
     Again present to me   5
In better sort the *Things* which I did see.
   Imaginations *Reall* are,
   Unto my Mind again repair:
Which makes my Life a Circle of Delights;
A hidden Sphere of obvious Benefits: 10
An Earnest that the Actions of the Just
Shall still revive, and flourish in the Dust.

POEMS FROM
CHRISTIAN ETHICKS

I

For Man to Act as if his Soul did see
The very Brightness of Eternity;
For Man to Act as if his Love did burn
Above the Spheres, even while its in its *Urne*;
5   For Man to Act even in the Wilderness,
As if he did those Sovereign Joys possess,
Which do at once confirm, stir up, enflame,
And perfect Angels; having not the same!
It doth increase the Value of his Deeds,
10   In this a Man a Seraphim exceeds:
    To Act on Obligations yet unknown,
To Act upon Rewards as yet unshewn,
To keep Commands whose Beauty's yet unseen,
To cherish and retain a Zeal between
15   Sleeping and Waking; shews a constant care;
And that a deeper Love, a Love so Rare,
That no Eye Service may with it compare.
    The Angels, who are faithful while they view
His Glory, know not what themselves would do,
20   Were they in our Estate! A Dimmer Light
Perhaps would make them erre as well as We;
And in the Coldness of a darker Night,
Forgetful and Lukewarm Themselves might be.
Our very Rust shall cover us with Gold,
25   Our Dust shall sparkle while their Eyes behold
The Glory Springing from a feeble State,
Where meer Belief doth, if not conquer Fate,
Surmount, and pass what it doth Antedate.†

'For Man to Act . . .'. From *Christian Ethicks*, chap. xxi. See Appendix (p. 419) for the context of this and the following fragments, and Introduction, p. xiii.
   25. *sparkle* emended by Dobell from 'sprinkle'.

II

For there are certain Periods and fit Bounds,
Which he that passeth, all his Work confounds.

III

All Musick, Sawces, Feasts, Delights and Pleasures,
Games, Dancing, Arts consist in govern'd Measures;
Much more do Words, and Passions of the Mind
In Temperance their sacred Beauty find.

IV

As in a Clock, 'tis hinder'd-Force doth bring
The Wheels to order'd Motion, by a Spring;
Which order'd Motion guides a steddy Hand
In useful sort at Figures just to stand;
Which, were it not by Counter-ballance staid,   5
The Fabrick quickly would aside be laid
As wholly useless: So a Might too Great,
But well proportion'd, makes the World compleat.
Power well-bounded is more Great in Might,
Than if let loose 'twere wholly Infinite.   10
He could have made an endless Sea by this,
But then it had not been a Sea of Bliss;
A Sea that's bounded in a finite shore,
Is better far because it is no more.
Should Waters endlessly exceed the Skies,   15
They'd drown the World, and all whate'er we prize.
Had the bright Sun been Infinite, its Flame
Had burnt the World, and quite consum'd the same.
That Flame would yield no splendor to the Sight,
'Twould be but Darkness though 'twere Infinite.   20
One Star made Infinite would all exclude,
An Earth made Infinite could ne're be view'd.
But all being bounded for each others sake,
He bounding all did all most useful make.
And which is best, in Profit and Delight,   25
Though not in Bulk, he made all Infinite.

'For there are certain Periods . . .'. As M points out, this as well as III and IV must have
formed part of the 'Poem on Moderation' quoted in C III. 19 and 21. IV provided Dobell
with final proof of T's authorship of the *Centuries* and *Poems*, and III has done the same for
the MS newly discovered by Dr. James Osborn (see TLS 8.10.64).

He in his Wisdom did their use extend,
By all, to all the World from End to End.
In all Things, all Things service do to all:
30   And thus a Sand is Endless, though most small.
        And every Thing is truly Infinite,
        In its Relation deep and exquisite.

V

Were all the World a Paradice of Ease
        'Twere easie then to live in Peace.
Were all men Wise, Divine, and Innocent,
        Just, Holy, Peaceful, and Content,
5   Kind, Loving, True, and alwaies Good,
                As in the Golden-Age they stood;
                        'Twere easie then to live
In all Delight and Glory, full of Love,
        Blest as the Angels are above.

10   But we such Principles must now attain,
                (If we true Blessedness would gain)
As those are, which will help to make us reign
                Over Disorders, Injuries,
                        Ingratitudes, Calamities,
15   Affronts, Oppressions, Slanders, Wrongs,
                        Lies, Angers, bitter Tongues,
The reach of Malice must surmount, and quell
        The very Rage, and Power of Hell.

VI

I

Mankind is sick, the World distemper'd lies,
        Opprest with Sins and Miseries.
Their Sins are Woes; a long corrupted Train
        Of Poyson, drawn from *Adam*'s vein,
5   Stains all his Seed, and all his Kin
        Are one Disease of Life within.
                They all torment themselves!
The World's one *Bedlam*, or a greater Cave
        Of Mad-men, that do alwaies rave.

2

·The Wise and Good like kind Physicians are, 10
  That strive to heal them by their Care.
They Physick and their Learning calmly use,
  Although the *Patient* them abuse.
  For since the Sickness is (they find)
  A sad Distemper of the Mind; 15
   All railings they impute,
All Injuries, unto the sore Disease,
  They are expresly come to ease!

3

If we would to the Worlds distemper'd Mind
  Impute the Rage which there we find, 20
We might, even in the midst of all our Foes,
  Enjoy and feel a sweet Repose.
  Might pity all the Griefs we see,
  Anointing every Malady
   With precious Oyl and Balm; 25
And while ourselves are Calm, our Art improve
  To rescue them, and shew our Love.

4

But let's not fondly our own selves beguile;
  If we Revile 'cause they Revile,
Our selves infected with their sore Disease, 30
  Need others Helps to give us ease.
  For we more Mad then they remain,
  Need to be cut, and need a Chain
   Far more than they. Our Brain
Is craz'd; and if we put our Wit to theirs, 35
  We may be justly made their Heirs.

5

But while with open eyes we clearly see
  The brightness of his Majesty;
While all the World, by Sin to Satan sold,
  In daily Wickedness grows old, 40

33. *cut*: the surgeon's knife or, as M thinks possible, a misprint for 'cur'd'.

L

Men in Chains of Darkness lye,
In Bondage and Iniquity,
        And pierce and grieve themselves!
The dismal Woes wherein they crawl, enhance
45   The Peace of our Inheritance.

                            6

We wonder to behold our selves so nigh
        To so much Sin and Misery,
And yet to see our selves so safe from harm!
        What *Amulet*, what hidden Charm
50   Could fortifie and raise the Soul
        So far above them; and controul
                Such fierce Malignity!
The brightness and the glory which we see
        Is made a greater Mystery.

                            7

55 And while we feel how much our GOD doth love
        The Peace of Sinners, how much move,
And sue, and thirst, intreat, lament, and grieve,
        For all the Crimes in which they live,
        And seek and wait, and call again,
60   And long to save them from the pain
                Of Sin, from all their Woe!
With greater thirst, as well as grief we try,
        How to relieve their Misery.

                            8

The life and splendour of Felicity,
65   Whose floods so overflowing be,
The streams of Joy which round about his Throne,
        Enrich and fill each Holy One,
        Are so abundant, that we can
        Spare all, even all to any Man!
70   And have it all our selves!
Nay have the more! We long to make them see
        The sweetness of Felicity.

9

While we contemplate their Distresses, how,
    Blind Wretches, they in bondage bow,
And tear and wound themselves, and vex and groan,   75
    And chafe and fret so near His Throne,
    And know not what they ail, but lye
    Tormented in their Misery
        (Like Mad-men that are blind)
In works of darkness nigh such full Delight: 80
    That they might find and see the sight,

10

What would we give! that they might likewise see
    The Glory of his Majesty!
The joy and fulness of that high delight,
    Whose Blessedness is infinite!   85
    We would even cease to live, to gain
    Them from their misery and pain,
        And make them with us reign.
For they themselves would be our greatest Treasures
    When sav'd, our own most Heavenly Pleasures.   90

11

O holy JESUS who didst for us die,
    And on the Altar bleeding lie,
Bearing all Torment, pain, reproach and shame,
    That we by vertue of the same,
    Though enemies to GOD, might be   95
    Redeem'd, and set at liberty.
        As thou didst us forgive,
So meekly let us Love to others shew,
    And live in Heaven on Earth below!

12

Let's prize their Souls, and let them be our Gems,   100
    Our Temples and our Diadems,
Our Brides, our Friends, our fellow-Members, Eyes
    Hands, Hearts and Souls, our Victories,

And Spoils and Trophies, our own Joyes!
Compar'd to Souls all else are Toyes!
O JESUS, let them be
Such unto us, as they are unto thee,
Vessels of Glory and Felicitie!

13

How will they love us, when they find our Care
Brought them all thither where they are!
When they conceive, what terrour 'tis to dwell
In all the punishments of Hell:
And in a lively manner see,
O Christ, eternal Joyes in thee!
How will they all delight
In praising thee for us, with all their might,
How sweet a Grace, how infinite!

VII

Contentment is a sleepy thing!
If it in Death alone must die;
A quiet Mind is worse than Poverty!
Unless it from Enjoyment spring!
That's Blessedness alone that makes a King!
Wherein the Joyes and Treasures are so great,
They all the powers of the Soul employ,
And fill it with a Work compleat,
While it doth all enjoy.
True Joyes alone Contentment do inspire,
Enrich Content, and make our Courage higher.
Content alone's a dead and silent Stone:
The real life of Bliss
Is Glory reigning in a Throne,
Where all Enjoyment is.
The Soul of Man is so inclin'd to see,
Without his Treasures no man's Soul can be,

VII. From chapter xxvii, 'Of Contentment'.
1-2. The meaning seems to be that bare contentment (at death having no added quality of active joy) is valueless.

Nor rest content Uncrown'd!
Desire and Love
Must in the height of all their Rapture move,   20
Where there is true Felicity.
Employment is the very life and ground
Of Life it self; whose pleasant Motion is
The form of Bliss:
All Blessedness a life with Glory Crown'd.   25
Life! Life is all: in its most full extent
Stretcht out to all things, and with all Content!

VIII

And if the Glory and Esteem I have,
Be nothing else than what my Silver gave;
If for no other ground
I am with Love or Praises crown'd,
'Tis such a shame, such vile, such base Repute   5
'Tis better starve, than eat such empty Fruit.

VIII. From chapter xxviii, 'Of Magnanimity'.

POEMS FROM *HEXAMERON* OR *MEDITATIONS ON THE SIX DAYS OF THE CREATION*[1]

First Day

Hail, sacred Light, which highly dost excel,
And dost our Sorrows and our Fears dispel!
When first appearing thou didst strike the Sight
With darting Beams, all glorious fair and bright,
5   And wondrous charming, Oh! how great and full
Of sparkling Glory! Oh! how beautiful!
How sweet thy Shine! How ravishing thy Rays!
Proclaiming loud thy great Creator's Praise,
When marvellously he had now decreed,
10   That Day should Night, and Night should Day succeed;
That this His Works and Wonders might display,
And shadow forth his own eternal Day;
Whilst that should temper the Day's increasing Drought,
Moisten the Air, and make the Earth to sprout.
15   He gave the Word, and Day did straight appear,
Till Day at length declin'd, and Night drew near.
Night, which hovering with her sable Wing,
Doth Ease and Rest to wearied Mortals bring.
Thus Nights and Days, and Days and Nights do fly,
20   Returning in their Course successively;
Each with its Comforts, though of diff'rent kinds,
Both for our active and our drooping Minds.
Since then both Day and Night such Blessings bring,
By Day and Night let's bless our Lord and King,
25   The King of all the World, in whom we move
And live, and are, the mighty God above.

                                    Amen.

[1] See Introduction, p. xv. The meditations for the First and Second Days are based on passages from Sylvester's *Du Bartas*—see M. ii. 399–400.

Second Day

    Hark how God's Word the Waters does command,
That they forthwith obey, and parted stand!
Two different ways, how does it them divide?
Some upwards mount, and some again subside.
In Vapours part ascend, the Clouds to fill,   5
Part to refresh the Earth, in Rain distill.
Mark how his Voice doth cut the Flames of Fire,
What whist'ling Winds do blow, and then retire;
How through the Air his pointed Arrows fly,
And how his Thunder rattles in the Sky: 10
He thunders, and the proudest Atheist quakes;
From Heaven roars, and Hell's Foundation shakes.
His Voice the Mountains and the Rocks doth rend,
And tallest Cedars fall at his Command.
Which yet to lowly Shrubs no Hurt will bring;   15
These, and their humble Valleys, laugh and sing,
Sing, O ye Valleys, whom the Lord doth crown;
On you he drops his welcome Blessings down.
When I perceive it rain in timely Showers,
I see on you he fruitful Favours pours: 20
But when from Clouds a watry Torrent spins,
Methinks Heav'n weeps for our unwept-for Sins.
And when on high I spy his beauteous Bow,
By this he does his Truth and Mercy show.
Oh that I could to him make some Return,   25
And that I cannot do it better, mourn!
Oh from these Eyes that Floods of Tears might fall!
Tears for my Sins, which for them loudly call;
And that my Thoughts, as Vapours, may arise,
And mount to thee, my God, above the Skies;   30
To own my Guilt, and Pardon supplicate,
And never cease thy Praise to celebrate.

                                      AMEN.

Third Day

Lo here, within the Waters liquid Womb
The unborn Earth lay, as in native Tomb;
Whilst she at first was buried in the Deep,
And all her Forms and Seeds were fast asleep.
5   Th' Almighty Word then spake, and streight was heard,
The Earth her Head up from the Waters rear'd.
The Waters soon, as frighted, fled apace,
And all were swiftly gather'd to one Place.
See now the Earth, with Life and Verdure crown'd,
10 Spring from her Bed, gay, vigorous, and sound:
Her Face ten thousand Beauties now adorn,
With Blessings numberless from Plenty's Horn.
Here, there, and ev'ry where they richly flow,
For us Almighty Bounty them does strow.
15 The Hills and Dales, the Lawns and Woods around,
God's Wisdom, Goodness, and his Pow'r resound.
Both far and near his Wonders they proclaim.
How vilely then is wretched Man to blame,
If he forget to praise that liberal Hand,
20 Out-spread from Sea to Sea, from Land to Land?
AMEN.

Fourth Day

1

Thou Lamp of God, and spacious World's vast Light,
Of thee how shall I sing? of thee how write?
   For here I find the Danger is,
    With Bards of old, the Way to miss.
5 Of thee a God, they strangely wond'ring made,
And to thy Fire devoutly Homage paid.

2

The ancient Bards did see, and do, no more.
But I a brighter Sun than thee adore.
   The Sun, I mean, that gave thee Light,
10   A Sun ten thousand times more bright.

Ah! who can thee sufficiently admire,
O God, my Sun, or thee enough desire?

3

Hail, thou faint Image of th' Eternal Sun!
Oh that with thee my Race I now could run!
    Oh that I could with thee obey!   15
    And oh that I did never stray!
But with thee always keep within my Line,
And with thee always in his Service join.

4

Thy influential Heat all Places warms,
And every Creature feels thy living Charms.   20
    The Fields do laugh, the Woods do sing,
    The Hills do dance, the Valleys spring.
The Fields and Groves, the Meads and Pastures live
By Heat, which God to thee at first did give.

5

The Plants, and Birds, and Beasts do all conspire   25
In this; and thee do eagerly Desire.
    Nothing we meet with here below,
    But what by thee doth live and grow.
Oh! how thou dost with Youth and Vigour fill
Thy Subject Earth, which Lifeless would be still!   30

6

Me with new Life from God thou dost inspire,
That seeing thee I burn with rapt'rous Fire.
    Thou art the Glory of thy Lord:
    Thou art the Image of his Word:
And I with thee now praise my LORD and thine,   35
That he my Sun, may ever on me shine.
                         AMEN.

Fifth Day

The Waters now are truly living made,
But how is this? Th' Almighty Word has said;
He said, *Now let the Waters living be.*
Th' admiring Angels then did Wonders see.
5   For streight the mighty Product of the Deep,
As if awaken'd from their watry Sleep,
Did now in numerous Shoals themselves display,
And made appear a Fifth more glorious Day,
Fairer than any that had gone before.   ⎫
10   Oh! who can God sufficiently adore,   ⎬
Who this Day gen'rated so rich a Store?   ⎭
A Day most fair! when his Almighty Skill
Did all the Seas, and Lakes, and Rivers fill.
Armies of Birds out of the Waters rise.
15   And soaring mount towards the smiling Skies.
Here skipping Fishes cut the lambent Air,
There living Castles mighty things declare;
And swiftly rolling through the spacious Main,
This Day proclaim, with all their finny Train.
20   O let not Man forget with these to raise
Both Heart and Voice to his great Maker's Praise.
                                                    AMEN.

Sixth Day

1

When first the teeming Waters had brought forth
Their Births, from East to West, from South to North,
    Fish fill'd the Sea, and Fowls the Air,
    The Earth alone remaining bare.
5   For though it had been furnish'd out so well,
Yet no Inhabitant on Earth did dwell.

2

The Earth was all throughout as *Eden* fair;
How fine, how goodly were the Plants she bare?

But yet no Animal was seen,
Nothing with Sense on Earth had been.   10
Till now th' Almighty did from Heaven look,
And into Being living Forms bespoke.

3

The pregnant Earth a second time did bear,
Not Herbs, nor Shrubs, nor Trees did now appear,
    As at the first, from her to spring;   15
    But nobler Births did to her cling.
With Life and Sense endu'd, these from her came,
Compleatly good, and naught in them to blame.

4

The harmless Lion with the Lamb did play,
And Leopards on the Sheep did never prey: 20
    There nothing was that did destroy:
    There nothing was that did annoy:
But all was Love, and perfect Harmony;
All did the Maker's Goodness testify.

5

But still the Heir was wanted to appear,   25
Till God at length was pleased to draw near:
    And as the Earth his Feet did touch,
    The blooming Earth did streightway blush;
Her Dust a lovely red did richly die:
No *Tyrian* Stain could with it ever vie.   30

6

And from this ruddy Earth there did arise
A beauteous Form, such as no mortal Eyes
    Have ever yet on Earth beheld,
    Since hither we have been expell'd,
From *Eden's* glorious East, with Beasts to dwell   35
In this vile World, which Sin has made an Hell.

7

The Beasts and Birds did all admiring stand,
So fair a Shape to view, which God's own Hand
    Had just produc'd with Art divine,
    In which all Beauties did combine.   40

And, lo! a rushing Breath from Heaven came,
Which kindled presently† the vital Flame.

8

The noble Godlike Form was then proclaim'd
The King of Earth, and God's Vicegerent nam'd.
His Subjects him did recognize,
Whose Glory did them all surprize.
It was God's Glory which on him did rest,
And with majestick Awe did him invest.

9

Whilst infinitely greater Majesty,
And Awe, and Dread, and justest Sov'reignty,
In his Creator does appear;
Enough to challenge ev'ry where
The utmost Duty Angels or Men can pay,
The strictest Service, and without Delay.

10

For shame then, O my guilty Soul, begin
To weep, lament, and wash away thy Sin.
Begin before it be too late;
Beg Pardon for thy Faults so great;
Repent, amend thy Life, amend thy Ways.
He's blest that his Creator's Will obeys.

11

And since to please thee nothing I can do
Without thy Grace, thy Grace do thou bestow,
O God, that furnish'd I may be
With sufficient Strength from thee,
To conquer all Temptations that arise
To whatsoever sort of Sin, or Vice.

12

That thankful, holy, happy I may be,
May please thee here, and to Eternity
May bless thee with a cheerful Voice,
And with the Saints, who all rejoice
To warble forth thy Praises, may
Enjoy thee in an everlasting Day.   AMEN.

POEMS FROM
THE CHURCH'S YEAR BOOK[1]

1

Unto the Spring of Purest Life
    Aspires my Withered Heart,
My Soul confined in this Flesh
    Employs both Strength and Art
Working, Strugling, Suing still,   5
    From Exile, home to part.

2

Who can utter the full Joy
    Which that High Place doth hold,
Where all the Buildings founded are
    On Orient Pearls untold.   10
And all the Work of those High rooms
    Doth Shine with Beams of Gold.

3

The Season is not Changd, but still
    Both Sun and Moon are Bright
The Lamb of this fair City is   15
    That Clear Immortal Light
Whose Presence makes Eternal Day
    Which never Ends in Night.

4

Nay all the Saints themselvs shall shine,
    As Bright as Brightest Sun;   20
In fullest Triumph Crowned, They
    To Mutual Joys shall run:
And safely count their Fights and Foes
    When once the War is don.

---

[1] M's title. See my Introduction, p. xv.
'Unto the Spring . . .': abridged and adapted by T from a translation of St. Peter Damian's hymn 'Ad Perennis Vitae Fontem'. The final stanza is completely recast. See M. ii. 401-2.

5

25   For being freed from all Defect,
       They feel no fleshly War;
Or rather both the Flesh and Mind
       At length united are.
For Joying in so Rich a Peace,
30   They can admit no Jar:

6

Being Cheerfull, Clear, and Content,
       They from Mishaps are Free.
No Sickness there can threaten Health,
       Nor Yong men Old can be.
35   There they Enjoy such Happy State,
       That in't no Change they see.

7

Who Know the Knower of all Things,
       What can they chuse but Know?
They all behold each others Hearts
40   And all their Secrets Shew.
One Act of Will, and of not Will,
       From all their Minds do flow.

8

Tho all their Merits Divers be
       According to their Pains,
45   Yet Lov doth make that evry ones
       Which any other gains.
And all which doth belong to One
       To all of them pertains.

9

O Happy Soul, which shalt behold
50   This King still present there;
And mayst from thence behold the World
       Run round, Secure from fear;
With Stars and Planets, Moon and Sun,
       Still moving in their Sphere!

10

O King of Kings giv me such Strength   55
    In this Great War depending;
That I may here prevail at length,
    And ever be Ascending.
Till I at last Arrive to Thee
The Source of all FELICITY.   60

1

Com Holy Ghost Eternal God
    Our Hearts with Life Inspire
Inkindle Zeal in all our Souls
And fill us with thy Heavenly fire.

2

Send forth thy Beams, and Let thy Grace   5
    Upon my Spirit shine:
That I may all thy Works enjoy,
Revive, Sing Praises, be Divine.

An Hymne upon St Bartholomews Day

1

What Powerfull Spirit livs within!
What Active Angel doth inhabit here!
    What Heavenly Light inspires my Skin;
Which doth so like a DIETIE appear!
A LIVING TEMPLE of all Ages I   5
    Within me see,
    A TEMPLE OF ETERNITIE!
    All Kingdoms I Descrie
    In Me.

60. Followed by a deleted line: 'No Greater Joy can be!'
'Com Holy Ghost . . .': a free translation of part of the Latin hymn 'Veni Creator Spiritus'
—see No. 88 in the *Oxford Book of Medieval Latin Verse*.

2

An Inward Omnipresence here,
Mysteriously like His with in me stands;
 Whose Knowledg is a Sacred Sphere,
That in it self at once Includes all Lands.
There is som ANGEL that within Me can
    Both Talk and Move
 And Walk and flie and See and love
   A Man on Earth, a Man
     Above.

3

 Dull Walls of Clay my SPIRIT leavs
And in a Forrein Kindom doth appear,
 This Great Apostle it receivs,
Admires his WORKS and sees them, standing here.
Within My Self from East to West I move,
    As If I were
 At once a CHERUBIM and Sphere,
   Or was at once abov,
    And here.

4

 The Soul's a Messenger wherby
Within our Inward Temple We may be
 Even like the very Dietie,
In all the parts of His Eternitie.
O liv within and leav unweildy Dross!
   Flesh is but Clay!
 O fly my Soul, and haste away
  To Jesus THRONE, or CROSS.
    Obey!

POEMS FROM A NOTEBOOK[1]

On the Bible

1

When Thou dost take
  this sacred Book into thy hand;
Think not that Thou
  th' included sence dost understand.

2

It is a signe   5
  thou wantest sound Intelligence;
If that Thou think
  thy selfe to understand the Sence.

3

Bee not deceived
  Thou then on it in vain mayst gaze   10
The way is intricate
  that leads into a Maze.

4

Heer's nought but whats Mysterious
  to an Understanding Eye:
Where Reverence alone stands Ope,   15
  And Sence stands By.

                            TT[2]

1

Rise noble soule and come away;
Lett us no longer wast the day:
Come lett us hast to yonder Hill,
  where Pleasures fresh are growing still.

[1] For the derivation of these poems, see Introduction, p. xv.
[2] After T's own signature-initials is a fragment partly torn away:
          These verses very neer, to . . .
          strangely seen in . . .
'Rise noble soule'. The poem is crossed through in MS.

5 The way at first is rough and steep;
And something hard for to ascend:
But on the Toppe do Pleasures keep
And Ease and Joyes doe still attend.

2

Come lett us goe: and doe not fear
10 the hardest way, while I am neer.
My heart with thine shall mingled bee;
Thy sorrowes mine, my Joyes with Thee.
And all our Labours as wee goe
True Love shall sweeten still.
15 and strew our way with Flowers too,
whilest wee ascend the Hill.

3

The hill of rest, where Angels live:
where Blisse her Palace hath to give;
where Thousands shall Thee welcom make,
20 and Joy, that Thou their Joyes do'st take.
o come lett's hast to this sweet place,
I pray thee quickly heal thy mind!
sweet lett us goe with joyfull pace
And leave the baser world behind.

4

25 Come letts unite; and wee'l aspire
like brighter Flames of heavenly fire;
That with sweet Incense do ascend,
still purer to their Journeys End.
Two—rising Flames—in one weel bee,
30 And with each other twining play,
And How, twill be a joy to see,
weel fold and mingle all the way.
T.T.

Finis

Epitaphium

Annae Cholmeley sacrum.
written on her grave stone.

Though stone I am, yet must I weep
   And sweat forth Teares of woe;
That such a Treasure I should keep,   5
   Beneath Mee buried soe.

But yet lett not the Reader weep,
   Unlesse it be for Joy;
The Cabinet alone I keep,
   Where in this Treasure Lay: 10

The Soule above with God on High,
   Lives in Eternall Blisse;
Where crowned with the Company,
   of glorious Saints she is.
                      T.T.

She is not Dead but sleepeth.

Job. cap. 19. v. 25. 26. 27

Memento mori.

Beneath that Stone, lies buried One,
   Confin'd in narrow roome;
Whose vaster Mind, noe Rest could find,
   Till laid within this Tombe.

Whil'st upon earth he was alive,
   All was but aire and wind;   5
The World too narrow was to give
   Contentment to his Mind.

Annae Cholmeley: see note to p. 162.

Not all the Treasures, nor the Pleasures,
    Where with the Earth is fill'd;
Can meat afford, fitt for the Board,
    where Soules are to bee still'd.
Life is the Shadow of a Dreame,
    Which He for sleep did rightly take;
Till Death did Jogge him from the same,
    He never truely was awake.

But now mine Eies, (above the Skies)
    are open; and I see
Things in the Light, not in the Night,
    but cleerly shewne to Mee.
Yea Lord! though here my body lies
    confus'd with other Earth;
At thy Command my Crummes shal rise,
    The same as at my Birth.
                                        T.T.

In Obitum[1]

viri optimi J: C. Eirenarchae.

Heer lies pure and precious Dust,
    Enclosed in this Urne;
which at the Resurrection must
    To life againe returne.

For though his dust in silence lies,
    with other Earth engrost;
It is a Treasure of such price,
    A graine shall not bee lost.

---

12. *still'd*: a possible reading; the word has been corrected.

[1] *In Obitum . . . J. C.* M considers it beyond a doubt that this is John Cholmeley of Creden-hill, who was one of T's sponsors when he was first appointed Rector there in 1657. Anne Cholmeley (see p. 161) was probably his daughter. Neither of the stones survives, but there is a monument in the chancel to John Cholmeley, who died in 1660.

This Grave must him againe restore,
    when the last Trump shall sound;   10
And hee alive (as hereto-fore)
    with endlesse Joyes bee crownd.

Here lie his bones, his Soule above,
    Doth Heav'nly blisse enjoy;
His Memory enbalm'd with Love,   15
    With us on earth doth stay.

Mistake not Reader; I don't meane,
    As if twere here alone,
That his dear Memory doth remaine,
    Grav'd on this obscure Stone: 20

Tis not this Stone which after Death,
    Doth make his Name to live;
It was his Life which so much breath,
    To this dumbe Stone did give.
                    T.T.

Yee that Towers so much prize,
Know not where a Kingdom lies!
Riches doe not make a King;
nor purple Robes that Tyrians bring.
nor Gold inlaid on shining Beams,   5
nor yet Majestick Diadems.

Hee's a King thats void of Care,
In whose Brest no Terrours are:
Whom Ambition doth not move
nor the giddy Peoples Love.   10

Who in safety plac'd on high
All things doth beneath Him 'spie:
And with cheerfullness can die.
In a Good mind a Kingdom lives;
Each man t'himselfe this Kingdom gives.   15

    1. 'Yee that Towers'. A translation of lines 342–52, 365–8, 380, and 390 of Seneca's
Thyestes. See M.
    4. *purple . . . bring*, corr. from 'a woollen Purple thing'.

THE CENTURIES

TRAHERNE corrected this manuscript himself with some care, and I have used his final version, without noting the variants except where the correction has made the sense obscure, or deleted something important. I have reproduced the vagaries of the original, with minor exceptions: the common abbreviations have been expanded; where words are inadvertently repeated, I have not included them; where stops have been omitted at the edge of the page or the end of a paragraph, I have put them in; and where a capital letter is needed after a deletion, I have added it.

T often uses a full point where it does not mark the end of a sentence, and is not followed by a capital letter. In modern punctuation this would be represented sometimes by a colon, sometimes by a lighter stop. Rather than resort to interpretation, I have used a centre stop in these places.

It is not possible to be certain as to whether T intends a capital or not, where the letters C, E, K, M, N, O, P, S, U, V, W are concerned, and some of my guesses, especially with the letter P, differ from those of Margoliouth.

The word *Century* does not appear until after the first hundred meditations, and the full title *Centuries of Meditations* was added to the manuscript by a later hand.

This book unto the friend of my best friend[1]
As of the Wisest Love a Mark I send
That she may write my Makers prais therin
And make her self therby a Cherubin.

[1] See Introduction, p. xvi.

[THE FIRST CENTURY]

I

An Empty Book is like an Infants Soul, in which any Thing may be Written. It is Capable of all Things, but containeth Nothing. I hav a Mind to fill this with Profitable Wonders. And since Love made you put it into my Hands I will fill it with those Truths you Love, without Knowing them: and with those Things which, if 5 it be Possible, shall shew my Lov; To you, in Communicating most *Enriching Truths*; to Truth, in Exalting Her Beauties in such a Soul.

2

Do not Wonder, that I promise to fill it, with those Truths you love, but know not: For tho it be a Maxime in the Scholes, That there is no Lov of a thing unknown; yet I hav found, that Things unknown have a Secret Influence on the Soul: and like the Centre of the Earth unseen, violently Attract it. We lov we know not what: and 5 therfore evry Thing allures us. As Iron at a Distance is drawn by the Loadstone, there being some Invisible Communications between them: So is there in us a World of Lov to somwhat, tho we know not what in the World that should be. There are Invisible Ways of Conveyance, by which som Great Thing doth touch our 10 Souls, and by which we tend to it. Do you not feel your self Drawn with the Expectation and Desire of som Great Thing?

3

I will open my Mouth in Parables: I will utter Things that have been Kept Secret from the foundation of the World. Things Strange, yet Common; Incredible, yet Known; Most High, yet Plain; infinitly Profitable, but not Esteemed. Is it not a Great Thing, that you should be Heir of the World? Is it not a very 5 Enriching Veritie? In which the Fellowship of the Mystery, which from the beginning of the World hath been hid in GOD, lies concealed! The Thing hath been from the Creation of the World, but hath not so been Explained, as that the interior Beauty should be understood. It is my Design therfore in such a plain maner to 10 unfold it, that my Friendship may appear, in making you Possessor of the Whole World.

4

I will not by the Nois of Bloody Wars, and the Dethroning of
Kings, advance you to Glory: but by the Gentle Ways of Peace
and Lov. As a Deep Friendship meditats and intends the Deepest
Designes for the Advancement of its Objects, so doth it shew it self
5 in Chusing the Sweetest and most Delightfull Methods, wherby
not to Weary, but Pleas the Person, it desireth to advance. Where
Lov administers Physick, its Tenderness is exprest in Balms and
Cordials. It hateth Corrosives, and is Rich in its Administrations.
Even so God, Designing to shew his Lov in exalting you hath
10 chosen the Ways of Eas and Repose, by which you should ascend.
And I after his Similitude will lead you into Paths Plain and
Familiar. Where all Envy, Rapine, Bloodshed, Complaint, and
Malice shall be far removed; and nothing appear but Contentment
and Thanksgiving. Yet shall the End be so Glorious, that Angels
15 durst not hope for so Great a One till they had seen it.

5

The fellowship of the Mystery that hath been hid in God, since the
Creation, is not only the Contemplation of his Lov in the Work
of Redemption: Tho that is Wonderfull: But the End, for which
we are Redeemd: A Communion with Him in all His Glory · for
5 which caus, S Peter saith The God of all Grace, hath called us
unto His Eternal Glory by Jesus Christ. His Eternal Glory by the
Methods of His Divine Wisdom being made ours: and our Fruition
of it, the End for which our Savior Suffered.

6

True Lov, as it intendeth the Greatest Gifts, intendeth also the
Greatest Benefits. It contenteth not it self in Shewing Great Things
unless it can make them Greatly Usefull. For Lov greatly De-
lighteth in seeing its Object continualy seated in the Highest
5 Happiness. Unless therfore I could advance you Higher by the
uses of what I give, my Lov could not be satisfied, in Giving you
the Whole World. But becaus when you Enjoy it, you are Advanced
to the Throne of God, and may see His Lov; I rest well Pleased
in Bestowing it. It will make you to see your own Greatness, the
10 Truth of the Scriptures, the Amiableness of Virtu, and the Beauty
of Religion. It will enable you also, to contemn the World, and to
overflow with Praises.

7

To Contemn the World, and to Enjoy the World, are Things contrary to each other. How then can we contemn the World which we are Born to Enjoy? Truly there are two Worlds. One was made by God, the other by Men. That made by GOD, was Great and Beautifull. Before the Fall, It was Adams Joy, and the 5 Temple of his Glory. That made by men is a Babel of Confusions: Invented Riches, Pomps and Vanities, brought in by Sin. Giv all (saith Thomas a Kempis) for all. Leav the one that you may enjoy the other.

8

What is more Easy and Sweet then Meditation? yet in this hath God commended his Lov, that by Meditation it is Enjoyed. As Nothing is more Easy then to Think, so nothing is more Difficult then to Think Well. The Easiness of Thinking we received from God, the Difficulty of thinking Well, proceedeth from our selvs. 5 Yet in Truth, it is far more Easy to think well then Ill, becaus Good Thoughts be sweet and Delightfull: Evil Thoughts are full of Discontent and Trouble. So that an Evil Habit, and Custom hav made it Difficult to think well, not Nature. For by Nature, nothing is so Difficult as to Think amiss.   10

9

Is it not Easy to conceiv the World in your Mind? To think the Heavens fair? The Sun Glorious? The Earth fruitfull? The Air Pleasant? The Sea Profitable? And the Giver Bountifull? Yet these are the Things which it is difficult to retain. For could we always be Sensible of their Use and Value; we should be always 5 Delighted with their Wealth and Glory.

10

To think well is to serv God in the Interior Court: To hav a Mind composed of Divine Thoughts, and set in frame, to be Like Him within. To Conceiv aright and to Enjoy the World, is to Conceiv the Holy Ghost, and to see His Lov; Which is the Mind of the Father. And this more Pleaseth Him then Many Worlds, 5 could we Creat as fair and Great as this. For when you are once acquainted with the World, you will find the Goodness and Wisdom of God, so manifest therin, that it was Impossible another, or

Better should be made. Which being made to be Enjoyed, Nothing
10 can Pleas or serv Him more then the Soul that Enjoys it. For that
Soul doth accomplish the End of His Desire in Creating it.

11

Lov is Deeper then at first it can be thought. It never ceaseth but
in Endless Things. It ever Multiplies. Its Benefits and its Designes
are always Infinit. Were you not Holy Divine and Blessed in
Enjoying the World, I should not care so much to Bestow it. But
5 now in this you accomplish the End of your Creation, and serv
God best, and Pleas Him most: I rejoyce in Giving it. For to Enable
you to Pleas GOD, is the Highest Service a Man can do you. It is
to make you Pleasing to the King of Heaven, that you may be the
Darling of His Bosom.

12

Can you be Holy without Accomplishing the End for which you
are Created? Can you be Divine unless you be Holy? Can you
Accomplish the End for which you were Created, unless you be
Righteous? Can you then be Righteous, unless you be Just in
5 rendering to Things their Due Esteem? All Things were made to
be yours. And you were made to Prize them according to their
value: which is your Office and Duty, the End for which you were
Created, and the Means wherby you Enjoy. *The End for which you*
were Created is that by Prizing all that God hath don, you may Enjoy
10 *your self and Him in Blessedness.*

13

To be Holy is so Zealously to Desire, so vastly to Esteem, and so
Earnestly to Endeavour it, that we would not for millions of Gold
and Silver, Decline, nor fail, nor Mistake in a Tittle. For then we
Pleas God when we are most like Him. We are like Him when our
5 Minds are in Frame. Our Minds are in Frame when our Thoughts
are like his. And our Thoughts are then like his when we hav such
Conceptions of all objects as God hath, and Prize all Things accord-
ing to their value. For God doth Prize all Things rightly. Which
is a Key that Opens into the very Thoughts of his Bosom. It
10 seemeth Arrogance to pretend to the Knowledg of his Secret
Thoughts. But how shall we hav the Mind of God, unless we

Know his Thoughts? Or how shall we be led by his Divine Spirit,
till we hav his Mind? His Thoughts are Hidden: but he hath
revealed unto us the Hidden Things of Darkness. By his Works and
by his Attributs we know His Thoughts. And by Thinking the same 15
are Divine and Blessed.

14

When Things are ours in their Proper Places, nothing is needfull
but Prizing, to Enjoy them. God therfore hath made it infinitly
Easy to Enjoy, by making evry Thing ours, and us able so Easily to
Prize them. Evry thing is ours that serves us in its Place. The Sun
servs us as much as is Possible, and more then we could imagine. 5
The Clouds and Stars Minister unto us, the World surrounds us
with Beauty, the Air refresheth us the Sea revives the Earth and us.
The Earth it self is Better then Gold becaus it produceth fruits and
flowers. And therfore in the Beginning, was it made Manifest to be
mine, becaus Adam alone was made to Enjoy it. By making One, 10
and not a Multitud, God evidently Shewed One alone to be the
End of the World, and evry one its Enjoyer · for evry one may
Enjoy it as much as He.

15

Such Endless Depths lie in the Divinity, and the Wisdom of God,
that as He maketh one, so He maketh evry one the End of the
World: the Supernumerary Persons being Enrichers of his In-
heritance. Adam and the World are both mine. And the Posterity of
Adam enrich it Infinitly. Souls are Gods Jewels. Evry one of which 5
is worth many Worlds. They are his Riches becaus his Image · and
mine for that reason. So that I alone am the End of the World.
Angels and Men being all mine. And if others are so, they are made
to Enjoy it for my further Advancement. God only being the
Giver, and I the Receiver. So that Seneca Philosophized rightly, 10
when he said, *Deus me dedit solum toti Mundo, et totum Mundum
mihi soli.* God gave me alone to all the World, and all the World to
me alone.

16

That all the World is yours, your very Senses and the Inclina-
tions of your Mind declare. The Works of God manifest, his Laws
testify and his Word doth prove it. His Attributes most sweetly

make it evident. The Powers of your Soul confirm it. So that in
5 the midst of such rich Demonstrations, you may infinitly Delight
in God as your Father Friend and Benefactor, in your self as his
Heir Child and Bride, in the Whole WORLD, as the Gift and
Token of His Lov. Neither can any thing but Ignorance Destroy
your Joys · for if you know your self, or God, or the World; you
10 must of Necessity Enjoy it. ·

17

To know GOD is Life Eternal. There must therfore some Exceed-
ing Great Thing be always attained in the Knowledge of Him.
To Know God is to Know Goodness; It is to see the Beauty of
infinit Lov: To see it attended with Almighty Power and Eternal
5 Wisdom; and using both those in the Magnifying of its Object.
It is to see the King of Heaven and Earth take infinit Delight in'
Giving. Whatever Knowledge els you hav of God, it is but Super-
stition. Which Plutarch rightly Defineth, *to be an Ignorant Dread
of his Divine Power, without any Joy in his Goodness.* He is not an
10 Object of Terror, but Delight. To know Him therfore as He is, is
to frame the most Beautifull Idea in all Worlds. He Delighteth in
our Happiness more then we: and is of all other the most Lovly
Object. An infinit Lord, who having all Riches Honors and Pleasures
in his own Hand, is infinitly Willing to give them unto me. Which
15 is the fairest Idea that can be Devised.

18

The WORLD is not this little Cottage of Heaven and Earth. Tho
this be fair, it is too small a Gift. When God made the WORLD,
He made the Heavens and the Heavens of Heavens, and the Angels
and the Celestial Powers. These also are Parts of the World: so are
5 all those infinit and Eternal Treasures that are to abide for ever,
after the Day of Judgement. Neither are these, some here, and
some there, but all evry where, and at once to be Enjoyed. The
WORLD is unknown, till the Value and Glory of it is seen: till the
Beauty and the Serviceableness of its Parts is Considered. When
10 you enter into it, it is an illimited feild of Varietie and Beauty:
where you may lose your self in the Multitude of Wonders and
Delights. But it is an Happy Loss to lose one self in Admiration† at
ones own Felicity: and to find GOD in exchange for oneself. Which
we then do when we see Him in His Gifts, and Adore his Glory.

19

You never Know your self, till you Know more then your Body.
The Image of God was not seated in the features of your face, but
in the Lineaments of your Soul. In the Knowledg of your Powers,
Inclinations and Principles, the Knowledg of your self cheifly
consisteth. Which are so Great that even to the most Learned of 5
men their Greatness is Incredible; and so Divine, that they are
infinit in Value. Alass the WORLD is but a little Centre in Com-
parison of you. Suppose it Millions of Miles from the Earth to the
Heavens, and Millions of Millions above the Stars, both here and
over the heads of our Antipodes: it is surrounded with infinit 10
and Eternal Space: And like a Gentlemans house to one that is
Travelling; It is a long time before you com unto it, you passe it in
an Instant, and leave it for ever. The Omnipresence and Eternity
of God are your Fellows and Companions. And all that is in them
ought to be made your familiar Treasures. Your Understanding 15
comprehends the World like the Dust of a Ballance, measures
Heaven with a Span and esteems a thousand yeers but as one Day.
So that Great Endless Eternal Delights are only fit to be its Enjoy-
ments.

20

The Laws of GOD, which are the Commentaries of his Works,
shew them to be yours: becaus They teach you to lov God with
all your Soul, and with all your Might. Whom if you lov with all
the Endless Powers of your Soul, you will lov Him in Him self, in
His Attributs, in His Counsels, in all his Works, in all His Ways: 5
and in evry Kind of Thing wherin He appeareth, you will Prize
Him, you will Honor Him, you will Delight in Him, you will ever
desire to be with him and to pleas Him. For to lov Him includeth
all this. You will feed with Pleasure upon evry Thing that is His.
So that the World shall be a Grand Jewel of Delight unto you: 10
a very Paradice; and the Gate of Heaven. It is indeed the Beautifull
Frontispiece of Eternitie · the Temple of God, the Palace of his
children. The Laws of God Discover all that is therin to be Created
for your sake. For they command you to lov all that is Good, and
when you see well, you enjoy what you lov. They apply the Endless 15
Powers of your Soul to all their Objects: And by ten thousand
Methods make evry Thing to serv you. They command you to

lov all Angels and Men, They command all Angels and Men to lov you. When you lov them, they are your Treasures; when They
20 lov you, to your great advantage you are theirs. All things serv you for serving them whom you lov, and of whom you are Beloved. The Enterance of His Words giveth Light to the Simple. You are Magnified among Angels and Men: Enriched by them, and Happy in them.

21

By the very Right of your Sences you Enjoy the World. Is not the Beauty of the Hemisphere present to your Ey? Doth not the Glory of the Sun pay Tribut to your Sight. Is not the Vision of the WORLD an Amiable Thing? Do not the Stars shed Influences to
5 Perfect the Air? Is not that a marvellous Body to Breath in? To visit the Lungs: repair the Spirits: revive the Sences: Cool the Blood: fill the Empty Spaces between the Earth and Heavens; and yet giv Liberty to all Objects? Prize these first: and you shall Enjoy the Residue. Glory, Dominion, Power, Wisdom, Honor, Angels,
10 Souls, Kingdoms, Ages. *Be faithfull in a little, and you shall be Master over much.* If you be not faithfull in esteeming these, who shall put into your Hands the true Treasures. If you be Negligent in Prizing these, you will be Negligent in Prizing all. There is a Diseas in Him who Despiseth present mercies, which till it be cured, he can never
15 be Happy. He esteemeth nothing that he hath, but is ever Gaping after more: which when he hath He despiseth in like manner. Insatiableness is Good, but not Ingratitud.

22

It is of the Nobility of Mans Soul that He is Insatiable · for he hath a Benefactor so Prone to Give, that He delighteth in us for Asking. Do not your Inclinations tell you that the WORLD is yours? Do you not covet all? Do you not long to hav it; to Enjoy it; to
5 Overcom it? To what End do Men gather Riches, but to Multiplie more? Do they not like Pyrrhus the King of Epire, adde hous to hous and Lands to Lands, that they may get it all? It is storied of that Prince, that having conceived a Purpose to invade Italy, he sent for Cineas, a Philosopher and the Kings friend: to whom
10 he communicated his Designe, and desired his Counsel. Cineas asked him to what Purpose he invaded Italie? He said, To Conquer

it. And what will you do when you hav Conquerd it? Go into
France said the King, and Conquer that. And what will you do when
you have Conquerd France? Conquer Germany. And what then?
said the Philosopher. Conquer Spain. I perceive said Cineas, you 15
mean to conquer all the World. What will you do when you have
conquerd all? Why then said the King we will return, and Enjoy
our selvs at Quiet in our own Land. So you may now said the
Philosopher without all this adoe. Yet could he not Divert him
till he was ruind by the Romans. Thus men get one Hundred 20
Pound a year that they may get another; and having two covet
Eight, and there is no End of all their Labor; becaus the Desire of
their Soul is Insatiable. Like Alexander the Great they must
hav all: and when they hav got it all be quiet. And may they
not do all this before they begin? Nay it would be well, if they 25
could be Quiet. But if after all, they shall be like the stars, that
are seated on high, but hav no Rest, what gain they more, but
Labor for their Trouble? It was wittily fained that that Yong
man sate down and Cried for more Worlds. So insatiable is Man
that Millions will not Pleas him. They are no more then so many 30
Tennis-Balls, in Comparison of the Greatness and Highness of his
Soul.

23

The Noble Inclination wherby Man thirsteth after Riches and
Dominion, is his Highest Virtu, when rightly Guided: and Carries
him as in a Triumphant Chariot, to his Soveraign Happiness. Men
are made Miserable only by abusing it. Taking a fals way to Satisfy
it, they Persue the Wind: Nay labor in the very fire, and after all 5
reap but Vanitie. Wheras, as Gods Lov, which is the fountain of all,
did cost us Nothing: so were all other Things prepared by it,
to satisfy our Inclinations in the Best of Manners, freely, without
any cost of ours. Being therfore all Satisfactions are near at hand,
by going further we do but leav them: And Wearying our selvs 10
in a long way round about, like a Blind man, forsake them. They
are immediatly near to the very Gates of our Sences. It becometh
the Bounty of God to prepare them freely: to make them Glorious,
and their Enjoyment Easy. For becaus His Lov is free so are his
Treasures. He therfore that will Despise them becaus he hath them 15
is Marvellously Irrational. The Way to Possess them is to Esteem

N

them. And the true Way of Reigning over them, is to break the
WORLD all into Parts, to examine them asunder. And if we
find them so Excellent that Better could not Possibly be made,
20 and so made that they could not be more ours, [we are] to rejoyce in
all with Pleasure answerable to the Merit of their Goodness. We
being then Kings over the Whole World, when we restore the
Pieces to their Proper Places, being Perfectly Pleased with the
whole Composure. This shall giv you a thorow grounded Con-
25 tentment, far beyond what troublesom Wars, or Conquests can
acquire.

24

Is it not a sweet Thing to hav all Covetousness and Ambition
satisfied, Suspicion, and infidelity removed, Courage and Joy in-
fused? Yet is all this in the fruition of the World attained · for
therby God is seen in all His Wisdom, Power, Goodness, and Glory.

25

Your Enjoyment of the World is never right, till you so Esteem it,
that evry thing in it, is more your Treasure, then a Kings Exchequer
full of Gold and Silver. And that Exchequer yours also in its Place
and Service. Can you take too much Joy in your fathers Works?
5 He is Himself in evry Thing. Som Things are little on the outside,
and Rough and Common · but I remember the Time, when the
Dust of the Streets were as precious as Gold to my Infant Eys,
and now they are more precious to the Ey of Reason.

26

The Services of Things, and their Excellencies are Spiritual: being
Objects not of the Ey, but of the Mind: And you more Spiritual by
how much more you Esteem them. Pigs eat Acorns, but neither
consider the Sun that gav them Life, nor the Influences of the
5 Heavens by which they were Nourished, nor the very Root of the
Tree from whence they came. This being the Work of Angels. Who
in a Wide and Clear Light see even the Sea that gave them Moysture.
And feed upon that Acorn Spritualy, while they Know the Ends
for which it was Created · and feast upon all these, as upon a World
10 of Joys within it: while to Ignorant Swine that eat the Shell, it is an
Empty Husk of no Taste nor Delightfull Savor.

27

You never Enjoy the World aright, till you see how a Sand Ex-
hibiteth the Wisdom and Power of God: And Prize in evry Thing
the Service which they do you, by Manifesting His Glory and
Goodness to your Soul, far more then the Visible Beauty on their
Surface, or the Material Services, they can do your Body. Wine by 5
its Moysture quencheth my Thirst, whether I consider it or no:
but to see it flowing from his Lov who gav it unto Man, Quencheth
the Thirst even of the Holy Angels. To consider it, is to Drink it
Spiritualy. To Rejoice in its Diffusion is to be of a Publick Mind.
And to take Pleasure in all the Benefits it doth to all is Heavenly · 10
for so they do in Heaven. To do so, is to be Divine and Good · and
to imitat our Infinit and Eternal Father.

28

Your Enjoyment of the World is never right, till evry Morning
you awake in Heaven: see your self in your fathers Palace: and
look upon the Skies and the Earth and the Air, as Celestial Joys:
having such a Reverend Esteem of all, as if you were among the
Angels. The Bride of a Monarch, in her Husbands Chamber, hath 5
no such Causes of Delight as you.

29

You never Enjoy the World aright, till the Sea it self floweth in
your Veins, till you are Clothed with the Heavens, and Crowned
with the Stars: and perceiv your self to be the Sole Heir of the whole
World: and more then so, becaus Men are in it who are evry one
Sole Heirs, as well as you. Till you can Sing and Rejoyce and De- 5
light in GOD, as Misers do in Gold, and Kings in Scepters, you
never Enjoy the World.

30

Till your Spirit filleth the whole World, and the Stars are your
Jewels, till you are as Familiar with the Ways of God in all Ages
as with your Walk and Table: till you are intimatly Acquainted with
that Shady Nothing out of which the World was made: till you lov
Men so as to Desire their Happiness, with a Thirst equal to the zeal 5
of your own: till you Delight in GOD for being Good to all: you
never Enjoy the World. Till you more feel it then your Privat
Estate, and are more present in the Hemisphere, Considering the

Glories and the Beauties there, then in your own Hous. Till you
10 remember how lately you were made, and how wonderfull it was
when you came into it: and more rejoyce in the Palace of your
Glory, then if it had been made but to Day Morning.

31

Yet further, you never Enjoy the World aright, till you so lov the
Beauty of Enjoying it, that you are Covetous and Earnest to Per-
suade others to Enjoy it. And so perfectly hate the Abominable
Corruption of Men in Despising it, that you had rather suffer the
5 flames of Hell then willingly be Guilty of their Error. There is so
much Blindness, and Ingratitud, and Damned folly in it. The
World is a Mirror of infinit Beauty, yet no Man sees it. It is a Temple
of Majesty yet no Man regards it. It is a Region of Light and Peace,
did not Men Disquiet it. It is the Paradice of God. It is more to
10 Man since he is faln, then it was before. It is the Place of Angels,
and the Gate of Heaven. When Jacob waked out of His Dream,
he said, *God is here and I wist it not. How Dreadfull is this Place!*
This is none other, then the Hous of God, and the Gate of Heaven.

32

Can any Ingratitud be more Damned then that which is fed by
Benefits? Or folly Greater then that which bereaveth us of infinit
Treasures? They Despise them meerly becaus they hav them: And
invent Ways to make them selvs Miserable in the Presence of
5 Riches. They Study a thousand New fangled Treasures, which
God never made: and then Griev and Repine that they be not
Happy. They Dote on their own Works, and Neglect Gods. Which
are full of Majesty Riches and Wisdom. And having fled away
from them becaus they are Solid Divine and True, Greedily per-
10 suing Tinsild vanities, they walk on in Darkness, and will not
understand. They do the Works of Darkness, and Delight in the
Riches of the Prince of Darkness, and follow them till they com
into Eternal Darkness. According to that of the Psalmist *All the*
foundations of the Earth are out of course.

33

The Riches of Darkness are those which Men hav made, during
their Ignorance of God Almightie's Treasures. That lead us from
the Lov of all, to Labor and Contention Discontentment and

Vanity. The Works of Darkness are Repining, Envy, Malice, Covet-
ousness, fraud, Oppression, Discontent and Violence: All which 5
proceed from the Corruption of men, and their mistake in the Chois
of Riches: For having refused those which God made, and taken
to themselvs Treasures of their own, they invented scarce and
Rare, Insufficient, Hard to be Gotten, litle, movable and useless
Treasures. Yet as violently Persue them as if they were the most 10
Necessary and Excellent Things in the whole World. And tho they
are all Mad, yet having made a Combination they seem Wise; and
it is a hard matter to persuade them either to Truth or Reason.
There seemeth to be no Way, but theirs: wheras God Knoweth
They are as far out of the Way of Happiness, as the East is from 15
the West. For by this means, they hav let in Broyls and Dissatisfac-
tions into the World, and are ready to Eat and Devour one another,
Particular and feeble Interests, fals Proprieties, Insatiable Long-
ings, fraud, Emulation, Murmuring and Dissension being evry
where seen, Theft and Pride and Danger and Cousenage Envy and 20
Contention Drowning the Peace and Beauty of Nature as Waters
cover the sea. O how they are ready to sink always under the Burden
and Cumber of Devised† Wants! Verily, the Prospect of their Ugly
Errors, is able to turn ones Stomach: they are so Hideous and
Deformed.
25

34

Would one think it Possible for a man to Delight in Gauderies
like a Butterflie, and Neglect the Heavens? Did we not daily see
it, it would be Incredible. They rejoyce in a Piece of Gold more
then in the Sun: and get a few little Glittering Stones and call them
Jewels. And Admire them becaus they be Resplendent like the 5
Stars, and Transparent like the Air, and Pellucid like the Sea. But
the Stars them selvs which are ten thousand Times more usefull
Great and Glorious, they Disregard. Nor shall the Air it self be
Counted any Thing, tho it be worth all the Pearls and Diamonds in
ten thousand Worlds, a WORK so Divine by reason of its Precious 10
and Pure Transparency, that all Worlds would be worth Nothing
without such a Treasure.

35

The Riches of the Light are the Works of God, which are the
Portion and Inheritance of his sons, to be seen and enjoyed in

Heaven and Earth, the Sea, and all that is therin · the Light and the Day. Great, and fathomless in use and Excellency, True, Necessary. Freely Given, Proceeding wholy from his Infinit Lov, As Worthy as they are Easy to be Enjoyed. Obliging us to lov Him, and to Delight in Him, filling us with Gratitud, and making us to over flow with Praises and Thanksgivings. The Works of Contentment and Pleasure are of the Day. So are the Works which flow from the Understanding of our Mutual Serviceableness to each other: Arising from the Sufficiency and Excellency of our Treasures, Contentment, Joy, Peace, Unitie, Charity &c. wherby we are all Knit together, and Delight in each others Happiness. For while evry one is Heir of all the World, and all the rest his Superadded Treasures · all the World servs Him in Himself, and in them, as his Superadded Treasures.

36

The Common Error which makes it Difficult to believ all the World to be wholy ours, is to be shund as a Rock of Shipwrack: or a Dangerous Quicksands. For the Poyson which they Drank hath infatuated their fancies and now they Know not, neither will they understand, they walk on in Darkness. *All the foundations of the Earth are out of Cours.* It is Safety not to be with them. And a Great Part of Happiness to be freed from their Seducing and Enslaving Errors. That while Others liv in a Golgotha or Prison, we should be in Eden, is a very Great Mystery. And a Mercy it is that we should be Rejoycing in the Temple of Heaven, while they are Toyling and Lamenting in Hell, for the World is both a Paradice and a Prison to different Persons.

37

The Brightness and Magnificence of this World, which by reason of its Height and Greatness is hidden from Men, is Divine and Wonderfull. It Addeth much to the Glory of that Temple in which we live. Yet is it the Caus why men understand it not. They think it too Great and Wide to be Enjoyed. But since it is all filled with the Majesty of His Glory who Dwelleth in it: and the Goodness of the Lord filleth the World, and His Wisdom shineth evry where within it and about it; and it aboundeth in an infinit Varietie of Services; we need nothing but open Eys, to be Ravished like the

Cherubims. Well may we bear the Greatness of the World, since 10
it is our Storehous and Treasurie. That our Treasures should be
Endless is an Happy Inconvenience: that all Regions should be
full of Joys: and the Room infinit wherin they are Seated.

38

You never Enjoy the World aright, till you see all things in it so
perfectly yours, that you cannot desire them any other Way:
and till you are Convinced, that all Things serv you Best in their
Proper Places. For can you desire to Enjoy any thing a Better
Way then in Gods Image? *It is the Height of Gods Perfection that* 5
hideth His Bounty: And the Lowness of your Base and Sneaking
Spirit, that make you Ignorant of his Perfection. (Evry one hath
in Him a Spirit, with which he may be Angry.) Gods Bounty is
so Perfect that *He giveth all Things in the Best of Manners*: making
those to whom He Giveth so Noble, Divine and Glorious, that 10
they shall Enjoy in His Similitude. Nor can they be fit to Enjoy
in His presence, or in Communion with Him, that are not truly
Divine and Noble. So that you must hav Glorious Principles
implanted in your Nature; a clear Eye able to see afar off, A Great
and Generous Heart, Apt to Enjoy at any Distance: a Good 15
and Liberal Soul Prone to Delight in the Felicity of all, and an
infinit Delight to be their Treasure. Neither is it any Prejudice to
you that this is required · for *there is Great Difference between a*
Worm and a Cherubim. And it more concerneth you to be an
Illustrious Creature, then to hav the Possession of the whole 20
World.

39

Your Enjoyment is never right, till you esteem evry Soul so Great
a Treasure as our Savior doth: and that the Laws of God are
sweeter then the Hony and Hony Comb becaus they command
you to lov them all in such Perfect Maner. For how are they Gods
Treasures? Are they not the Riches of His Lov? Is it not his 5
Goodness that maketh Him Glorious to them? Can the Sun or
Stars serv Him any other Way, then by serving them? And how
will you be the Son of God, but by having a Great Soul like unto
your Fathers. *The Laws of God command you to live in His Image* ·
and to do so, is to live in Heaven. God commandeth you to lov all 10

like Him, becaus He would hav you to be his Son, all them to be
your Riches, you to be Glorious before them, and all the Creatures
in serving them to be your Treasures, while you are his Delight,
like him in Beauty, and the Darling of his Bosom.

40

Socrates was wont to say, *They are most Happy and neerest the Gods
that needed Nothing.* And coming once up into the Exchange at
Athens, where they that Traded Asked Him, What will you Buy;
what do you lack? After he had Gravely Walkt up into the Middle,
5 spreading forth his Hands and turning about, *Good Gods,* saith he,
*who would hav thought there were so many Things in the World which
I do not want!* And so left the Place under the Reproach of Nature.
He was wont to say, *That Happiness consisted not in Having Many,
but in Needing the Fewest Things: for the Gods Needed Nothing at
10 all, and they were most like them that least Needed.* We Needed
Heaven and Earth, our Sences, Such Souls and Such Bodies, with
infinit Riches in the Image of God to be Enjoyed: Which God of
his Mercy having freely prepared, they are most Happy that so live
in the Enjoyment of those, as to need no Accidental Trivial Thing.
15 No Splendors, Pomps and Vanities. Socrates perhaps being an
Heathen, knew not that all Things proceeded from God to Man,
and by Man returned to God: but we that know it: must need All
Things as God doth that we may receiv them with Joy, and liv
in His Image.

41

As Pictures are made Curious by Lights and Shades, which without
Shades, could not be: so is Felicitie composed of Wants and Sup-
plies, without which Mixture there could be no Felicity. Were
there no Needs, Wants would be Wanting themselvs: And Supplies
5 Superfluous. Want being the Parent of Celestial Treasure. It
is very Strange; Want it self is a Treasure in Heaven: And so
Great an one, that without it there could be no Treasure. GOD
did infinitly for us, when He made us to Want like GODS, that
like GODS, we might be satisfied. The Heathen DIETIES
10 wanted nothing, and were therfore unhappy; For they had no
Being. But the LORD GOD of Israel the Living and True GOD,
was from all Eternity, and from all Eternity Wanted like a GOD.

He Wanted the Communication of His Divine Essence, and Persons to Enjoy it. He Wanted Worlds, He wanted Spectators, He wanted Joys, He wanted Treasures. He wanted, yet he wanted not, for he 15 had them.

42

This is very strange that GOD should Want · for in Him is the Fulness of all Blessedness: He overfloweth Eternaly. His Wants are as Glorious as Infinit. Perfectiv needs that are in His Nature, and ever Blessed, becaus always Satisfied. He is from Eternity full of Want: Or els He would not be full of Treasure. Infinit Want 5 is the very Ground and Caus of infinit Treasure. It is Incridible, yet very Plain: Want is the Fountain of all His Fulness. Want in GOD is a Treasure to us. For had there been no Need He would not hav Created the World, nor Made us, nor Manifested his Wisdom, nor Exercised his Power, nor Beautified Eternity, nor 10 prepared the Joys of Heaven. But He Wanted Angels and Men, Images, Companions. And these He had from all Eternitie.

43

Infinit Wants Satisfied Produce infinit Joys; And, in the Possession of those Joys, are infinit Joys themselvs. *The Desire Satisfied is a Tree of Life.* Desire imports som thing absent: and a Need of what is Absent. GOD was never without this Tree of Life. He did Desire infinitly · yet He was never without the Fruits of this 5 Tree, which are the Joys it produced. I must lead you out of this, into another World, to learn your Wants. For till you find them you will never be Happy. Wants themselvs being sacred Occasions and Means of Felicitie.

44

You must Want like a GOD, that you may be Satisfied like GOD. Were you not made in His *Image?* He is infinitly Glorious, becaus all His Wants and Supplies are at the same time in his Nature from Eternity. He had, and from Eternity He was without all His Treasures. From Eternity He needed them, and from Eternity 5 He enjoyed them. For all Eternity is at once in Him · both the Empty Durations before the World was made, and the full ones after. His Wants are as Lively as His Enjoyments: And always

present with Him. For His Life is Perfect, and He feels them both.
10 His Wants put a Lustre upon His Enjoyments, and make them
infinit. His Enjoyments being infinit Crown his Wants, and make
them Beautifull even to GOD Himself. His Wants and Enjoy-
ments being always present, are Delightfull to each other, stable
Immutable Perfectiv of each other, and Delightfull to Him.
15 Who being Eternal and Immutable, Enjoyeth all His Wants and
Treasures together. His Wants never Afflict Him, His Treasures
never Disturb Him. His Wants always Delight Him, His
Treasures never Cloy Him. The Sence of His Wants is always
as Great, as if his Treasures were removed: and as lively upon
20 Him. The Sence of His Wants, as it Enlargeth His Life, so it
infuseth a Valu, and continual Sweetness into the Treasures He
Enjoyeth.

45

This is a Lesson long enough: which you may be all your Life in
Learning, and to all Eternity in Practising. *Be Sensible of your
Wants, that you may be sensible of your Treasures.* He is most like
GOD that is sensible of evry Thing. Did you not from all Eternity
5 Want som one to give you a Being? Did you not Want one to give
you a Glorious Being? Did you not from all Eternity Want som
one to giv you infinit Treasures? And som one to give you Spec-
tators, Companions, Enjoyers? Did you not Want a Dietie, to
make them Sweet and Honorable by His infinit Wisdom? What
10 you wanted from all Eternity, be sensible of to all Eternity. Let
your Wants be present from Everlasting. Is not this a Strange Life
to which I call you? Wherin you are to be present with Things
that were before the World was made? And at once present even
like GOD with infinit Wants and infinit Treasures? Be present
15 with your Want of a Diety, and you shall be present with the Dietie.
You shall Adore and Admire Him, Enjoy and Prize Him; Believ
in Him, and Delight in Him: See Him to be the Fountain of all
your Joys· and the Head of all your Treasures.

46

It was His Wisdom made you Need the Sun. It was His Goodness
made you need the Sea. Be Sensible of what you need, or Enjoy
neither. Consider how much you need them. For thence they

Derive their Value. Suppose the Sun were Extinguished: or the
Sea were Drie. There would be no Light, no Beauty, no Warmth, 5
no Fruits, no Flowers, no Pleasant Gardens, Feasts, or Prospects.
No Wine no Oyl no Bread, no Life, no Motion. Would you not
give all the Gold and Silver in the Indies for such a Treasure?
Prize it now you have it, at that Rate, and you shall be a Grateful
Creature: Nay you shall be a Divine and Heavenly Person. For they 10
in Heaven do Prize Blessings when they hav them. They in Earth
when they hav them Prize them not, They in Hell Prize them,
when they hav them not.

47

To hav Blessings and to Prize them is to be in Heaven; To hav
them, and not to prize them, is to be in Hell, I would say upon
Earth: To prize them and not to hav them, is to be in Hell. Which
is Evident by the Effects. To Prize Blessings while we hav them is to
Enjoy them, and the effect therof is Contentation Pleasure Thanks- 5
giving Happiness. To Prize them when they are gone produceth
Envy, Covetousness, Repining, Ingratitud, Vexation, Miserie.
But it was no Great Mistake to say, That to hav Blessings, and not
to Prize them is to be in Hell. For it maketh them ineffectual, as if
they were Absent. Yea in som respect it is Worse then to be in Hell. 10
It is more vicious, and more Irrational.

48

They that would not upon Earth see their Wants from all Eternity,
shall in Hell see their Treasures to all Eternity. Wants here may be
seen and Enjoyed, Enjoyments there shall be seen, but wanted.
Wants here may be Blessings, there they shall be Curses. Here
they may be fountains of Pleasure and Thanksgiving; there they 5
will be fountains of Wo and Blasphemie. No Miserie is Greater then
that of Wanting in the Midst of Enjoyments, Of Seeing and Desiring
yet never Possessing. Of beholding others Happy, being seen by
them ourselvs in Misery. They that look into Hell here may avoid it
herafter. They that refuse to look into Hell upon Earth, to consider 10
the maner of the Torments of the Damned; shall be forced in Hell to
see all the Earth, and remember the Felicities which they had when
they were Living. Hell it self is a Part of GODs Kingdom, to wit
His Prison. It is fitly mentioned in the Enjoyment of the World:
And is it self by the Happy Enjoyed, as a Part of the world.   15

49

The Misery of them who hav and Prize not, Differeth from theirs,
who Prize and hav not. The one are more Odious and less sensible;
more foolish, and more vicious: The sences of the other are Exceed-
ing Keen and Quick upon them; yet are they not so foolish and
5 Odious as the former. The one would be Happy and cannot, the
other may be Happy and will not. The one are more vicious, the
other more Miserable. But How can that be? Is not he most
Miserable that is most vicious? Yes, that is true. But they that
Prize not what they hav are Dead; their sences are laid asleep, and
10 when they com to Hell they wake: And then they begin to feel their
Misery. He that is most Odious is most Miserable, and he that is
most Pervers is most Odious.

50

They are Deep Instructions that are taken out of Hell, and Heavenly
Documents that are taken from abov. Upon Earth we learn nothing
but Vanitie. Where People Dream, and Loyter and Wander, and
Disquiet themselvs in vain, to make a vain shew; but do not Profit,
5 becaus they prize not the Blessings they hav received. To prize
what we hav is a Deep and Heavenly Instruction. It will make us
Righteous, and Serious, Wise and Holy, Divine and Blessed. It will
make us Escape Hell and attain Heaven. For it will make us Carefull
to pleas Him from whom we hav received all· that we may liv in
10 Heaven.

51

Wants are the Bands and Cements between God and us. Had
we not Wanted, we could never hav been Obliged. Wheras now
we are infinitly Obliged, becaus we Want infinitly. From Eter-
nity it was requisit that we should Want. We could never els
5 have Enjoyed any Thing: Our own Wants are Treasures. And if
Want be a Treasure, sure evry Thing is so. Wants are the Liga-
tures between God and us. The Sinews that convey Sences from
him into us: wherby we liv in Him, and feel his Enjoyments. For
had we not been Obliged by having our Wants Satisfied, we
10 should not hav been Created to lov Him. And had we not been
Created to lov Him, we could never have Enjoyed his Eternal
Blessedness.

52

Lov has a marvellous Property of feeling in another. It can Enjoy
in another, as well as Enjoy Him. Lov is an infinit Treasure to its
Object, and its Object is so to it. GOD is LOV, and you are His
Object. You are Created to be his Lov: and He is yours. He is
Happy in you, when you are Happy: as Parents in their Children. 5
He is Afflicted in all your Afflictions. And whosoever toucheth you
toucheth the Apple of His Ey. Will not you be happy in all his
Enjoyments? He feeleth in you, will not you feel in Him? He hath
Obliged you to lov Him. And if you lov Him you must of necessity
be Heir of the World, for you are Happy in Him. All His Praises 10
are your Joys, all his Enjoyments are your Treasures, all His
Pleasures are your Enjoyments. In GOD you are Crowned, in GOD
you are concerned. In Him you feel, in Him you liv, and mov and
hav your Being · in Him you are Blessed. Whatsoever therfore
serveth Him serveth you and in Him you inherit all Things.   15

53

O the Nobility of Divine Friendship! Are not all his Treasures
yours, and yours His? Is not your very Soul and Body His; Is not
His Life and Felicity yours? Is not His Desire yours? Is not His
Will yours? And if His will be yours, the Accomplishment of it is
yours, and the end of all is your Perfection. You are infinitly Rich 5
as He is: Being Pleased in evry thing as He is. And if His Will be
yours, yours is His · for you will what He Willeth, which is to be
truly Wise and Good and Holy. And when you Delight in the same
Reasons that moved Him to Will, you will Know it. He willed the
Creation not only that He might Appear but be[1]: wherin is seated 10
the Mystery of the Eternal Generation of his Son. Do you will it
as He did, and you shall be Glorious as he is. He Willed the Happi-
ness of Men and Angels not only that He might appear, but be Good
and Wise and Glorious. And He willed it with such infinit Desire,
that He is infinitly Good: infinitly Good in Him self, and infinitly 15
Blessed in them. Do you will the Happiness of Men and Angels as
He did, and you shall be Good, and Infinitly Blessed as He is.
All their Happiness shall be your Happiness as it is His. He willed
the Glory of all Ages, and the Government and Welfare of all

[1] *Glorious*, deleted.

20 Kingdoms and the Felicity also of the Highest Cherubims. Do
you extend your Will like Him, and you shall be Great as He
is, and concernd and Happy in all these. He willed the Redemp-
tion of Mankind, and therfore is His Son Jesus Christ an infinit
Treasure. Unless you will it too, He will be no Treasure to you.
25 Verily you ought to will these Things so Ardently: that GOD
Himself should be therfore your Joy because He Willed them.
Your Will ought to be United to His in all Places of His Dominion.
Were you not Born to hav Communion with Him? And that
cannot be without this Heavenly Union. Which when it is what
30 it ought, is Divine and Infinit. You are GODs Joy for Willing what
he willeth. For He loves to see you Good and Blessed. And will
not you lov to see Him Good? Verily if ever you would enjoy
God, you must enjoy His Goodness. All His Goodness to all
His Hosts in Heaven and Earth. And when you do so, you are the
35 Universal Heir of God and All Things. GOD is yours and the
Whole World. You are His, and you are all; Or in all, and
with all.

54

He that is in all, and with all, can never be Desolat. All the Joys
and all the Treasures, all the Counsels and all the Perfections, all
the Angels and all the Saints of GOD are with Him. All the King-
doms of the World and the Glory of them are continualy in his
5 Ey: The Patriarchs Prophets and Apostles are always before Him.
The Counsels and the fathers, the Bishops and the Doctors minister
unto Him. All Temples are Open before Him, The Melodie of
all Quires reviveth Him, the Learning of all Universities doth
employ him, the Riches of all Palaces Delight him, The Joys of
10 Eden Ravish Him, the Revelations of S. John Transport Him,
The Creation and the Day of Judgment pleas Him, The Hosannas
of the Church Militant, and the Hallelujahs of the Saints Trium-
phant fill Him, the Splendor of all Coronations entertain Him,
The Joys of Heaven surround Him, And our Saviors Cross like
15 the Centre of Eternity is in Him, It taketh up his Thoughts,
and exerciseth all the Powers of his soul, with Wonder Admiration
Joy and Thanksgiving. The Omnipotence of God is His Hous,
and Eternity his Habitation.

55

The Contemplation of Eternity maketh the Soul Immortal. Whose
Glory it is, that it can see before and after its Existence into End-
less Spaces. Its Sight is its Presence. And therfore is the Presence
of the Understanding Endless, becaus its Sight is so. O what
Glorious Creatures should we be, could we be present in Spirit 5
with all Eternity! How Wise, would we esteem this presence of the
understanding, to be more real then that of our Bodies! When
my Soul is in Eden with our first Parents, I my self am there in a
Blessed Maner. When I walk with Enoch, and see his Translation,
I am Transported with Him. The present Age is too little to contain 10
it. I can visit Noah in His Ark, and swim upon the Waters of the
Deluge. I can see Moses with his Rod, and the children of Israel
passing thorow the Sea. I can Enter into Aarons Tabernacle, and
Admire the Mysteries of the Holy Place. I can Travail over the
Land of Canaan, and see it overflowing with Milk and Hony; 15
I can visit Solomon in his Glory, and go into his Temple, and
view the sitting of His servants, and Admire the Magnificence
and Glory of his Kingdom. No Creature but one like unto the
Holy Angels can see into all Ages. Sure this Power was not given
in vain· but for some Wonderfull Purpose; worthy of itself to 20
Enjoy and fathom. Would Men consider what GOD hath don, they
would be Ravished in Spirit with the Glory of His Doings. For
Heaven and Earth are full of the Majesty of His Glory. And how
Happy would Men be could they see and Enjoy it! But abov all
these our Saviors Cross is the Throne of Delights. That Centre 25
of Eternity, *That Tree of Life* in the midst of the Paradice of
GOD!

56

There are we Entertained with the Wonder of all Ages. There
we enter into the Heart of the Univers. There we Behold the
Admiration of Angels. There we find the Price and Elixar of our
Joys. As on evry side of the Earth all Heavy things tend to the
Centre; so all Nations ought on evry Side to flow in unto it. It is 5
not by going with the feet, but by Journeys of the Soul, that we
Travail thither. By withdrawing our Thoughts from Wandering
in the Streets of this World, to the Contemplation and Serious
Meditation of his Bloody Sufferings. Where the Carcase is thither

10 will the Eagles be Gathered together. Our Eys must be towards
it, our Hearts set upon it, our Affections Drawn and our Thoughts
and Minds united to it. When I am lifted up saith the Son of man
I will draw all Men unto me. As fishes are Drawn out of the Water,
as Jeremie was Drawn out of the Dungeon, as S. Peters Sheet was
15 Drawn up into heaven; so shall we be Drawn by that Sight from
Ignorance and Sin and Earthly vanities, idle Sports Companions
Feasts and Pleasures, to the Joyfull Contemplation of that Eternal
Object. But by what Cords? The Cords of a Man, and the Cords
of Lov.

57

As Eagles are Drawn by the Sent of a Carcais, As Children are
Drawn together by the Sight of a Lion, As People flock to a Corona-
tion, and as a Man is Drawn to his Beloved Object, so ought we.
As the Sick are Drawn by the Credit of a Physician, as the Poor
5 are Drawn by the Liberality of a King, as the Devout are Drawn
by the fame of the Holy, and as the Curious are Drawn by the
Nois of a Miracle so ought we. As the stones were Drawn to the
Building of Thebes by the Melodie of Amphion, as the Hungry
are Drawn with the Desire of a Feast, and the Pitifull Drawn to
10 a Wofull Spectacle so ought we. What Visible Chains or Cords
draw these? What Invisible Links allure? They follow all, or
flock together of their own accord. And shall not we much more?
Who would not be Drawn to the Gate of Heaven, were it open
to receiv him? Yet nothing compels Him, but that which forceth
15 the Angels· Commoditie and Desire. For these are Things which
the Angels desire to look into. And of Men it is Written, They
shall look on Him whom they hav Peirced. Verily the Israelites
did not more Clearly see the Brazen Serpent upon the Pole in
the Wilderness, then we may our Savior upon the Cross. The
20 Serpent was seen with their Eys, the Slayer of the Serpent is seen
with our Souls. They had less need to see the one, then we to see
the other.

58

The Cross is the Abyss of Wonders, the Centre of Desires, the
Schole of Virtues, the Hous of Wisdom, the Throne of Lov, the
Theatre of Joys and the Place of Sorrows; It is the Root of Happi-
ness, and the Gate of Heaven.

59

Of all the Things in Heaven and Earth it is the most Peculiar. It is the most Exalted of all Objects. It is an Ensign lifted up for all Nations, to it shall the Gentiles seek, His Rest shall be Glorious: the Dispersed of Judah shall be gathered together to it, from the four Corners of the Earth. If Lov be the Weight of the Soul, and 5 its Object the Centre · All Eys and Hearts may convert and turn unto this Object: cleave unto this Centre, and by it enter into Rest. There we might see all Nations Assembled with their Eys and Hearts upon it. There we may see Gods Goodness Wisdom and Power: yea his Mercy and Anger displayed. There we may see 10 Mans Sin and infinit value. His Hope and Fear, his Misery and Happiness. There we might see the Rock of Ages, and the Joys of Heaven. There we may see a Man Loving all the World, and a GOD Dying for Mankind(.) There we may see all Types and Ceremonies, figures and Prophesies. And all Kingdoms Adoring 15 a Malefactor: An Innocent Malefactor, yet the Greatest in the World. There we may see the most Distant Things in Eternity united: all Mysteries at once couched together and Explained. The only reason why this Glorious Object is so Publickly Admired by Churches and Kingdoms, and so little thought of by Particular 20 men, is becaus it is truly the most Glorious. It is the Root of Comforts, and the Fountain of Joys. It is the only Supreme and Soveraign Spectacle in all Worlds. It is a Well of Life beneath in which we may see the face of Heaven abov: and the only Mirror, wherin all things appear in their Proper Colors · that is sprinkled in the 25 Blood of our Lord and Savior.

60

The Cross of Christ is the Jacobs ladder by which we Ascend into the Highest Heavens. There we see Joyfull Patriarchs, Expecting Saints, and Prophets Ministering, Apostles Publishing and Doctors Teaching. All Nations concentering, and Angels Praising. That Cross is a Tree set on fire with invisible flame, that Illuminateth all 5 the World. The Flame is Lov. The Lov in His Bosom who died on it. In the light of which we see how to possess all the Things in Heaven and Earth after His Similitud. For He that Suffered on it, was the Son of GOD as you are: tho He seemed a Mortal Man. He had Acquaintance and Relations as you hav, but He was a Lover of Men 10

O

and Angels. Was He not the Son of GOD and Heir of the Whole
World? To this poor Bleeding Naked Man did all the Corn and
Wine and Oyl, and Gold and Silver in the World minister in an
Invisible Maner, even as he was exposed Lying and Dying upon
15 the Cross.

61

Here you learn all Patience, Meekness, Self Denial, Courage,
Prudence, Zeal, Lov, Charity, Contempt of the World, Joy,
Penitence, Contrition, Modestie, Fidelity, Constancy Persever-
ance, Holiness, Contentation and Thanksgiving. With whatsoever
5 els is requisit for a Man, a Christian or a King. This Man Bleeding
here was Tutor to King Charles the Martyr: and Great Master
to S. Paul the Convert who learned of Him Activity, and Zeal unto
all Nations. Well therfore may we take up with this Prospect, and
from hence behold all the Things in Heaven and Earth. Here we
10 learn to imitat Jesus in his Lov unto all.

62

LORD JESUS what Lov shall I render unto Thee, for thy Lov
unto me! Thy eternal Lov! Oh what fervor, what Ardor, what
Humiliation, what Reverence, what Joy, what Adoration, what
Zeal, what Thanksgiving! Thou that art Perfect in Beauty, Thou
5 that art the King of Eternal Glory, Thou that reignest in the Highest
Heavens camest down from Heaven to Die for me! And shall not
I liv unto Thee? O my joy! O my Sovereign Friend! O my Life,
and my All! I beseech Thee let those Trickling Drops of Blood
that run down Thy flesh drop upon me. O let Thy Lov enflame
10 me. Which is so deep and infinit, that Thou didst suffer the Wrath
of GOD for me: And Purchase all Nations and Kingdoms to be
my Treasures. O Thou that Redeemedst me from Hell, and when
Thou hadst Overcom the Sharpness of Death didst open the
Kingdom of Heaven to all Believers; What shall I do unto Thee?
15 What shall I do for Thee, O Thou Preserver of Men. Liv, Lov,
and Admire; and learn to becom such unto Thee as Thou unto
me. O Glorious Soul! whose Comprehensiv understanding at
once contains all Kingdoms and Ages! O Glorious Mind! Whose
Lov extendeth to all Creatures! O miraculous and Eternal GOD-
20 head, now suffering on the Cross for me: As Abraham saw thy

Day and was Glad, so didst Thou see me and this Day from all
Eternitie, and seeing me wast Gracious and Compassionat Towards
me. (All Transeunt Things are Permanent in God) *Thou settest me*
before Thy Face forever.) O let me This Day see Thee, and be united
to Thee in Thy Holy Sufferings. Let me learn O GOD such 25
Lessons from Thee, as may make me Wise, and Blessed as an
Angel of GOD!

63

Why Lord Jesus dost Thou lov men; why are they thy Treasures?
What Wonder is this, that Thou shouldst esteem them so as to
Die for them? Shew me the Reasons of thy Lov, that I may Lov
them too. O Goodness ineffable! they are the Treasures of thy
Goodness · who so infinitly lovest them that Thou gavest thy self 5
for them. Thy Goodness delighted to be communicated to them
whom thou hast saved. O Thou who art most Glorious in Good-
ness, make me Abundant in this Goodness like unto Thee, That I
may as Deeply pitty others Miserie, and as Ardently Thirst their
Happiness as Thou doest. Let the same mind be in me that is in 10
Christ Jesus. For He that is not led by the Spirit of Christ is none
of His. Holy Jesus I Admire† thy Lov I admire thy Lov unto me
also. O that I could see it through all those Wounds! O that I could
feel it in all those Stripes! O that I could hear it in all those Groans!
O that I could Taste it beneath that Gall and Vinegre! O that I could 15
smell the Savor of thy sweet Oyntments, even in this Golgotha
or Place of a Skull. I Pray Thee teach me first thy Lov unto Me,
and then unto Man Kind! But in thy Lov unto Mankind I am
Beloved.

64

These Wounds are in themselvs Orifices too small to let in my
Sight, to the vast Comprehensions of thine Eternal Lov. These
Wounds Engraven in thy Hands but Shady Impressions; unless
I see the Glory of thy Soul, in which the fulness of the GOD-
HEAD Dwelleth Bodily. These Bloody Characters are too Dim 5
to let me read it, in its Lustre and Perfection. Till I see thy Person:
and Know thy Ways! O Thou that Hangest upon this Cross before
mine Eys, Whose face is Bleeding, and coverd over with Tears

---

63. 12. T deleted 'unto me also' as first written, and then added it above the line with a
second 'I admire thy Lov'.

and filth and Blows! Angels Adore the GLORY of Thy GOD-
10 HEAD in the Highest Heavens! Who in evry Thought, and in evry
Work didst Glorious Things for me from Everlasting. What Could
I O my Lord Desire more then such a World! Such Heavens and
such an Earth! Such Beasts and Fowls and fishes made for me.
All these Do Homage unto me, and I hav Dominion over them
15 from the Beginning! The Heavens and the Earth Minister unto
me, as if no Man were Created but I alone. I willingly Acknow-
ledg it to be thy Gift! Thy Bounty unto Me! How many thousand
Ways do Men also minister unto me! O what Riches hast Thou
prepared out of Nothing for me! All Creatures labor for my sake,
20 and I am made to Enjoy all thy Creatures. O what Praises shall
I return unto Thee, the Wisdom of the father, and the Brightness
of the Glory of his Eternal Goodness! Who didst make all for me
before thou didst redeem me.

65

Had I been alive in Adams steed, how should I hav Admired the
Glory of the world! What a Confluence of Thoughts and Wonders
and Joys and Thanksgivings would hav replenished me in the sight
of so Magnificent a Theatre, so Bright a Dwelling Place; so Great
5 a Temple, so Stately a Hous replenished with all Kind of Treasure,
raised out of Nothing Created for me and for me alone. Shall I now
Despise them? When I consider the Heavens which Thou hast
made, the moon and stars which are the Works of thy Fingers;
what is Man that Thou art Mindfull of Him, or the Son of Man,
10 that Thou Visitest Him! Thou hast made Him a little lower then
the Angels and Crowned him with Glory and Honor! O what Lov
must that needs be, that prepared such a Palace! Attended with
what Power! With what Wisdom Illuminated! Abounding with
what Zeal! And how Glorious must the King be, that could out
15 of Nothing Erect such a Curious, so Great, and so Beautifull
a Fabrick! It was Glorious while new: and is as new as it was
Glorious.

66

But this is Small. What O my Lord could I desire to be which
Thou hast not made me! If Thou hast exprest Thy Lov in furnish-
ing the Hous · How Gloriously doth it Shine in the Possessor!

My Lims and Members when rightly Prized, are Comparable to the fine Gold; The Topaz of Ethiopia and the Gold of Ophir are not to 5 be compared to them. What Diamonds are Equal to my Eys; What Labyrinths to mine Ears; What Gates of Ivory, or Rubie Leaves to the Double Portal of my Lips and Teeth? Is not Sight a Jewel? Is not Hearing a Treasure? Is not Speech a Glory! O my Lord Pardon my Ingratitud and pitty my Dulnes, who am not Sensible 10 of these Gifts. The freedom of thy Bounty hath deceived me. These things were too near to be considered. Thou preventedst me with thy Blessings, and I was not aware. But now I giv Thanks and Adore and Prais Thee for these Inestimable favors. I believ Thou lovest me, becaus Thou hast endued me, with these Sacred 15 and Living Treasures. Holy Father, hence forth I more Desire to esteem them, then Palaces of Gold! yea tho they were given me by Kings. I confess unto Thee that I am Richer in them. O what Joy, what Delight and Jubilee should there always be, would men Prize the Gifts of God according to their Value! 20

67

But what Creature could I desire to be which I am not Made? There are Angels and Cherubim. I rejoyce O Lord in their Happiness; and that I am what I am by thy Grace and favor. Suppose O my Soul there were no Creature made at all, And that GOD making Thee alone offered to make Thee what Thou wouldst. What 5 couldst Thou Desire; or what wouldst Thou wish, or Crave to be? Since GOD is the most Glorious of all Beings, and the most Blessed, couldst thou wish any more then to be His IMAGE! O my Soul, He hath made [thee] His Image. Sing O ye Angels, and Laud His Name ye Cherubims: Let all the Kingdoms of the Earth be Glad, 10 and let all the Hosts of Heaven rejoyce · for He hath made His Image, the Likeness of himself, his own Similitude. What Creature what Being what Thing more Glorious could there be! GOD from all Eternity was infinitly Blessed and desired to make one infinitly Blessed. He was infinit LOV, and being Lovly in being so, Would 15 prepare for Himself a Most Lovly Object. Having Studied from all Eternity, He saw none more Lovly then the Image of His Lov, His own Similitude. O Dignity Unmeasurable! O Exaltation Passing Knowledge! O Joy Unspeakable! Triumph O my Soul and Rejoyce for ever! I see that I am infinitly Beloved. For *infinit* 20

67. 17. T deleted words here, but forgot to delete the comma after *saw*.

Lov hath exprest and pleased it self in Creating an Infinit Object.
GOD is LOV, and my Soul is Lovely! God is Loving, and His
Image Amiable. O my Soul these are the Foundations of an Eternal
Friendship between GOD and Thee. He is infinitly Prone to Lov,
25 and Thou art Like Him. He is infinitly Lovly and Thou art Like
Him. What can more Agree then that which is infinitly Lovly, and
that which is infinitly Prone to lov! Where both are so Lovly, and
so Prone to lov, what Joys and Affections will be Excited between
them! What infinit Treasures will they be to each other! O my
30 GOD Thou hast Glorified thy self, and thy Creature infinitly,
in making thine Image! It is fitted for the Throne of GOD! It is
meet to be thy Companion! It is so Sublime and Wonderfull and
Amiable, that all Angels and Men were Created to Admire it. As
it was Created to Admire Thee, and to liv in Communion with
35 Thee for ever.

68

Being made alone, O my Soul, thou wouldst be in thy Body like
GOD in the World, an Invisible Mysterie, too Great to be Com-
prehended by all Creatures. Thou wouldst have all the Goodness ·
of GOD towards Thee to enjoy, in that thy Creation. Whatever is
5 in Him would be thy Treasure. But had He Determined to Creat
no more: there had been no Witnesses of thy Glory. No Spec-
tators of thy Communion with GOD. No other Treasures beside
GOD and Thou. One would think those were Sufficient. But
Infinit Goodness loves to Abound. And to overflow infinitly with
10 Infinit Treasures. Lov lovs to do somwhat for its Object more
then to Creat it. It is always more stately being surrounded with
Power, and more Delightfull being Inaccessible in a Multitude of
Treasures, and more Honorable in the midst of Admirers: and
more Glorious when it reigneth over many Attendants. Lov ther-
15 fore hath prepared all these for it self and its Object. And becaus
it is always more Great, by how much the Greater they are that
minister unto it, It maketh its Attendants, the most Glorious that
can be, and infinitly Delighteth in giving them all with all its
Treasures to its Beloved. Had GOD Created Thee alone, He had
20 not been so Good as He is. He is Good to Innumerable Millions
now whom he Createth besides, And more good unto thee, infinitly
and ever[1] He Glorifieth His Eternal Wisdom, in making His

---

[1] A possible reading; the word is almost illegible.

Goodness unto all Them Wholy thine, and wholy infinit unto each
of them yet wholy and soly thine in all. Friendship will Manifest
it self in doing all it can for its Beloved. Since therfore GOD will 25
make some other Creatures, what kind of Creatures doth thy Soul
Desire. *Wish Wisely Thou shalt receiv a Grant*. Since Lov is so sweet ·
and Thou art by GODs Lov so infinitly exalted: What canst Thou
Desire but Creatures like unto thy Creator? Behold therfore
Angels and Men produced by his Goodness and made to Delight 30
Thee.

69

O Adorable *Trinity*! What hast Thou don! Thou hast made me
the End of all Things, and all the End of me. I in all, and all in
Me. In evry Soul whom Thou hast Created Thou hast given me
the Similitude of thy self, to Enjoy!·Could my Desires hav Aspired
unto such Treasures? Could my Wisdom hav Devised such Sub- 5
lime Enjoyments! Oh! Thou hast don more for us then we could
ask or think. I prais and Admire and rejoyce in Thee: who art
infinitly infinit in all thy Doings.

70

But what Laws O my Soul wouldst Thou desire? By which the
Lives of those Creatures, should be Guided towards Thee? A
Friend commandeth all in His Jurisdiction to lov his Friend: And
therin Supremely manifesteth his Lov. GOD Himself Exalteth
Thee and causeth Thee to Reign in His Soul. He Exalteth Thee 5
by His Laws and causeth Thee to reign in all others [in] the World.
And souls are like his thy Heavenly Mansions. The Lawgiver of
Heaven and Earth Employeth all His Authority for Thee. He Pro-
moteth Thee in His Eternal Palace, and maketh Thee His Friend,
and telleth His Nobles and all His Subjects. Whatsoever ye do unto 10
Him ye do unto Me. Joseph was not so great in Pharoahs Court,
Nor Haman in the Court of Ahasuerus, as Thou art in Heaven.
He Tendereth Thee as the Apple of His Ey. He hath set His
Heart upon Thee. Thou art the sole Object of His Ey, and the End
of all His Endeavors.
15

70. 6–7. T added 'the World . . . Mansions' above the line, omitting the stop after it and
leaving in an unwanted stop after 'others'.

71

But what Life wouldst Thou lead? And by what Laws wouldst
Thou thy self be guided? For none are so Miserable as the Lawless
and Disobedient. Laws are the Rules of Blessed Living. Thou must
therfore be guided by som Laws. What wouldst Thou chuse?
5 Surely since thy Nature and GODs are so Excellent, the Laws of
Nature, are the most pleasing as the Laws of Blessedness. GOD
loved Thee with an infinit Lov, and became by doing so thine
infinit Treasure. Thou art the End unto Whom He liveth For all
the Lines of His Works and Counsels end in Thee, and in thy
10 Advancement. Wilt not Thou becom to Him an Infinit Treasure,
by loving Him according to His Desert. It is impossible but to lov
Him that loveth. Lov is so Amiable that it is Irresistible. There is
no Defence against that Arrow, nor any Deliverance in that War,
nor any Safeguard from that Charm. Wilt Thou not liv unto Him?
15 Thou must of Necessity liv unto som Thing. And what so Glorious
as His Infinit Lov? Since therfore Laws are requisit to lead Thee,
what Laws can thy Soul desire, then those that Guid thee in the
most Amiable Paths to the Highest End? By lov alone is GOD
Enjoyed. By Lov alone Delighted in, by Lov alone approached or
20 Admired. His Nature requires Lov. Thy Nature requires Lov.
The Law of Nature Commands Thee to lov Him. The Law of His
Nature, and the Law of thine.

72

There is in Lov two Strange Perfections, that make it infinit in
Goodness. It is infinitly Diligent in doing Good; And it infinitly
Delighteth in that Goodness. It taketh No Pleasure Comparable
in any thing to that it taketh in Exalting and Blessing. And therfore
5 hath it made Thee a Comprehension infinit to see all Ages, and an
Affection Endless to lov all Kingdoms, and a Power fathomless to
Enjoy all Angels. And a Thirst unsatiable to desire and Delight in
them. And a never Wearied faculty alsufficient to see, Number
take in Prize and Esteem all the Varieties of Creatures and their
Excellencies in all Worlds that Thou mayst Enjoy them in Com-
munion with Him. It is all Obligation, that He requires it. What
Life wouldst Thou lead? wouldst Thou lov God alone? GOD alone
cannot be Beloved. He cannot be loved with a finit Lov, becaus He
is infinit. Were He Beloved alone, His Lov would be limited. He

must be Loved in all with an Illimited Lov, even in all His Doings, 15
in all His friends in all His Creatures. Evry where · in all Things
Thou must meet His Lov. And this the Law of Nature Commands.
And it is thy Glory That Thou art fitted for it. His Lov unto thee
is the Law and Measure of thine unto him, his Lov unto all others
the Law and Obligation of thine unto all. 20

73

His Nature requireth that Thou lov all those whom He loveth.
And receiv Him in all those Things wherin He giveth Him self
unto Thee. Their Nature loveth to be Beloved and being Amiable
require Lov; as well as Delight in it. They require it both by Desert
and Desire. Thy Nature urgeth it · for without Loving Thou art 5
Desolat, and by Loving Thou Enjoyest. Yea by Loving Thou
Expandest and Enlargest thy self. And the more Thou lovest art
the more Glorious. Thou lovest all thy Friends Friends; and
needest not to fear any Dearth of Lov or Danger of Insufficiency.
For the more Thou lovest thy Friend, thy Soveraign friend, 10
the more Thou lovest all his. Which showeth the Endless Prone-
ness of Lov to increas and never to Decay. O my Soul Thou livest
in all those whom Thou lovest: and in them Enjoyest all their
Treasures.

74

Miraculous are the Effects of Divine Wisdom. He loveth evry one:
maketh evry one infinitly Happy: and is infinitly Happy in evry
one. He giveth all the World to one, He giveth it to evry one, He
giveth it to evry one in giving it to all, and Giveth it wholy to me ·
in giving it to evry one for evry ones sake. He is infinitly Happy 5
in Evry one, as many Times therefore as there are Happy Persons.
He is infinitly Happy. Evry one is infinitly Happy in evry one,
Evry one therfore is as many Times infinitly Happy as there are
Happy Persons. He is infinitly Happy abov all their Happiness in
Comprehending all. And I Comprehending His and theirs, am, 10
Oh how Happy! Here is Lov! Here is a Kingdom! Where all are
Knit in infinit Unity · all are Happy in each other · all are like
Dieties. Evry one the End of all Things evry one supreme, evry
one a Treasure and the Joy of all, and evry one most infinitly
Delighted in being so. All things are ever Joys for evry ones sake, 15

and infinitly Richer to evry one for the sake of all. The same Thing
is Multiplied by being Enjoyed. And He that is Greatest is most my
Treasure. This is the Effect of Making Images. And by all their
Lov is evry Image infinitly Exalted. Comprehending in his Nature
20 all Angels all Cherubims all Seraphims all Worlds all Creatures,
and GOD over all Blessed for ever.

75

Being to lead this Life within I was Placed in Paradice without,
with som Advantages which the Angels hav not. And being De-
signed to Immortality and an Endless Life, was to Abide with GOD
from everlasting to everlasting in all His Ways. But I was Deceived
5 by my Appetite, and fell into Sin. Ingratefully I despised Him that
gav me my Being. I offended in an Apple against Him that gave
me the whole World: But Thou O Savior art here upon the Cross
suffering for my Sins. What shall I render unto Thee for so Great
a Mercy! All Thanksgiving is too Weak. And all Expression too
10 feeble. I giv Thee my self· my Soul and Body I offer unto Thee.
It is unworthy of Thee, but Thou lovest me. Wash me with thy
Blood from all my Sins: And fill me with thy Holy Spirit that I
may be like unto Thee. So shall I Prais thy Name Acceptably for
ever more. Amen.

76

And now O Lord Heaven and Earth are infinitly more valuable
then they were before · being all bought with thy Precious Blood.
And Thou O Jesus art a Treasure unto me far Greater then all
those. At what Rate or Measure shall I Esteem Thee! Thou hast
5 restored me again to the Friendship of GOD, to the Enjoyment of
the World, To the Hope of Eternal Glory, To the Lov of Angels
Cherubims and Men, To the Enjoyment and Obedience of thy
Holy Laws: which alone are Sweeter to me then the Hony and the
Hony Comb, and more precious then Thousands of Gold and
10 Silver. Thou hast restored me abov all to the Image of GOD.
And Thou hast Redeemed all Ages and Kingdoms for me alone!
Who am commanded to lov them as Thou doest. O that I might be
unto them as Thou art! O that I might be unto Thee as Thou art
to Me. As glorious and as Rich in Lov! O that I might Die for
15 Thee! O that I might ever live unto Thee! In evry Thought, in

evry Action of my Life, in evry Moment I Bless Thee for Renewing
the old commandement; upon New Obligations among Sinners,
As I hav loved you, so do ye also lov one another. O let Thy Lov be in
me · that thy Joy may be fulfilled in me for evermore.   5

77

Now O Lord I see the Greatness of Thy Lov wherwith Thou Diest.
And by thy Actions more then by thy Sufferings Admire Thee. But
henceforth I will more Admire Thee by Thy Sufferings · for con-
sidering that such Actions went before; what lov must move Thee
to com into the Place of Guilty Sinners!   5

78

Lord I lament, and Abhor my self that I hav been the Occasion of
these thy Sufferings. I had never known the Dignity of my Nature,
hadst not Thou esteemed it: I had never seen, nor Understood its
Glory, hadst not Thou Assumed it. Be Thou Pleased to unite me
unto Thee in the Bands of an Individual Lov, that I may evermore   5
liv unto Thee, and Liv in Thee. And by how much the more Vile
I hav been, let my lov be so much O Lord the more Violent Hence-
forth and fervent unto Thee. O Thou who wouldst never hav per-
mitted sin, hadst Thou not known how to Bring good out of Evil,
hav Pitty upon me: Hear my Prayer. O my GOD since Pitty En- 10
balmes Lov, let thine com Enricht, and be more precious to me
Miserable Sinner. Let the Remembrance of all the Glory wherin
I was Created make me more Serious and Humble, more Deep and
Penitent more Pure and Holy before Thee. And since the World 15
is Sprinkled with thy Blood, and Adorned with all Kingdoms and
Ages for me: which are Heavenly Treasures and Vastly Greater
then Heaven and Earth · Let me see thy Glory in the Preparation of
them, and thy Goodness in their Government. Open unto me
the Gate of Righteousness, that I may enter in to the New Jeru-
salem.   20

79

My Lord, Thou Head of the Holy Catholic Church · I Admire
and Prais Thee for Purchasing to thy self such a glorious Bride:
and for Uniting us all by the Blood of thy Crosse. I beseech Thee
let my Lov unto all be Regular like thine, and Pure, and Infinit.

5 Make it Divine, and make it Holy. I confess I can see· but I cannot Moderat, nor Lov as I ought. I Pray Thee for thy Loving kindness sake supply my Want in this Particular. And so make me to lov all, that I may be a Blessing to all: and welpleasing to Thee in all. Teach me Wisdom, How to Expend my Blood Estate Life and 10 Time in thy service for the Good of all, and make all them that are round about me Wise and Holy as Thou art. That we might all be Knit together in GODly Lov, and united in thy service to Thy Honor and Glory.

80[1]

My Excellent friend, you see that there are Treasures in Heaven and Earth fit to be Enjoyed, besides those of Kings Courts and Taverns. The Joys of the Temple are the Greatest Joys were they understood; they are the most Magnificent Solemn and Divine. 5 There are Glorious Entertainments in this Miserable World, could we find them out. What more Delightfull can be imagined, then to see a Savior at this Distance Dying on the Cross to Redeem a man from Hell, and to see one self the Beloved of GOD and all Kingdoms, yea the Admired of Ages, and the Heir of the whole 10 World? Hath not His Blood united you and me, Cannot we see and Lov and Enjoy each other at 100 Miles Distance? In Him is the only Sweet and Divine Enjoyment. I Desire but an Amiable Soul in any Part of all Eternity, and can lov it unspeakably: And if lov it, Enjoy it. For Lov implies Pleasure, becaus it is ever pleased 15 with what is Beloved. Lov GOD and Jesus Christ and Angels and Men, which you are made to do as naturaly as the Sun is made to shine, and the Beauty of the Holy Ghost Dwelling in you will make you my Delight, and the Treasure of the Holy Angels. You will at last be seen by me and all others, in all your Thoughts and 20 in all your Motions. In the mean time, Delight only in the Lov of JESUS, and Direct all your Lov unto Him. Adore Him, Rejoyce in Him, Admire His Lov and Prais Him, Secretly and in the Congregation. Enjoy His Saints that are round about you, make your self Amiable that you may be Admitted to their Enjoyment, 25 by Meekness Temperance, Modesty Humility Charity Chastitie Devotion Cheerfulness Gratitude Joy Thanksgiving. Retire from them that you may be the more Precious, and com out unto them

---

[1] This section is crossed through for deletion in the manuscript.

the more Wise. So shall you make the Place wherin you live a
Nest of Sweet Perfumes, and evry Soul that is round about you
will be a Bed of Honor and Sweet Repose unto you.   30

81

My Goodness extendeth not to Thee O Lord, but to Thy Saints,
and to the Excellent in the Earth in whom is all my Delight. To
Delight in the Saints of God is the Way to Heaven. One would
think it Exceeding easy and reasonable, to Esteem those whom
Jesus purchased with his precious Blood. And if we do so how can 5
we chuse but inherit all Things. All the Saints of all Ages and all
Kingdoms are his Inheritance, his Treasures, his Jewels. Shall
they not be yours since they are His whom you love so infinitly?
There is not a cup of cold Water given to a Disciple in the name
of a Disciple, but He accepteth it as don to Himself. Had you been 10
with Mary Magdalen, would you not hav annointed his feet, and
washed them in tears and wiped them with the Hairs of your
head? His poor Servants, his Contemptible and Disguised Mem-
bers here upon Earth are his Feet, yea more, the Apple of His Ey:
yea more, for He gave his Eys and Heart and Hands and feet for 15
them. O therfore universaly in all places tender them and at all
times be ready and Willing to Minister unto them. And that with
infinit Joy, Knowing the Excellency of your Duty · for you are
Enjoying the World, and Communicating your self like God unto
them. You are laying up Treasure in Heaven and Enlarging your 20
Soul, Beautifying your Life, and Delighting the Holy Angels,
Offering up sacrifices unto God, and perfuming the World; Em-
bracing Jesus Christ, and caressing your Savior while you are
Dispensing Charities among them. Every Alms Deed is a Precious
Stone in the Crown of Glory.   25

82

But there are a sort of Saints meet to be your Companions, in
another maner · But that they lie concealed. You must therfore
make your self exceeding Virtuous, that by the very Splendor of
your Fame you may find them out. While the Wicked are like
Heaps of Rubbish, these few Jewels lie buried in the Ruins of Man- 5
kind: and must Diligently be Digd for. You may Know them by
their Lustre · and by the very Desire and Esteem they hav of you

when you are virtuous. For as it is the Glory of the Sun that Darkness cannot approach it, becaus it is always encompassed with
10 its own Beams; so it is the Priviledge of Holy Souls, that they are
always secure in their own Light, which driveth away Divels and
Evil Men: And is accessible by none, but Lovers of Virtue. Beginners and Desirers will give you the Opportunity of infusing your
self and your Principles into them. Practicers and Growers will
15 mingle souls and be Delightfull Companions, The Sublime and
Perfect, in the Lustre of their Spirit will shew you the Image
of Almighty God and the Joys of Heaven. They will Allure Protect Encourage Comfort Teach Honor and Delight you. But you
must be very Good, for that is the way to find them. And very
20 Patient to endure som time, and very Diligent to observ where
they are.

<h1 style="text-align:center">83</h1>

They will Prais our Savior with you and turn the World into
Heaven. And if you find those of Noble and Benevolent Natures,
Discreet and Magnanimous, Liberal and Cheerfull, Wise and
Holy as they ought to be, you will hav in them Treasures Greater
5 then all Relations whatsoever. They will Exchange Souls with you,
Divide Estates, Communicate Comforts, Counsels and Honors,
And in all Tenderness Constancy Fidelity and Lov be more yours
then their own. There are exceeding few such Heavenly Lovers
as Jesus was, who imparted his own Soul unto us. Yet som may
10 Doubtlessly be found. And half a Dozen such as these wisely
chosen will represent unto us the New Jerusalem: Entertain us
always with Divine Discourses, Pleas us always with Heavenly
Affections, Delight us always with Melodie and Praises · and ever
make us near unto our Savior.

<h1 style="text-align:center">84</h1>

Yet you must Arm yourself with Expectations of their Infirmities,
and resolv nobly to forgive them: not in a sordid and Cowardly
maner, by taking no notice of them: nor in a Dim and Lazy maner,
by letting them alone: but in a Divine and Illustrious maner, by
5 chiding them meekly, and vigorously rendering and showering
down all kind of Benefits. Cheerfully continuing to do Good, and
whatever you suffer by your Piety and charity, Confidence or Lov,

to be like our Savior, Unwearied: who when he was abused, and
had often been evil intreated among men, proceeded couragiously
through all Treacheries and Deceits to die for them. So shall you 10
turn their very Vices, into Virtues to you, and as our Savior did make
of a Wreath of Thorns, a Crown of Glory. But set the Splendor of
Virtues before you, and when som fail, think with your self, there
are some Sincere and Excellent, And why should not I be the most
Virtuous?
15

85

With all their Eys behold our Savior, with all their Hearts Adore
Him, with all their Tongues and Affections praise him. See how
in all Closets, and in all Temples; in all Cities and in all feilds; in
all Nations and in all generations they are lifting up their hands
and Eys unto his Cross; and Delight in all their Adorations. This 5
will Enlarge your Soul and make you to Dwell in all Kingdoms and
Ages: Strengthen your Faith and Enrich your Affections: fill you
with their Joys and make you a Lively Partaker in Communion with
them. It will make you a Possessor Greater then the World. Men
do mightily wrong themselvs: when they refuse to be present in 10
all Ages: and Neglect to see the Beauty of all Kingdoms, and
Despise the Resentments† of evry Soul, and Busie them selvs only
with Pots and Cups and things at home, or Shops and Trades and
things in the street. But do not liv to God Manifesting Himself in
all the World, nor care to see, (and be present with Him, in) all the 15
Glory of his Eternal Kingdom. By seeing the Saints of all Ages we
are present with Them. By being present with them becom too
Great for our own Age, and near to our Savior.

86

O Jesu, Thou King of Saints, whom all Adore: and the Holy
Imitat, I Admire the perfection of thy Lov in evry soul! Thou
lovest evry one Wholy as if Him alone: Whose Soul is so Great
an Image of thine Eternal Father, that Thou camest down from
Heaven to die for Him, and to Purchase Mankind that they might 5
be his Treasures. I Admire to see thy Crosse in evry Understand-
ing, thy Passion in evry Memory, thy Crown of Thorns in evry
Ey, and thy Bleeding, Naked Wounded Body in evry Soul. Thy

Death liveth in evry Memory, thy Crucified Person is Enbalmed
10 in evry Affection, thy pierced feet are Bathed in evry ones Tears,
thy Blood all droppeth on evry Soul: Thou wholy Communicatest
thy self to evry Soul in all Kingdoms, and art wholy seen in every
Saint, and wholy fed upon by evry Christian. It is my Priviledge
that I can enter with Thee into evry Soul, and in evry Living Temple
15 of thy Manhood and thy Godhead, behold again, and Enjoy thy
Glory.

87

Oh how do thine Affections extend like the Sun Beams unto all
the stars in heaven and to all the Kingdoms in the World. Thine at
once Enlighten both Hemispheres. Quicken us with Life, Enable
us to digest the Nourishment of our Souls, caus Us to see the
5 Greatness of our Nature, the Lov of God, and the Joys of Heaven:
Melt us into Tears, Comfort and Enflame us, and do all in a Celestial
maner, that the Sun can do in a Terrene and Earthly. O Let me
so long Eye Thee, till I be turned into Thee, and look upon me till
Thou art formed in me, that I may be a Mirror of thy Brightness,
10 an Habitation of thy Lov and a Temple of thy Glory. That all thy
Saints might live in me, and I in them: enjoying all their felicities
Joys and Treasures.

88

O Thou Sun of Righteousness, Ecclypsed on the Cross, overcast
with Sorrows, and covered with the shadow of Death, remov the
vail of thy flesh that I may see thy Glory. Those cheeks are shades,
those Lims and Members clouds, that hide the Glory of thy Mind,
5 thy Knowledg and thy Lov from us. But were they removed those
inward Excellencies would remain Invisible. As therfore we see
thy Flesh with our fleshly Eys, and handle thy Wounds with our
Bodily Sences, let us see thy Understanding with our Understand-
ings, and read thy Lov with our own. Let our Souls hav Communion
10 with thy Soul, and let the Ey of our Mind enter into thine. Who
art Thou who Bleeding here causest the Ground to Tremble and
the Rocks to rend, and the Graves to Open? Hath thy Death In-
fluence so high as the Highest Heavens? That the Sun also Mourneth
and is Clothed in Sables? Is thy Spirit present in the Temple,

that the vail rendeth in twain at thy Passion? O let me leav Kings 15
Courts to com unto Thee, and chuse rather in a Cave to serve Thee,
then on a Throne to despise Thee. O my Dying Gracious Lord, I
perceiv the virtu of thy Passion evry where: Let it I beseech Thee
enter into my Soul, and rent my Rocky Stony Heart, and tear the
vail of my flesh that I may see into the Holy of Holies! O Darken 20
the Sun of Pride and Vain Glory. Yea let the Sun it self be Dark in
Comparison of thy Lov! And open the Grave of my flesh, that my
Soul may arise to Prais Thee. Grant this for thy Mercy sake.
Amen!

89

Is this He that was transfigured upon Mount Tabor! Pale,
Withered! Extended! Tortured! Soyld with Blood and Sweat
and Dust! Dried! Parched! O Sad! O Dismal Spectacle! All His
Joynts are dissolved, all His Blood is shed: to the last Drop! All his
Moysture is consumed! What is here but a Heap of Desolations! 5
a Deformed Carcais! a Disfigured Countenance! A Mass of
Miseries; and silent Footsteps of Innumerable Sufferings! Can this
be a Joy! Can this be an Entertainment! Can this Delight us!
O JESUS the more vile I here behold Thee, the more I Admire
Thee. Into what Low Abysses didst thou Descend; in what Depths 10
of misery dost Thou now lie! Oh what Contusions, what Stripes and
Wounds, what Desolations and Deformities didst Thou suffer for
our sakes! In all the Depths of thy Humiliation I here Adore Thee!
I prize and Desire always to see these Stripes and these Deformities.
It is sweeter to be with Thee in thy Sufferings, then with Princes 15
on their Thrones, and more do I rejoyce with Thee in thy Miseries,
then in all their Solemnities. I Tremble also to see thy Condescen-
tions. The Great Effects and Expressions of thy Lov! Thou wast
slain for me: and shall I leav thy Body in the feild O Lord? Shall
I go away and be Merry, while the Love of my Soul and my only 20
Lover is Dead upon the Cross. Groans here, in the sight and Ap-
prehension of thy Lov, are beyond all Melodie, and the solemn
sorrows of a loving Soul, a faithfull Friend, a Tender Spouse, a
Deep and Compassionat Tru Lover, beyond all the Entertainments
in the World. Thine O Jesus will I ever be while I hav any 25
Being.

88. 16. *and*. M reads the ampersand as *I*.

P

90

This Body is not the Cloud, but a Pillar assumd to manifest His
Lov unto us. In these Shades doth this Sun break forth most
Oriently. In this Death is His Lov Painted in most lively colours.
GOD never shewd Himself more a GOD, then when He appeared
5 Man. Never gained more Glory then when He lost all Glory. Was
never more Sensible of our Sad Estate, then when He was bereaved
of all Sence. O let thy Goodness shine in me! I will lov all O Lord
by thy Grace Assisting as Thou doest: And in Death it self, will
I find Life, and in Conquest Victory. This Sampson by Dying
10 Kild all His Enemies: And then carried the Gates of Hell and
Death away, when being Dead, Himself was born to his Grave.
Teach me O Lord these Mysterious Ascentions. By Descending
into Hell for the sake of others, let me Ascend into the Glory of the
Highest Heavens. Let the Fidelity and Efficacy of my Lov appear,
15 in all my Care and Suffering for Thee.

91

O Jesu Lord of Lov· and Prince of Life! who even being Dead,
art Greater then all Angels Cherubims and Men. Let my Lov unto
Thee be as Strong as Death: and so Deep that No Waters may
be able to Drown it. O let it be ever Endless and Invincible! O that
5 I could realy so lov Thee, as rather to suffer with S. Anselm the
Pains of Hell then to Sin against Thee. O that no Torments, no
Powers in Heaven or Earth, no Stratagems no Allurements might
Divide me from Thee. Let the Length and Bredth and Height and
Depth of my Love unto Thee be like Thine unto me. Let un-
10 dreinable fountains, and unmeasurable Abysses be hidden in it.
Let it be more vehement then flame, more Abundant then the sea,
more Constant then the Candle in Aarons Tabernacle that burned
day and night. Shall the sun shine for me; and be a Light from the
Beginning of the World to this very day that never goeth out, and
15 shall my Lov ceas, or intermit, O Lord, to shine or burn. O Let it
be a Perpetual fire on the Altar of my Heart, and let my Soul it self
be thy Living Sacrifice.

92

It is an inestimable Joy that I was raised out of Nothing, to see
and Enjoy this Glorious World: It is a Sacred Gift wherby the

children of Men are made my Treasures, but O Thou who art fairer then the Children of Men, how great and unconceivable is the Joy of thy Lov! That I who was lately raised out of the dust, 5 hav so Great a Friend, that I who in this life am born to mean Things according to the world should be called to inherit such Glorious Things in the way of Heaven: Such a Lord, so Great a Lover, such Heavenly Mysteries, such Doings, and such sufferings, with all the Benefit and pleasure of them in thy Intelligible King- 10 dom: it amazeth, it transporteth and ravisheth me. I will leave my fathers house and com unto Thee; For Thou art my Lord, and I will Worship Thee. That all Ages should appear so visibly before me, and all thy Ways be so lively Powerfull and present with me, that the Land of Canaan should be so near, and all the Joys in 15 Heaven and Earth so sweet to comfort me! This O Lord declareth thy Wisdom, and sheweth thy Power. But O the Riches of thine infinit Goodness in making my Soul an Interminable Temple, out of which nothing can be, from which Nothing is removed, to which nothing is afar off; but all things immediatly near, in Real true and 20 Lively Maner. O the Glory of that Endless Life, that can at once extend to all Eternity! Had the Cross been 20 Millions of Ages further, it had still been equaly near, nor is it possible to remov it, for it is with all Distances in my Understanding, and tho it be removed many thousand Millions of Ages more is as clearly seen 25 and Apprehended. This Soul for which Thou diedst, I desire to Know more perfectly, O my Savior. That I may prais thee for it, and believ it worthy, in its Nature, to be an Object of thy Lov; tho unworthy by reason of sin: and that I may use it in thy Service, and Keep it pure to thy Glory.

30

93

As my Body without my Soul is a Carcase, so is my Soul without thy Spirit. A chaos, a Dark Obscure Heap of Empty faculties: Ignorant of it self, unsensible of thy Goodness, Blind to thy Glory: Dead in Sins and Trespasses. Having Eys I see not, having Ears I hear not, having an Heart I understand not the Glory of thy Works 5 and the Glory of thy Kingdom. O Thou who art the Root of my Being, and the Captain of my Salvation, look upon me. Quicken me O Thou Life-giving and Quickening Seed. Visit me with thy Light and thy Truth, let them lead me to thy Holy Hill: and make me to

10 see the Greatness of thy Lov in all its Excellencies, Effects, Emana-
tions Gifts and Operations. O my Wisdom! O my Righteousness,
Sanctification and Redemption; let thy Wisdom Enlighten me,
let thy Knowledg illuminat me, let thy Blood redeem me, wash
me and Cleans me, let thy Merits justify me, O Thou who art Equal
15 unto GOD, and didst suffer for me. Let thy Righteousness clothe
me. Let thy Will imprint the Form of itself upon mine; and let my
Will becom Conformable to thine: that thy Will and mine, may be
united, and made one for evermore.

94

Thy Will O Christ and thy Spirit in Essence are one. As therfore
thy Human Will is conformable to thy Divine; let my Will be
conformable to thine. Thy Divine Will is all Wisdom, Goodness,
Righteousness, Holiness, Glory and Blessedness. It is all Light and
5 Life and Love. It extendeth to all Things in Heaven and Earth, It
illuminateth all Eternity, it Beautifies the Omnipresence of GOD
with Glory without Dimensions. It is infinit in Greatness and
Magnifieth all that are united to it. Oh that my Will being made
Great by thine, might becom Divine, Exalted, Perfected! O Jesu
10 without Thee I can do nothing. O Thou in whom the fulness of
the GODhead Dwelleth I desire to learn of Thee, to becom in
Spirit like unto Thee. I desire not to learn of my Relations, Acquain-
tance, Tradesmen Merchants or Earthly Princes to be like unto
them; but like unto Thee the King of Glory, and to those who are
15 thy Sons and Friends in another World. Grant therfore, O Thou
of whom the whole Familie in Heaven and Earth is named, that
being Strengthened with Might by thy Spirit in the Inner Man,
I may be able to Comprehend with all Saints, what is the Bredth
and Length and Depth and Heighth, and to know that Lov of Christ
20 which Passeth Knowledg, that I may be filled with all the fulness of
GOD.

95

O Thou who Ascendedst up on High, and ledst Captivity Captiv,
and gavest Gifts unto Men, as after thy Ascension into Heaven
thou didst send thy Holy Spirit down upon thine Apostles in the
form of a Rushing Mighty Wind, and in the shape of cloven fiery

Tongues; send down the Holy Ghost upon me: Breath upon 5
me, Inspire me, Quicken Me, Illuminat me, Enflame me, fill me
with the Spirit of GOD; that I may overflow with Praises and
Thanksgivings as they did · fill me with the Riches of thy Glory,
that Christ may Dwell in my Heart by faith, that I being rooted
and Grounded in Lov may speak the Wonderfull Works of GOD. 10
Let me be Alive unto them: let me see them all, let me feel them
all, let me enjoy them all: that I may Admire the Greatness of thy
Lov unto my Soul, and rejoyce in Communion with Thee for ever-
more. How Happy O Lord am I, Who am called to a Communion
with GOD the father Son and Holy Ghost, in all their Works 15
and Ways, in all their Joys, in all their Treasures, in all their
Glory! Who hav such a Father, having in Him the Fountain
of Immortality Rest and Glory, and the Joy of seeing Him Creating
all Things for my sake! Such a Son, Having in Him the Means of
Peace and felicity, and the Joy of seeing Him redeeming my Soul, 20
by his sufferings on the Cross, and doing all things that pertain
to my salvation between the father and Me: Such a Spirit and
such a Comforter dwelling in me to Quicken, Enlighten and
Enable me, and to awaken all the Powers of my Soul, that night
and day the same Mind may be in me that was in Christ 25
Jesus!

96

O Thou who hast Redeemed me to be a Son of God, and called
me from vanity to inherit All Things, I Prais Thee, that having
Loved me, and Given thy self for me, Thou commandest us Saying,
As I hav loved you, so do ye also love one another. Wherin Thou
hast commanded all Men, so to lov me, as to lay down their Lives 5
for my Peace and Welfare. Since Lov is the End for which Heaven
and Earth was made, enable me to see and discern the Sweetness
of so great a Treasure. And since Thou hast Advanced me into the
Throne of GOD, in the Bosom of all Angels and Men; commanding
them by this Precept, to giv me an Union and Communion with 10
Thee in their Dearest Affection; in their Highest Esteem; and in
the most near and inward Room and Seat in their Hearts: Give
me the Grace which S. Paul prayed for, that I may be Acceptable
to the Saints; fill me with thy Holy Spirit, and make my Soul and
Life Beautifull, make me all Wisdom Goodness and Lov, that I may 15

be Worthy to be Esteemed and Accepted of them. That being
Delighted also with their Felicity, I may be Crowned with thine,
and with their Glory.

97

O Jesu, who having prepared all the Joys in Heaven and Earth
for me, and redeemed me to Inherit thy Fathers Treasures; hast
prepared for me the most Glorious Companions, in whose presence
and Society I may Enjoy them: I Bless Thee for the Communion
5 of Saints; and for thy Adorning the same, with all maner of Beauties,
Excellencies, Perfections and Delights. O what a Glorious Assembly
is the Church of the First Born, How Blessed and Divine! What
Perfect Lovers! How Great and Honorable! How Wise! How
sweet and Delightfull! Evry one being the End, evry one the
10 King of Heaven; evry one the Son of GOD in Greatness and
Glory; evry one the Intire and Perfect Friend of all the Residu;
evry one the Joy of each others Soul; evry one the Light and
Ornament of thy Kingdom; evry one thy Peculiar Friend, yet
Loving evry one as thy Peculiar friend: and rejoycing in the
15 Pleasures and Delights of evry one! O my God, make me one of
that Happy Assembly. And let me lov evry one for whom Christ
died, with a Lov as Great and Lively as His. That I may Dwell
in Him, and He in me · and that we all may be made perfect in
one, even as Thou O Jesus art in the Father and the Father is
20 in Thee: that thy Lov may be in us, and Thou in me for ever-
more.

98

Wisely, O Jesu, didst Thou tell thy Disciples, when Thou Pro-
misedst them the Comforter, that the World cannot receiv the
Spirit of Truth: becaus it seeth Him not neither Knoweth Him.
But ye Know Him, for He Dwelleth with you, and shall be in
5 you. O let the Spirit of Truth dwell with me, and then little matter
for any other Comforter. When I see my self Beloved of the Father:
when I know the Perfection of thy Love, when the Father and the
Son loveth me, and both manifest themselvs unto me; when they
are near unto me and Abide with me for ever and ever: little Harm
10 can death do, or Sickness and Poverty. I can never be alone becaus
the Father and Son are with me. No Reproaches can Discomfort

me, no Enemies can hurt me. O let me Know Thee Thou Spirit of Truth, be Thou always with me, and Dwell within me. How is it Possible, but Thou shouldst be an infinit Comforter; Who givest me a Being as Wide as Eternity; a Well Being as Blessed 15 as the Dietie, a Temple of Glory in the Omnipresence of GOD, and a Light wherin to Enjoy the New Jerusalem! An unmovable Inheritance, and an Everlasting Kingdom that cannot be shaken! Thou art He who Shewest me all the Treasures in Heaven and Earth, who enablest me to turn Afflictions into Pleasures, and to 20 Enjoy mine Enemies: Thou Enablest me to lov as I am Beloved, and to be Blessed in GOD: Thou sealest me up unto the Day of Redemption, and givest me a foretast of Heaven upon Earth. Thou art my God and my Exceeding Joy, my Comforter and my Strength for evermore. Thou representest all things unto me, which the 25 Father and the Son hath don for me. Thou fillest me with Courage against all Assaults and Enablest me to overcom in all Temptations; Thou makest me Immovable by the very Treasures and the Joys which Thou shewest to me. O Never leav me nor forsake me, but remain with me, and be my Comfort forever. 30

99

Wisely doth S. John say, We are the Sons of God; but the World knoweth us not becaus it knew Him not. He that Knoweth not the Spirit of God, can never Know a Son of GOD, nor what it is to be His Child. He made us the sons of GOD in Capacity by giving us a Power, to see Eternity, to Survey His Treasures, to 5 love his children, to know and to lov as He doth, to becom Righteous and Holy as He is; that we might be Blessed and Glorious as He is. The Holy Ghost maketh us the Sons of God in Act, when we are Righteous as He is Righteous, and Holy as He is Holy. When we prize all the Things in Heaven and Earth, as He Prizeth Him, 10 and make a Conscience of doing it as He doth after His similitude; then are we actualy present with them, and Blessed in them, being Righteous and Holy, as He is · then the Spirit of GOD dwelleth in us, and then are we indeed the Sons of God, a Chosen Generation, a Royal Priesthood, an Holy Nation, a Peculiar 15 People, Zealous of Good Works, shewing forth the Praises of Him, who hath called us out of Darkness, into His Marvellous Light.

100

Christ Dwelling in our Hearts by Faith is an infinit Mystery ·
which may thus be understood. An Object Seen, is in the Faculty
Seeing it, and by that in the Soul of the Seer, after the Best of
Maners. Wheras there are eight maners of In-being, the In-being
5 of an Object in a Faculty is the Best of all. Dead Things are in a
Room containing them in a vain maner; unless they are Objec-
tivly in the Soul of a Seer. The Pleasure of an Enjoyer, is the very
End why Things placed are in any Place. The Place and the Thing
Placed in it, being both in the Understanding of a Spectator of
10 them. Things Dead in Dead Place Effect nothing. But in a Living
Soul, that seeth their Excellencies, they Excite a Pleasure answer-
able to their value, a Wisdom to Embrace them, a Courage not
to Forsake them, a Lov of their Donor, Praises and Thanksgivings;
and a Greatness and a Joy Equal to their Goodness. And thus all
15 Ages are present in my Soul, and all Kingdoms, and GOD Blessed
forever. And thus Jesus Christ is seen in me and dwelleth in me,
when I believ upon Him. And thus all Saints are in me, and I in
them. And thus all Angels and the Eternity and Infinity of GOD
are in me for evermore. I being the Living TEMPLE and Com-
20 prehensor of them. Since therfore all other ways of In-being would
be utterly vain, were it not for this: And the Kingdom of God (as
our Savior saith, this Way) is within you; let us ever think and
Meditat on Him, that His conception Nativity Life and Death may
be always within us. Let Heaven and Earth, Men and Angels,
25 God and his Creatures be always within us · that is in our Sight,
in our Sence, in our Lov and Esteem: that in the Light of the Holy
Ghost we may see the Glory of His Eternal Kingdom, and Sing
the Song of Moses, and the Song of the Lamb saying, Great and
Marvellous are thy Works Lord GOD Almighty, Just and true
30 are thy Ways Thou King of Saints.

THE SECOND CENTURY

1

The Services which the World doth you, are transcendent to all
Imagination. Did it only sustain your Body and preserv your Life,
and Comfort your sences, you were bound to valu it as much as
those services were worth: but it Discovers the Being of GOD
unto you, It opens His Nature, and shews you his Wisdom Good- 5
ness and Power, It Magnifies His Lov unto you, It serves Angels
and Men for you, It entertains you with many Lovely and Glorious
Objects, It feeds you with Joys, and becomes a Theme that fur-
nishes you with perpetual Praises and Thanksgivings, It enflameth
you with the Lov of God, and is the Link of your Union and 10
Communion with Him. It is the Temple wherin you are Exalted
to Glory and Honor, and the visible Porch or Gate of Eternitie.
A Sure Pledge of Eternal Joys, to all them that Walk before God
and are Perfect in it.

2

If you desire Directions how to enjoy it, Place yourself in it as if
no one were Created besides your self. And consider all the services
it doth, even to you alone. Prize those services with a Joy answer-
able to the value of them, be Truly Thankfull, and as Gratefull
for them, as their Merit deserves. And remember always how 5
Great soever the World is, it is the Beginning of Gifts. The first
Thing which GOD bestows to evry Infant, by the very Right of
His Nativity. Which becaus Men are Blind they cannot see; and
therfore know not that GOD is Liberal: from that first Error they
proceed, and multiply their Mistaking all along. They know not 10
themselvs nor their own Glory, they understand not His Com-
mandments, they see not the Sublimity of Righteous Actions, they
know not the Beauty of Truth, nor are acquainted with the Glory
of the Holy Scriptures.

3

Till you see that the World is yours, you cannot weigh the Greatnes
of Sin, nor the Misery of your fall, nor Prize your Redeemers Lov.

One would think these should be Motives Sufficient to stir us
up, to the Contemplation of GODs Works, wherin all the Riches
5 of His Kingdom will appear. For the Greatness of Sin proceedeth
from the Greatness of His Lov whom we hav offended[,] from the
Greatness of those Obligations which were laid upon us, from
the Great Blessedness and Glory of the Estate wherin we were
placed, none of which can be seen, till Truth is seen, a great Part
10 of which is, That the World is ours. So that indeed the Knowledg
of this is the very real Light, wherin all Mysteries are Evidenced
to us.

4

The Misery of your fall ariseth Naturaly from the Greatness of
your Sin. For to Sin against infinit Lov is to make one self infinitly
Deformed: To be infinitly Deformed, is to be infinitly Odious in
His Eys, whose Lov of Beauty is the Hatred of Deformity. To be
5 infinitly odious in His Eys who once loved us with infinit Lov:
to hav sind against all Obligations, and to hav faln from infinit
Glory and Blessedness is infinit Misery: But cannot be seen, till
the Glory of the Estate from which we are faln is Discerned. To
be infinitly Odious in His Eys who infinitly loved us, maketh us
10 unavoidably Miserable: becaus it bereaveth us of the End for
which we were Created, which was to Enjoy his Lov: and of the
End also of all the Creatures which were made only to Manifest
the same. For when we are bereaved of these, we liv to no purpose:
and having lost the End to which we were Created, our Life is
15 cumbersom and irksom to us.

5

The Counsel which our Savior giveth in the Revelation, to the
Church of Ephesus, is by all Churches, and by every Soul diligently
to be observed. *Remember from whence thou art faln, and Repent.*
Which intimates our Duty of Remembering our Happiness in
5 the Estate of Innocence. For without this we can never Prize our
Redeemers Lov: He that Knows not to what He is redeemed cannot
Prize the Work of Redemption. The Means cannot there be valued,
where the End is despised. Since therfore by the Second Adam,
we are restored to that we lost in the first: unless we valu that we
10 lost in the first, we cannot truly rejoyce in the second. But when we

do, then all things receiv an infinit Esteem, and an Augmentation
infinitly infinit, that follows after. Our Saviors Lov, His Incarna-
tion, His Life and Death, His Resurrection, His Ascension into
Heaven, His Intercession for us &c being then seen, and infinitly
prized in a Glorious Light: as also our Deliverance from Hell, and 15
our Reconciliation unto God.

6

The Consideration also of this Truth, that the World is mine
confirmeth my Faith. GOD having placed the Evidences of Religion
in the Greatest and Highest Joys. For as long as I am Ignorant that
the World is mine, the Lov of GOD is Defectiv to me. How can I
believ that He gave His Son to die for me, who having Power to do 5
otherwise gave me nothing but Rags and Cottages? But when I see
once that He gave Heaven and Earth to me, and made me in His
Image to Enjoy them in His Similitude, I can easily believ that He
gave His Son also for me. Especialy since He commanded all
Angels and Men to lov me as Him self: And so highly Honoreth 10
me, that whatsoever is don unto me, He accounteth don unto
Him.

7

Place yourself therfor in the midst of the World as if you were
alone: and Meditat upon all the Services which it doth unto you.
Suppose the Sun were absent, and conceiv the World to be a
Dungeon of Darkness and Death about you: you will then find
His Beams more Delightfull then the Approach of Angels: and 5
loath the Abomination of that Sinfull Blindness, wherby you see
not the Glory of so Great and Bright a Creature, becaus the Air
is filled with its Beams. Then you will think that all its Light shineth
for you, and Confesse that GOD hath manifested Himself indeed,
in the Preparation of so Divine a Creature. You will abhor the 10
Madness of those who esteem a Purs of Gold more then it. Alass,
what could a Man do with a Purse of Gold in an Everlasting Dun-
geon? And shall we prize the sun less then it, which is the Light and
fountain of all our Pleasures? You will then abhor the preposterous
Method of those, who in an evil sence are Blinded with its Beams, 15
and to whom the presence of the Light is the Greatest Darkness.

For they who would repine at GOD without the Sun, are un-
thankfull, having it: and therfore only despise it, becaus it is
Created.

8

It raiseth Corn to supply you with food, it melteth Waters to Quench
your Thirst, It infuseth Sence into all your Members, It illuminates
the World to entertain you with Prospects, It surroundeth you with
the Beauty of Hills and Valleys, It moveth and laboreth Night and
5 Day for your Comfort and Service; It sprinkleth flowers upon
the Ground for your Pleasure, and in all these Things sheweth
you the Goodness and Wisdom of a GOD that can make one
Thing so Beautifull, Delightfull, and Serviceable having ordained
the same to Innumerable Ends. It concocteth Minerals, raiseth
10 Exhalations, begetteth Clouds, sendeth down the Dew and Rain
and Snow, that refresheth and repaireth all the Earth. And is far
more Glorious in its Diurnal Motion, then if there were two suns
to make on either side a Perpetual Day: the Swiftness wherby it
moves in 24 hours about so vast an Universe manifesteth the
15 Power and Care of a Creator, more then any station or Quiet could
do. And producing innumerable Effects it is more Glorious, then
if Millions of Agents diversly did do them.

9

Did the Sun stand still that you might hav a perpetual Day, you
would not know the sweetness of Repose: the Delightfull vicissi-
tudes of Night and Day, the Early Sweetness and Spring of the
Morning[,] the Perfume and Beauty in the cool of the Evening,
5 would all be swallowed up in Meridian Splendor: all which now
entertain you with Delights. The Antipodes would be empty,
perpetual Darkness and Horror there, and the Works of God on the
other side of the World in vain.

10

Were there two suns, that day might be alike in both Places, stand-
ing still, there would be nothing but Meridian Splendor under
them, and nothing but continual morning in other places, they
would absume and Dry up all the Moysture of the Earth, which
5 now is repaired as fast as it Decayeth, And perhaps when the Nature

of the Sun is Known, it is impossible there should be Two: At least
it is impossible they should be more Excellent then this one: that we
might Magnify the Diety and rest satisfied in Him, for making the
Best of all possible Works for our Enjoyment.

11

Had the Sun been made one infinit Flame, it had been worse then
it is · for there had been no Living; it had filled all Space, and
devoured all other Things. So that it is far better being finit, then if
it were infinit.

Even as the Sea within a finit Shore   5
Is far the Better 'caus it is no more.

Whence we may easily perceiv the Divine Wisdom hath atcheived
things more then infinit in Goodness and Beauty. As a sure Token
of their Perfect Excellency.

12

Entering thus far into the Nature of the Sun, we may see a little
Heaven in the Creatures. And yet we shall say less of the rest in
Particular: tho evry one in its Place be as Excellent as it: and this
without these cannot be sustained. Were all the Earth filthy Mires,
or Devouring Quicksands; firm Land would be an unspeakable 5
Treasure. Were it all Beaten Gold it would be of no value. It is a
Treasure therfor of far Greater valu to a noble Spirit, then if the
Globe of the Earth were all Gold. A Noble Spirit being only that
which can Survey it all, and Comprehend its Uses. The Air is
Better, being a living Miracle as it now is, then if it were Cramd 10
and fild with Crowns and Scepters. The Mountains are better then
Solid Diamonds, and those Things which Scarcity maketh Jewels
(when you enjoy these) are yours in their Places. Why should you
not render Thanks to God for them all? You are the Adam, or the
Eve that Enjoy them. Why should you not Exult and Triumph in 15
His Lov who hath done so Great Things for you? Why should you
not rejoyce and sing His Praises? Learn to Enjoy what you hav
first, and covet more if you can afterwards.

13

Could the seas serv you were you alone, more then now they do?
Why do you not render Thanks for them? They serv you better

11. 5-6. See C III, 21, 7-8.

then if you were in them: evry thing serving you best in its Proper
Place. Alone you were Lord over all: and bound to Admire His
5 Eternal Lov who raised you out of Nothing into this Glorious
World which He Created for you. To see infinit Goodness Wisdom
and Power, making the Heavens and the Earth the Seas, the Air
the Sun and Stars! what Wonder, what Joy, what Glory, what
Triumph, what Delight should this afford! It is more yours then
10 if you had been made alone.

14

The Sun is but a little Spark of His infinit Lov. The Sea is but one
Drop of His Goodness. But what flames of Lov ought that Spark
to Kindle in your Soul; what Seas of Affection ought to flow for that
Drop in your Bosom! The Heavens are the Canopy and the Earth is
5 the footstool of your Throne: who reign in Communion with GOD:
or at least are called so to do. How lively should his Divine Good-
ness appear unto you; how continualy should it rest upon you; how
deeply should it be impressed in you. Verily its Impressions ought
to be so deep, as to be always remaining: always felt, always Ad-
10 mired, always seen, and rejoyced in. You are never truly Great till
all the World is yours: and the Goodness of the Donor so much
your Joy, that you think upon it all day long. Which King David,
the Royal Man well understood, when He said; My Lips shall be
filled with thy Prais, and thy Honor all the Day. I will make Men-
15 tion of thy Loving Kindness in thy Holy Temple.

15

The world servs you, as in serving those Cattle which you feed
upon, so in serving those Men, that Build, and Plow, and Plant,
and Govern for you. It servs you in those that Pray and Adore and
Prais for you, that fill the World with Beauty and vertue; that are
5 made to lov· and Honor, to Pleas and Advance you with all the
Services that the Art of man can devise. So that you are alone in
the World, tho there are Millions in it beside. You are alone to
Enjoy and rejoyce in all, being the Adequat Object of His Eternal
Lov, and the End of all. Thus the world servs to promote and
10 Advance you.

16

These services are so Great, that when you enter into them, they are ample fields and Territories of Joy: tho on the outside, they seem so contemptible, that they promise Nothing. The Magnified Pleasures of this corrupted World, are like the Egyptian Temples in old time, that were Magnifica in frontispicio Ridicula in Pene- 5 trali: They hav a Royal Frontispiece, but are Ridiculous when you com in. These Hidden Pleasures: becaus they are Great Common and Simple, are not understood.

17

Besides these immediat Pleasures here beneath, there are many Sublime and Celestial Services which the World doth do. It is a Glorious Mirror wherin you may see the verity of all Religion: Enjoy the Remainders of Paradice and Talk with the Dietie. Apply yourself Vigorously to the Enjoyment of it. For in it you shall see the 5 face of God: and by Enjoying it, be wholy Converted to Him.

18

You shall be Glorified, you shall liv in Communion with Him, you shall ascend into the Throne of the Highest Heavens; you shall be Satisfied, you shall be made Greater then the Heavens, you shall be Like Him, when you enjoy the World as He doth; you shall converse with His Wisdom Goodness and Power abov all 5 Worlds, and therfore shall Know Him. To know whom is a Sublime thing: for it is Life Eternal.

19

They that Quarrel at the maner of GODs revealing Himself, are troubled, becaus He is Invisible. Yet is it Expedient that He should be so: for whatsoever is Visible is a Body: whatsoever is a Body excludeth other Things out of the place where it self is. If GOD therfore being infinit, were Visible, He would make it Impossible 5 for any thing to have a Being Besides. Bulk as such, in it self is Dead. Whatsoever is Visible is so in like maner. That which inspireth Bulk with Motion Life and Sence is Invisible; and in it self distinct from the Bulk which it inspireth. Were GOD therfore pure Bulk, He could neither move nor Will nor desire any thing, but being 10 invisible, He leaveth Room for, and Effecteth all Things. He filleth

nothing with a Bodily presence but includeth all. He is Pure Life, Knowledg, and Desire, from which all things flow: Pure Wisdom Goodnes and Lov to which all Things return.

20

Hence we may know the Reason why GOD appeareth not in a visible maner, is, becaus indeed He is invisible. They who are angry with the Diety for not shewing Himself to their Bodily Eys are not displeased with that maner of Revelation, but that He is such
5 a God as He is. By pretending to be visible He would but Delude the World, which as Plato observeth [is contrary to the nature of the Dietie]. But tho He is invisible, yet say they, He may assume a Body, and make Himself visible therin. We ask therfore what kind of Body they desire · for if He should take upon Him self a visible
10 Body, that Body must represent som of His Perfections. What Perfections then would they hav that Body to Express? If His Infinity, that Body then must be infinit. Upon which the same Absurdity would follow as before · for being infinit it would exclude all Being beside out of Place. If His Eternity; that cannot be a Body be
15 represented. Neither is any sence able to judge of Infinity or Eternity · for if He should represent Himself by an infinit Wall; sight being too short might apprehend it self Defectiv, and be assured that it could not apprehend the Ends of that Wall; but whether it had Ends, which it self was not able to discern, it
20 could not be satisfied. Would you therfore hav it to Express some other of His Perfections; as Particularly that of His Beauty? Beauty being a thing consisting of Variety, that Body could not be one simple Being, but must be sweetly temperd of a Manifold and delightfull Mixture of figures and Colors: be som such Thing
25 as Ezekiel saw in his Vision · for uniform Beauty the Sun is the most Delightfull: yet is not the Sun the most Delightfull Thing that is Possible. A Body more Beautifull then it may be made. Suppose therfore the most Beautifull that is Possible were created. What would follow? Being a silent and Quiet Object of the Ey,
30 it would be no more noted, then if it had not a Being. The most Beautifull Object, being always present, grows common and despised. Even as a Picture is at first admired, but at length no more

5-7. *By . . . Dietie.* These words were deleted from line 2, and in writing them again lower down, T omitted the words between the square brackets.

regarded then the bare Wall. Since therfore the most Beautifull thing that is Possible, being always continued, would grow into contempt; how do we know, but the World is that Body, which the 35 Diety hath assumed to manifest His Beauty, and by which He maketh Himself as visible, as it is possible He should?

21

When Amasis the King of Egypt sent to the Wise Men of Greece, to Know, Quid Pulcherrimum? upon due and Mature Consideration, they answered, The WORLD. The World certainly being so Beautiful that nothing visible is capable of more. Were we to see it only once, that first Appearance would amaze us. But being daily seen, 5 we observ it not. Ancient Philosophers hav thought GOD to be the *Soul of the World*. Since therfore this visible World is the Body of GOD, not his Natural Body, but which He hath assumed; let us see how Glorious His Wisdom is, in Manifesting Himself therby. It hath not only represented His infinity and Eternity which we 10 thought impossible to be represented by a Body, but His Beauty also, His Wisdom, Goodness, Power, Life and Glory, His Righteousness, Lov, and Blessedness: all which as out of a plentifull Treasurie, may be taken and collected out of this World.

First His Infinity; for the Dimensions of the World are unsearch- 15 able. An infinit Wall is a poor thing to Expresse his Infinity · a Narrow Endless Length is nothing: might be, and if it were, were unprofitable · but the World is round, and endlessly unsearchable every Way. What Astronomer, what Mathematician, what Philosopher did ever comprehend the Measures of the World? The 20 very Earth alone being round and Globous, is illimited. It hath neither Walls nor Precipices, nor Bounds, nor Borders. A man may lose himself in the midst of Nations and Kingdoms. And yet it is but a Centre compared to the Univers. The Distance of the Sun, the Altitude of the Stars, the Wideness of the Heavens on evry 25 side passeth the Reach of Sight, and Search of the Understanding. And whether it be infinit or no, we cannot tell. The Eternity of GOD is so apparent in it, that the Wisest of Philosophers[1] thought the World Eternal. We com into it and leav it as if it had neither beginning nor Ending. Concerning its Beauty I need say 30

---

[1] 'Aristotle by name', deleted.

Q

nothing. No man can turn unto it, but must be ravished with its Appearance · only thus much, Since these things are so Beautifull, how much more Beautifull is the Author of them? Which was the Note and Observation of the Wise Man in the Book
35 of   But the Beauty of GOD is Invisible it is all Wisdom, Goodness, Life and Lov, Power, Glory, Blessedness &c. How therfore shall these be Expressed in a Material World? His Wisdom is expressed in manifesting His Infinity in such a commodious maner. He hath made a Penetrable Body in which we may stand,
40 to wit the Air, and see the Heavens and the Regions of the Earth, at Wonderfull Distances. His Goodness is manifest in making that Beauty so Delightfull, and its Varieties so Profitable. The Air to breath in, the Sea for Moisture, the Earth for fertility, the Heavens for Influences, the Sun for Productions, the Stars and
45 Trees wherwith it is Adorned for innumerable Uses. Again His Goodness is seen, in the End to which He guideth all this Profitableness, in making it serviceable to supply our Wants and Delight our Sences: to Enflame us with His Lov, and make us Amiable before Him, and Delighters in His Blessedness: GOD
50 having not only shewed us His Simple Infinity in an Endless Wall, but in such an Illustrious Maner, by an infinit variety, that He hath drowned our Understanding in a Multitude of Wonders: Transported us with Delights, and Enriched us with innumerable Diversities of Joys and Pleasures. The very Greatness of our felicity
55 convinceth us, that there is a GOD.

22

His Power is evident by Upholding it all. But how shall His Life appear in that which is Dead. Life is the Root of Activity and Motion. Did I see a Man sitting in a Chair, as long as he was quiet, I could not tell but His Body was inanimat: but if He stirred, if He
5 moved his Lips, or stretched forth his Arms, if he breathd or twinkled with his Eys: I could easily tell He had a Soul within Him. Motion being a far greater Evidence of Life, then all Lineaments whatsoever. Colors and features may be in a dead picture, but Motion is always attended with life. What shall I think therfore
10 when the Winds Blow, the Seas roar, the Waters flow, the Vapours ascend, the Clouds flie, the Drops of rain fall, the Stars march forth

35. The blank is in MS. The reference is to Wisdom 13$^{1-5}$, as Dobell noted.

in Armies, the Sun runneth Swiftly round about the World? Can
all these things move so without a Life, or Spring of Motion? But
the Wheels in Watches mov, and so doth the Hand that pointeth out
the figures. This being a Motion of Dead things. Therfore hath 15
GOD created Living ones: that by Lively Motions, and Sensible
Desires, we might be Sensible of a Diety. They Breath, they see,
they feel, they Grow, they flourish, they know, they lov. O what a
World of Evidences. We are lost in Abysses, we now are absorpt in
Wonders, and Swallowed up of Demonstrations. Beasts Fowls 20
and Fishes teaching and evidencing the Glory of their Creator.
But these by an Endless Generation might succeed each other
from Everlasting. Let us therfore survey their Order, and see by
that whether we cannot Discern their Governer. The Sun and Moon
and Stars shine, and by shining minister influences to Herbs and 25
flowers · these Grow and feed the Cattle: the seas also and springs
minister unto them, as they do unto fowls and fishes. All which are
subservient unto Man, a more Noble creature, endued with under-
standing to Admire His Creator Who being King and Lord of this
World, is able to Prize all in a Reflexiv maner, and render Praises 30
for all with Joy, living Blessedly in the fruition of them. None can
Question the Being of a Dietie, but one that is ignorant of Mans
Excellencies, and the Glory of his Dominion over all the Creatures.

23

Abov all, Man Discovereth the Glory of GOD: who being Him-
self Immortal, is the Divinest Creature. He hath a Dominion over
all the rest and GOD over Him. By Him, the Fountain of all these
Things is the End of them: for He can return to their Author de-
served Praises. Sences cannot resemble that which they cannot 5
apprehend; nor express that which they cannot resemble, but in
a shady maner. But Man is made in the Image of GOD, and ther-
fore is a Mirror and Representativ of Him. And therfore in Himself
He may see GOD, which is His Glory and Felicitie. His Thoughts
and Desires can run out to Everlasting. His Lov can extend to all 10
Objects, His Understanding is an endless Light, and can infinitly
be present in all Places, and see and Examine all Beings, survey
the reasons, surmount the Greatness, exceed the Strength, con-
templat the Beauty, Enjoy the Benefit, and reign over all it sees
and Enjoys like the Eternal GODhead. Here is an Invisible Power, 15

an Indivisible Omnipresence, a Spiritual Supremacy; an Inward,
Hidden, unknown Being Greater than all · a Sublime and Sover-
aign Creature meet to live in Communion with GOD in the fruition
of them.

24

That you are a Man should fill you with Joys, and make you to
overflow with Praises. The Priviledge of your Nature being infinitly
infinit. And that the World servs you in this fathomless maner,
Exhibiting the Dietie, and ministering to your Blessedness, ought
5 daily to Transport you with a Blessed Vision, into Ravishments
and Extasies. What Knowledg could you have had of God by an
unprofitable Wall tho endless and infinit? For tho as Things now
are, nothing can be, but it exhibits a Dietie; as the Apostle saith,
By Things that are seen the Invisible things of GOD are mani-
10 fested, even His power and Godhead · becaus evry thing is a
Demonstration of His Goodness and Power; by its Existence and
the End to which it is guided: yet an Endles Wall could never
manifest His Being, were it present with you alone: for it would
deny that Infinity by its unprofitableness, which it sheweth by its
15 Endlessness. The true exemplar of GODs infinity is that of your
Understanding, which is a lively Patern and Idea of it. It excludeth
Nothing, and containeth all Things. Being a Power that Permitteth
all Objects to be, and is able to Enjoy them. Here is a Profitable
Endlessness of infinit valu, becaus without it infinit Joys and Bless-
20 ings would be lost, which by it are Enjoyed. How Great doth God
appear, in Wisely preparing such an Understanding to Enjoy his
Creatures; such an Endles Invisible and Mysterious Receiver?
And how Blessed and Divine are you, to whom GOD hath not only
simply appeared, but whom He hath exalted as an Immortal King
25 among all His Creatures?

25

You are able to see His Righteousness and Blessedness and Glory,
which are invisible. Yea, which is infinitly more, to resemble and
attain them, to Express them in your self, Enjoying them and the
Similitud of them. No Beast can see what Righteousness is. Nor is
5 any Bruit capable of Imitating it. You are: being admitted into the

fellowship and Order of Angels. Which have neither Eys nor Ears, and yet see and understand things, which are infinitly Higher then the Sphere of Sences. You are able to Discern, that in all these Things He is Lov to you; and that Lov is a fountain of infinit Benefits. That being Lov to you He hath don the Best of all Pos- 10 sible Things, and made you the End of all Things · for Lov is a fountain of infinit Benefits, and doth all that is Possible for its Beloved Object. It endlessly desireth to Delight it self, and its Delight is to Magnify its Beloved. You are able to see the Righteous- ness of Lov in this. For in doing the Best of all Possible Things 15 it is Right Wise to it self and to all other Beings. Right wise to it self in Glorifying it self in the Best of Maners, and to all other Things in making them most Excellent. Right Wise to it self in preparing for it self the Best of Treasures, and to its Object in like maner, in making its Beloved the most Blessed. Right Wise unto it 20 self, in satisfying it self in its infinit Desire of becoming Delightfull to its Object, in preparing for it self infinit Pleasures, and in making for it self the most Delightfull Object that can Possibly be made. Right Wise unto you, in making you that Object: and providing all the Treasures of it self for you, and making it self 25 infinitly Joyous and Delightfull to you. Nothing is so Righteous, or Right-wise as Lov. For by Making it self Glorious it becometh infinit: and by loving its Object infinitly it enableth it self to Delight infinitly in its Objects Happiness: and Wisely prepareth infinit Treasures, Right wisely therby at once enriching it self and 30 its Object. So that you are áble evidently to Discern that GOD is Lov, and therin to contemplat all His Perfections.

26

You are able therin to see the infinit Glory of your High Estate. For if GOD is Lov, and Lov be so Restles a Principle in Exalting its Object: and so Secure that it always promoteth and Glorifieth and Exalteth it self therby, where will there be any Bounds in your Exaltation? How Dreadfull, how Amiable how Blessed, how Great, 5 how unsearchable, how incomprehensible must you be in your true real inward Happiness? The Object of Lov is infinitly Exalted. Lov is infinitly Delightfull to its Object, GOD by all His Works mani- festeth Himself to be Lov, and you being the End of them, are evidently its Object. Go where you will, here alone shall you find 10

your Happiness. Contemplat therfore the Works of GOD, for they serv you not only in manifesting Him, but in making you to know yourself and your Blessedness.

27

As Lov is Righteous in Glorifying it self and making its Object Blessed: so is it in all its Dealings and Dispensations towards it. Having made it Amiable it cannot but lov it. Which it is Righteous in doing, for to lov what is Lovly is a Righteous Thing. To make
5 it infinitly Amiable is a Righteous Thing to infinit Lov: and to lov it infinitly being infinitly Amiable. For therby infinit Lov doth right to itself and its Measure: yea to it self and its Object. To tender what is Amiable is a Righteous Thing: to Hurt it is Evil. Lov therfore is infinitly Righteous in being infinitly tender of its
10 Objects Welfare: and in hating infinitly the Sin of Hurting it. It is Righteous in commanding others to promote it, and in punishing those that injure or offend it. And thus have you a Gate, in the Prospect even of this World, wherby you may see into GODs Kingdom. For by His Works you see that God is Lov, and by His Lov
15 see the Nature of all Righteousness opened and unfolded: with the Ground and foundations of Rewards and Punishments.

28

But GOD being infinit, is infinitly Righteous. His Lov therfore is Righteous to it self and all its Works as well as its Object. To it self in requiring that be infinitly Esteemed, of which it is infinitly Desirous. The Contemners of it therfore it infinitly Punisheth. To
5 its Works not only in making them the Best that may be, but in requiring an Exact and due esteem, from the Enjoyers of them. Is not Lov Jealous of the Honor of its Gifts? Doth not a Contempt of its Presents, redound upon it self? The World therfore serveth you abundantly in teaching you your Duty. They daily cry in a
10 Living maner, with a silent, and yet most loud voice · We are all His Gifts: We are Tokens and Presents of His Lov. You must therfore Esteem us according to the Beauty and Worth that is in us, and the Lov from whence we came. Which to do, is certainly the most Blessed Thing in all Worlds, as not to do it is most Wicked
15 and most Miserable.

29

Lov further manifests it self in joyning Righteousness and Blessed-
ness together. For wherin can Lov appear more then in making
our Duty most Blessed. Which here is don by Making Obedience
the fruition of ones Blessedness. GOD cannot therfore but be
infinitly provoked, when we break His Laws. Not only becaus 5
Lov is Jealous and Cruel as the Grave, but becaus also our Duty
being so Amiable, which it imposeth on us with infinit Obligations,
they are all Despised. His Lov it self, our most Beautifull Duty and
all its Obligations. So that His Wrath must be very Heavy, and his
Indignation infinit.   10

30

Yet Lov can forbear, and Lov can forgiv. Tho it can never be
reconciled to an unlovly Object. And hence it is, that tho you hav
so little considered the Works of God, and prized his Lov, yet you
are permitted to live: and live at ease, and enjoy your Pleasure. But
Lov can never be reconciled to an Unlovely Object, and you are 5
infinitly unlovly by Despising GOD, and His Lov so long. Yea one
Act only of Despite done to the smallest Creature made you infinitly
deformed. What shall becom of you therfore since GOD cannot be
reconciled to an Ugly Object? Verily you are in Danger of Perishing
Eternaly. He cannot indeed be reconciled to an ugly Object as it is 10
Ugly· but as it is capable of being otherwise He may. He can never
therfore be reconciled to your sin, becaus sin it self is uncapable of
being Altered: but He may be reconciled to your Person, becaus
that may be restored: and which is an infinit Wonder, to Greater
Beauty and Splendor then before.   15

31

By how much the greater His Lov was, by so much the Greater
may his Sorrow be at the Loss of His Object: and by so much the
Greater His Desire also of its Restauration. His Lov therfore being
infinit, may do infinit Things for an Object infinitly valued. Being
infinit in Wisdom it is able also to Devise a Way Inscrutable to us, 5
wherby to Sever the Sin from the Sinner: and to satisfy its Right-
eousness in Punishing the Transgression, yet satisfy it self in saving
the Transgressor: And to purge away the Dross and incorporated
filth and Leprosy of sin: restoring the Soul to its Primitiv Beauty

10 Health and Glory. But then it doth this at an infinit Expense
wherin also it is more Delighted. And especialy Magnified, for it
giveth another equaly Dear unto it self to suffer in its steed. And
thus we com again by the Works of God to our Lord JESUS
CHRIST.

32

Whoever suffereth innocently and justly in anothers steed, must
becom a Suerty by His voluntary Act. And this an Angel or a
Cherubim might hav done. He might also perhaps hav suffered
an infinit Punishment in the Removal of that Lov of GOD which
5 he infinitly prized: and perhaps also He might hav payed an
Obedience which He owed not. For the Angels are bound to lov
God with all their Might, and Men as themselvs, while they are
innocent: and to liv by loving them in their Blessedness and Glory;
yet they are not bound by vertu of this Law to die for men being
10 Wicked and Deformed, and therfore in undertaking this might hav
undertaken more then was their Duty: and perhaps Loving God
infinitly, (had they seen his Lov to man) they would. Yea perhaps
also they might hav sufferd in our Nature; and been able to hav
sustained infinit Wrath; which are all the Conditions usualy
15 reckoned up and numberd by Divines, as requisit in a Mediator
and Redeemer of others · for they might hav been Hypostaticaly
united to our Nature and tho they were Creatures: yet almighty
Power can sustain a Creature under as Great a Punishment as
Almighty Power can inflict. Almighty Power upholding it being
20 like the nether Milstone, and almighty Power Punishing like the
Upper Milstone, between which two it is infinitly tormented. We
must therfore Search Higher: into the Causes of our Saviors Pre-
lation above them.

33

One Great Caus why no Angel was admitted to this office, was
becaus it was an Honor infinitly too Great and Sublime for them.
GOD accounting none but His own Son worthy of that Dignity.
Wherfore it is written, No man taketh this Honor to Himself, but
5 He that is called of God, as was Aaron. Neither did Jesus (tho He
were the Son of GOD) make Himself an High Priest, but He that
said unto Him Thou art a Priest for ever after the order of Melchi-

sedec. Nor yet was it forced or imposed upon Him, but He volun-
tarily undertook it · for which caus God hath highly exalted him
and given Him a Name which is abov every Name in Heaven and
Earth, becaus being in the Form of God, he thought it not Robbery
to be Equal with God, yet took upon him the form of a Servant,
and being found in the fashion of a Man would humble Himself to
the Death of the Cross for our sakes.

Where we learn several strange and Admirable Things · first
How High an Honor it is to suffer for God in this World · secondly
In what an infinit Dignity Man is exalted for whom God counted
none Worthy to suffer but His own son. And Thirdly the Equity of
Gods Proceeding in Chastising another for our sins: (against the
Socinians who being Blind in this Mysterie, are the Enemies of our
Saviors Diety in this World.) For had He imposed this task upon one
that was unwilling it had been Injustice. Had he imposed it upon one
that was unable to perform it it had been folly: had he imposed it
upon any one to his Harm, Cruelty: But laying it upon one that was
Willing and Able, to his Highest Benefit, it was Righteousnes Wis-
dom and Glory. All Mercy Goodnes and Lov on evry side.

34

How vile are they and Blind and Ignorant, that will not see evry
one to be the Heir of the World, for whose sake all this was done!
He that spared not his own Son but gav Him up for us all, how shall
He not with Him also freely giv us all Things? Is not He an Object
of infinit Lov for whom our savior Died? Shall not all Things in
Heaven and Earth serv Him in Splendor and Glory, for whom the
Son of God came down, to Minister in Agonies and Sufferings?
O here Contemplat the Glory of Man, and his High Exaltation in
the Throne of GOD. Here consider how you are Beloved, and be
Transported with Excess of Joy at this Wonderfull Mystery · leave
the Trash and vanities of the World, to live here in communion with
the Blessed Trinity. Imitate S. Paul, who counted all Things but
Dross and Dung, for the Excellency of the Knowledg of GOD in
Christ. And thus the Works of GOD serv you in teaching you the
Knowledg of our Lord and Savior.

35

Another reason for which our Redemption was denied to Angels
and reserved only to be wrought by our Savior, is the Dignity of

Man· *for the Redemption of their Soul is Precious, and ceaseth for ever.*
None of them can by any Means redeem Him, nor giv to GOD
5 a ransom for him. Having Sinned he must be Clothed in the
Righteousness of GOD or perish for ever. All the Angels and
Cherubims in Heaven, tho their Righteousness should be imputed
to Him could not justify Him. No Created Righteousness is able
to Cover Him. The Exceeding Glory of His Primitiv Estate being
10 so great, that it made His Sin infinitly infinit.

36

Yet further another reason why this Office was delegated to none
of them, was this: He that Died for us must by His own Merits
save us. [It was not Convenient that the Righteousness of the Judg
Himself should be accepted for ours: but the Righteousness of
5 another, who on our Behalf should appear before our Judge · for
which caus it was necessary that another, and not the Judge, should
be Righteous in our steed. And that in suffering, as well as doing.
Now no Angel could be Righteous in suffering· becaus tho by
Almighty Power sustaining he might be upheld to suffer infinit
10 Punishments, yet by His own Strength He could not suffer infinit
Punishments, at least not so, as to be Virtuous and Meritorious
in suffering them, for us. For to suffer Virtuously and Meritoriously
is so to suffer as to lov the Inflicter in the Midst of Sufferings. Which
no Angel under Infinit Torments by His own Strength was able
15 to do, being Hated of GOD.] Being therfore our Savior was to
Merit for us, by His own Actions, it was necessary that He should
be such an one, who, by His own Power could sustain infinit
Punishments, and offer them up to GOD on our behalf with infinit
Lov as a Voluntary Obedience. Which only Christ was able to do
20 out of the Treasurie of His own Fulness. For the Divine Essence
in Him could overcom infinit Punishments, and infinitly lov the
inflicter of them: without any Repining, Despondency, or Hatred,
returned for the same. Where it is Curious to observ, how fully our
Savior satisfied for us. We Hated GOD when He loved us: our
25 Savior not only Loved GOD, while GOD loved Him; but loved
Him also with infinit Lov, even while He expressed Hatred against
Him.

36. 3-15. Deleted in MS.

37

Finaly another reason, was the Dignity of our Saviors Person. Who being infinitly more Excellent then all Angels, was in His Condescentions infinitly more Acceptable. Which Excellency both of His Person and Condescention is not a little Magnified by His Eternity. By His Sufferings He brought in Eternal Righteousnes. 5 That He should stoop down for our sakes was infinitly Meritorious. And since the Will before GOD is the Highest Deed: Accepting this from all Eternity, it is as if from all Eternity He had suffered for us. His Lov to GOD and Man, in this Act, was infinit and Eternal. And therfore is it said, That He through the Eternal Spirit, 10 offered up Himself a Sacrifice to GOD for us. His Eternal Spirit from Everlasting offered up it self, when He said, Lo, I com: in the volum of the Book is it written of me: to do thy will O GOD: And He offered up Himself through the Eternal Spirit in Time when He was slain upon the Cross. Now no Creature can offer up it self 15 Eternaly, becaus it was not from Everlasting. Nor can any thing Work Eternal Righteousness for us, but GOD alone.

38

How then should we be saved? Since Eternal Righteousnes must be paid for our Temporal Iniquity, Since one must suffer by his own strength on our Behalf, and out of his own Fulness defray our Debt of infinit charity, and that in the midst of sufferings; which no Angel nor Seraphim is able: since He must Pay an Obedience 5 which He did not owe: both in Loving men when themselvs were Hatefull, and in Loving God when He was Hated of Him: since none but GOD could do this, and it was inconvenient† for GOD to do it: whither shall we flie for Refuge? Verily we are in a great Strait: but in the midst of these Exigences Lov prepareth for it self an 10 Offering. One Mighty to Save concerning whom it is Written, *This Day hav I begotten Thee.*

39

GOD by Loving Begot His Son. For GOD is Lov. And by loving He begot His Lov. He is of Him self, and by Loving He is what He is: *Infinit Lov.* GOD is not a Mixt and Compounded Being, so

No. 39 originally began as follows: 'It is a very Great Mystery that God by Loving Begot Himself. Yet very plain . . .'.

that His Lov is one thing and Himself another: but the most Pure
5 and Simple of all Beings, All Act, and Pure Lov in the Abstract.
Being Lov therfore it self, by Loving He begot Lov. Had He not
loved He had not been what He now is, The GOD of Lov. The
most Righteous of all Beings, in being infinitly Righteous to Him
self, and all. But by Loving He is infinitly Righteous to Himself,
10 and all. For He is of Himself, Infinitly Blessed and Most Glorious;
And all His Creatures are of Him, in whom they are infinitly
Delighted and Blessed and Glorious.

40

In all Lov there is a Lov begetting, a Lov begotten, and a Lov
Proceeding. Which tho they are one in Essence, subsist Neverthe-
less in Three Several Maners. For Lov is Benevolent Affection to
another. Which is of it self, and by it self relateth to its Object. It
5 floweth from it self, and resteth in its Object. Lov proceedeth of
Necessity from it self · for unless it be of it self it is not Lov. Con-
straint is Destructiv and Opposit to its Nature. The Lov from
which it floweth, is the Fountain of Love · the Lov which streameth
from it is the communication of Lov, or Lov communicated · and
10 the Lov which resteth in the Object is the Lov which Streameth
to it. So that in all Lov the Trinity is Clear. By secret Passages
without Stirring it proceedeth to its Object, and is as Powerfully
present as if it did not Proceed at all. The Lov that lieth in the
Bosom of the Lover, being the Lov that is perceived in the Spirit
15 of the Beloved: that is, the same in Substance, tho in the Maner of
Substance, or Subsistence, different. Lov in the Bosom is the Parent
of Lov, Lov in the Stream is the Effect of Lov, Lov seen, or Dwell-
ing in the Object proceedeth from both. Yet are all three one and
the self same Lov: tho three loves.

41

Lov in the Fountain, and Lov in the Stream are both the same.
And therfore are they both Equal in Time and Glory. For Lov
communicateth it self: And therfore Lov in the fountain is the very
Lov communicated to its Object. Lov in the fountain is Lov in the
5 Stream, and Lov in the Stream Equaly Glorious with lov in the
Fountain. Tho it Streameth to its Object it abideth in the Lover,
and is the Lov of the Lover.

42

Where Lov is the Lover, Lov streaming from the Lover, is the Lover; the Lover streaming from Himself: and Existing in another Person.

43

This Person is the Son of GOD: Who as He is the Wisdom of the Father, so is He the Lov of the Father. For the Lov of the Father is the Wisdom of the Father. And this Person did God by loving us beget, that He might be the Means of all our Glory.

44

This Person differs in Nothing from the Father but only in this that He is Begotten of Him. He is Eternal with the Father, as Glorious and as Intelligent. He is of the same Mind in evry Thing in all Worlds, Loveth the same Objects in as infinit a Measure. Is the Means by which the Father Loveth, Acteth, Createth Redeemeth 5 Governeth and Perfecteth all Things. And the Means also by which we see and Lov the Father: our Strength and our Eternity. He is the Mediator between GOD and His Creatures. God therfore being willing to redeem us by His own Blood (Act 20.) by Him redeemed us, and in His Person died for us.   10

45

How Wonderfull is it, that GOD by being Lov should prepare a Redeemer to Die for us? But how much more Wonderfull, that by this means Himself should be: and be GOD by being LOV! By this means also He refineth our Nature, and enableth us to Purge out the Poyson and the filthy Plague of Sin· for Lov is so Amiable and 5 Desirable to the Soul that it cannot be resisted. Lov is the Spirit of GOD. In Himself it is the Father, or els the Son, For the Father is in the Son, and the Son is in the father: In us it is the Holy Ghost. The Lov of GOD being seen, being GOD in us. Purifying, Illuminating, Strengthening and Comforting the Soul of the Seer. For 10 GOD by shewing communicateth Himself to Men and Angels. And when He Dwelleth in the Soul, Dwelleth in the Sight. And when He Dwelleth in the Sight Atchieving all that lov can do for such a Soul. And thus the World serveth you as it is a Mirror wherin

15 you Contemplat the Blessed Trinity · for it Plainly sheweth that
GOD is Lov, and in His being Lov you see the Unity of the Blessed
Trinity, and a Glorious Trinity in the Blessed Unitie.

46

In all Lov there is some Producer, som Means, and som End:
all these being Internal in the Thing it self. Lov Loving is the
Producer, and that is the father; Lov produced is the Means, and
that is the Son: for Lov is the Means by which a Lover loveth.
5 The End of these Means is Lov: for it is Lov, by loving: and that
is the Holy Ghost. The End and the Producer being both the same,
by the Means attained · for by Loving Lov attaineth it self and
Being. The Producer is attained by Loving, and is the End of
Himself. That Lov is the End of it self, and that GOD loveth that
10 He might be lov, is as evident to him that considers spiritual Things,
as the Sun. Becaus it is impossible there should be a Higher End,
or a Better proposed. What can be more Desirable then the most
Delightfull Operation; what more Eligible, then the most Glorious
Being; what further can be proposed then the most Blessed and
15 Perfect Life. Since GOD therfore chuseth the most Perfect Life,
what can be more Perfect, then that Life and that Being which is
at once the fountain, and the End of all Things? There being in it
the Perpetual Joy of Giving and Receiving infinit Treasures. To
be the Fountain of Joys and Blessings is Delightfull. And by being
20 Lov GOD is the fountain of all Worlds. To receiv all and to be the
End of all is Equaly Delightfull, and by Being Lov GOD receiveth,
and is the End of all. For all the Benefits that are don unto all, by
Loving all, Himself receiveth. What Good could heaven and Earth
do Him, were it not for His Lov to the children of Men? By being
25 what He is, which is Lov unto all, He Enjoyeth all.

47

What Life can be more Pleasant, then that which is Delighted in
it self, and in all Objects; in which also all Objects infinitly Delight?
What Life can be more Pleasant, then that which is Blessed in all
and Glorious before all? Now this Life is the Life of Lov. For this
5 End therfore did He desire to Lov, that He might be LOV. Infinitly
Delightfull to all Objects, infinitly Delighted in all, and infinitly
Pleased in Himself, for being infinitly Delightfull to all, and

Delighted in all. All this He attaineth by Lov. For Lov is the Most Delightfull of all Employments: all the Objects of Lov are Delightfull to it, and Lov is Delightfull to all its Objects. Well then may 10 Lov be the End of Loving, which is so Compleat. It being a Thing so Delightfull, that GOD infinitly rejoyceth in Him self for being Lov. And thus you see how GOD is the End of Himself. *He doth what He doth, that He may be what He is*: Wise and Glorious and Bountifull and Blessed in being Perfect Lov.   15

48

Lov is so Divine and Perfect a Thing, that it is Worthy to be the very End and Being of the Dietie. It is His Goodness, and it is His Glory. We therfore so Vastly Delight in Lov, becaus all these Excellencies and all other, Whatsoever lie within it. By Loving a Soul does Propagat and beget it self. By Loving it does Dilate and 5 Magnify it self. By Loving it does Enlarge and Delight it self. By Loving also it Delighteth others, as by Loving it doth Honor and Enrich it self. But abov all by Loving it does attain it self. Lov also being the End of Souls, Which are never Perfect, till they are in Act, what they are in Power. They were made to lov and are Dark and 10 Vain and Comfortless till they do it. Till they lov they are Idle, or misemployed. Till they lov they are Desolat; without their Objects: and Narrow and Little and Dishonorable: but when they Shine by Lov upon all Objects, they are accompanied with them and Enlightened by them. Till we becom therfore all Act as GOD is, we can 15 never rest, nor ever be Satisfied.

49

Lov is so Noble, that it Enjoyeth others Enjoyments. Delighteth in giving all unto its Object, and in seeing all Given to its Object. So that Whosoever loveth all Mankind, He Enjoyeth all the Goodness of GOD to the whole WORLD: and Endeavoreth the Benefit of Kingdoms and Ages. With all Whom He is present by Lov, which is 5 the best maner of Presence that is Possible.

50

GOD is present by Lov alone. By Lov alone He is Great and Glorious. By Lov alone He liveth and feeleth in other Persons. By Lov alone He enjoyeth all the Creatures, by Lov alone He is

Pleasing to Him self. By Lov alone He is Rich and Blessed. O why
5 dost not Thou by Lov alone seek to Atchiev all these! By Lov alone
attain another Self. By Lov alone live in others. By Lov attain thy
Glory. The Soul is shriveld up and Buried in a Grave that does not
Lov. But that which does love Wisely and Truly is the Joy and End
of all the World, the King of Heaven and the Friend of GOD, the
10 shining Light and Temple of Eternity: The Brother of Christ Jesus,
and One Spirit with the Holy Ghost.

51

Lov is far more Glorious Being then flesh and Bones. If thou wilt
it is Endless and infinitly more Sweet then thy Body can be to Thee
and others. Thy Body is confined, and is a Dull Lump of Heavy
Clay, by which thou art retarded, rather then doest move: It was
5 given thee to be a Lantern only to the Candle of Lov that shineth
in thy soul. By it Thou dost see and feel and eat and drink: but the
End of all is, that Thou mightst be as GOD is: a Joy and Blessing
by being Lov. Thy Lov is illimited. Thy Lov can Extend to all
Objects. Thy Lov can see GOD and Accompany His Lov through-
10 out all Eternity. Thy Lov is infinitly Profitable to thy self and others·
to thy self for therby mayst thou receiv infinit Good things: to
others, for therby thou art prone to do infinit Good to all. Thy
Body can receiv but few pleasures. Thy lov can feed upon all: Take
into it self all Worlds, and all Eternities above all Worlds and all the
15 Joys of God before and after. Thy flesh and Bones can do but little
Good: nor that little unles as by Lov it is inspired and directed.
A Poor Carcase thy Body is; But Lov is Delightfull and Profitable
to thousands. O liv therfore by the more Noble Part. Be like Him
who Baptizeth with fire· feel thy Spirit, Awaken thy Soul, be an
20 Enlarged Seraphim· an infinit GOOD, or like unto Him.

52

The true WAY we may go unto His Throne, and can never Exceed,
nor be too High. All Hyperbolies are but little Pigmies, and Diminu-
tiv Expressions, in Comparison of the Truth. All that Adam could
propose to Himself or hope for was laid up in Store for Him, in
5 a Better Way then.he could Ask or think: but in seeking for it
a fals way, He lost all: what He had in Hope, and what He had in

20. *GOOD*, corr. from 'God'.

Fruition. To be as GODs, we are Prompted to Desire by the
Instinct of Nature. And that we shall be by Loving all as He doth.
But by loving Him? What, O What shall we be? By loving Him
according to the greatness of His Lov unto us, according to His 10
Amiableness, as we ought, and according to the Obligations that lie
upon us; we shall be no Man can devise what. We shall lov Him
infinitly more then our selvs, and therfore liv infinitly more in Him
then in our selvs: and be infinitly more Delighted with His Eternal
Blessedness then our own. We shall infinitly more delight him 15
then our selvs. All Worlds all Angels all Men All Kingdoms
all Creatures will be more ours in Him then in our selvs: so will
His Essence and Eternall GODHEAD. Oh Lov what hast Thou
don!

53

And He will so lov us, when all this Beauty of Lov is within us,
that tho we by our Lov to Him seem more Blessed in His Blessed-
ness then He, He is infinitly more Blessed then we even in our
Blessedness. We being so united to each other, that Nothing can
Divide us for evermore.   5

54

Lov is infinitly Delightfull to its Object, and the more Violent the
more glorious. It is infinitly High, Nothing can hurt it. And infinitly
Great in all Extremes: of Beauty and Excellency. Excess is its true
Moderation: Activity its Rest: and burning Fervency its only Re-
freshment. Nothing is more Glorious yet nothing more Humble: 5
Nothing more Precious, yet nothing more Cheap: Nothing more
familiar, yet nothing so inaccessible: Nothing more Nice, yet Noth-
ing more Laborious: Nothing more Liberal, yet Nothing more
Covetous: It doth all things for its Objects sake, yet it is the most self
Ended thing in the Whole World: for of all things in Nature it can 10
least endure to be Displeased. Since therfore it containeth so many
Miracles It may well contain this one more, that it maketh evry one
Greatest, and among Lovers evry one is Supreme and Soveraign.

55

GOD by Lov wholy Ministereth to others, and yet Wholy ministere-
eth to Himself. Lov having this Wonder in it also, that among in-
numerable Millions, it maketh evry one the sole and single End of

R

all Things: It attaineth all Unattainables: and Atchieveth Im-
5 possibles · that is seeming Impossibles to our Inexperience, and
Real Impossibles to any other Means or Endeavors · for indeed
it maketh evry one more then the End of all Things: and infinitly
more then the Sole Supreme and Soveraign of all · for it maketh Him
so first in Himself: and then in all. For while All Things in Heaven
10 and Earth fall out after my Desire, I am the End and Soveraign of
all: which conspiring always to Crown my Friends with Glory and
Happiness: And Pleasing all in the same maner whom I lov as my
self: I am in evry one of them the End of all things again: being as
much concerned in their Happiness as my own.

56

By Loving a Soul does Propagat and beget it self · becaus before it
loved it lived only in it self: after it loved, and while it loveth it
liveth in its Object. Nay it did not so much as live in it self, before
it loved · for as the sun would be unseen, did it not Scatter, and
5 spread abroad its Beams; by which alone it becometh Glorious: so
the Soul without Extending, and living in its Object, is Dead within
it self. An Idle Chaos of Blind and confused Powers · for which when
it loveth, it gaineth Three Subsistences in it self by the Act of Lov-
ing. A Glorious Spirit that Abideth within: a Glorious Spirit that
10 floweth in the Stream. A glorious Spirit that resideth in the Object.
Insomuch that now it can Enjoy a Sweet Communion with it self:
in contemplating what it is in it self, and to its Object.

57

Lov is so vastly Delightfull in the Lover, becaus it is the Com-
munication of His Goodness · for the Natural End of Goodness is
to be Enjoyed: it Desireth to be anothers Happiness. Which Good-
ness of GOD is so deeply implanted in our Natures, that we never
5 Enjoy our selvs but when we are the Joy of others: of all our Desires
the Strongest is to be Good to others. We Delight in Receiving,
more in Giving. We lov to be Rich: but then it is, that we therby
might be more Greatly Delightfull · thus we see the Seeds of
Eternity Sparkling in our Natures.

58

Lov is so vastly Delightfull to Him that is Beloved, becaus it is the
fountain of all Affections Services and Endeavors; a Spring of

Honor and Liberality, and a secure Pledge of future Benefits. It
is the sole Title by which we reign in anothers Bosom, and the only
Throne by which we are exalted. The Body and Soul of Him that 5
loves is His that is Beloved. What then can Lov deny? All Greatness
Power and Dominion befalleth Him that is Beloved, in the Soul
that loveth Him. So that while all the Glorious Creatures in all
Worlds Lov you, you Reign in all Souls, are the Image of GOD,
and exalted like GOD in evry Bosom.   10

59

Tho No Riches follow, yet we are all naturaly Delighted with Lov:
both for what we receiv, and for what we give. When we are
Beloved we receiv the Quintessence and Glory of anothers Soul,
the End of Heaven and Earth, the cream and flower of all Per-
fections. The Tribute of GOD almighty, Peace and Welfare 5
Pleasure and Honor, Help and Safety, all in readiness. And som
thing infinitly more which we are not able to Express. When we are
beloved we attain the End of Riches in an immediat maner; and
having the End need not regard the Means. For the End of Riches is
that we may be Beloved · we receiv Power to see our selvs Amiable in 10
anothers Soul, and to Delight and Pleas another Person. For it is
impossible to Delight a Luke Warm Person, or an Alienated Affec-
tion with giving Crowns and Scepters, so as we may a Person that
violently loves us with our very presence and Affections.

60

By this we may Discern what Strange Power GOD hath given to
us by loving us infinitly. [Who more Prizeth our Naked Lov then
Temples full of Gold: Whose Naked Lov is more Delightfull to us
then all Worlds: And Whose Greatest Gifts and Treasures are
Living Souls and Friends, and Lovers. Who as He hath Manifested 5
His Lov by giving us His Son, hath Manifested it also by giving us
all His Sons and Servants. Commanding them to lov us with that
precious Lov wherwith they do them selvs · but most] He giveth us
a Power more to pleas him, then if we were able to Creat Worlds and
present them unto Him.   10

61

How Happy we are that we may liv in all, as well as one; and how
All sufficient Lov is, we may see by this: The more we liv in all the
60. The words between square brackets are deleted in the MS.

more we liv in one. For while He seeth us to live in all, we are a
more Great and Glorious Object unto Him; the more we are
5 Beloved of all, the more we are Admired by Him; The more we
are the Joy of all, the more Blessed we are to Him. The more Blessed
we are to Him the Greater is our Blessedness. We are all Naturaly
Ambitious of being Magnified in others, and of seeming Great in
others. Which Inclination was implanted in us that our Happiness
10 might be Enlarged by the Multitud of Spectators.

62

Lov is the true Means by which the World is Enjoyed. Our Lov
to others, and Others Lov to us. We ought therfore abov all Things
to get acquainted with the Nature of Lov · for Lov is the Root and
Foundation of Nature: Lov is the Soul of Life, and Crown of
5 Rewards. If we cannot be satisfied in the Nature of Lov we can
never be satisfied at all. The very End for which GOD made the
World was that He might Manifest His Lov. Unless therfore we
can be satisfied with his Lov so manifested we can never be satisfied.
There are many Glorious Excellencies in the Material World, but
10 without Lov they are all Abortiv. We might spend Ages in Con-
templating the Nature of the Sun, and entertain our selvs many
yeers with the Beauty of the Stars, and Services of the Sea: but the
Soul of Man is above all these, it comprehendeth all Ages in a
Moment; and unless it perceiv somthing more Excellent, is very
15 Desolat. All Worlds being but a Silent Wilderness, without som
living Thing, more Sweet and Blessed after which it Aspireth.
Lov in the fountain, and Lov in the End is the Glory of the World,
and the Soul of Joy. Which it infinitly preferreth abov all Worlds,
and delighteth in, and loveth to Contemplat, more then all Visible
20 Beings that are Possible. So that you must be sure to see Causes,
wherfore infinitly to be Delighted with the Lov of GOD, if ever
you would be Happy.

63

See Causes also wherfore to be Delighted in your Lov to Men, and
Lov of Men to you. For the World serves you to this End, that you
might lov them and be Beloved of them. And unless you are pleased
with the End for which the World serves you, you can never be
5 pleased with the Means leading to that End. Abov all things

therfore Contemplat the Glory of Loving Men, and of being
Beloved of them. For this End our Savior Died, and for this End
He came into the World, that you might be restored from Hatred,
which is the Greatest Misery. From the Hatred of GOD and Men
which was due for Sin, and from the Misery of Hating GOD and 10
Men; for to Hate and be Hated is the Greatest Misery. The Neces-
sity of Hating GOD and Men being the Greatest Bondage, that Hell
can impose.

64

When you lov men, the World Quickly becometh yours: and your
self becom a Greater Treasure then the World is. For all their Per-
sons are your Treasures, and all the Things in Heaven and Earth
that serv them, are yours. For those are the Riches of Lov, which
minister to its Object.
                                                               5

65

You are as Prone to lov, as the Sun is to shine. It being the most
Delightfull and Natural Employment of the Soul of Man: without
which you are Dark and Miserable, Consider therfore the Extent
of Lov, its Vigor and Excellency. For certainly He that Delights not
in Lov makes vain the Univers, and is of Necessity to Himself the 5
Greatest Burden. The Whole World ministers to you as the Theatre
of your Lov. It sustains you and all Objects that you may continu to
lov them. Without which it were Better for you to hav no Being.
Life without Objects is Sensible Emptiness. Objects without Lov
are the Delusion of Life. The Objects of Lov are its Greatest 10
Treasures: and without Lov it is impossible they should be Treas-
ures. For the Objects which we lov are the Pleasing Objects, and
Delightfull Things. And whatsoever is not pleasing and delightfull
to us can be no Treasure. Nay it is Distastefull, and Worse then
Nothing, since we had rather it should hav no Being.
                                                               15

66

That Violence wherwith som times a man doteth upon one Creature,
is but a little spark of that lov, even towards all, which lurketh in
His Nature. We are made to lov: both to satisfy the Necessity of our
Activ Nature, and to answer the Beauties in evry Creature. By Lov
our souls are married and sodderd to the creatures: and it is our 5

Duty like GOD to be united to them all. We must lov them infinitly
but in God, and for God: and God in them: namely all His Excel-
lencies Manifested in them. When we dote upon the Perfections
and Beauties of som one Creature: we do not lov that too much, but
10 other things too little. Never was any thing in this World loved too
much, but many Things hav been loved in a fals Way: and all in
too short a Measure.

67

Suppose a River or a Drop of Water, an Apple or a Sand, an Ear
of Corn, or an Herb: GOD knoweth infinit Excellencies in it
more then we: He seeth how it relateth to Angels and Men; How
it proceedeth from the most perfect Lover to the most Perfectly
5 Beloved; how it representeth all His Attributs; How it conduceth
in its place, by the best of Means to the Best of Ends: And for this
Caus it cannot be Beloved too much. GOD the Author and GOD
the End is to be Beloved in it: Angels and Men are to be Beloved
in it: And it is highly to be Esteemed for all their Sakes. O what
10 a Treasure is evry Sand when truly understood! Who can lov any
Thing that God made too much? His infinit Goodness and Wisdom
and Power and Glory are in it. What a World would this be, were
evry thing Beloved as it ought to be!

68

Suppose a Curious and fair Woman. Som have seen the Beauties
of Heaven, in such a Person. It is a vain Thing to say they loved
too much. I dare say there are 10000 Beauties in that Creature
which they hav not seen. They loved it not too much but upon fals
5 causes. Nor so much upon fals ones, as only upon som little ones.
They lov a Creature for Sparkling Eys and Curled Hair, Lillie
Brests and Ruddy Cheeks; which they should love moreover for
being GODs Image, Queen of the Univers, Beloved by Angels,
Redeemed by Jesus Christ, an Heires of Heaven, and Temple of
10 the Holy Ghost: a Mine and fountain of all Vertues, a Treasurie of
Graces, and a Child of GOD. But these Excellencies are unknown.
They lov her perhaps, but do not lov God more: nor Men as much:
nor Heaven and Earth at all. And so being Defectiv to other Things,
perish by a seeming Excesse to that. We should be all Life and
15 Mettle and Vigor and Lov to evry Thing. And that would Poys us.

I dare Confidently say, that evry Person in the Whole World ought
to be Beloved as much as this: And she if there be any caus of Differ-
ence more then she is. But GOD being Beloved infinitly more, will
be infinitly more our Joy, and our Heart will be more with Him.
So that no Man can be in Danger by loving others too much, that 20
loveth GOD as He ought.

69

The Sun and Stars Pleas me in Ministering to you. They Pleas
me in ministering to a thousand others as well as you. And you pleas
me becaus you can live and lov in the Image of GOD: not in a Blind
and Bruitish maner, as Beasts do; by a meer Appetite and rude
Propensitie, but with a Regulated well orderd Lov Upon Clear 5
Causes, and with a Rational Affection, guided to Divine and
Celestial Ends. Which is to lov with a Divine and Holy Lov,
Glorious and Blessed. We are all Prone to Love, but the Art lies in
Managing our Love: to make it truly Amiable and Proportionable.
To lov for GODs sake, and to this End, that we may be Wel 10
Pleasing unto Him: to lov with a Design to imitate Him, and to
satisfy the Principles of Intelligent Nature and to becom Honor-
able: is to lov in a Blessed and Holy maner.

70

In one Soul we may be entertained and taken up with innumerable
Beauties. But in the Soul of Man there are innumerable Infinities.
One Soul in the Immensity of its Intelligence, is Greater and more
Excellent then the whole World. The Ocean is but the Drop of a
Bucket to it, the Heavens but a Centre, the Sun Obscurity, and all 5
Ages but as one Day. It being by its Understanding a Temple of
Eternity, and GODs Omnipresence · between which and the whole
World there is no Proportion. Its Lov is a Dominion Greater then
that which Adam had in Paradice: And yet the fruition of it is but
Solitary. We need Spectators; and other Diversities of Friends and 10
Lovers, in whose Souls we might likewise Dwell, and with whose
Beauties we might be Crowned and entertained. In all whom we can
dwell exactly: and be present with them fully. Lest therfore the
other Depths and Faculties of our Souls, should be Desolat and Idle,
they also are Created to entertain us. And as in many Mirrors we 15

are so many other selvs, so are we Spritualy Multiplied when
we meet our selvs more Sweetly, and liv again in other Persons.

71

Creatures are Multiplied, that our Treasures may be Multiplied ·
their Places enlarged, that the Territories of our Joyes might be
Enlarged. With all which our Souls may be present in immediat
maner. For Since the Sun which is a poor little Dead Thing, can
5 at once shine upon many Kingdoms, and be wholy present, not
only in many Cities and Realms upon Earth, but in all the Stars
in the firmament of Heaven: surely the Soul which is a far more
perfect Sun, nearer unto GOD in Excellency and Nature, can do
far more. But that which of all Wonders is the most Deep is, that
10 a Soul, wheras one would think it could Measure but one soul,
which is as large as it: can exceed that, and Measure all Souls,
wholy and fully. This is an infinit Wonder indeed · for Admit
that the Powers of one Soul were fathomles and infinit: are not the
Powers so also of another? One would think therfore, that one
15 Soul should be lost in another: And that two Souls should be
exactly Adaequate.† Yet my Soul can examine and search all the
Chambers and Endles Operations of another: being prepared to
see innumerable Millions.

72

Here is a Glorious Creature! But that which maketh the Wonder
infinitly infinit, is this. That one Soul which is the Object of mine,
can see all Souls, and all the Secret Chambers, and endless Perfec-
tions, in evry Soul: Yea and All Souls with all their Objects in evry
5 Soul. Yet mine can Accompany all these in one Soul: and without
Deficiency exceed that Soul, and accompany all these in evry other
Soul. Which shews the Work of GOD to be deep and Infinit.

73

Here upon Earth perhaps where our Estate is imperfect this is
Impossible: but in Heaven where the Soul is all Act it is necessary.
For the Soul is there all that it can be: Here it is to rejoyce in what
it may be. Till therfore the Mystes of Error and Clouds of Ignorance
5 that confine this Sun be removed: it must be present in all King-
doms and Ages virtualy,† as the Sun is by Night. If not by Clear

Sight and Lov, at least by its Desire. Which are its Influences and
its Beams. Working in a latent and obscure maner on Earth, abov
in a Strong and Clear.

74

The World serveth you therfore, in maintaining all People in all
Kingdoms · which are your fathers Treasures, and your as yet
Invisible Joys, that their Multitudes at last may come to Heaven,
and make those Innumerable Thousands, whose Hosts and Em-
ployments will be your Joy. Whose Order Beauty Melody and 5
Glory will be your Eternall Delights. And of whom you hav many
a Sweet Description in the Revelation. These are they of whom it is
said, After this I beheld, and lo a great Multitude which no man
could number of all Nations and Kindred and People and Tongues
stood before the Throne and before the Lamb, clothed with White 10
Robes and Palms in their Hands, and they cried with a loud voice,
saying Salvation to our GOD which sitteth upon the Throne and to
the Lamb: of which it is said, They fell down before the Lamb,
having evry one of them Harps and Golden Vials full of Odors
which are the Prayers of the Saints, and they sung a new song, 15
saying Thou art Worthy to take the Book and to open the Seals
therof: for Thou wast slain, and hast redeemed us to God by thy
Blood, out of evry Kindred and Tongue and People and Nation:
And hast made us unto our GOD Kings and Priests · of whom it is
said, I saw a Sea of Glass, and they that had gotten the Victory 20
over the Beast standing on it, and they Sing the Song of Moses the
Servant of God, and the Song of the Lamb, saying *Great and*
Marvellous are thy works Lord GOD Almighty; Just and True
are thy Ways Thou King of Saints. Who shall not fear Thee O Lord
and Glorify thy Name, for Thou only art Holy: for all Nations 25
shall com and Worship before Thee, becaus thy Judgements are made
Manifest.

75

That all the Powers of your Soul shall be turned into Act in the
Kingdom of Heaven is manifest by what S. John writeth, in the Isle
Patmos. And I beheld and I heard the Voice of many Angels round
about the Throne: and the Beasts and the Elders, and the Number
of them was ten thousand times ten thousand, and Thousands of 5

Thousands: saying, With a loud Voice, *Worthy is the Lamb that was slain, to receiv Power and Riches and Wisdom, and Strength and Honor and Glory and Blessing. And evry Creature which is in Heaven and on earth, and under the Earth, and such as are in the Sea, And all* 10 *that are in them, heard I saying, Blessing and Honor and Glory and Power, be unto Him that sitteth upon the Throne and unto the Lamb for ever and ever.*

76

These Things shall never be seen with your Bodily Eys · but in a more perfect maner. You shall be present with them in your Understanding. You shall be In them to the very centre and they in you. As Light is in a Piece of Chrystal, so shall you be with every Part and 5 Excellency of them. An Act of the Understanding is the presence of the Soul, which being no Body but a Living Act, is a Pure Spirit, and Mysteriously fathomless in its true Dimensions. By an Act of the Understanding therfore be present now with all the Creatures among which you live: and hear them in their Beings and Operations 10 Praising GOD in an Heavenly Maner. Som of them Vocaly, others in their Ministery, all of them Naturaly and Continualy. We infinitly wrong our selvs by Laziness and Confinement. All Creatures in all Nations and Tongues and People Prais God infinitly; and the more, for being your Sole and Perfect Treasures. You are never what you 15 ought till you go out of yourself and walk among them.

77

Were all your Riches here in som little place: all other Places would be Empty. It is necessary therfore for your Contentment, and true Satisfaction, that your Riches be Dispersed evry where. Whether is more Delightfull; to have som few privat Riches in one, and all 5 other Places void, or to hav all places evry where filled with our Proper Treasures? Certainly to hav Treasures in all Places · for by that means we are entertained evry where with Pleasures, are evry where at home Honered and delighted, evry where Enlarged, and in our own Possessions. But to hav a few Riches in som narrow Bounds, 10 tho we should suppose a Kingdom full, would be to hav our Delights Limited, and Infinit Spaces Dark and Empty, wherin we might wander without Satisfaction. So that God must of necessity to satisfy His Lov give us infinit Treasures. And we of Necessity seek for our Riches in all Places.

78

The Heavens and the Earth serv you, not only in shewing unto you your fathers Glory, as all Things without you are your Riches and Enjoyments. But as within you also, they Magnify, and Beautify and Illuminat your Soul. For as the Sun Beams Illuminat the Air and All Objects, yet are them selvs also Illuminated by them, so 5 fareth it with the Powers of your Soul. The Rays of the Sun carry Light in them as they Pass through the Air, but go on in vain till they meet an Object: and there they are Expresst. They Illuminat a Mirror, and are Illuminated by it. For a looking glass without them would be in the Dark, and they without the Glass unperceived. 10 There they revive and overtake them selvs, and represent the Effigies from whence they came; both of the Sun and Heavens and Trees and Mountains, if the Glass be seated conveniently to receiv them. Which were it not that the Glass were present there one would have thought even the Ideas of them absent from the Place. 15 Even so your Soul in its Rays and Powers is unknown: and no man would believ it present evrý where, were there no Objects there to be Discerned. Your Thoughts and Inclinations pass on and are unperceived. But by their Objects are discerned to be present: being illuminated by them · for they are Present with them and Activ 20 about them. They recover and feel them selvs, and by those Objects live in Employment. Being turned into the figure and Idea of them. For as Light varieth upon all objects whither it cometh, and returneth with the Form and figure of them: so is the Soul Transformed into the Being of its Object. Like light from the Sun, its first 25 Effigies is simple Life, the Pure resemblance of its Primitive fountain, but on the Object which it meeteth it is quickly changed, and by Understanding becometh All Things.

79

Objectiv Treasures are always Delightfull: and tho we travail Endlessly, to see them all our own is infinitly Pleasant: and the further we go the more Delightfull. If they are all ours wholly and soly, and yet nevertheless evry ones too, it is the most Delightfull Accident that is Imaginable · for therby two Contrary Humors are 5 at once Delighted, and two Inclinations, that are both in our Natures, yet seem Contradictory are at once Satisfied. The one is the Avaricious Humor and Lov of Propriety: Wherby we refer all

unto our selvs and naturaly desire to hav all alone in our Private
10 Possession, and to be the alone and single End of all Things. This
we perceiv our selvs becaus all universaly and evry where is ours.
The other is the Communicativ Humor that is in us, wherby we
desire to hav Companions in our Enjoyments to tell our Joys, and
to spread abroad our Delights, and to be our selvs The Joy and
15 Delight of other Persons. For Thousands Enjoy all as well as wee:
and are the End of all: And God communicateth all to them as
well as us. And yet to us alone, becaus He communicateth them
to us, and maketh them our Rich and Glorious Companions: to
whom we may tell our Joys and be Blessed again. How much ought
20 we to Prais GOD, for satisfying two such Insatiable Humors that
are contrary to each other. One would think it Impossible that both
should be pleased, and yet His Divine Wisdom hath made them
Helpfull and Perfectiv to each other.

80

Infinit Lov cannot be Expressed in finit Room: but must hav
infinit Places wherin to utter and shew it self. It must therfore fill
all Eternity and the Omnipresence of God with Joys and Treasures
for my Fruition. And yet it must be Exprest in a finit Room: by
5 making me able in a Centre to Enjoy them. It must be infinitly
exprest in the smallest Moment by making me able in evry Moment
to see them all. It is both ways infinit, for my Soul is an Infinit
Sphere in a Centre. By this may you know that you are infinitly
Beloved: GOD hath made your Spirit a Centre in Eternity Compre-
10 hending all: and filled all about you in an Endless maner with
infinit Riches: Which shine before you and surround you with
Divine and Heavenly Enjoyments.

81

Few will believ the Soul to be infinit: yet Infinit is the first Thing
which is naturaly Known. Bounds and Limits are Discerned only
in a Secondary maner. Suppose a Man were Born Deaf and Blind.
By the very feeling of His Soul He apprehends infinit about Him,
5 infinit Space, infinit Darkness. He thinks not of Wall and Limits
till He feels them and is stopt by them. That things are finit therfore
we learn by our Sences · but Infinity we know and feel by our Souls:
and feel it so Naturaly, as if it were the very Essence and Being of

the Soul. The truth of it is, It is individualy in the Soul: for GOD
is there, and more near to us then we are to our selvs. So that we 10
cannot feel our Souls, but we must feel Him, in that first of Proper-
ties infinit Space. And this we know so Naturaly, that it is the only
Primo et Necessario Cognitum in Rerum naturâ · Of all Things the
only first and most Necessarily Known · for we can unsuppose
Heaven and Earth, and Annihilat the World in our Imagination · 15
but the Place where they stood will remain behind, and we cannot
unsuppose or Annihilat that do what we can. Which without us
is the Chamber of our Infinit Treasures, and within us the Reposi-
torie, and Recipient of them.

82

What shall we render unto God for this infinit Space in our Under-
standings! Since in Giving us this He hath laid the foundation of
infinit Blessedness, manifested infinit Lov, and made us in Capacity
infinit Creatures. In this He hath glorified and Gratified infinit
Goodnes; Exerted infinit Power: and made Himself therby infinitly 5
Delightfull · and infinitly Great, in being Lord and Upholder of such
infinit Creatures · for Being wholy evry where, His omnipresence
was wholy in evry Centre: and He could do no more, then that
would bear: Communicat Himself wholy in evry Centre. His
Nature and Essence being the foundation of His Power, and of our 10
Happiness: of His Glory and our Greatness of His Goodness and
our Satisfaction. For we could never believ that He loved us
infinitly unless He Exerted all His Power · for κατὰ Δύναμιν · is one
of the principal Properties of Lov: as wel as ἐκείνου ἔνεκα · To the
utmost of its Power, as well as for His Sake.   15

83

He therfore hath not made us infinit Treasures only in Extent:
and Souls infinit to see and Enjoy them: which is to measure and
run Parallel with them: but in Depth also they are evry where
infinit being infinit in Excellency. And the Soul is a Miraculous
Abyss of infinit Abysses, an Undrainable Ocean, an inexhausted 5
fountain of Endles Oceans, when it will exert it self to fill and
fathom them · for if it were otherwise, Man is a Creature of such

Noble Principles and Severe Expectations, that could he perceiv
the least Defect to be in the Diety, it would infinitly Displeas Him.
10 The smallest Distaste, Spreading like a Cloud from a Hand over all
the Heavens. Neither will any pretence serv the turn to cover our
Cowardice: which we call Modesty, in not Daring to say or expect
this of the Dietie. Unless we expect this with infinit Ardency, we are
a Lazy Kind of Creatures Good for Nothing. Tis Mans Holiness
15 and Glory to Desire Absolut Perfection in GOD, with a Jealousy
and Care infinitly Cruel: for when we so desire it, that without this
We should be infinitly Displeased, and altogether lost and Desperat
for ever: finding GOD to hav exceeded all our Desires: it becometh
the foundation of infinit Lov. In the fruition of the fruits of which,
20 we are to liv in Communion with Him for ever more.

Space perfects its stature
Objects its lineaments
Affections its Colors
Actions its Graces

84

Your Soul being naturaly very Dark, and Deformed and Empty
when Extended through infinit but empty Space: the World servs
you in Beautifying and filling it with Amiable Ideas; for the Per-
fecting of its Stature in the Ey of GOD · for the thorow Under-
5 standing of which you must know, That GOD is a Being whose
Power from all Eternity was prevented with Act. And that He is
One infinit Act of KNOWLEDG and *Wisdom*, which is infinitly
Beautified with many Consequences of Lov &c. Being one Act of
Eternal Knowledge · He Knows all which He is Able to Know.
10 All Objects in all Worlds being seen in His Understanding. His
Greatness is the presence of His Soul with all Objects in infinit
Spaces: and His Brightness the Light of Eternal Wisdom. His
Essence also is the Sight of Things. For He is all Ey and all Ear.
Being therfore Perfect, and the Mirror of all Perfection, He hath
15 Commanded us to be perfect as He is Perfect: And we are to Grow
up into Him till we are filled with the Fulness of His GODhead.
We are to be Conformed to the Image of His Glory: till we becom
the Resemblance of His Great Exemplar. Which we then are, when
our Power is Converted into Act, and covered with it · we being
20 an Act of KNOWLEDG and Wisdom as He is. When our Souls are

Present with all Objects, and Beautified with the Ideas and figures of them all. For then shall we be *Mentes* as He is *Mens*. We being of the same Mind, with him who is an infinit Eternal mind. As both Plato and Cato with the Apostle term Him.

> Si Deus est Animus sit Pura Mente Colendus.   25
> If GOD as verses say a Spirit be
> We must in Spirit like the Dietie
> Becom. We must the Image of His Mind
> And Union with it in our Spirit find.

Heaven and Earth, Angels and Men, GOD and All Things 30 must be contained in our Souls, that we may becom Glorious Personages, and like unto Him in all our Actions.

85

You know that Lov receivs a Grandure of Valu and Esteem from the Greatness of the Person, from whom it doth proceed. The Lov of a King is naturaly more Delightfull then the Lov of a Beggar. The Lov of God more Excellent then the Lov of a King. The Lov of a Beautifull Person is more Pleasing then that of one Deformed. 5 The Love of a Wise Man is far more Precious then the love of a fool. When you are so Great a Creature as to fill Ages and Kingdoms with the Beauty of your Soul, and to reign over them like the Wisdom of the father filling Eternity with Light and Glory, your Lov shall be Acceptable and Sweet and Precious. The World therfore serveth 10 you, not only in furnishing you with Riches, and Making you Beautifull, and Great and Wise, when it is Rightly used: but in Doing that which doth infinitly concern you, in making your Lov precious. For abov all Things in all Worlds you naturaly desire most Violently that your Lov should be Prized: and the reason 15 is, becaus that being the Best Thing you can do or giv, all is Worthless that you can do besides: and you have no more Power left to be Good, or to Pleas, or to do any Thing, when once your Lov is despised.

86

Since therfore Lov does all it is able, to make it self accepted · both in increasing its own vehemence, and in Adorning the Person of the Lover; as well as in offering up the most chois and Perfect

24. *The Apostle*: St. John.   25. *Disticha Catonis* I. See M.

Gifts. With what care ought [you] to Express your Lov in Beautify-
5 ing your self with this Wisdom, and in making your Person
Acceptable? Especialy since your Person is the Greatest Gift,
your Lov can offer up to GOD Almighty. Clothe your self with
Light as with a Garment, when you com before Him: Put on the
Greatness of Heaven and Earth, Adorn your self with the Excel-
10 lencies of GOD Himself: When you prepare your self to Speak to
Him, be all the KNOWLEDG and Light you are able, as Great as
Clear and as Perfect as is Possible. So at length shall you appear
before GOD in Sion: and as GOD convers with GOD for evermore.

87

GOD hath made it Easy to convert our Soul into a Thought con-
taining Heaven and Earth, not that it should be Contemptible
becaus it is Easy: but don, becaus it is Divine. Which Thought is
as easily Abolished, that by a Perpetual Influx of Life it may be
5 maintained. If He would but suspend his Power, no doubt but
Heaven and Earth would strait be abolished, which He upholds
in him self as easily and as continualy, as we do the Idea of them in
our own Mind. Since therfore All Things depending so Continualy
upon His Care and Lov, the Perpetual Influx of His Almighty
10 Power is infinitly Precious and His Life exercised incessantly in
the Manifestation of Eternal Lov, in that evry Moment throughout
all Generations He continueth without failing to uphold all Things
for us. We likewise ought to Shew our infinit Lov by Upholding
Heaven and Earth, Time and Eternity, GOD and all Things in our
15 Souls, without Wavering or Intermission: by the perpetual Influxe
of our Life. To which we are by the Goodnes of All Things infinitly
Obliged. Once to ceas is to draw upon our selvs infinit Darkness,
after we hav begun to be so Illuminated: for it shews a forgetfulnes
and Defect in Lov: and it is an infinit Wonder that we are afterward
20 restored.

89

Being that we are here upon Earth Turmoiled with Cares and often
Shaken with Winds and by Disturbances distracted: It is the infinit
Mercy of GOD, that we are permitted to Breath and be Diverted.
For all the Things in Heaven and Earth attend upon us, while we
5 ought to Answer and Observ them, by upholding their Beauty

89. Through a mistake in T's numbering, there is no § 88.

within: But we are spared and GOD winketh at our Defect, all the
World attending us while we are about some little Trifling Business.
But in the Estate of Glory the least Intermission would be an
Eternal Apostasie. But there by reason of our infinit Union with
GOD it is Impossible.

10

90

We could easily shew that the Idea of Heaven and Earth in the
Soul of Man, is more Precious with GOD then the Things them
selvs, and more Excellent in nature. Which becaus it will surprize
you a little, I will. What would Heaven and Earth be Worth, were
there no Spectator, no Enjoyer? As much therfore as the End is 5
better then the Means, the Thought of the World wherby it is En-
joyed is Better then the World. So is the Idea of it in the Soul of Man,
better then the World in the Esteem of GOD: It being the End of
the World, without which Heaven and Earth would be in vain. It
is better to you, becaus by it you receiv the World, and it is the 10
Tribut you pay. It more immediatly Beautifies and Perfects your
Nature. How Deformed would you be should all the World stand
about you and you be Idle? Were you able to Creat other Worlds,
GOD had rather you should think on this · for therby you are
united to Him. The Sun in your Ey, is as much to you as the Sun in 15
the Heavens · for by this, the other is Enjoyed. It would shine on all
Rivers Trees and Beasts, in vain to you, could you not think upon it.
The Sun in your Understanding illuminates your Soul, the Sun
in the Heavens inlightens the Hemisphere. The World within you
is an offering returned. Which is infinitly more Acceptable to GOD 20
Almighty, since it came from him, that it might return unto Him.
Wherin the Mysterie is Great. For GOD hath made you able to
Creat Worlds in your own mind, which are more Precious unto
Him then those which He Created: And to Give and offer up the
World unto Him, which is very Delightfull in flowing from Him, 25
but much more in Returning to Him. Besides all which in its own
Nature also a Thought of the World, or the World in a Thought
is more Excellent then the World, becaus it is Spiritual and Nearer
unto GOD. The Material World is Dead and feeleth Nothing. But
this Spiritual World tho it be Invisible hath all Dimensions, and 30
is a Divine and Living Being, the Voluntary Act of an Obedient
Soul.

91

Once more, that I might Close up this Point with an infinit Wonder;
As among Divines it is said, That evry Moments Preservation is
a New Creation: and therfore Blessings continued must not be
Despised, but be more and more esteemed: becaus evry Moments
5 Preservation is another Obligation: even so in the Continual Series
of Thoughts wherby we continue to uphold the Frame of Heaven
and Earth in the Soul towards God, evry Thought is another World
to the Diety as Acceptable as the first. Yea the Continuance puts
an infinit Worth and Lustre on them. For to be Desultory and
10 Inconstant is the Part of a fickle and careless Soul: and make[s] the
Imagination of it Worthless and Despised. But to continu Serious
in Upholding these Thoughts for GODs sake, is the Part of a
Faithfull and Loving Soul: which as it therby continues Great
and Honorable with GOD, so is it therby Divine and Holy: and
15 evry Act of it of infinit Importance: and the Continuance of its Life
Transcendently Esteemed. So that tho you can build or demolish
such Worlds as often as you pleas; yet it infinitly concerneth you
faithfully to continue them: and Wisely to Repair them · for tho to
make them suddainly be to a Wise Man very easy: yet to uphold
20 them always is very Difficult, a Work of unspeakable Diligence, and
an Argument of infinit Lov.

92

As it becometh you to retain a Glorious sence of the World, becaus
the Earth and the Heavens and the Heaven of Heavens are the
Magnificent and Glorious Territories of GODs Kingdom, so are
you to remember always the unsearchable Extent and illimited
5 Greatness of your own Soul; the Length and Bredth and Depth
and Height of your own Understanding. Becaus it is the Hous of
GOD, a Living Temple, and a Glorious Throne of the Blessed
Trinity, far more Magnificent and Great then the Heavens: yea a
Person that in Union and Communion with GOD, is to see Eternity,
10 to fill His Omnipresence, to Possess his Greatness, to Admire his
Lov, to receiv his Gifts, to Enjoy the World, and to live in His
Image. Let all your Actions proceed from a sence of this Greatness,
let all your Affections extend to this Endles Wideness, let all your
Prayers be animated by this Spirit and let all your Praises arise

and ascend from this fountain. For you are never your true self, 15
till you live by your Soul more then by your Body, and you never
live by your Soul, till you feel its incomparable Excellency, and
rest satisfied and Delighted in the Unsearchable Greatness of its
Comprehension.

93

The World does serv you, not only as it is the Place and Receptacle
of all your Joys, but as it is a Great Obligation laid upon all Mankind,
and upon evry Person in all Ages to lov you as Himself: as it also
Magnifieth all your Companions, and sheweth your heavenly
Fathers Glory. Yea as it Exalteth you in the Eys of the Illuminat, and 5
maketh you to be Honored and Reverenced by the Holy. For there is
not a Man in the Whole World that Knows GOD, or Him self, but
he must Honor you: not only as an Angel or a Cherubim, but as one
Redeemed by the Blood of Christ, Beloved by all Angels Cherubims
and Men, an Heir of the World, and as much Greater then the 10
Universe, as He that possesseth the Hous, is Greater then the Hous.
O what a Holy and Blessed Life would men Lead, what Joys and
Treasures would they be to each other, in what a Sphere of Excel-
lency would evry Man mov, how Sublime and Glorious would
their Estate be, how full of Peace and Quiet would the world be, 15
yea of Joy and Honor, Order and Beauty, did Men perceiv this of
themselvs, and had they this Esteem for one another!

94

As the World servs you by shewing the Greatness of GODs Lov
to you, so doth it serv you as fuel to foment and increas your
Praises. Mens Lips are closed, becaus their Eys are Blinded: Their
Tongues are Dumb becaus their Ears are Deaf: and there is no
Life in their Mouths, becaus Death is in their Hearts. But did they 5
all see their Creators Glory, which appeareth chiefly in the Great-
ness of His Bounty; did they all know the Blessedness of their
Estate, O what a Place full of Joys, what an Amiable Region and
Territory of Praises would the World becom; yea, what a Sphere of
Light and Glory! As no man can Breath out more Air then he 10
draweth in: so no man can offer up more Praises, then he receiveth
Benefits, to return in Praises. For Praises are Transformed and

returning Benefits. And therfore doth GOD so Greatly desire the
Knowledg of Him, becaus GOD when He is Known is all Lov: and
15 the Praises which He desires, are the Reflexion of His Beams: which
will not return till they are Apprehended. The World therfore is not
only the Temple of these Praises, and the Altar wheron they are
offered, but the fuel also that Enkindles them, and the very Matter
that composeth them. Which so much the more servs you, becaus it
20 enkindles a Desire in you, that GOD should be praised, and moves
you to take Delight in all that Prais Him. So that as it incites yours,
it gives you an Interest in others Praises: And is a Valley of Vision,
wherin you see the Blessed Sight, of all Mens Praises Ascending,
and of all Gods Blessings coming down upon them.

95

The World serves you, as it teaches you more abundantly to Prize
the Lov of Jesus Christ. For since the Inheritance is so Great to
which you are restored, and no less then the Whole World is the
Benefit of your Saviors Lov, how much are you to Admire that
5 Person, that redeemed you from the Lowest Hell to the fruition of
it? Your forfeiture was unmeasurable and your Sin infinit, your
Despair insupportable, and your Danger Eternal: How Happy are
you therfore, that you hav so Great a Lord, whose Lov rescued
you from the Extremest Misery? Had you seen Adam turned into
10 Hell, and going out of this fair Mansion which the Lord had given
him, into Everlasting Torments, or Eternal Darkness: you would
hav thought the World a Glorious Place, which was Created for
him, and the Light of Eden would hav appeared in Greater Lustre
then it did before: and his Lov by whom He was recovered the
15 Greatest Jewel. It is a Heavenly thing to understand His Lov,
and to see it well. Had Adam had no Esteem for the Place
to which he was restored, he had not valued the Benefit of His
Restitution. But now looking upon it with those Eys wherwith
Noble Men look upon their Territories and Palaces, when they
20 are going to Die, His Mercy who died for Him, that He after his
Condemnation might return again into his Dear Enjoyments,
maketh Him by whom they were purchased the Best and Greatest
of all Enjoyments. Darius when he had Conquerd Babylon, by
the Art of Zopyrus, who cut of(f) His Nose and Ears and Lips,
25 that making the Babylonians to confide in him, he might deliver

up the City into the Kings hands; Admiring the fidelity and Lov
of Zopyrus protested, that He had rather hav one Zopyrus whole,
then ten Babylons. Even so We were our Spirits Divine and Noble
and Genuin, should by the Greatness of the Benefit be Excited
abov our selvs, and to exceed the Gift, in the Lov of our Savior. 30
Being afterwards Asked upon the Sight of a Pomgranat slit in the
Midst, What Thing he would above all other desire, might he hav
as many of them as there were Seeds in that Pomgranat, answered,
Tot Zopyrorum: As Many Zopyruses. One Savior is worth in-
numerable Worlds.   35

96

The World is a Pomgranat indeed, which GOD hath put into
mans Heart, as Solomon observeth in the Ecclesiastes, becaus it
containeth the Seeds of Grace and the Seeds of Glory. All Virtues
lie in the World, as Seeds in a Pomgranate: I mean in the fruition
of it · out of which when it is sown in Mans Heart they Naturaly 5
arise. The fidelity of Zopyrus and the Lov of Darius are included
in it. For when we Consider, how Great a Lord gave us so Great
a Dominion: we shall think it abominable to be Treacherous and
Unfaithfull in the Midst of his Dominions. When we consider we
cannot chuse but Sin, if we sin at all, being surrounded with His 10
Gifts. And that the land we tread on is of his Munificence: how
can we erre against Him who gav it to us? Can we forsake Him,
whose Gifts we cannot leav? The Whole World is Better then
Babylon: and at Greater Expence then Zopyrus Lips was it pur-
chasd for us.   °   15

97

This visible World is Wonderfully to be Delighted in and Highly
to be Esteemed, becaus it is the Theatre of GODs Righteous King-
dom. Who as Himself was Righteous becaus He made it freely, so
He made it that We might freely be Righteous too. For in the King-
dom of Glory it is impossible to fall. No man can sin that clearly 5
seeth the Beauty of Gods face: Becaus no Man can sin against his
own Happiness · that is, none can when he sees it Clearly willingly
and Wittingly forsake it. Tempter, Temptation, Loss and Danger
being all seen: but here we see His Face in a Glasse, and more Dimly
behold our Happiness as in a Mirror: by faith therfore we are to live, 10

and to sharpen our Ey that we may see his Glory, We are to be
Studious and Intent in our Desires and Endeavors. For we may sin,
or we may be Holy. Holiness therfore and Righteousness naturaly
flow out of our fruition of the World: For who can vilify and debase
15 Himself by any Sin, while he Actualy considers he is the Heir of it?
It exalts a Man to a Sublime and Honorable life: it lifts him abov
Lusts and Makes Him Angelical.

98

It makes Him sensible of the Reality of Happiness: it feeds Him
with Contentment, and fils Him with Gratitude · it delivers him
from the Lov of Mony which is the Root of all Evil · it causes him to
reign over the Pervers Customs and Opinions that are in the World:
5 it opens his Eys, and makes him to see Mens Blindness and
Errors · it sateth His Covetousness, feedeth his Curiosity and
pleaseth his Ambition · it makes him too Great for Preferments
and Allurements · it causeth him to delight in Retirement: and to
be in lov with Prayer and Communion with GOD · it lifteth him
10 up abov mens Scandals and Censures · it maketh him Zealous
of the Salvation of all · it filleth him with Courage on the Behalf
of GOD · it makes him to rejoyce in a present visible immovable
Treasure, to which the rest of the World is Blind, and strengthens
his faith and Hope of Invisible · yea it makes Him Wise, and many
15 invisible Joys doth He see in this. Glory and Dominion are in-
visible Joys. And so is that Great Interest a Man hath to all King-
doms and Ages. Which a true Possessor of the World is more
sensible off, then of his Houses and Lands. It makes him Meek
in Pardoning all injuries, becaus He is abov the Reach of his
20 Enemies: and infinitly Secure in the midst of His Fruitions. How
Great a Thing is the Enjoyment of the World, how highly to be
esteemed and how zealously to be thirsted after, that eminently
containeth all these! Verily it is a Thing so Divine and Heavenly,
that it makes vices and virtues almost visible to our very Eys.

99

Varro citeth 288 Opinions of Philosophers concerning Happiness:
they were so Blind in the Knowledg of it, and so different in their
Apprehension. All which Opinions fall in here, as all Rivers fall

into the Sea, and Agree together. Som Placed Happiness in Riches, and som in Honor, som in Pleasure, and som in the Contempt of all Riches Honor and Pleasure; som in Wisdom, and som in firm Stability of Mind, som in Empire, and som in Lov. Som in bare and Naked Contentment, som in Contemplation, and som in Action: som in Rest, and som in Sufferings, and som in Victory and Triumph. All which occur here. For here is Victory and Triumph over our Lusts, that we might live the Life of Clear Reason, in the fruition of all Riches Honors and Pleasures which are by Wisdom to be seen, and by Lov to be Enjoyed in the Highest Empire, with Great Contentation, in Solitud alone, in Communion with all, by Action and Contemplation, attaining it by Sufferings, and resting in the Possession, with Perfect Victory and Triumph over the World and evil Men, or Sin Death and Hell, Maugre all the Oppositions of Men and Divels. Neither Angels nor Principalities nor Power, nor Height nor Depth, nor Things present nor Things to com, being able to seperat us, from the Lov of God which is in Christ Jesus our Lord.

100

Felicity is a Thing coveted of all. The Whole World is taken with the Beauty of it: and he is no Man, but a Stock or Stone that does not desire it. Nevertheless Great Offence hath been don by the Philosophers and Scandal given, through their Blindness, many of them in making Felicity to consist in Negativs. They tell us it doth not consist in Riches, it doth not consist in Honors, it doth not consist in Pleasures. Wherin then saith a Miserable Man, doth it consist. Why, in Contentment, in Self sufficiency, in Vertues, in the Right Government of our Passions, &c. Were it not better to shew the Amiableness of Vertues and the Benefit of the Right Government of our Passions, the Objects of Contentment, and the Grounds of Self sufficiency by the truest Means? Which these never do. Ought they not to Distinguish between true and fals Riches as our Savior doth; between Real and fained Honors? between Clear and Pure Pleasures, and those which are Muddy and unwholsom? The Honor that cometh from abov, the Tru Treasures, those Rivers of Pleasure that flow at his right hand for evermore are by all to be sought and by all to be desired. For it is the Affront of Nature, a making vain the Powers, and a Baffling the Expectations of the

20 Soul, to deny it all Objects, and a Confining it to the Grave, and a
Condemning of it to Death to tie it to that inward unnatural mis-
taken Self sufficiency and Contentment they talk of. By the true
Government of our Passions, we disentangle them from Impedi-
ments, and fit and guid them to their proper Objects. The Amiable-
25 ness of Virtue consisteth in this, that by it all happiness is either
attained or Enjoyed. Contentment and Rest ariseth from a full
Perception of infinit Treasures. So that whosoever will Profit in
the Mystery of Felicity, must see the Objects of His Happiness,
and the Maner how they are to be Enjoyed, and discern also the
30 Powers of His Soul by which He is to enjoy them, and perhaps the
Rules that shall Guid Him in the Way of Enjoyment. All which
you have here. GOD, THE WORLD, YOUR SELF. *All Things*
in Time and Eternity being the Objects of your Felicity. GOD the
Giver, and you the Receiver.

THE THIRD CENTURY

1

Will you see the Infancy of this sublime and celestial Greatness? Those Pure and Virgin Apprehensions I had from the Womb, and that Divine Light wherewith I was born, are the Best unto this Day, wherin I can see the Universe. By the Gift of GOD they attended me into the World, and by his Special favor I remember 5 them till now. Verily they seem the Greatest Gifts His Wisdom could bestow · for without them all other Gifts had been Dead and Vain. They are unattainable by Book, and therfore I will teach them by Experience. Pray for them earnestly: for they will make you Angelical, and wholy Celestial. Certainly Adam in Paradise had not 10 more sweet and Curious Apprehensions of the World, then I when I was a child.

2

All appeared New, and Strange at the first, inexpressibly rare, and Delightfull, and Beautifull. I was a little Stranger which at my Enterance into the World was Saluted and Surrounded with innumerable Joys. My Knowledg was Divine: I knew by Intuition those things which since my Apostasie, I Collected again, by the 5 Highest Reason. My very Ignorance was Advantageous. I seemed as one Brought into the Estate of Innocence. All Things were Spotles and Pure and Glorious: yea, and infinitly mine, and Joyfull and Precious. I knew not that there were any Sins, or Complaints, or Laws. I Dreamed not of Poverties Contentions or Vices. All 10 Tears and Quarrels, were hidden from mine Eys. Evry Thing was at Rest, Free, and Immortal. I knew Nothing of Sickness or Death or Exaction, in the Absence of these I was Entertained like an Angel with the Works of GOD in their Splendor and Glory; I saw all in the Peace of Eden; Heaven and Earth did sing my Creators 15 Praises, and could not make more Melody to Adam, then to me. All Time was Eternity, and a Perpetual Sabbath. Is it not Strange, that an Infant should be Heir of the World, and see those Mysteries which the Books of the Learned never unfold?

3

The Corn was Orient† and Immortal Wheat, which never should
be reaped, nor was ever sown. I thought it had stood from Ever-
lasting to Everlasting. The Dust and Stones of the Street were as
Precious as GOLD. The Gates were at first the End of the World,
5 The Green Trees when I saw them first through one of the Gates
Transported and Ravished me; their Sweetnes and unusual Beauty
made my Heart to leap, and almost mad with Extasie, they were such
strange and Wonderfull Thing[s]: The Men! O what Venerable and
Reverend Creatures did the Aged seem! Immortal Cherubims! And
10 yong Men Glittering and Sparkling Angels and Maids strange
Seraphick Pieces of Life and Beauty! Boys and Girles Tumbling in
the Street, and Playing, were moving Jewels. I knew not that they
were Born or should Die. But all things abided Eternaly as they were
in their Proper Places. Eternity was Manifest in the Light of the
15 Day, and som thing infinit Behind evry thing appeared: which talked
with my Expectation and moved my Desire. The Citie seemed to
stand in Eden, or to be Built in Heaven. The Streets were mine, the
Temple was mine, the People were mine, their Clothes and Gold
and Silver was mine, as much as their Sparkling Eys fair Skins and
20 ruddy faces. The Skies were mine, and so were the Sun and Moon
and Stars, and all the World was mine, and I the only Spectator
and Enjoyer of it. I knew no Churlish Proprieties,† nor Bounds
nor Divisions: but all Proprieties and Divisions were mine: all
Treasures and the Possessors of them. So that with much adoe
25 I was corrupted; and made to learn the Dirty Devices of this
World. Which now I unlearn, and becom as it were a little Child
again, that I may enter into the Kingdom of GOD.

4

Upon those Pure and Virgin Apprehensions which I had in my
Infancy, I made this Poem.[1]

I

That Childish Thoughts such Joys Inspire,
Doth make my Wonder, and His Glory higher;
His Bounty, and my Wealth more Great:
It shews His Kingdom, and His Work Compleat.
5   In which there is not any Thing,
Not meet to be the Joy of Cherubim.

[1] 'The Approach.' See p. 21.

2

He in our Childhood with us Walks,
And with our Thoughts Mysteriously He talks;
   He often Visiteth our Minds,
But cold Acceptance in us ever finds.   10
   We send Him often grievd away,
Who els would shew us all His Kingdoms Joy.

3

O Lord I Wonder at Thy Lov,
Which did my Infancy so Early mov:
   But more at that which did forbear   15
And mov so long, tho sleighted many a yeer:
   But most of all, at last that Thou
Thy self shouldst me convert, I scarce know how.

4

Thy Gracious Motions oft in vain
Assaulted me: My Heart did hard remain   20
   Long time! I sent my God away
Grievd much, that He could not giv me His Joy.
   I careless was, nor did regard
The End for which He all those Thoughts prepard.

5

But now, with New and Open Eys,   25
I see beneath, as if I were abov the Skies:
   And as I backward look again
See all His Thoughts and mine most Clear and Plain.
   He did approach, He me did Woe.
I Wonder that my GOD this thing would doe.   30

6

From Nothing taken first I was;
What Wondrous things His Glory brought to pass!
   Now in the World I Him behold,
And Me, Inveloped in Precious Gold;
   In deep Abysses of Delights,   35
In present Hidden Glorious Benefits.

7

Those Thoughts His Goodness long before
Prepard as Precious and Celestial Store:
With Curious Art in me inlaid,
40 That Childhood might it self alone be said
My Tutor Teacher Guid to be,
Instructed then even by the Dietie.

5

Our Saviors Meaning, when He said, He must be Born again and
becom a little Child that will enter into the Kingdom of Heaven:
is Deeper far then is generaly believed. It is not only in a Careless
Reliance upon Divine Providence, that we are to becom Little
5 Children, or in the feebleness and shortness of our Anger and
Simplicity of our Passions: but in the Peace and Purity of all our
Soul. Which Purity also is a Deeper Thing then is commonly
apprehended · for we must disrobe our selvs of all fals Colors, and
unclothe our Souls of evil Habits; all our Thoughts must be Infant-
10 like and Clear: the Powers of our Soul free from the Leven of this
World, and disentangled from mens conceits and customs. Grit in
the Ey or the yellow Jandice will not let a Man see those Objects
truly that are before it. And therfore it is requisit that we should
be as very Strangers to the Thoughts Customs and Opinions of men
15 in this World as if we were but little Children. So those Things
would appear to us only which do to Children when they are first
Born. Ambitions, Trades, Luxuries, inordinat Affections, Casual
and Accidental Riches invented since the fall would be gone, and
only those Things appear, which did to Adam in Paradice, in the
20 same Light, and in the same Colors. GOD in His Works, Glory in
the Light, Lov in our Parents, Men, our selvs, and the Face of
Heaven. Evry Man naturaly seeing those Things, to the Enjoyment
of which He is Naturaly Born.

6

Evry one provideth Objects, but few prepare Senses wherby, and
Light wherin to see them. Since therfore we are Born to be a Burn-
ing and Shining Light, and whatever men learn of others, they
see in the Light of others Souls: I will in the Light of my Soul
5 shew you the Univers. Perhaps it is Celestial, and will teach you

how Beneficial we may be to each other. I am sure it is a Sweet and Curious Light to me: which had I wanted: I would hav given all the Gold and Silver in all Worlds to hav Purchased. But it was the Gift of GOD and could not be bought with Mony. And by what Steps and Degrees I proceeded to that Enjoyment of all Eternity which 10 now I possess I will likewise shew you. A Clear, and familiar Light it may prove unto you.

7

The first Light which shined in my Infancy in its Primitive and Innocent Clarity was totaly Ecclypsed: insomuch that I was fain to learn all again. If you ask me how it was Ecclypsed? Truly by the Customs and maners of Men, which like Contrary Winds blew it out: by an innumerable company of other Objects, rude vulgar 5 and Worthless Things that like so many loads of Earth and Dung did over whelm and Bury it: by the Impetuous Torrent of Wrong Desires in all others whom I saw or knew that carried me away and alienated me from it: by a Whole Sea of other Matters and Concernments that Covered and Drowned it: finaly by the Evil Influence of 10 a Bad Education that did not foster and cherish it. All Mens thoughts and Words were about other Matters; They all prized New Things which I did not dream of. I was a stranger and unacquainted with them; I was little and reverenced their Authority; I was weak, and easily guided by their Example: Ambitious also, and Desirous 15 to approve my self unto them. And finding no one Syllable in any mans Mouth of those Things, by Degrees they vanishd, My Thoughts, (as indeed what is more fleeting then a Thought) were blotted out. And at last all the Celestial Great and Stable Treasures to which I was born, as wholy forgotten, as if they had never been. 20

8

Had any man spoken of it, it had been the most easy Thing in the World, to hav taught me, and to hav made me believ, that Heaven and Earth was GODs Hous, and that He gav it me. That the Sun was mine and that Men were mine, and that Cities and Kingdoms were mine also: that Earth was better then Gold, and that Water 5 was, every Drop of it, a Precious Jewel. And that these were Great and Living Treasures: and that all Riches whatsoever els was Dross in Comparison. From whence I clearly find how Docible our

Nature is, in natural Things, were it rightly entreated. And that our
10 Misery proceedeth ten thousand times more from the outward
Bondage of Opinion and Custom, then from any inward corruption
or Depravation of Nature: And that it is not our Parents Loyns,
so much as our Parents lives, that Enthrals and Blinds us. Yet
is all our Corruption Derived from Adam: inasmuch as all the Evil
15 Examples and inclinations of the World arise from His Sin. But I
speak it in the presence of GOD and of our Lord Jesus Christ,
in my Pure Primitive Virgin Light, while my Apprehensions were
natural, and unmixed, I can not remember, but that I was ten
thousand times more prone to Good and Excellent Things, then
20 evil. But I was quickly tainted and fell by others.

9

It was a Difficult matter to persuade me that the Tinsild Ware
upon a Hobby hors was a fine thing. They did impose upon me,
and Obtrude their Gifts that made me believ a Ribban or a Feather
Curious. I could not see where the Curiousness or fineness: And to
5 Teach me that A Purs of Gold was of any valu seemed impossible,
the Art by which it becomes so, and the reasons for which it is
accounted so were so Deep and Hidden to my Inexperience. So
that Nature is still nearest to Natural Things · and farthest off from
preternatural, and to esteem that the Reproach of Nature, is an
10 Error in them only who are unacquainted with it. Natural Things
are Glorious, and to know them Glorious: But to call things pre-
ternatural,† Natural, Monstrous. Yet all they do it, who esteem
Gold Silver Houses Lands Clothes &c. the Riches of Nature, which
are indeed the Riches of Invention. Nature knows no such Riches ·
15 but Art and Error makes them. Not the God of Nature, but Sin
only was the Parent of them. The Riches of Nature are our Souls
and Bodies, with all their Faculties Sences and Endowments. And
it had been the Easiest thing in the whole World, that all felicity
consisted in the Enjoyment of all the World, that it was prepared for
20 me before I was born, and that Nothing was more Divine and
Beautifull.

10

Thoughts are the most Present things to Thoughts, and of the
most Powerfull Influence. My Soul was only Apt and Disposed
to Great Things; But Souls to Souls are like Apples to Apples,

one being rotten rots another. When I began to speak and goe·
Nothing began to be present to me, but what was present in their 5
Thoughts. Nor was any thing present to me any other way, then it
was so to them. The Glass of Imagination was the only Mirror,
wherin any thing was represented or appeared to me. All Things
were Absent which they talkt not of. So I began among my Play
fellows to prize a Drum, a fine Coat, a Peny, a Gilded Book &c. 10
who before never Dreamd of any such Wealth. Goodly Objects to
drown all the Knowledg of Heaven and Earth: As for the Heavens
and the Sun and Stars they disappeared, and were no more unto me
than the bare Walls. So that the Strange Riches of Mans Invention
quite overcame the Riches of Nature. Being learned more 15
laboriously and in the second place.

11

By this let Nurses, and those Parents that desire Holy Children
learn to make them Possessors of Heaven and Earth betimes · to
remove silly Objects from before them, to Magnify nothing but
what is Great indeed, and to talk of God to them and of His Works
and Ways before they can either Speak or go. For Nothing is so Easy 5
as to teach the Truth becaus the Nature of the Thing confirms the
Doctrine. As when we say The Sun is Glorious, A Man is a Beauti-
full Creature, Soveraign over Beasts and Fowls and Fishes, The .
Stars Minister unto us, The World was made for you, &c. But to
say This Hous is yours, and these Lands are another Mans and this 10
Bauble is a Jewel and this Gugaw a fine Thing, this Rattle makes
Musick &c. is deadly Barbarous and uncouth to a little Child; and
makes him suspect all you say, becaus the Nature of the Thing
contradicts your Words. Yet doth that Blot out all Noble and
Divine Ideas, Dissettle his foundation, render him uncertain in all 15
Things, and Divide him from GOD. To teach him those Objects
are little vanities, and that tho GOD made them, by the Ministery
of Man, yet Better and more Glorious Things are more to be
Esteemed, is Natural and Easy.

12

By this you may see who are the Rude and Barbarous Indians. For
verily there is no Salvage Nation under the Cope of Heaven, that
is more absurdly Barbarous than the Christian World. They that

go Naked and Drink Water and liv upon Roots are like Adam, or
5 Angels in Comparison of us. But they indeed that call Beads and
Glass Buttons Jewels, and Dress them selvs with feather, and buy
pieces of Brass and broken hafts of Knives of our Merchants are
som what like us. But We pass them in Barbarous Opinions, and
Monstrous Apprehensions: which we Nick Name Civility, and
10 the Mode, amongst us. I am sure those Barbarous People that go
naked, com nearer to Adam God and Angels: in the Simplicity of
their Wealth, tho not in Knowledg.

13

You would not think how these Barbarous Inventions spoyle your
Knowledg. They put Grubs and Worms in Mens Heads: that are
Enemies to all Pure and True Apprehensions, and eat out all their
Happines. They make it impossible for them, in whom they reign,
5 to believ there is any Excellency in the Works of GOD, or to taste
any Sweetness in the Nobility of Nature, or to Prize any Common,
tho never so Great a Blessing. They alienat men from the Life of
GOD, and at last make them to live without GOD in the World. To
liv the Life of GOD is to live to all the Works of GOD, and to enjoy
10 them in His Image · from which they are wholy Diverted that follow
fashions. Their fancies are corrupted with other Gingles.

14

Being Swallowed up therfore in the Miserable Gulph of idle talk
and worthless vanities, thenceforth I lived among Shadows, like a
Prodigal Son feeding upon Husks with Swine. A Comfortless
Wilderness full of Thorns and Troubles the World was, or wors:
5 a Waste Place covered with Idleness and Play, and Shops and
Markets and Taverns. As for Churches they were things I did not
understand. And Scholes were a Burden: so that there was nothing
in the World worth the having, or Enjoying, but my Game and
Sport, which also was a Dream and being passed wholy forgotten.
10 So that I had utterly forgotten all Goodness Bounty Comfort and
Glory: which things are the very Brightness of the Glory of GOD:
for lack of which therfore He was unknown.

15

Yet somtimes in the midst of these Dreams, I should com a litle
to my self· so far as to feel I wanted som thing, secretly to Expostu-
late with GOD for not giving me Riches, to long after an unknown

Happiness, to griev that the World was so Empty, and to be dis-
satisfied with my present State becaus it was vain and forlorn. 5
I had heard of Angels, and much admired that here upon earth
nothing should be but Dirt and Streets and Gutters · for as for the
Pleasures that were in Great Mens Houses I had not seen them : and
it was my real Happiness they were unknown · for becaus Nothing
Deluded me, I was the more Inquisitive.   10

16

Once I remember (I think I was about 4 yeer old, when) I thus
reasoned with my self · sitting in a little Obscure Room in my
Fathers poor House. If there be a God, certainly He must be
infinit in Goodness. And that I was prompted to, by a real Whisper-
ing Instinct of Nature. And if He be infinit in Goodness, and a 5
Perfect Being in Wisdom and Love, certainly He must do most
Glorious Things: and giv us infinit Riches; how comes it to pass
therfore that I am so poor? of so Scanty and Narrow a fortune,
enjoying few and Obscure Comforts? I thought I could not believ
Him a GOD to me, unless all His Power were Employd to Glorify 10
me. I knew not then my Soul, or Body: nor did I think of the
Heavens and the Earth, the Rivers and the Stars, the Sun or the
Seas: all those were lost, and Absent from me. But when I found
them made out of Nothing for me, then I had a GOD indeed, whom
I could Prais, and rejoyce in.   15

17

Som times I should be alone, and without Employment, when
suddainly my Soul would return to it self, and forgetting all Things
in the whole World which mine Eys had seen, would be carried
away to the Ends of the Earth: and my Thoughts would be deeply
Engaged with Enquiries, How the Earth did End? Whether Walls 5
did Bound it, or Suddain Precipices · or Whether the Heavens by
Degrees did com to touch it; so that the face of the Earth and
Heaven were so neer, that a Man with Difficulty could Creep under?
Whatever I could imagin was inconvenient, and my Reason being
Posed was Quickly Wearied. What also upheld the Earth (becaus it 10
was Heavy) and kept it from falling; Whether Pillars, or Dark
Waters? And if any of these, What then upheld those, and what

T

again those, of which I saw there would be no End? Little did I
think that the Earth was Round, and the World so full of Beauty,
15 Light, and Wisdom. When I saw that, I knew by the Perfection of
the Work there was a GOD, and was satisfied, and Rejoyced. People
underneath and feilds and flowers with another Sun and another
Day Pleased me mightily: but more when I knew it was the same
Sun that served them by night, that served us by Day.

18

Som times I should Soar abov the Stars and Enquire how the
Heavens Ended, and what was beyond them? concerning which
by no means could I receiv satisfaction. Som times my Thoughts
would carry me to the Creation, for I had heard now, that the
5 World which at first I thought was Eternal, had a Beginning: how
therfore that Beginning was, and Why it was; Why it was no sooner,
and what was before; I mightily desired to Know. By all which
I easily perceiv that my Soul was made to live in Communion with
GOD, in all Places of his Dominion, and to be satisfied with the
10 Highest Reason in all Things. After which it so Eagerly aspired,
that I thought all the Gold and Silver in the World but Dirt, in
comparison of Satisfaction in any of these. Som times I Wondered
Why Men were made no Bigger? I would have had a Man as Big
as a Giant, a Giant as big as a Castle, and a Castle as big as the
15 Heavens. Which yet would not serv: for there was infinit Space
beyond the Heavens, and all was Defectiv and but little in Com-
parison: And for him to be made infinit, I thought it would be to no
Purpose, and it would be inconvenient. Why also there was not
a Better Sun, and better Stars, a Better Sea and Better Creatures
20 I much admired.† Which thoughts produced that Poem upon
Moderation, which afterwards was written. Som part of the verses
are these

19

In Making Bodies Lov could not Express
It self, or Art; unless it made them less.
O what a Monster had in Man been seen,
Had every Thumb or Toe a Mountain been!
5 What Worlds must He devour when he did eat?
What Oceans Drink! yet could not all His Meat,

Or Stature, make Him like an Angel Shine;
Or make His Soul in Glory more Divine.
A Soul it is that makes us truly Great,
Whose little Bodies make us more Compleat.   10
An Understanding that is Infinit,
An Endles Wide and Everlasting Sight,
That can Enjoy all Things and nought exclude,
Is the most Sacred Greatnes may be viewd.
Twas inconvenient that His Bulk should be   15
An Endless Hill; He nothing then could see.
No figure hav, no Motion, Beauty, Place,
No Color, feature, Member, Light or Grace.
A Body like a Mountain is but Cumber.
An Endless Body is but idle Lumber.   20
It Spoils Convers, and Time it self devours,
While Meat in vain, in feeding idle Powers.
Excessiv Bulk being most injurious found,
To those Conveniences which Men have Crownd.
His Wisdom did His Power here repress,   25
GOD made Man Greater while He made Him less.

20

The Excellencies of the Sun I found to be of another Kind then
that Splendor after which I sought, even in unknown and invisible
Services; And that GOD by Moderation Wisely Bounding His
Almighty power, had to my Eternal Amazement and Wonder, made
all Bodies far Greater then if they were infinit: there not being a 5
Sand nor Mote in the Air that is not more Excellent then if it were
infinit. How Rich and Admirable then is the Kingdom of GOD;
where the Smallest is Greater then an infinit Treasure! Is not this
Incredible? Certainly to the Placits and Doctrines of the Scholes:
Till we all Consider, That infinit Worth shut up in the Limits of a 10
Material Being, is the only way to a Real Infinity. GOD made
Nothing infinit in Bulk, but evry thing there where it ought to be.
Which, becaus Moderation is a Vertu observing the Golden Mean,
in som other parts of the former Poem, is thus Expressed.

21

His Power Bounded, Greater is in Might,
Then if let loos, twere wholy infinit.
He could hav made an Endless Sea by this.
But then it had not been a Sea of Bliss.
Did Waters from the Centre to the Skies
Ascend, twould drown whatever els we Prize
The Ocean bounded in a finit Shore,
Is better far becaus it is no more.
No Use nor Glory would in that be seen,
His Power made it Endless in Esteem.
Had not the Sun been bounded in its Sphere,
Did all the World in one fair flame appear
And were that flame a real Infinit
Twould yeeld no Profit Splendor nor Delight.
Its Corps confind, and Beams extended be
Effects of Wisdom in the Dietie.
One Star made infinit would all Exclude.
An Earth made infinit could nere be Viewd.
But one being fashioned for the others sake,
He bounding all, did all most usefull make:
And which is best, in Profit and Delight
Tho not in Bulk, they all are infinit.

22

These Liquid Clear Satisfactions, were the Emanations of the
Highest Reason, but not atchieved till a long time afterwards. In
the mean time I was som times tho seldom visited and inspired
with New and more vigorous Desires after that Bliss which Nature
Whispered and Suggested to me. Evry New Thing Quickened my
Curiosity and raised my Expectation. I remember once, the first
time I came into a Magnificent or Noble Dining Room, and was
left there alone, I rejoyced to see the Gold and State and Carved
Imagery · but when all was Dead, and there was no Motion, I was
weary of it, and departed Dissatisfied. But afterwards, when I saw
it full of Lords and Ladies and Musick and Dancing, the Place
which once seemed not to differ from a Solitary Den, had now
Entertainment and nothing of Tediousness but pleasure in it.

§ 21. These lines occur in a variant form in 'Christian Ethicks' (see p. 141) and provided
Dobell with the final proof of T's authorship (see G. I. Wade's edition, p. xci).

By which I perceived (upon a Reflexion made long after) That
Men and Women are when well understood a Principal Part of our 15
True felicity. By this I found also that nothing that stood still, could
by doing so be a Part of Happiness: and that Affection, tho it were
invisible, was the best of Motions. But the August and Glorious
Exercise of Virtue, was more Solemn and Divine which yet I saw
not. And that all Men and Angels should appear in Heaven. 20

23

Another time, in a Lowering and sad Evening, being alone in the
field, when all things were dead and quiet, a certain Want and
Horror fell upon me, beyond imagination. The unprofitableness
and Silence of the Place dissatisfied me, its Wideness terrified me,
from the utmost Ends of the Earth fears surrounded me. How did 5
I know but Dangers might suddainly arise from the East, and
invade me from the unknown Regions beyond the Seas? I was a
Weak and little child, and had forgotten there was a man alive in
the Earth. Yet som thing also of Hope and Expectation comforted
me from every Border. This taught me that I was concernd in all 10
the World: and that in the remotest Borders the Causes of Peace
delight me, and the Beauties of the Earth when seen were made to
entertain me: that I was made to hold a Communion with the
Secrets of Divine Providence in all the World: that a Remembrance
of all the Joys I had from my Birth ought always to be with me: 15
that the Presence of Cities Temples and Kingdoms ought to Sustain
me, and that to be alone in the World was to be Desolate and Miser-
able. The Comfort of Houses and friends, and the clear Assurance
of Treasures evry where, Gods Care and Lov, His Goodnes Wis-
dom and Power, His presence and Watchfulness in all the Ends of 20
the Earth, were my Strength and Assurance for ever: and that these
things being Absent to my Ey, were my Joys and consolations: as
present to my Understanding as the Wideness and Emptiness of
the Universe which I saw before me.

24

When I heard of any New Kingdom beyond the seas, the Light
and Glory of it pleased me immediatly, enterd into me, it rose up
within me and I was Enlarged Wonderfully. I entered into it,
I saw its Commodities, Rarities, Springs, Meadows Riches,

5 Inhabitan[t]s, and became Possessor of that New Room, as if it had
been prepared for me, so much was I Magnified and Delighted in
it. When the Bible was read my Spirit was present in other Ages.
I saw the Light and Splendor of them: the Land of Canaan, the
Israelites entering into it, the ancient Glory of the Amorites, their
10 Peace and Riches, their Cities Houses Vines and Fig trees, the
long Prosperity of their Kings, their Milk and Honie, their slaughter
and Destruction, with the Joys and Triumphs of GODs People,
all which Entered into me, and GOD among them. I saw all and
felt all in such a lively maner, as if there had been no other Way to
15 those Places, but in Spirit only. This shewd me the Liveliness of
interior presence, and that all Ages were for most Glorious Ends,
Accessible to my Understanding, yea with it, yea within it · for
without changing Place in my self I could behold and enjoy all
those. Any thing when it was proposed, tho it was 10000 Ages agoe,
20 being always before me.

25

When I heard any News I received it with Greediness and Delight,
becaus my Expectation was awakend with som Hope that My
Happiness and the Thing I wanted was concealed in it. Glad
Tidings you know from a far Country brings us our Salvation: And
5 I was not deceived. In Jury was Jesus Killed, and from Jerusalem
the Gospel came. Which when I once knew I was very Confident
that evry Kingdom contained like Wonders and Causes of Joy,
tho that was the fountain of them. As it was the First fruits so was it
the Pledg of what I shall receiv in other Countries. Thus also when
10 any curious Cabinet, or secret in Chymistrie, Geometry or Physick
was offered to me, I diligently looked in it, but when I saw it to the
Bottom and not my Happiness I despised it. These Imaginations
and this Thirst of News occasioned these Reflexions.

26

On News

I

News from a forrein Country came,
As if my Treasure and my Wealth lay there:
So much it did my Heart Enflame!
Twas wont to call my Soul into mine Ear.

On News. See p. 79.

Which thither went to Meet   5
　　The Approaching Sweet:
And on the Threshhold stood,
To entertain the Unknown Good.
　　　It Hoverd there,
　　As if twould leav mine Ear.   10
And was so Eager to Embrace
The Joyfull Tidings as they came,
Twould almost leav its Dwelling Place,
　　To Entertain the Same.

2

As if the Tidings were the Things,   15
My very Joys themselvs, my forrein Treasure,
　　Or els did bear them on their Wings;
With so much Joy they came, with so much Pleasure.
　　My Soul stood at the Gate
　　　To recreat   20
　　It self with Bliss: And to
Be pleasd with Speed. A fuller View
　　It fain would take
　　Yet Journeys back would make
Unto my Heart: as if twould fain   25
Go out to meet, yet stay within
To fit a place, to Entertain,
　　And bring the Tidings in.

3

What Sacred Instinct did inspire
My Soul in Childhood with a Hope so Strong?   30
What Secret Force movd my Desire,
To Expect my Joys beyond the Seas, so Yong?
　　Felicity I knew
　　　Was out of View:
　　And being here alone,   35
I saw that Happiness was gone,
　　From Me! for this,
　　I Thirsted Absent Bliss,

And thought that sure beyond the Seas,
40   Or els in som thing near at hand
I knew not yet, (since nought did pleas
I knew·) my Bliss did stand.

4

But little did the Infant Dream
That all the Treasures of the World were by:
45   And that Himself was so the Cream
And Crown of all, which round about did lie.
Yet thus it was. The Gem,
The Diadem,
The Ring Enclosing all
50   That Stood upon this Earthy Ball;
The Heavenly Ey,
Much Wider then the Skie,
Wher in they all included were
The Glorious Soul that was the King
55   Made to possess them, did appear
A Small and little thing!

27

Among other things, there befel me a most infinit Desire of a Book
from Heaven · for observing all things to be rude and superfluous
here upon Earth I thought the Ways of felicity to be known only
among the Holy Angels: and that unless I could receiv informa-
5 tion from them, I could never be Happy. This Thirst hung upon
me a long time; Till at last I perceived that the God of Angels had
taken Care of me, and prevented† my Desires. For He had sent the
Book I wanted before I was Born: and prepared it for me, and also
commended, and sent it unto me, in a far better maner then I was
10 able to imagine. Had som Angel brought it to me, which was the
best way wherin I could then desire it, it would hav been a peculiar
favor, and I should hav thought myself therin Honored abov all
Mankind. It would hav been the Soul of this world, the Light of
my Soul, the Spring of Life, and a fountain of Happiness. You
15 cannot think what Riches and Delights I promised myself therin.
It would hav been a Mine of Rarities, Curiosities and Wonders,

to hav entertained the Powers of my Soul, to hav directed me in the
Way of Life, and to hav fed me with Pleasures unknown to the
whole World.

28

Had som Angel brought it miraculously from Heaven, and left
it at my foot, it had been a Present meet for Seraphims. Yet had
it been a Dream in comparison of the Glorious Way wherin GOD
prepared it. I must hav spent time in studying it, and with great
Diligence, hav read it daily to drink in the Precepts and Instruc- 5
tions it contained. It had in a narrow Obscure maner com unto me,
and all the World had been Ignorant of felicity, but I. Wheras
now there are thousands in the World, of whom I being a Poor
Child was Ignorant, that in Temples, Universities and Secret
Closets enjoy felicity, whom I saw not in Shops, or Scholes or 10
Trades; whom I found not in Streets, or at feasts, or Taverns: and
therfore thought not to be in the World: Who Enjoy Communion
with God, and hav fellowship with the Angels evry Day. And these
I discerned to be a Great Help unto me.

29

This put me upon two things: upon Enquiring into the Matter
contained in the Bible, and into the Maner wherin it came unto
me. In the matter I found all the Glad Tidings my Soul longed
after, in its Desire of News · in the maner, that the Wisdom of
GOD was infinitly Greater then mine and that He had appeared 5
in His Wisdom, exceeding my Desires. Abov all things I desired
som Great Lord or Mighty King, that having Power in his hand,
to give me all Kingdoms Riches and Honors, was willing to do it.
And by that Book I found that there was an Eternal GOD, who
loved me infinitly, that I was his Son, that I was to overcom Death, 10
and to liv forever, that He Created the World for me, that I was to
Reign in His Throne, and to inherit all Things. Who would hav
believed this had not that Book told me? It told me also that I was
to liv in Communion with Him, in the Image of His Life and Glory,
that I was to Enjoy all His Treasures and Pleasures, in a more 15
perfect maner then I could Devise, and that all the truly Amiable
and Glorious Persons in the World were to be my friends and
Companions.

30

Upon this I had enough. I desired no more the Honors and Pleasures
of this World, but gav my self to the Illimited and Clear fruition
of that: and to this Day see nothing wanting to my Felicity but mine
own Perfection. All other Things are well; I only, and the Sons
5 of Men about me are Disorderd. Nevertheless could I be what I
ought, their very Disorders would be my Enjoyments · for all
things shall work together for Good to them that lov GOD. And
if the Disorders then certainly the Troubles, and if the Troubles,
much more the Vanities of Men would be mine. Not only their
10 Enjoyments, but their very Errors and Distractions increasing my
Felicity. So that being Heir of the Whole World alone, I was to walk
in it, as in a Strange Marvellous and Amiable Possession, and alone
to render Praises unto God for its Enjoyment.

31·

This taught me that those Fashions and Tinsild vanities, which
you and I despised ere while, fetching a litle Cours about, became
ours. And that the Wisdom of God in them also was very Conspicu-
ous. For it becometh His Goodness to make all Things Treasures:
5 and His Power is able to bring Light out of Darkness, and Good out
of Evil. Nor would His Lov endure, but that I also should hav a Wis-
dom, wherby I could draw Order out of Confusion. So that it is my
Admiration and Joy, that while so many thousand wander in Dark-
ness, I am in the Light; and that while so many Dote upon fals
10 Treasures and Pierce themselvs thorow with many Sorrows; I liv
in Peace, and Enjoy the Delights of God and Heaven.

32

In respect of the Matter, I was very sure that Angels and Cheru-
bims could not bring unto me better Tidings then were in the
Scriptures contained: could I but believ them to be true · but I was
Dissatisfied about the Maner, and that was the Ground of my
5 Unbelief. For I could not think that GOD being LOV would
neglect His Son, and therfore surely I was not His Son, nor He
Lov: becaus He had not Ascertaind me more carefully, that the
Bible was His Book from Heaven. Yet I was encouraged to hope
well, becaus the Matter was so Excellent, abov my Expectation.
10 And when I searched into it, I found the Way infinitly better then
if all the Angels in Heaven had brought it to me.

33

Had the Angels brought it to me alone, these Several Inconveniences had attended the Vision. 1. It had been but one Suddain Act wherin it was sent me: wheras Now GOD hath been all Ages in preparing it. 2. It had been don by inferior Ministers, whereas now it is don by GOD Himself. 3. Being Satan is able to Transform Him self into an Angel of Light, I had been still Dubious, till having recours to the Excellency of the Matter, by it I was informed and Satisfied. 4. Being Corrupted, that one Miracle would hav been but like a Single Spark upon green Wood, it would hav gon out immediatly: wheras I needed 10000 Miracles to Seal it, yea and to awaken me to the Meditation of the Matter that was revealed to me. 5. Had it been revealed no other Way, all the World had been Dark and Empty round about me: Wheras now it is my Joy and my Delight and Treasure, being full of Knowledg, Light, and Glory. 6. Had it been revealed at no other Time, God had now only been Good unto me, wheras He hath Manifested His Lov in all Ages, and been Carefully and most Wisely Revealing it from the Beginning of the World. 7. Had He revealed it to no other Person, I had been Weak in faith being Solitary, and sitting alone like a Sparrow upon the Hous top, who now have the Concurrent and joynt affections of Kingdoms and Ages. Yea notwithstanding the Disadvantage of this Weakness, I must hav gon abroad, and Published this faith to others, both in lov to God, and Lov to Men · for I must hav don my Duty, or the Book would hav don me no Good, and Lov to God and Men must hav been my Duty · for without that I could never be Happy. Yea finaly had not the Book been revealed before neither had GOD been Glorious, nor I Blessed, for He had been Negligent of other Persons, His Goodness had been Defectiv to all Ages, Whom now I Know to be GOD by the Universality of His Lov unto Mankind: and the Perfection of His wisdom to evry Person.

34

To talk now of the Necessity of bearing all Calamities and Persecutions in preaching, is little: to consider the Reproaches, Mockings and Derisions I must have endured of all the World, while they scoffed at me, for pretending to be the only man, that had a Book from Heaven; is Nothing: nor is it much to Mention the

Impossibility of Convincing others, all the World having been full
of Darkness, and God always Silent before. All Ages had been
void of Treasure had not the Bible been revealed till the other Day,
wherin now I can Expatiat with Perfect Liberty, and evry where
See the Lov of GOD to all Mankind. Lov to me alone. All the
World being adorned with Miracles Prophets Patriarchs Apostles,
Martyrs, Revelations from Heaven, Lively Examples, Holy Souls,
Divine Affairs, for my Enjoyment. The Glory of God and the
Light of Heaven appearing evrywhere, as much as it would hav
don in that seeming Instant, had the Book I desired com unto me
any other Way.

35

You will not believ what a World of Joy this one Satisfaction and
Pleasure brought me. Thenceforth I thought the Light of Heaven
was in this World: I saw it Possible, and very Probable, that I was
infinitly Beloved of Almighty God, the Delights of Paradice were
round about me, Heaven and Earth were open to me, all Riches
were little Things, this one Pleasure being so Great that it ex-
ceeded all the Joys of Eden. So Great a Thing it was to me, to be
satisfied in the Maner of Gods Revealing Himself unto Mankind.
Many other Enquiries I had concerning the Maner of His Reveal-
ing Himself, in all which I am infinitly satisfied.

36

Having been at the University, and received there the Taste and
Tincture of another Education, I saw that there were Things in
this World of which I never Dreamed, Glorious Secrets, and
Glorious Persons past Imagination. There I saw that Logick,
Ethicks, Physicks, Metaphysicks, Geometry, Astronomy, Poesie,
Medicine, Grammer, Musick, Rhetorick, all kind of Arts Trades
and Mechanicismes that Adorned the World pertained to felicity.
At least there I saw those Things, which afterwards I knew to per-
tain unto it: And was Delighted in it. There I saw into the Nature of
the Sea, the Heavens, the Sun, the Moon and Stars, the Elements,
Minerals and Vegetables. All which appeared like the Kings
Daughter, All Glorious within, and those Things which my Nurses
and Parents should hav talkt of, there were taught unto Me.

37

Nevertheless som things were Defectiv too. There was never a
Tutor that did professely Teach Felicity: tho that be the Mistress
of all other Sciences. Nor did any of us Study these things but as
Aliena, which we ought to hav Studied as our own Enjoyments.
We Studied to inform our Knowledg, but knew not for what End ₅
we so Studied. And for lack of aiming at a Certain End, we Erred in
the Maner. How beit there we received all those Seeds of Know-
ledg that were afterwards improved; and our Souls were Awakened
to a Discerning of their faculties, and Exercise of their Powers.

38

The Maner is in evry thing of greatest Concernment. Whatever
Good thing we do, neither can we pleas God, unless we do it
Well: nor can He pleas us, whatever Good He does, unless He do
it *well*. Should He giv us the most Perfect Things in Heaven and
Earth to make us Happy, and not giv them to us in the Best of all ₅
Possible Maners, He would but Displeas us, and it were Impossible
for Him to make us Happy. It is not Sufficient therfore for us to
Study, the most excellent Things unless we do it in the most Excel-
lent of Maners. And what that is it is impossible to find till we are
Guided therunto by the Most Excellent End · with a Desire of ₁₀
which I flagrantly Burned.

39

The Best of all Possible Ends is the Glory of GOD, but Happiness
was that I thirsted after. And yet I did not erre · for the Glory of God
is to make us Happy. Which can never be don but by giving us most
Excellent Natures and Satisfying those Natures: by Creating all
Treasures of infinit Valu, and giving them to us in an infinit maner, ₅
to wit both in the Best that to Omnipotence was possible. This led
me to Enquire, Whither All Things were Excellent and of Perfect
Valu, and whither they were mine in Propriety?

40

It is the Glory of God to giv all Things to us in the Best of all
possible maners. To Study Things therfore under the Double
Notion of Interest and Treasure, is to study all Things in the Best
of all possible Maners. Becaus in Studying so we Enquire after

5 GODs Glory and our own Happiness. And indeed enter into the Way that leadeth to all Contentments Joys and Satisfactions, to all Praises Triumphs and Thanksgivings, to All Virtues Beauties Adorations and Graces, to all Dominion Exaltation Wisdom and Glory, to all Holiness, Union and Communion with GOD, 10 to all Patience and Courage and Blessedness, which it is impossible to meet any other Way. So that to Study Object for Ostentation, vain Knowledg or Curiosity is fruitless Impertinence · tho GOD Himself, and Angels, be the Object. But to Study that which will Oblige us to lov Him, and Feed us with Nobility and 15 Goodness toward Men, that is Blessed. And so is it to Study that, which will lead us to the Temple of Wisdom, and Seat us in the Throne of Glory.

41

Many Men Study the same Things, which hav not the Taste of, nor Delight in them. And their Palates vary according to the Ends, at which they Aim. He that Studies Politie Men and Maners, meerly that He may know how to behav Himself and get Honor 5 in this World · has not that Delight in his Studies, as He that Contemplats these things that He might see the Ways of God among them: and Walk in Communion with Him. The Attainments of the one are narrow, the other Grows a Celestial King of all Kingdoms. Kings Minister unto Him, Temples are His Own, 10 Thrones are his Peculiar Treasure. Governments Officers Magistrates and Courts of Judicature are His Delights in a way ineffable, and a maner unconceivable to the others Imagination. He that Knows the Secrets of Nature with Albertus Magnus, or the Motions of the Heavens with Galilao, or the Cosmography of the Moon 15 with Hevelius, or the Body of Man with Galen, or the Nature of Diseases with Hippocrates, or the Harmonies in Melody with Orpheus, or of Poesie with Homer, or of Grammer with Lilly, or of whatever els with the greatest Artist; He is nothing · if he Knows them meerly for Talk or idle Speculation, or Transeunt and Ex- 20 ternal Use. But He that Knows them for Valu, and Knows them His own: shall Profit infinitly. And therfore of all Kind of Learnings, Humanity and Divinity are the most Excellent.

42

By Humanity we search into the Powers and Faculties of the Soul,
enquire into the Excellencies of Humane Nature, consider its
Wants, Survey its Inclinations Propensities and Desires. Ponder its
Principles Proposals and Ends, Examine the Causes and fitness of
all, the Worth of all, the Excellency of all. Wherby we com to know 5
what Man is in this World, What his Soveraign End and Happiness,
and what is the Best Means by which He may attain it. And by this
we com to see what Wisdom is: Which namely is a Knowledg Exer-
cised in finding out the Way to Perfect Happiness, by discerning
Mans real Wan[t]s and Soveraign Desires. We com more over to 10
Know Gods Goodness, in seeing into the Causes, wherfore He im-
planted such faculties and Inclinations in us, and the Objects, and
Ends prepared for them. This leadeth us to Divinity. For God
gav Man an Endless Intellect to see All Things, and a Proneness
to covet them, becaus they are His Treasures; and an infinit 15
Variety of Apprehensions and Affections, that he might hav an
Allsufficiency in Him self to Enjoy them: A Curiositie Profound
and Unsatiable to stir him up to look into them: An Ambition Great
and Everlasting to Carry him to the Highest Honors Thrones and
Dignities. An Emulation wherby he might be animated and 20
Quickned by all Examples, a Tendernes and Compassion wherby
He may be united to all Persons; A Sympathy and Lov to Vertu,
a Tenderness of His Credit in evry Soul, that He might Delight to
be Honored in all Persons: an Ey to behold Eternity and the
Omnipresence of GOD, that He might see Eternity and Dwell 25
within it: A Power of Admiring Loving and Prizing, that seeing the
Goodness and Beauty of God, He might be United to it for ever-
more.

43

In Divinity we are entertained with all Objects from Everlasting
to Everlasting: becaus with Him whose Outgoings from Ever-
lasting: being to Contemplat GOD, and to Walk with Him in all
His Ways: And therfore to be Entertained with all Objects, as He
is the Fountain, Governor, and End of them. We are to Contem- 5
plat GOD in the Unity of His Essence, in the Trinity of Persons,
in His Manifold Attributes, in all His Works, Internal and External,
in his Counsels and Decrees, in the Work of Creation, and in His

Works of Providence. And Man, as he is a Creature of GOD,
10 capable of Celestial Blessedness, and a Subject in His Kingdom:
in his fourfold Estate of Innocency, Misery, Grace and Glory.
In the Estate of Innocency we are to Contemplate the Nature and
Maner of His Happiness, the Laws under which He was governed,
the Joys of Paradice, and the Immaculat Powers of His Immortal
15 Soul. In the Estate of Misery we hav his Fall, the Nature of Sin
Original and Actual, His Manifold Punishments Calamity Sickness
Death &c. In the Estate of Grace; the Tenor of the New Covenant,
the maner of its Exhibition under the various Dispensations of the
Old and New Testament, the Mediator of the Covenant, the Con-
20 ditions of it Faith and Repentance, the Sacraments or Seals of it,
the Scriptures Ministers and Sabbaths, the Nature and Govern-
ment of the Church, its Histories and Successions from the Begin-
ning to the End of the World. &c. In the State of Glory; the Nature
of Seperat Souls, their Advantages Excellencies and Privileges,
25 the Resurrection of the Body the Day of Judgement and Life
Everlasting. Wherin further we are to see and understand the
Communion of Saints, Heavenly Joys, and our Society with
Angels. To all which I was naturaly Born, to the fruition of all
which I was by Grace redeemed, and in the Enjoyment of all
30 which I am to liv Eternaly.

44

Natural Philosophy teaches us the Causes and Effects of all Bodies
simply and in them selvs. But if you extend it a little further, to
that indeed which its Name imports, signifying the Lov of Nature,
it leads us into a Diligent inquisition into all Natures, their Qualities,
5 Affections, Relations, Causes and Ends, so far forth as by Nature
and Reason they may be Known. And this Noble Science, as such
is most Sublime and Perfect, it includes all Humanity and
Divinity together GOD, Angels, Men, Affections, Habits, Actions,
Virtues; Evry Thing as it is a Solid intire Object singly proposed,
10 being a Subject of it, as well as Material and visible Things. But
taking it as it is usualy Bounded in its Terms, it treateth only of
Corporeal Things, as Heaven, Earth, Air, Water, Fire, the Sun
and Stars, Trees Herbs, flowers, Influences, Winds, Fowles
Beasts Fishes Minerals and Precious Stones; with all other Beings
15 of that Kind. And as thus it is taken it is Nobly Subservient to

the Highest Ends: for it Openeth the Riches of Gods Kingdom, and the Nature of His Territories Works and Creatures in a Wonderfull Maner, Clearing and preparing the Ey of the Enjoyer.

45

Ethicks teach us the Mysteries of Moralitie, and the Nature of Affections Virtues and Maners, as by them we may be Guided to our Highest Happiness. The former for Speculation, this for Practice. The former furnisheth us with Riches, this with Honors and Delights, the former feasteth us, and this instructeth us. For by this 5 we are taught to liv Honorably among men, and to make our selvs Noble and Usefull among them. It teacheth us how to Manage our Passions, to Exercise Virtues, and to form our Maners, so as to liv Happily in this World. And all these put together Discover the Materials of Religion to be so Great, that it Plainly manifesteth the 10 Revelation of GOD to be Deep and Infinit. For it is impossible for Language, Miracles, or Apparitions to teach us the Infallibility of GODs Word or to shew us the Certainty of true Religion, without a Clear Sight into Truth it self that is into the Truth of Things. Which will them selvs when truly seen, by the very Beauty and 15 Glory of them, best Discover, and Prov Religion.

46

When I came into the Country, and being seated among silent Trees, had all my Time in mine own Hands, I resolved to Spend it all, whatever it cost me, in Search of Happiness, and to Satiat that burning Thirst which Nature had Enkindled, in me from my Youth. In which I was so resolut, that I chose rather to liv upon 5 10 pounds a yeer, and to go in Lether Clothes, and feed upon Bread and Water, so that I might hav all my time clearly to my self: then to keep many thousands per Annums in an Estate of Life where my Time would be Devoured in Care and Labor. And GOD was so pleased to accept of that Desire, that from that time to this 10 I hav had all things plentifully provided for me, without any Care at all, my very Study of Felicity making me more to Prosper, then all the Care in the Whole World. So that through His Blessing I liv a free and a Kingly Life, as if the World were turned again into Eden, or much more, as it is at this Day. 15

47

1

A life of Sabbaths here beneath!
Continual Jubilees and Joys!
The Days of Heaven, while we breath
On Earth! Where Sin all Bliss Destroys.
This is a Triumph of Delights!
That doth exceed all Appetites.
No Joy can be Compard to this,
It is a Life of Perfect Bliss.

2

Of perfect Bliss! How can it be?
To Conquer Satan, and to Reign
In such a Vale of Miserie,
Where Vipers, Stings and Tears remain;
Is to be Crownd with Victorie.
To be Content, Divine and free,
Even here beneath is Great Delight
And next the Beatifick Sight.

3

But inward Lusts do oft assail,
Temptations Work us much Annoy.
Weel therfore Weep, and to prevail
Shall be a more Celestial Joy.
To hav no other Enemie,
But one; and to that one to Die:
To fight with that and Conquer it,
Is better then in Peace to sit.

4

Tis Better for a little time:
For He that all His Lusts doth quell,
Shall find this Life to be His Prime,
And Vanquish Sin and Conquer Hell.
The Next shall be His Double Joy:
And that which here seemd to Destroy,
Shall in the Other Life appear
A Root of Bliss; a Pearl each Tear.

48

Thus you see I can make Merry with Calamities, and while I griev at Sins, and War against them, abhorring the World, and my self more: Descend into the Abysses of Humilitie, and there Admire a New Offspring and Torrent of Joys, GODs Mercies. Which accepteth of our fidelity in Bloody Battails, tho every Wound defile 5 and Poyson; and when we slip or fall, turneth our true Penitent Tears into Solid Pearl, that shall abide with Him for evermore. But Oh let us take heed that we never Willingly commit a Sin against so Gracious a Redeemer, and so Great a Father.

49

Sin!
O only fatal Woe,
That makst me Sad and Mourning go!
That all my Joys dost Spoil,
His Kingdom and my Soul Defile!   5
I never can Agree
With Thee!

2

Thou!
Only Thou! O Thou alone,
(And my Obdurat Heart of Stone,)   10
The Poyson and the Foes
Of my Enjoyments and Repose,
The only Bitter Ill:
Dost Kill!

3

Oh!   15
I cannot meet with Thee,
Nor once approach thy Memory,
But all my Joys are Dead,
And all my Sacred Treasures fled;
As if I now did Dwell   20
In Hell.

4

Lord!
O hear how short I Breath!
See how I Tremble here beneath!
A Sin! Its Ugly face
More Terror, then its Dwelling Place,
Contains, (O Dreadfull Sin)
Within!

50

The Recovery

Sin! wilt Thou vanquish me!
And shall I yeeld the victory?
Shall all my Joys be Spoild,
And Pleasures soild
By Thee!
Shall I remain
As one thats Slain
And never more lift up the Head?
Is not my Savior Dead!
His Blood, thy Bane; my Balsam, Bliss, Joy, Wine;
Shall Thee Destroy; Heal, Feed, make me Divine.

51

I cannot meet with Sin, but it Kils me, and tis only by Jesus Christ
that I can Kill it, and Escape. Would you blame me to be confounded,
when I have offended my Eternal Father, who gav me all the Things
in Heaven and Earth? One Sin is a Dreadfull Stumbling Block in
the Way to Heaven. It breeds a long Parenthesis in the fruition of
our Joys. Do you not see my Friend, how it Disorders and Disturbs
my Proceeding? There is no Calamity but Sin alone.

52

When I came into the Country, and saw that I had all time in my
own hands, having devoted it wholy to the Study of Felicitie,
I knew not where to begin or End; nor what Objects to chuse,
upon which most profitably I might fix my Contemplation. I saw
my self like som Traveller, that had Destined his Life to journeys,
and was resolvd to spend his Days in visiting Strange Places: who

might wander in vain, unless his Undertakings were guided by som
certain Rule; and that innumerable Millions of Objects were pre-
sented before me, unto any of which I might take my journey · fain
I would hav visited them all, but that was impossible. What then 10
should I do? Even imitat a Traveller, who becaus He cannot visit
all Coasts, Wildernesses, Sandy Deserts, Seas, Hills, Springs and
Mountains, chuseth the most Populous and flourishing Cities,
where he might see the fairest Prospects, Wonders, and Rarities,
and be entertained with greatest Courtesie: and where indeed he 15
might most Benefit himself with Knowledg Profit and Delight:
leaving the rest, even the naked and Empty Places unseen. For
which caus I made it my Prayer to GOD Almighty, that He, whose
Eys are open upon all Things, would guid me to the fairest and
Divinest.

                                                                  20

53

And what Rule do you think I walked by? Truly a Strange one,
but the Best in the Whole World. I was Guided by an Implicit Faith
in Gods Goodness: and therfore led to the Study of the most
Obvious and Common Things. For thus I thought within my self:
GOD being, as we generaly believ, infinit in Goodness, it is most 5
Consonant and Agreeable with His Nature, that the Best Things
should be most Common · for nothing is more Naturall to infinit
Goodness, then to make the Best Things most frequent; and only
Things Worthless, Scarce. Then I began to Enquire what Things
were most Common: Air, Light, Heaven and Earth, Water, the 10
Sun, Trees, Men and Women, Cities Temples &c. These I found
Common and Obvious to all: Rubies Pearls Diamonds Gold and
Silver, these I found scarce, and to the most Denied. Then began
I to consider and compare the value of them, which I measured by
their Serviceableness, and by the Excellencies which would be 15
found in them, should they be taken away. And in Conclusion I
saw clearly, that there was a Real Valuableness in all the Common
things; in the Scarce, a feigned.

54

Besides these Common things I hav named, there were others as
Common, but Invisible. The Laws of God, the Soul of Man,
Jesus Christ and His Passion on the Crosse, with the Ways of GOD
in all Ages. And these by the General Credit they had Obtained

5 in the World confirmed me more. For the Ways of God were
transeunt Things, they were past and gon; our Saviors Sufferings
were in one particular Obscure Place, the Laws of God were no
Object of the Ey, but only found in the Minds of Men; these ther-
fore which were so Secret in their own Nature, and made common
10 only by the Esteem Men had of them, must of Necessity include
unspeakable Worth for which they were celebrated, of all, and so
generaly remembered. As yet I did not see the Wisdom and Depths
of Knowledg, the Clear Principles, and Certain Evidences wherby
the Wise and Holy, the Ancients and the Learned that were abroad
15 in the World knew these Things, but was led to them only by the
fame which they had vulgarly received. Howbeit I believed that
there were unspeakable Mysteries contained in them, and tho they
were Generaly talkt of their valu was unknown. These therfore
I resolved to Study, and no other. But to my unspeakable Wonder,
20 they brought me to all the Things in Heaven and in Earth, in
Time and Eternity, Possible and Impossible, Great and Little,
Common and Scarce, and Discovered them all to be infinit
Treasures.

55

That any thing may be found to be an infinit Treasure, its Place
must be found in Eternity, and in Gods Esteem. For as there is a
Time, so there is a Place for all Things. Evry thing in its Place is
Admirable Deep and Glorious: out of its Place like a Wandering
5 Bird, is Desolat and Good for Nothing. How therfore it relateth
to God and all Creatures must be seen before it can be Enjoyed.
And this I found by many Instances. The Sun is Good, only as
it relateth to the Stars, to the Seas, to your Ey, to the feilds, &c.
As it relateth to the Stars it raiseth their Influences; as to the Seas
10 it melteth them and maketh the Waters flow; as to your Ey, it
bringeth in the Beauty of the World; as to the feilds; it clotheth
them with Fruits and flowers: Did it not relate to others it would
not be Good. Divest it of these Operations, and Divide it from
these Objects it is Useless and Good for nothing. And therfore
15 Worthless, because Worthles and Useless go together. A Piece of
Gold cannot be Valued, unless we Know how it relates to Clothes,
to Wine, to Victuals, to the Esteem of Men, and to the Owner.
Som little Piece in a Kingly Monument severd from the rest hath

no Beauty at all. It enjoys its valu in its Place, by the Ornament it
gives to, and receivs from all the Parts. By this I discerned, that 20
even a little Knowledg could not be had in the Mysterie of Felicity,
without a great deal. And that that was the reason why so many
were ignorant of its nature, and why so few did attain it · for by the
Labor required to much Knowledg they were discouraged, and for
lack of much did not see any Glorious motives to allure them.   25

56

Therfore of Necessity they must at first believ that Felicity is a
Glorious tho an unknown Thing. And certainly it was the infinit
Wisdom of God, that did implant by Instinct so strong a Desire
of felicity in the Soul, that we might be excited to labor after it,
tho we know it not, the very force wherwith we covet it supplying 5
the place of Understanding. That there is a Felicyty we all know
by the Desires after, that there is a most Glorious felicity we know by
the Strength and vehemence of those Desires: And that nothing
but Felicity is worthy of our Labor, becaus all other things are the
Means only which conduce unto it. I was very much animated by 10
the Desires of Philosophers, which I saw in Heathen Books aspiring
after it. But the misery is *It was unknown.* An altar was erected to
it like that in Athens with this inscription TO THE UNKNOWN
GOD.

57

Two things in Perfect Felicity I saw to be requisite: and that
Felicity must be perfect, or not Felicity. The first was the Perfection
of its Objects, in Nature Serviceableness Number and Excellency.
The second was the Perfection of the Maner wherin they are
Enjoyed, for Sweetness Measure and Duration. And unless in these 5
I could be satisfied I should never be contented. Especialy about
the later · for the Maner is always more Excellent [than] the Thing.
And it far more concerneth us that the Maner wherin we enjoy be
compleat and Perfect: then that the Matter which we Enjoy be
compleat and Perfect. For the Maner as we contemplat its Excel- 10
lency is it self a great Part of the Matter of our Enjoyment.

58

In Discovering the Matter or Objects to be Enjoyed, I was greatly aided by remembering that we were made in Gods Image. For thereupon it must of Necessity follow that GODs Treasures be our Treasures, and His Joys our Joys. So that by enquiring what
5 were GODs, I found the Objects of our felicity Gods Treasures being ours· for we were made in his Image that we might liv in His similitud. And herin I was mightily confirmed by the Apostles Blaming the Gentiles, and charging it upon them as a very great Fault that they were alienated from the life of God, for herby I
10 perceived that we were to liv the Life of God: when we lived the tru life of Nature according to Knowledg: and that by Blindness and Corruption we had Strayed from it. Now GODs Treasures are his own Perfections, and all His Creatures.

59

The Image of God implanted in us, guided me to the maner wherin we were to Enjoy· for since we were made in the similitud of God, we were made to Enjoy after his Similitude. Now to Enjoy the Treasures of God in the Similitud of God, is the most perfect
5 Blessedness God could Devise. For the Treasures of GOD are the most Perfect Treasures and the Maner of God is the most perfect Maner. To Enjoy therfore the Treasures of God after the similitud of God is to Enjoy the most perfect Treasures in the most Perfect Maner. Upon which I was infinitly satisfied in God, and knew
10 there was a Dietie, becaus I was Satisfied. For Exerting Himself wholy in atchieving thus an infinit felicity He was infinitly Delightfull Great and Glorious, and my Desires so August and Insatiable that nothing less then a Deity could satisfy them.

60

This Spectacle once seen, will never be forgotten. It is a Great Part of the Beatifick Vision. A Sight of Happiness is Happiness. It transforms the Soul and makes it Heavenly, it powerfully calls us to Communion with God, and weans us from the Customs of
5 this World. It puts a Lustre upon GOD and all his Creatures, and makes us to see them in a Divine and Eternal Light. I no sooner discerned this but I was (as Plato saith, In summâ Rationis Arce Quies habitat) seated in a Throne of Repose and Perfect Rest.

All Things were well in their Proper Places, I alone was out of
frame and had need to be Mended · for all things were Gods 10
Treasures in their Proper places, and I was to be restored to Gods
Image. Wherupon you will not believ how I was withdrawn from
all Endeavors of altering and Mending Outward Things. They lay
so well methoughts, they could not be Mended: but I must be
Mended to Enjoy them.   15

61

The Image of God is the most Perfect Creature. Since there cannot
be two GODs the utmost Endeavor of Almighty Power is the
Image of GOD. It is no Blasphemy to say that GOD cannot
make a GOD: the Greatest Thing that He can make is His Image:
A most Perfect Creature, to enjoy the most perfect Treasures, 5
in the most perfect Maner. A Creature endued with the most
Divine and perfect Powers, for Measure Kind Number Dura-
tion Excellency is the most Perfect Creature: Able to see all
Eternity with all its Objects, and as a Mirror to Contain all it
seeth: Able to Lov all it contains, and as a Sun to shine upon its 10
loves. Able by Shining to communicat it self in Beams of Affec-
tion, and to Illustrat all it Illuminats with Beauty and Glory:
Able to be Wise Holy Glorious Blessed in it self as God is, being
adorned inwardly with the same kind of Beauty, and outwardly
Superior to all Creatures.   15

62

Upon this I began to believ that all other Creatures were such that
GOD was Himself, in their Creation · that is *Almighty Power
wholy exerted:* And that evry Creature is indeed as it seemed in
my infancy: not as it is commonly apprehended. Evry Thing being
Sublimely Rich and Great and Glorious. Evry Spire of Grass 5
is the Work of His Hand: And I in a World where evry Thing is
mine, and far better then the Greater sort of Children esteem
Diamonds and Pearls. Gold and Silver being the very Refuse of
Nature, and the Worst Things in Gods Kingdom. Howbeit truly
Good in their Proper Places.   10

63

To be satisfied in God is the Highest Difficulty in the whole
World. And yet most easy to be don. To make it possible that
we should be satisfied in GOD was an Atchievment of infinit
Weight, before it was attempted, and the most difficult Thing in
5 all Worlds before it was Attchieved. For we naturaly expect infinit
Things of God: and can be satisfied only with the Highest Reason.
So that the Best of all Possible Things must be wrought in God,
or els we shall remain Dissatisfied. But it is most Easy at present,
becaus GOD is. For GOD is not a Being compounded of Body
10 and Soul, or Substance and Accident, or Power and Act but is
All Act, Pure Act, a Simple Being. Whose Essence is to be, Whose
Being is to be Perfect, so that He is most Perfect towards all and
in all. He is most Perfect for all and by all. He is in Nothing im-
perfect becaus His Being is to be Perfect. It is Impossible for Him
15 to be GOD, and Imperfect: And therfore do we so Ardently and
infinitly desire His Absolut Perfection.

64

Neither is it Possible to be otherwise. All his Power being turned
into Act, it is all Exerted: infinitly, and wholy. Neither is there any
Power in Him Which He is not Able, and Willing to use: or which
He cannot Wisely Guid to most Excellent Ends. So that we may
5 expect most Angelical and Heavenly Rarities in all the Creatures.
Were there any Power in GOD unimployed He would be Com-
pounded of Power and Act. Being therfore GOD is all Act, He is
a GOD in this, that Himself is Power Exerted. An infinit Act
becaus infinit Power infinitly Exerted· an Eternal Act becaus infinit
10 Power Eternaly Exerted. Wherin consisteth the Generation of His
son, the Perfection of His Lov, and the Immutability of GOD. For
GOD by Exerting Himself begot His Son, and doing [it] wholy, for
the sake of His Creatures is perfect Lov: and doing it wholy from all
Eternity, is an Eternal Act and therfore Unchangable.

65

With this we are Delighted becaus it is absolutly impossible that
any Power Dwelling with Lov should continu Idle. Since GOD
therfore was infinitly and Eternaly Communicativ, all Things were
Contained in Him from all Eternitie. As Nazianzen in his 38th
5 Oration admirably Expresseth it, in these Words, *Becaus it was*

by no means sufficient for GOODNESS to move only in the Con-
templation of it self: but it became what was GOOD to be Diffused
and Propagated, that more might be affected with the Benefit (for this
was the part of the Highest Goodness:) first He thought upon Angelical
and Celestial Vertues, and that Thought was the Work, which he 10
wrought by the WORD, and fulfilled by the Spirit. Atque ita Secundi
Splendores Procreati Sunt primi Splendoris Administri. And so were
there Second Splendors Created, and made to Minister to the first
Splendor, so that all Motions Successions Creatures and Opera-
tions with their Beginnings and Ends were in Him from Everlasting. 15
To whom Nothing can be Added, becaus from all Eternity He was,
whatsoever to all Eternity He can be. All Things being now to be
seen and Contemplated in His Bosom: and Advanced therfore into
a Diviner Light, being infinitly Older and more Precious then we
were aware. Time itself being in GOD Eternaly.   20

66

Little did I imagine that while I was thinking these Things I was
Conversing with GOD. I was so Ignorant that I did not think any
Man in the World had had such thoughts before. Seeing them
therfore so Amiable, I wonderd not a little, that nothing was
Spoken of them in former Ages· but as I read the Bible I was here 5
and there Surprized with such Thoughts, and found by Degrees
that these Things had been written of before, not only in the Scrip-
tures but in many of the Fathers and that this was the Way of
Communion with God in all Saints, as I saw Clearly in the Person
of David. Me thoughts a New Light Darted in into all his Psalmes, 10
and finaly spread abroad over the whole Bible. So that things which
for their Obscurity I thought not in being were there contained:
Things which for their Greatness were incredible, were made
Evident and Things Obscure, Plain. GOD by this means bringing
me into the very Heart of His Kingdom.   15

67

There I saw Moses blessing the Lord for the Precious Things of
Heaven, for the Dew and for the Deep that coucheth beneath:
and for the precious fruits brought forth by the Sun, and for the
precious things put forth by the Moon: and for the chief things of
the ancient Mountains and for the precious things of the lasting 5

Hills: and for the precious things of the Earth, and fulness therof. There I saw Jacob, with Awfull Apprehensions Admiring the Glory of the World, when awaking out of His Dream he said, How dreadfull is this Place? This is none other then the Hous of
10 GOD, and the Gate of Heaven. There I saw GOD leading forth Abraham, and shewing him the Stars of Heaven; and all the Countries round about him, and saying All these will I give Thee, and thy Seed after thee. There I saw Adam in Paradice, Surrounded with the Beauty of Heaven and Earth, void of all Earthly
15 Comforts to wit such as were devised, Gorgeous Apparel, Palaces, Gold and Silver, Coaches, Musical Instruments &c, And entertained only with Celestial Joys. The Sun and Moon and Stars, Beasts and fowles and fishes, Trees and fruits and flowers, with the other Naked and Simple Delights of Nature. By which I
20 evidently saw, that the Way to becom Rich and Blessed, was not by heaping Accidental and Devised Riches to make ourselvs great in the vulgar maner; but to approach more near, and to see more Clearly with the Ey of our understanding, the Beauties and Glories of the whole world: and to hav communion with the Diety in the
25 Riches of GOD and Nature.

68

I saw moreover that it did not so much concern us what Objects were before us, as with what Eys we beheld them; with what Affections we esteemed them, and what Apprehensions we had about them. All men see the same Objects, but do not equaly under-
5 stand them. Intelligence is the Tongue that discerns and Tastes them, Knowledg is the Light of Heaven. Lov is the Wisdom and Glory of GOD. Life Extended to all Objects, is the Sence that enjoys them. So that Knowledg Life and Lov, are the very means of all Enjoyment · which abov all Things we must seek for and
10 Labor after. All Objects are in God Eternal: which we by perfecting our faculties are made to Enjoy. Which then are turned into Act when they are exercised about their Objects · but without them are Desolat and Idle; or Discontented and forlorn. Wherby I perceived the Meaning of that Definition wherin Aristotle Describeth Felicity ·
15 when he saith Felicity is the Perfect Exercise of Perfect Virtu in a Perfect Life · for Life is perfect when it is perfectly Extended to all Objects, and perfectly sees them and perfectly loves them: which is don by a perfect Exercise of Virtu about them.

69

In Salem dwelt a Glorious King,
    Raisd from a Shepherds lowly State,
That did his Praises like an Angel sing
        Who did the World create.
    By many great and Bloody Wars,   5
    He was Advanced unto Thrones:
    But more Delighted in the Stars,
Then in the Splendor of His Precious Stones.
Nor Gold nor Silver did his Ey regard:
The Works of GOD were his Sublime Reward.   10

2

    A Warlike Champion he had been
    And Many feats of Chivalrie
Had don: in Kingly Courts his Ey had seen
        A Vast Variety
    Of Earthly Joys: Yet he despis'd   15
    Those fading Honors, and fals pleasures
    Which are by Mortals so much Prizd;
And placd his Happiness in other Treasures
No State of Life which in this World we find
Could yeeld contentment to his greater Mind.   20

3

    His fingars touchd his Trembling Lyre,
    And evry Quavering String did yeeld,
A Sound that filled all the Jewish Quire
        And Ecchoed in the Field.
    No Pleasure was so Great to Him   25
    As in a Silent Night to see
    The Moon and Stars: A Cherubim
Abov them even here He seemd to be.
Enflamd with Lov it was his great Desire,
To Sing Contemplat Ponder and Admire.   30

4

    He was a Prophet, and foresaw
    Things extant in the World to com:
He was a Judg, and ruled by a Law
        That then the Hony Comb

§ 69. After this poem about David, T quotes freely from the Psalms until § 94.

35   Was Sweeter far: He was a Sage,
   And all His People could Advise;
   An Oracle, whose evry Page
Contain'd in vers the Greatest Mysteries
But most He then Enjoyd Himself, when he
40 Did as a Poet prais the Dietie.

     5

   A Shepherd, Soldier, and Divine,
   A Judge, a Courtier, and a King,
Priest, Angel, Prophet, Oracle did shine
    At once; when He did sing.
45   Philosopher and Poet too
   Did in his Melodie appear;
   All these in Him did pleas the View
Of Those that did his Heavenly Musick hear
And evry Drop that from his flowing Quill
50 Came down, did all the World with Nectar fill.

     6

   He had a Deep and perfect Sence
   Of all the Glories and the Pleasures
That in Gods Works are hid, the Excellence
    Of such Transcendent Treasures
55   Made him on Earth an Heavenly King,
   And fil'd his Solitudes with Joy;
   He never did more Sweetly Sing
Then when alone, tho that doth Mirth destroy.
Sence did his Soul with Heavenly Life inspire
60 And made him seem in Gods Celestial Quire.

     7

   Rich Sacred Deep and Precious Things
   Did here on Earth the Man surround
With all the Glory of the King of Kings
    He was most strangely Crownd.
65   His Clear Soul and Open Sight
   Among the Sons of GOD did see

Things filling Angels with Delight
His Ear did hear their Heavenly Melodie
And when He was alone He all became,
That Bliss implied, or did increas His Fame.   70

                    8

All Arts He then did Exercise
And as His GOD He did Adore
By Secret Ravishments abov the Skies
      He carried was, before
He died. His Soul did see and feel   75
What others know not; and became
While He before his GOD did kneel
A Constant Heavenly Pure Seraphick Flame.
Oh that I might unto His Throne Aspire;
And all His Joys abov the Stars Admire!   80

                    70

When I saw those Objects celebrated in His Psalmes which GOD
and Nature had proposed to me, and which I thought Chance only
presented to my view: you cannot imagine how unspeakably I was
delighted, to see so Glorious a Person, so Great a Prince, so Divine
a Sage, that was a Man after Gods own Heart by the testimony 5
of God Himself, rejoycing in the same things, meditating on the
same and Praising GOD for the same. For by this I perceived we
were led by one Spirit: and that following the clew of Nature into
this Labyrinth I was brought into the midst of Celestial Joys: and
that to be retired from Earthly Cares and fears and Distractions 10
that we might in sweet and heavenly Peace contemplat all the Works
of GOD, was to live in Heaven and the only way to becom what
David was a Man after Gods own Heart. There we might be en-
flamed with those Causes for which we ought to lov Him: there we
might see those Viands which feed the Soul with Angels food: 15
there we might Bath in those Streams of Pleasure that flow at His
Right Hand for evermore.

                    71

That Hymn of David in the eighth Psalm, was supposed to be made
by night, wherin he celebrateth the Works of God; becaus he
mentioneth the Moon and Stars, but not the Sun in his meditation.

When I consider the Heavens which Thou hast made, the Moon
5 and Stars which are the Works of thy fingars, What is Man that
Thou art Mindfull of him, or the Son of man that Thou visitest
him? Thou hast made him a little lower then the Angels, and hast
crowned him with Glory and Honor. Thou hast given him Dominion
over the Works of thy Hands, Thou hast put all things in Subjec-
10 tion under his feet: All Sheep and Oxen, yea and the Beasts of the
field: the fowls of the Air and the fishes of the Sea, and whatsoever
passeth through the Paths of the Sea. This Glory and Honor
wherwith Man is Crowned ought to affect evry Person, that is
Gratefull, with celestial Joy: and so much the rather, becaus it is
15 evry mans proper and sole Inheritance.

72

His Joyfull Meditation in the nineteenth Psalm directeth evry
Man to consider the Glory of Heaven and Earth. The Heavens
declare the Glory of God, and the firmament sheweth His Handy-
work. Day unto Day uttereth Speech, and Night unto Night
5 sheweth Knowledg. There is no Speech nor Language where their
voice is not heard. Their Line is gon throughout all the Earth,
and their voice to the End of the World. In them hath He set a
Tabernacle for the Sun, which is as a Bridegroom coming out of his
chamber, and rejoyceth as a Strong Man to run his Race. His going
10 forth is from the End of the heaven, and his Circuit to the Ends
of it, and nothing is hid from the heat therof. From thence he
proceedeth to the Laws of God, as Things more Excellent in their
Nature then His Works. The Law of the Lord is perfect converting
the Soul; the Testimony of the Lord is sure making Wise the
15 Simple. The Statutes of the Lord are right rejoycing the Heart,
the Commandment of the Lord is pure Enlightening the Eys.
The fear of the Lord is clean Enduring for ever, the Judgments of
the Lord are true and righteous altogether. More to be desired
are they then Gold, yea then much fine Gold; Sweeter also then
20 honey and the Honeycomb. Wherby he plainly sheweth that
Divine and Kingly Delights are in the Laws and Works of God
to be taken, by all those that would be Angelical and Celestial
Creatures. For that in the Kingdom of Heaven evry one being dis-
entangled from Particular Relations and Private Riches, as if he
25 were newly taken out of Nothing to the fruition of all Eternity, was
in these alone to Solace himself as his peculiar Treasures.

73

Ye that fear the Lord Prais Him; All ye Seed of Jacob Glorify Him,
and fear Him all ye Seed of Israel. For He hath not despised nor ab-
horred the Affliction of the Afflicted, neither hath He hid His face
from him, but when he cried unto Him, He heard. My Prais shall be
of Thee in the great Congregation; I will pay my vows before them   5
that fear Him. The Meek shall Eat and be satisfied. They shall Prais
the Lord that seek Him; your Heart shall liv for ever. All the Ends
of the World shall remember and turn unto the Lord, all the
Kindreds of the Nations shall Worship before Thee. For the King-
dom is the Lords, and He is the Governor among the Nations. All   10
they that be fat upon Earth shall Eat and Worship: all they that go
down to the Dust shall bow before Him, and none can Keep alive
his own Soul. A Seed shall serv Him, it shall be counted to the Lord
for a Generation. They shall com and declare His Righteousness to
a people that shall be born, that He hath don this. Here he sheweth   15
that it was his desire and Delight to hav all Nations Praising God:
and that the Condescention of the Almighty in Stooping down to
the Poor and Needy was the Joy of his Soul. He prophesieth also of
the Conversion of the Gentiles to the Knowledg of Jesus Christ,
which to see was to him an Exceeding Pleasure.   20

74

The Earth is the Lords and the fullness therof, the round World and
they that dwell therin. He observeth here that GOD by a compre-
hensiv Possession and by Way of Eminence, enjoyeth the whole
World; All Mankind and all the Earth, with all that is therin, being
His peculiar Treasures. Since therfore we are made in the Image of   5
God, to liv in his Similitud, as they are His, they must be our
Treasures. We being Wise and Righteous over all as He is. Becaus
they regard not the Works of the Lord, nor the Operation of His
hands, therfore shall He destroy them and not build them up.

75

By the Word of the Lord were the Heavens made, and all the Host
of them by the Breath of His Mouth. He gathereth the Waters of the
Sea together, He laieth up the Depth in Storehouses. Let all the
Earth fear the Lord, let all the Inhabitants of the World stand in
Awe of Him. For He spake, and it was don, He commanded and it   5

stood fast. He frequently meditateth upon the Works of God, and affirmeth the Contemplation of them to beget His fear in our Hearts · for that He being great in Strength, not one faileth.

76

All my Bones shall say, Lord who is like unto Thee, who deliverest the Poor from him that is too strong for him; yea the Poor and the Needy from him that Spoileth him! Thy Mercy O Lord is abov the Heavens and Thy Faithfulness reacheth to the clouds. Thy Right-
5 eousness is like the great Mountains, thy Judgments are a great Deep: O Lord thou preservest Man and Beast. How Excellent is Thy Loving Kindness O God! therfore the Children of Men put their Trust under the Shadow of thy Wings. They shall be abundantly satisfied with the fatness of thy Hous; and Thou shalt make them
10 Drink of the River of thy Pleasures. For with Thee is the fountain of Life. In thy Light we shall see Light. The Judgments of God, and his Loving Kindness, His Mercy and faithfulness, are the fatness of his Hous, and his Righteousness being seen in the Light of Glory is the Torrent of Pleasure at His right hand for evermore.

77

Hearken O Daughter and consider, and incline thine Ear; forget also thine own People and thy fathers hous · so shall the King greatly desire thy Beauty for He is thy Lord and Worship thou Him. ¶The Kings Daughter is all Glorious within, her clothing is of
5 wrought Gold. She shall be brought unto the King in Raiment of Needle Work, the virgins her companions that follow her, shall be brought unto Thee. With Gladness and rejoycing shall they be brought, they shall enter into the Kings Palace. Instead of thy fathers shall be thy children whom thou mayest make Princes in
10 all the Earth. The Psalmist here singeth an Epithalamium upon the Marriage between Christ and His Church: whom he persuadeth to forsake her countrey and her fathers hous, together with all the customs and vanities of this World: and to Dedicat her self wholy to our Saviors Service · since she is in exchange to enter into His
15 Palace and becom a Bride to so Glorious a Person. The Bridegroom and the Bride, the Palace (which is all the World) with all that is therin, being Davids Joy and his true Possession. Nay evry Child of this Bride, is if a Male a Prince over all the Earth; if a Female

Bride to the King of Heaven. And evry Soul that is a Spous of
Jesus Christ, esteemeth all the Saints her own Children and her 20
own Bowels.

78

There is a River the streams wherof shall make Glad the City of
God; the holy Place of the Tabernacle of the most High. He
praiseth the Means of Grace, which in the Midst of this World are
Great Consolations · and in all Distresses refresh our Souls. Com
behold the Works of the Lord, what Desolations he hath made in 5
the Earth. He exhorteth us to Contemplat Gods Works, which are
so perfect, that when His Secret and just Judgments are seen, the
very destruction of Nations, and laying waste of Cities, shall be
Sweet and Delightfull.

79

O clap your Hands all ye people shout unto God with the voice of
Triumph. For the Lord most High is Terrible, He is a Great King
over all the Earth. He shall chuse our Inheritance for us, the Excel-
lency of Jacob whom He loved. Beautifull for Situation, the Joy
of the whole Earth is Mount Sion, on the Sides of the North the 5
City of the Great King. God is known in her Palaces for a Refuge.
Walk about Sion and go round about her, tell the Towers therof:
Mark ye well her Bulwarks, Consider her Palaces, that ye may tell
it to the Generation following. For this God is our God for ever and
ever. He will be our Guid even unto Death.   10

80

As in the former Psalms, he proposeth true and Celestial Joys, so in
this following he discovereth the vanity of fals imaginations. They
that trust in their Wealth, and boast them selvs in the Multitude of
their Riches, None of them can by any Means redeem his Brother,
or giv unto God a Ransom for him · for the Redemption of their Soul 5
is precious and it ceaseth forever. For he seeth that wise men die,
likewise the fool and the Bruitish Person perish, and leav their
Wealth to others. Their inward thought is, that their houses shall
continu for ever, and their Dwelling Places to all Generations: They
call their Lands after their own Names. This their Way is their folly, 10
yet their Posterity approve their Sayings. Like sheep they are laid in
the Grave, Death shall feed sweetly on them, and the Upright shall

hav Dominion over them in the Morning: and their Beauty shall
consume in the Grave from their Dwelling. Man that is in Honor
15 and understandeth not, is like the Beast that Perisheth.

81

Hear O my People and I will speak; O Israel and I will testify
against thee. I am GOD even thy GOD. I will not reprov thee for
thy Sacrifices or thy Burnt offerings to hav been continualy before
me. I will take no Bullock out of thy Hous, nor He goats out of thy
5 folds. For evry Beast of the Forest is mine and the Cattle upon
a thousand Hills. I know all the Fowls of the Mountains, and the
Wilde Beasts of the field are mine. If I were Hungry I would not
tell thee: for the World is mine, and the fulness therof. Will I eat
the flesh of Buls or Drink the Blood of Goats? Offer unto God
10 Thanksgiving and pay thy Vows to the Most High. And call upon
me in the Day of Trouble; I will Deliver Thee, and Thou shalt
Glorify me. When I was a little child, I thought that evry one that
lifted up his Eys to behold the sun, did me in looking on it Wonder-
full service. And certainly being moved therby to Prais my Creator,
15 it was in it self a service Wonderfully Delightfull. For since GOD
so much esteemeth Praises, that He preferreth them abov thousands
of Rams and tens of thousands of Rivers of oyl: if I lov Him with
that enflamed Ardor and Zeal I ought: His Praises must needs be
Delightfull to me abov all Services and Riches whatsoever. That
20 which hinders us from seeing the Glory and Discerning the Sweet-
ness of Praises; hinders us also from Knowing the maner how we are
concerned in them · but God knoweth infinit reasons, for which he
preferreth them. If I should tell you what they are you would be
Apt to Despise them. Divine and Heavenly Mysteries being thirsted
25 after till, they are known, but by corrupted Nature undervalued.
Howbeit since Grace correcteth the Perversness of Nature, and
tasteth in a better maner, it shall not be long, till somwhere we
Disclose them.

82

Are not Praises the very End for which the World was created?
Do they not consist as it were of Knowledg, Complacency, and
Thanksgiving? Are they not Better then all the fowls and Beasts

and fishes in the World? What are the Cattel upon a thousand Hils
but Carcaises, without Creatures that can rejoyce in GOD, and 5
enjoy them? It is evident that Praises are infinitly more excellent
then all the creatures becaus they proceed from Men and Angels ·
for as streams do they derive an Excellency from their Fountains,
and are the last Tribut that can possibly be paid to the Creator.
Praises are the Breathings of interior Lov, the Marks and Symp- 10
toms of an Happy Life, Overflowing Gratitud, returning Benefits,
an Oblation of the Soul, and the Heart ascending upon the Wings
of Divine Affection to the Throne of GOD. GOD is a Spirit and
cannot feed on Carcases: but He can be Delighted with Thanks-
givings, and is infinitly pleased with the Emanations of our Joy, 15
becaus His Works are Esteemed, and Himself is Admired. What
can be more Acceptable to Lov then that it should be Prized and
Magnified. Becaus therfore God is Lov and his Measure infinit:
He infinitly desires to be Admired and Beloved: and so our Praises
enter into the very Secret of His Eternal Bosom, and mingle with 20
Him who Dwelleth in that Light which is inaccessible. What
Strengths are there even in flattery to Pleas a great Affection? Are
not your Bowels moved, and your Affections melted with Delight
and Pleasure, when your Soul is precious in the Ey of those you
lov? when your Affection is pleased; your Lov prized, and they 25
satisfied? To Prize Lov is the Highest Service in the Whole World
that can be don unto it. But there are a thousand Causes moving
GOD to Esteeme our Praises, more then we can well apprehend.
However let these Enflame you, and mov you to prais Him Night
and Day for ever.
30

83

Of our Savior it is said, Sacrifice and Offering Thou wouldst not
but a Body hast Thou prepared me, all Sacrifices being but Types
and figures of Himself, and Himself infinitly more Excellent then
they all. Of a Broken Heart also it is said, Thou desirest not Sacrifice
els I would giv it. Thou Delightest not in Burnt Offering The Sacri- 5
fices of God are a broken Spirit, a broken and a contrite Heart O
GOD Thou wilt not Despise. One Deep and Serious Groan is more
Acceptable to God, then the Creation of a World. In Spiritual
things we find the Greatest Excellency. As Praises becaus they are
the Pledges of our Mutual Affection, so Groans becaus they are the 10

Pledges of a Due Contrition are the Greatest Sacrifices. Both pro-
ceed from Lov. And in both we manifest and Exercise our friend-
ship. In contrition we show our Penitence for having offended,
and by that are fitted to rehears his Praises. All the Desire wherwith
15 He longs after a Returning Sinner, makes Him to esteem a Broken
heart. What can more melt and dissoīv a Lover then the Tears of
an offending and returning friend? Here also is the saying verified.
The Falling out of Lovers is the Beginning of Lov: the renewing,
the repairing and the Strengthening of it.

84

An Enlarged Soul that seeth all the World praising God, or penitent
by bewailing their Offences and converting to Him, hath his Ey
fixed upon the Joy of Angels. It needeth nothing but the Sence of
GOD, to inherit all Things. We must borrow and derive it from
5 Him by seeing His and Aspiring after it. Do but clothe your self
with Divine Resentments† and the World shall be to you the valley
of vision, and all the Nations and Kingdoms of the World shall
appear in Splendor and celestial Glory.

85

The Righteous shall rejoyce when he seeth the vengeance, he shall
Wash his feet in the Blood of the Wicked. But I will sing of thy
Power, yea I will sing aloud of thy Mercy in the Morning · for Thou
hast been my Defence in the Day of my Trouble. The Deliverances
5 of your former Life are Objects of your Felicity, and so is the
Vengeance of the Wicked · with both which in all Times and Places
you are ever to be present in your Memory and understanding · for
lack of Considering its Objects the Soul is Desolat.

86

My Soul thirsteth for Thee, my flesh longeth for Thee in a dry and
thirsty Land where no Water is. To see thy Power and thy Glory
so as I hav seen Thee in the Sanctuary. Becaus thy Loving Kind-
ness is better then Life my Lips shall prais Thee. Thus will I Bless
5 Thee while I live I will lift up my hands in thy Name. My soul shall
be satisfied as with Marrow and fatness, and my Mouth shall Prais
Thee with joyfull Lips. O Thou that hearest Prayer unto Thee shall
all flesh com. Blessed is the Man whom Thou chusest and causest
to approach unto Thee, that He may dwell in thy Courts. We shall

be satisfied with the Goodnes of thy Hous even of thy Holy Temple. 10
See how in the 65th Psal. He introduceth the Meditation of Gods
visible Works sweetly into the Tabernacle and maketh them to be
the fatness of his hous even of his Holy Temple. God is seen when
his Lov is manifested. God is enjoyed when his Lov is prized. When
we see the Glory of his Wisdom and Goodness, and his Power 15
exerted, then we see His Glory. And these we cannot see till we see
their Works. When therfore we see His Works, in them as in a
Mirror we see His Glory.

87

Make a Joyfull Nois unto God all ye Lands, sing forth the Honor of
his Name, make his Prais Glorious. Say unto God, How terrible art
Thou in thy Works? through the greatness of thy Power shall thine
Enemies submit them selvs unto Thee. All the Earth shall Worship
Thee and sing unto Thee, they shall sing to thy Name. Com and see 5
the Works of God He is Terrible in His doing towards the Children
of Men. The prospect of all Nations Praising Him, is far sweeter
then the Prospect of the feilds or silent Heavens serving them · tho
you see the Skies adorned with Stars, and the feilds covered with
corn and flocks of Sheep and Cattel. When the Ey of your Under- 10
standing shineth upon them, they are yours in Him, and all your
Joys.

88

God is my King of Old working Salvation in the midst of the
Earth. He divided the sea by His Strength. He brake the Heads of
Leviathan in Pieces. His Heart is always abroad in the midst of the
Earth: seeing and rejoycing in His Wonders there. His Soul is
busied in the Ancient Works of God for his People Israel. The 5
Day is thine, the Night also is thine, Thou hast prepared the Light
and the Sun. Thou hast set all the Borders of the Earth Thou hast
made Summer and Winter. He proposeth more Objects of our
felicity · in which we ought to meet the Goodness of God, that we
might rejoyce before Him. The Day and Night, the Light and the 10
Sun are Gods Treasures, and ours also.

89

In the 78th Psalm, he commandeth all Ages to record the Ancient
Ways of God, and recommendeth them to our Meditation, shew-
ing the Ordinance of God, that Fathers should teach their children,
and they another Generation. Which certainly since they are not
5 to be seen in the visible World, but only in the Memory and
Minds of Men. The Memory and Mind are a strange Region of
celestial Light, and a Wonderfull place as well as a large and sub-
lime one in which they may be seen. What is contained in the Souls
of Men being as visible to us as the very Heavens.

90

In the 84th Psalm He longeth earnestly after the Tabernacles of
God, and preferreth a Day in his Courts abov a thousand. Becaus
there as Deborah Speaketh in her song, was the Place of Drawing
Waters that is of repentance: and of rehearsing the Righteous Acts
5 of the Lord. Which it is more Blessed to do then to inherit the
Palaces of Wicked Men.

91

Among the Gods there is none like unto Thee. Neither are there
any Works like unto thy Works. All Nations whom Thou hast
made shall com and worship before Thee, O Lord, and shall glorify
thy Name. For Thou art Great, and doest Wondrous things Thou
5 art GOD alone. This is a Glorious Meditation, wherein the Psalmist
gives himself Liberty to Examine the Excellency of Gods Works,
and finding them infinitly Great and abov all that can be besides,
rejoyceth, and admireth the Goodnes of God, and resteth satisfied
with Complacency in them. That they were all his He Knew well,
10 being the Gifts of God made unto him · and that He was to hav
communion with God in the Enjoyment of them. But their Excel-
lency was a thing unsearchable, and their Incomparableness abov
all Imagination, which he found by much Study to his infinit
Delectation.

92

In his other Psalms he proceedeth to Speak of the Works of God
over and over again: somtimes stirring up all Creatures to Prais
God for the very Delight he took in their Admirable Perfection,
somtimes shewing Gods Goodness and Mercy by them, and

somtimes rejoycing Himself and Triumphing in them. By all this 5
teaching us what we ought to do, that we might becom Divine and
Heavenly. In the 103 psal. he openeth the Nature of Gods present
Mercies, both towards himself in particular and towards all in
general, turning Emergencies in this World into Celestial Joys.
In the 104. psal he insisteth wholy upon the Beauty of Gods Works 10
in the Creation, making all things in Heaven and Earth and in the
Heaven of Heavens, in the Wilderness and the Sea his Private and
personal Delights. In the 105 and 106 Psalmes he celebrateth the
Ways of God in former Ages with as much vehemency Zeal and
Pleasure as if they were New Things, and as if He were present with 15
them seeing their Beauty and Tasting their Delight that very
moment. In the 107 Psalm he Contemplates the Ways of God in the
Dispensations of his Providence, over Travellers sick men sea men
&c Shewing that the way to be much in Heaven, is to be much
employd here upon Earth in the Meditation of Divine and Celestial 20
Things · for such are these tho they seem Terrestrial. All which he
concludeth thus, Whoso considereth these things, even he shall
understand the Loving Kindness of the Lord. In the 119th Psalm,
like an Enamord Person, and a Man ravished in Spirit with Joy and
pleasure he treateth upon Divine Laws, and over and over again 25
maketh Mention of their Beauty and Perfection. By all which we
may see what inward life we ought to lead with God in the Temple.
And that to be much in the Meditation of Gods Works and Ways
and Laws, to see their Excellency, to Taste their Sweetnes to behold
their Glory, to Admire and Rejoyce and Overflow with Praises is 30
to live in Heaven. But unlesse we hav a Communion with David in
a Rational Knowledg of their Nature and Excellency We can never
understand the Grounds of his Complacency† or the Depth of his
Resentments.†

93

In our outward Life towards Men the Psalmist also is an Admirable
Precedent. In Weeping for those that forget Gods Law, in publish-
ing his Praises in the Congregation of the Righteous in speaking of
his Testimonies without Cowardice or shame even before Princes ·
in delighting in the Saints, in Keeping Promises tho made to his 5
Hurt, in tendering the Life of his Enemies and Clothing Himself
with Sack-cloth when they were sick, in shewing Mercy to the

Poor, in enduring the Songs and Mockings of the Drunkards, in
taking care to Glorify the Author of all Bounty with a Splendid
10 Temple and Musical Instruments in this World, in Putting his
Trust and Confidence in God among all his Enemies, evermore
promoting his honor and Glory, Instructing others in the Excel-
lency of His Ways, and endeavouring to Establish his Worship in
Israel. Thus ought we to the Best of our Power to express our
15 Gratitud and friendship to so Great a Benefactor in all the Effects
of Lov and fidelity. Doing his pleasure with all our Might, and
promoting his Honor with all our Power.

94

There are Psalmes more Clear wherin he Expresseth the Joy He
taketh in Gods Works and the Glory of them · wherin he teacheth
us at Divers times and in Divers manners to ponder on them.
Among which the 145 psal (and so onward to the last) are very
5 Eminent. In which he openeth the Nature of Gods Kingdom, and
so vigorously and vehemently Exciteth all Creatures to Praise
Him, and all Men to do it with all kind of Musical Instruments by
all Expressions, in all Nations for all Things as if 10000 vents were
not sufficient to eas his fulness, as if all the World were but one
10 Celestial Temple in which He was Delighted, as if all Nations were
present before him and he saw God face to face in this Earthly
Tabernacle, as if his Soul like an infinit Ocean were full of joys,
and all these but Springs and Chanels overflowing. So Purely so
Joyfully so Powerfully he walked with God, all Creatures, as they
15 brought a Confluence of Joys unto him, being Pypes to eas him.

95

His Soul recovered its Pristine Liberty and saw thorow the Mud
Walls of flesh and Blood. Being alive, he was in the Spirit all his
Days, while his Body therfore was inclosed in this World his Soul
was in the Temple of Eternity and clearly beholds the infinit Life
5 and Omnipresence of God · having Conversation with Invisible
Spiritual and Immaterial Things which were its companions it
self being Invisible Spiritual and Immaterial. Kingdoms and Ages
did surround him, as clearly as the Hills and Mountains: and ther-
fore the Kingdom of God was ever round about Him. Evry thing was
10 one way or other his soveraign Delight and Transcendent Pleasure,
as in Heaven evry thing will be evry ones Peculiar Treasure.

96

He saw these Things only in the Light of faith, and yet rejoyced as if he had seen them in the Light of Heaven, which argued the Strength and Glory of his faith. And wheras he so rejoyced in all the Nations of the Earth for praising God, he saw them doing it in the Light of Prophesie, not of History. Much more therfore should we rejoyce, who see these Prophesies fulfilled, since the fulfilling of them is so Blessed Divine and Glorious, that the very Praevision of their Accomplishment Transported and Ravished this Glorious Person· but we wither, and for lack of sence shrivell up into Nothing, who should be filled with the Delights of Ages.

97

By this we understand what it is to be the Sons of God and what it is to live in Communion with him, what it is to be Advanced to his Throne, and to reign in his Kingdom with all those other Glorious and Marvellous Expressions that are applied to Men in the Holy Scriptures. To be the Sons of God is not only to Enjoy the Privileges and the freedom of His Hous, and to bear the Relation of Children to so Great a father, but it is to be like him and to share with Him in all His Glory and in all his Treasures. To be like Him in Spirit and Understanding, to be Exalted above all Creatures as the End of them, to be present as He is by Sight and Lov, without Limit and without bound with all his Works, to be Holy towards all and Wise toward all as He is. Prizing all his Goodness in all with infinit Ardor, that as Glorious and Eternal Kings being Pleased in all we might reign over all for ever more.

98

This Greatness both of God towards us, and of our selvs towards him we ought always as much as possible to retain in our understanding. And when we cannot effectualy keep it alive in our Sences, to cherish the Memory of it in the centre of our Hearts, and do all things in the Power of it · for the Angels when they com to us, so fulfill their outward Ministery, that within they nevertheless maintain the Beatifick Vision: Ministering before the Throne of God, and among the Sons of Men at the same time. The reason wherof S. Greg. saith is this, Tho the Spirit of an Angel be limited and Circumscribed in it self, yet the Supreme Spirit, which is GOD,

is uncircumscribed. He is evry where and wholy evry where: which makes their Knowledg to be Dilated evry where · for being wholy evry where They are immediatly present with his Omnipresence in evry place and wholy. It filleth them for ever.

99

This Sence that God is so Great in Goodnes, and we so Great in Glory, as to be His Sons, and so Rich as to live in Communion with Him; And so individualy united to Him, that He is in us, and we in Him; will make us do all our Duties not only with incom-
5 parable Joy, but Courage also. It will fill us with Zeal and fidelity, and make us to overflow with Praises · for which one cause alone the Knowledg of it ought infinitly to be Esteemed · for to be Ignorant of this, is to sit in Darkness, and to be a Child of Darkness: it maketh us to be without God in the World, exceeding Weak Timer-
10 ous and feeble, Comfortless and Barren, Dead and Unfruitfull, Lukewarm, Indifferent Dumb, unfaithfull. To which I may adde that it makes us uncertain · for so Glorious is the Face of God and True Religion, that it is impossible to see it, but in Transcendent Splendor. Nor can we Know that God is, till we see Him infinit in
15 Goodness. Nothing therfore will make us certain of His Being but His Glory.

100

To Enjoy Communion with God is to abide with Him in the fruition of His Divine and Eternal Glory, in all His Attributes in all his Thoughts in all His Creatures; In His Eternity, Infinity, Almighty Power, Soveraignty &c. In all those Works which from
5 all Eternity He wrought in Himself; as the Generation of His Son, the Proceeding of the Holy Ghost, the Eternal Union and Com-munion of the Blessed Trinity, the Councels of His Bosom, the Attainment of the End of all His Endeavors wherin we shall see our selvs exalted and Beloved from all Eternity. We are to enjoy
10 Communion with Him in the Creation of the World, In the Government of Angels, in the Redemption of Mankind, in the Dispensations of His Providence in the Incarnation of his Son, in His Passion Resurrection and Ascension, in His shedding abroad the Holy Ghost in his Government of the Church in His Judgment
15 of the World, in the Punishment of his Enemies, in the Rewarding

of his friends, in Eternal Glory. All these therfore particularly
ought to be near us, and to be esteemed by us as our Riches;
being those Delectable Things that Adorn the Hous of GOD
which is Eternity; and those Living fountains, from whence we
suck forth the streams of Joy, that everlastingly overflow to refresh 20
our Souls.

THE FOURTH CENTURIE

1

Having spoken so much concerning his Enterance and Progress in
Felicity, I will in this Centurie speak of the Principles with which
your friend endued Himself to enjoy it! for besides Contemplativ,
there is an Activ Happiness; which consisteth in Blessed Operations.
5 And as som things fit a man for Contemplation, so there are others
fitting him for Action: which as they are infinitly necessary to
Practical Happiness, so are they likewise infinitly conduciv to
Contemplativ it self.

2

He thought it a Vain Thing to see Glorious Principles lie Buried
in Books, unless he did remove them into his Understanding; and
a vain thing to remov them unless he did revive them, and rais
them up by continual exercise. Let this therfore be the first Prin-
5 ciple of your soul. That to have no Principles, or to liv beside them,
is equaly Miserable. And that Philosophers are not those that
Speak, but Do great Things.

3

He thought that to be a Philosopher a Christian and a Divine,
was to be one of the most Illustrious Creatures in the World; and
that no man was a Man in Act, but only in Capacity, that was
not one of these; or rather all· for either of these Three include the
5 other two. A Divine includes a Philosopher and a Christian, a
Christian includes a Divine and a Philosopher, a Philosopher
includes a Christian and a Divine. Since no man therfore can be
a Man, unless he be a Philosopher, nor a true Philosopher unless
he be a Christian, nor a Perfect Christian unless he be a Divine;
10 evry man ought to Spend his time, in Studying diligently Divine
Philosophy.

4

This last Principle needs a little Explication. Not only becaus Philosophy is condemned for vain, but becaus it is Superfluous among inferior Christians, and impossible as som think unto them. We must distinguish therfore of Philosophy, and of Christians also. Som Philosophy, as St Paul saith is vain, but then it is 5 vain Philosophy. But there is also a Divine Philosophy, of which no Books in the World are more full then His own. That we are naturaly the Sons of GOD, (I speak of Primitiv and upright Nature,) that the Son of GOD is the first Beginning of evry Creature, that we are to be Changed from Glory to Glory into the same 10 Image, that we are Spiritual Kings, that Christ is the Express Image of His Fathers Person, that by Him all Things are made, whether they are Visible or Invisible, is the Highest Philosophy in the World, and so is it also to treat as he does of the Nature of Virtues and Divine Laws. Yet no Man I suppose will account 15 these Superfluous, or vain · for in the right Knowledg of these Eternal Life consisteth. And till we see into the Beauty and Blessedness of Gods Laws, the Glory of His Works, the Excellency of our Souls &c. we are but Children of Darkness, at least but Ignorant and imperfect: neither able to rejoyce in God, as we ought, 20 nor to liv in Communion with Him. Rather we should remember that Jesus Christ is the Wisdom of the father, and that since our Life is hid with Christ, in GOD; we should spend our Days in Studying Wisdom, that we might be like unto Him: that the Treasures of Heaven are the Treasures of Wisdom, and that they 25 are hid in him. As it is written, In Him are hid all the Treasures of Wisdom and Knowledg.

5

In distinguishing of Christians, we ought to Consider that Christians are of two sorts, Perfect or imperfect, Intelligent and Mature; or Weak and Inexperienced: (I will not say Ignorant, for an Ignorant Christian is a Contradiction in Nature. I say not that an Imperfect Christian is the most Glorious Creature in the whole 5 World, nor that it is necessary for him, if he loves to be Imperfect, to be a Divine Philosopher. But he that is Perfect is a Divine Philosopher, and the most Glorious Creature in the whole World. Is not a Philosopher a Lover of Wisdom? That is the Signification

10 of the very Word. And sure it is the Essence of a Christian or very
near it to be a Lover of Wisdom. Can a Christian be so degenerat,
as to be a Lover of Imperfection? Does not your very Nature abhor
Imperfection? Tis true a Christian so far as he is Defectiv and
imperfect may be Ignorant · yet still He is a Lover of Wisdom,
15 and a Studier of it. He may be defectiv, but so far as he is de-
fectiv he is no Christian · for a Christian is not a Christian in his
Blemishes, but his Excellencies. Nor is a Man indeed a Man in his
Ignorances, but his Wisdom. Blemishes may mar a Man, and spoil
a Christian, but they cannot make him. Defects may be in Him and
20 cleav unto him, but they are to be shaken off and repented. Evry
man therfore according to his Degree, so far forth as He is a
Christian, is a Philosopher.

6

Furthermore, doth not S. Paul command us *in understanding to be
Men?* That implies that with little Understanding we are but
Children, and without understanding are not Men · but insignificant
Shels, and meer Apparitions. Doth he not Earnestly Pray, that their
5 Hearts may be Comforted, being Knit together in Lov, unto all
the Riches of the full Assurance of Understanding to the Acknow-
ledgment of the Mystery of God, and of the Father and of Christ?
This plainly shews, that tho a Weak Christian may believ great
things by an implicit faith, yet it is very desirable, his faith should
10 be turned into Assurance, and that cannot be, but by the Riches
of Knowledg and Understanding · for He may beleiv that GOD
is and that Jesus Christ is his Savior, and that His Soul is im-
mortal, and that there are Joys in Heaven, and that the Scriptures
are Gods Word, and that GOD loves him &c. so far as to yeeld
15 Obedience in som measure, but he can never com to a full Assurance
of all this, but by seeing the Riches of the full Assurance i.e. those
things which are called the Riches of the full Assurance; becaus
being Known they giv us Assurance of the Truth of all Things.
The glory of GODs Laws, the True Dignity of His own Soul,
20 the Excellency of GODs Ways, the Magnificent Goodness of His
Works, and the Real Blessedness of the State of Grace. All which a
Man is so Clearly to see, that He is not more sensible of the Reality
of the Sun Beams. How els should he liv in Communion with GOD;
to wit, in the Enjoyment of them? for a full Assurance of the Reality
25 of his Joys, is infinitly necessary to the Possession of them.

7

This Digression steals me a little further. Is it not the shame and reproach of Nature, that men should spend so much time in studying Trades, and be so ready skild in the Nature of clothes, of Grounds, of Gold and Silver, &c. and think it much to spend a little time, in the study of God, Themselvs, and Happiness? 5 What hav men to do in this World, but to make them selvs Happy? Shall it ever be praisd, and despised? Verily Happiness being the Soveraign and Supreme of our Concerns, should hav the most peculiar portion of our Time: and other things what she can spare. It more concernes me to be Divine, then to hav a Purs 10 of Gold. And therfore as Solomon said, We must dig for her as for Gold and Silver; and that is the way to understand the fear of the Lord, and to find the Knowledg of God. It is a strange thing that Men will be such Enemies to them selvs: Wisdom is the Principal Thing yet all neglect her · wherfore Get Wisdom, and 15 with all thy Getting get understanding. Exalt her and she shall promote thee, she shall bring thee to Honor when thou dost embrace her. She shall giv to thy Head an Ornament of Grace, a Crown of Glory shall she deliver to Thee. Had you certain Tidings of a Mine of Gold, would the Care of your Ordinary 20 Affairs detain you, could you hav it for the Digging? Nothing more ruins the world, then a Conceit, that a little Knowledg is sufficient. Which is a mere lazy Dream, to cover our Sloth or Enmity against GOD. Can you go to a Mine of Gold, and not to Wisdom; (to dig for it;) without being guilty, either of a Base Despondency and 25 Distrust of Wisdom, that she will not bring you to such Glorious Treasures as is promised; or els of a vile and Lazy Humor that makes you despise them, becaus of that little, but long labor, you apprehend between? Nothing keeps men out of the Temple of Honor, but that the Temple of Vertue stands between. But this was 30 His Principle that loved Happiness, and is your friend. I came into this World only that I might be Happy. And whatsoever it cost me I will be Happy. A Happiness there is, and it is my desire to enjoy it.

8

Philosophers are not only those that Contemplat happiness, but Practise virtue. He is a Philosopher that subdues his vices, Lives by Reason, Orders his Desires, Rules his Passions, and submits

not to his sences, nor is guided by the Customs of this World.
5 He despiseth those Riches which Men esteem, he despiseth those
Honors which men esteem, he forsaketh those Pleasures which
Men Esteem. And having proposed to him self a Superior End,
then is commonly discerned, bears all Discouragements, breaks
thorow all Difficulties and lives unto it: That having seen the
10 Secrets, and the Secret Beauties of the Highest reason, orders his
Conversation, and lives by Rule: tho in this Age, it be held never
so strange that He should do so. Only He is Divine becaus he
does this upon Noble Principles, Becaus GOD is, becaus Heaven
is, becaus Jesus Christ hath Redeemd him, and becaus he Lovs
15 Him: not only becaus vertue is Amiable, and felicity Delightfull;
but for that also.

9

Once more we will distinguish of Christians. There are Christians,
that place and desire all their Happiness in another Life, and
there is another sort of Christians that desire Happiness in this.
The one can defer their Enjoyment of Wisdom till the World to
5 com: And dispence with the Increas and Perfection of Knowledg
for a little time: the other are instant and impatient of Delay; and
would fain see that Happiness here, which they shall enjoy herafter.
Not the vain Happiness of this World, falsly called Happiness,
truly vain: but the real Joy and Glory of the Blessed: which
10 Consisteth in the Enjoyment of the Whole World in Communion
with God, not this only, but the Invisible and Eternal: which they
earnestly covet to Enjoy immediatly: for which reason they daily
pray Thy Kingdom come; and travail towards it by learning
Wisdom as fast as they can. Whether the first sort be Christians
15 indeed, look you to that. They hav much to say for themselvs.
Yet certainly they that put of[f] felicity with long delays, are to
be much suspected · for it is against the Nature of Lov and desire
to defer. Nor can any reason be given, why they should desire it at
last, and not now. If they say Becaus God hath Commanded them,
20 that is fals: for He offereth it now, Now they are commanded to
have their Conversation in Heaven, now they may be full of Joy
and full of Glory. Ye are not streightned in me, but in your own
Bowels. Those Christians that can defer their felicity may be con-
tented with their Ignorance.

10

He that will not Exchange his Riches now, will not forsake them herafter. He must, but will hardly be persuaded to do it willingly. He will leav them, but not forsake them · for which caus two Dishonors cleav unto him; and if at Death, eternaly · first, he coms of [f] the Stage unwillingly, which is very unhandsom: and secondly 5 He prefers his Riches abov his Happiness. Riches are but servants to Happiness, when they are Impediments they ceas to be Riches. As long as they are Conduciv to Felicity they are desirable; but when they are incompitable Abominable · for what End are Riches endeavored, Why do we desire them but that we may be 10 more Happy? When we see the Persuit of them destructiv to Felicity, to desire them is of all things in Nature the most absurd and the most foolish. I ever thought that Nothing was desirable for it self but Happiness, and that whatever els we desire, it is of valu only in relation, and Order to it.   15

11

That Maxim also which your Friend used, is of very Great and Divine Concernment: *I will first spend a great deal of time in seeking Happiness, and then a Great deal more in Enjoying it.* For if Happiness be worthy to be Sought, it is worthy to be Enjoyed. As no folly in the world is more vile then that pretended by Alchymists, 5 of Having the Philosophers Stone, and being contented without using it: so is no Deceit more Odious, then that of Spending many Days in Studying, and none in Enjoying, Happiness. That Base pretence is an Argument of Falshood and meer forgery in them: that after so much toil in getting it they refuse to use it: 10 Their pretence is that they are so abundantly satisfied in having it, they care not for the use of it. So the Neglect of any Man that finds it, shews that indeed he hath lost of Happiness. That which he hath found is Counterfeit Ware, if he neglect to use it: Tis only becaus he cannot: Tru Happiness being to[o] precious, to ly by 15 Despised. Shall I forsake all Riches and Pleasures for Happiness, and persue it many Days and Moneths and yeers; and then neglect and Bury it when I hav it? I will now spend Days and Nights in Possessing it · as I did before in seeking it. It is better being Happy, then Asleep.   20

12

Happiness was not made to be Boasted, but enjoyed · tho others count me miserable, I will not believ them; if I know and feel my self to be Happy; nor fear them. I was not born to approv my self to them: but GOD. A Man may enjoy very Great Delights, with-
5 out telling them.

> Tacitus si pasci potuisset Corvus, haberet
> Plus Dapis; et rixæ minus, invidiæque.

> Could but the Crow in lonely Silence Eat,
> She then would hav less Envy, and more Meat.

10 Heaven is a Place where our Happiness shall be seen of all. We shall there enjoy the Happiness of being seen in Happiness, with-out the Danger of Ostentation: But here Men are Blind and Cor-rupted, and cannot see: if they could, we are corrupted, and in danger of abusing it. I knew a Man that was mightily derided
15 in his persuit of Happiness, till he was understood, and then Admired · but he lost all by his Miscarriage.†

13

One great Discouragement to Felicity, or rather to great Souls in the persuit of Felicity, is the Solitariness of the Way that leadeth to her Temple. A man that studies Happiness must sit alone like a Sparrow upon the Hous Top, and like a Pelican in the Wilder-
5 ness. And the reason is becaus all men prais Happiness and despise it · very few shall a Man find in the way of Wisdom: And few indeed that having given up their Names to Wisdom and felicity, that will persevere in seeking it. Either He must go on alone, or go back for company. People are tickled with the Name of it, and
10 som are persuaded to Enterprize a little, but quickly draw back when they see the trouble, yea cool of them selvs without any Trouble. Those Mysteries which while men are Ignorant of, they would giv all the Gold in the World for, I hav seen when Known to be despised. Not as if the Nature of Happiness were such that
15 it did need a vail: but the Nature of Man is such, that it is Odious and ingratefull. For those things which are most Glorious when most Naked, are by Men when most Nakedly reveald most Des-pised. So that GOD is fain for His very Names sake, lest His

Beauties should be scorned to conceal her Beauties: and for the
sake of Men, which naturaly are more prone to prie into secret 20
and forbidden things then into Open and common. Felicity is
amiable under a Vail, but most Amiable when most Naked. It hath
its times, and seasons for both. There is som Pleasure in breaking
the Shell: and many Delights in our Addresses, previous to the
Sweets in the Possession of her. It is som Part of Felicity that we 25
must seek her.

14

In order to this, he furnished him self with this Maxime. *It is a*
Good Thing to be Happy alone. It is better to be Happy in Com-
pany, but Good to be Happy alone. Men owe me the Advantage of
their Society, but if they deny me that just Debt, I will not be unjust
to my self, and side with them in bereaving me. I will not be Dis- 5
couraged, least I be Miserable for Company. More Company
increases Happiness, but does not leighten or Diminish Misery.

15

In Order to Interior or Contemplativ Happiness, it is a Good
Principle: that Apprehensions within are better then their Objects.
Morneys Simile of the Saw is admirable. If a man would cut with
a saw, he must not apprehend it to be a Knife, but a Thing with
Teeth; otherwise he cannot use it. He that mistakes his Knife to 5
be an Auger, or his Hand to be his Meat, confounds him self by
misapplications. These Mistakes are Ocular · but far more Absurd
ones are unseen. To mistake the World, or the Nature of ones
soul, is a more Dangerous Error. He that Thinks the Heavens and
the Earth not his, can hardly use them: he that thinks the Sons of 10
Men impertinent to his Joy and Happiness can scarcely lov them.
But he that Knows them to be Instruments and what they are will
delight in them, and is able to use them. Whatever we misapprehend
we cannot use. Nor well enjoy, what we cannot use. Nor can a thing
be our Happines, we cannot enjoy. Nothing therfore can be our 15
Happiness, but that alone which we rightly apprehend. To appre-
hend God our Enemie destroys our Happiness. Inward Apprehen-
sions are the very light of Blessednes, and the Cement of Souls
and their Objects.

16

Of what vast Importance right Principles are, we may see by this, *Things Prized are Enjoyed.* All Things are ours; All Things serv us and Minister to us, could we find the way: Nay they are ours, and serv us so perfectly, that they are best enjoyed in their proper
5 places: even from the Sun to a Sand, from a Cherubim to a Worm. I will not except Gold and Silver and Crowns and Precious Stones, nor any Delights or secret Treasures in Closets and Palaces. For if otherwise GOD would not be perfect in Bounty. But suppose the World were all yours if this Principle be rooted in you, to prize
10 nothing that is yours, it blots out all at one Dash, and bereavs you of a whole World in a Moment.

17

Tho God be yours, and all the Joys and Inhabitants in Heaven, if you be resolvd to prize nothing Great and Excellent, nothing Sublime and Eternal; you lay waste your Possessions; and make vain your Enjoyment of all permanent and Glorious Things. So
5 that you must be sure to inure yourself frequently to these Principles and to impresse them deeply; *I will Prize all I hav: And nothing shall with me be less esteemed, becaus it is Excellent. A Daily Joy shall be more my Joy, becaus it is continual. A Common Joy is more my Delight becaus it is Common. For all Mankind are my Friends. And*
10 *evry Thing is Enrichd in serving them.* A little Grit in the Ey destroyeth the sight of the very Heavens: and a little Malice or Envy a World of Joys. One wry Principle in the Mind is of infinit Consequence. *I Will ever Prize what I hav, and so much the more becaus I hav it.* To Prize a thing when it is gon breedeth Torment and
15 Repining: to Prize it while we hav it Joy and Thanksgiving.

18

All these relate to Enjoyment, but those Principles that relate to Communication are more Excellent. These are Principles of Retirement and Solitude; but the Principles that aid us in Conversation are far better: and help us tho not so immediatly to Enjoyment
5 in a far more Blessed and Diviner maner. For it is more Blessed to giv then to receiv: and we are more happy in Communication then Enjoyment, but only that Communication is Enjoyment; as indeed what we giv we best receiv · for the Joy of Communicating

and the Joy of receiving maketh perfect Happiness. And therfore are
the Sons of Men our Greatest Treasures, becaus they can give and 10
receiv: Treasures perhaps infinit as well as Affections. But this
I am sure they are our Treasures. And therfore is Conversation so
Delightfull becaus they are the Greatest.

19

The World is best enjoyed and most immediatly while we convers
Wisely and Blessedly with Men. I am sure it were desirable that
they could giv and receiv infinit Treasures. And perhaps they can ·
for whomsoever I lov as my self, to him I giv my self and all my
Happiness · which I think is infinit: and I receiv Him and all His 5
Happiness. Yea in him I receiv GOD, for GOD delighteth me for
being his Blessedness. So that a Man Obligeth me infinitly that
maketh Himself Happy; and by making Himself Happy giveth me
Himself and all His Happiness. Besides this he loveth me infinitly,
as GOD doth; and he dare do no less for Gods sake. Nay he loveth 10
God for loving Me, and Delighteth in Him for being Good unto
me. So that I am Magnified in his Affections, represented in his
Understanding Tenderly Beloved Caressed and Honored: and this
maketh Society Delightfull. But here upon Earth it is subject to
Changes. And therfore this Principle is always to be firm, as the 15
foundation of Bliss, GOD only is my Soveraign Happiness and
Friend in the World. Conversation is full of Dangers, and Friend-
ships are Mortal among the Sons of Men. But Communion with
GOD is infinitly Secure, and He my Happiness.

20

He from whom I received these things, always thought, that to be
Happy in the midst of a Generation of Vipers was becom his Duty ·
for men and he are faln into Sin. Were all men Wise and Innocent, it
were easy to be Happy · for no man would injure and molest another.
But he that would be Happy now must be Happy among Ingratefull 5
and Injurious Persons. That Knowledg which would make a man
Happy among just and Holy persons, is unusefull now: and those
Principles only Profitable that will make a Man Happy, not only in
Peace, but Blood. On every side we are environed with Enemies,
surrounded with Reproaches encompassed with Wrongs, beseiged 10
with offences, receiving evil for Good, being disturbed by fools, and

invaded with Malice. This is the true Estate of this World. Which
lying in Wickedness, as our savior Witnesseth, yeeldeth no better
fruits, then the bitter Clusters of folly and Perversness: the Grapes
15 of Sodom, and the Seeds of Gomorrah. Blind Wretches that Wound
themselvs, offend me. I need therfore the Oyl of Pitty and the Balm
of Lov to remedie and heal them. Did they see the Beauty of Holi-
ness or the face of Happiness, they would not do so. To think the
World therfore a General Bedlam, or Place of Madmen, and one
20 self a Physician, is the most necessary Point of present Wisdom:
an important Imagination, and the Way to Happiness.

21

He thought within himself that this World was far better then Para-
dice had men Eys to see its Glory, and their Advantages · for the very
Miseries and sins and offences that are in it, are the Materials of his
Joy and Triumph and Glory. So that He is to learn a Diviner Art
5 that wil now be Happy: and that is like a Royal Chymist to reign
among Poysons to turn Scorpions into fishes, Weeds into flowers
Bruises into Ornaments, Poysons into Cordials. And he that cannot
this Art, of Extracting Good out of Evil, is to be accounted Nothing.
Hertofore, to Enjoy Beauties, and be Gratefull for Benefits was
10 all the Art that was required to Felicity, but now a Man must like
a GOD, bring Light out of Darkness, and Order out of Confusion.
Which we are taught to do by His Wisdom, that Ruleth in the midst
of Storms and Tempests.

22

He generaly held, that Whosoever would enjoy the Happiness of
Paradice must put on the Charity of Paradice. And that Nothing
was his Felicity but his Duty. He called his Hous the Hous of Para-
dice: not only becaus it was the Place wherin he enjoyed the whole
5 World, but becaus it was evry ones hous in the whole world · for ob-
serving the Methods, and studying the Nature of Charity in Paradise,
he found that all men would be Brothers and Sisters throughout the
whole World · and evermore love one another as their own selvs,
tho they had never seen each other before · from whence it would
10 proceed that evry man approaching him, would be as welcom as an
Angel, and the coming of a Stranger as Delightfull as the Sun, all
things in his Hous being as much the forreiners as they were his own.
Especially if he could infuse any Knowledg or Grace into Him.

23

To establish him self thorowly in this Principle, he made much of
another. For he saw that in Paradice a great help to this Kind of
Life, was the Cheapness of commodities, and the natural fertility
of the then innocent and Blessed Ground. By which means it came
to pass that evry man had enough for him self, and all. But that now 5
the Earth being cursed and Barren, there was danger of want, a
necessity of Toyl and labor and Care, and Maintenance of Servants.
Therfore he concluded, That the Charity of Men ought to supply
the Earths Sterility · who could never want, were they all of a Mind,
and Liberal to each other. But since this also faileth, and mens 10
hearts are Cursed and Barren as the Ground, What is wanting in
them God will supply. And that to live upon Gods Provisions is
the most Glorious Dependance in the whole world. And so he made
the Lov of God his true foundation, and builded not his
Hopes on the charity of men, but fled unto God as his last Refuge. 15
Which he thought it very safe and blessed to do, becaus the Trial of
his faith was more Glorious, and the Lov of God supplied the Defect
of Charity in men: and he that had commanded had faithfully
promised and was able to perform.

24

He thought the Stars as fair now, as they were in Eden, the sun as
Bright, the Sea as Pure: and nothing pesterd the World with
Miseries, and destroyed its order Peace and Beautie, but sins and
vices. Rapine, covetousness envy Oppression Luxury Ambition
Pride &c. filled the World with Briars and Thorns, Desolations 5
Wars Complaints and Contentions. And that this made Enormities
to be vices. But Universal Charity did it breath among Men, would
blow all these away, as the Wind doth Chaff and Stubble: and that
then the Heavens would be as serene and fair, and the Lands as rich
as ever they were. And that as all things were improved by the Work 10
of Redemption, Trades and Occupations that were left behind,
would be pleasant Ornaments and Innocent Recreations · for
whence have we all our Cities Palaces and Temples, whence all
our Thrones and Magnificent Splendors, but from Trades and
Occupations.   15

25

But Order and Charity in the midst of these, is like a Bright Star
in an obscure Night, like a summers day in the Depth of Winter,
like a Sun shining among the clouds, like a Giant among his
Enemies, that receiveth Strength from their Numbers, like a King
5 sitting in the Midst of an Army. By how much the more scarce it
is, by so much the more Glorious · by how much the more Assaulted
by so much the more invincible, by how much the more lonely,
by so much the more pittied of God and Heaven. And surely He,
who being Perfect Lov, designed the felicity of the world with so
10 much Care, in the Beginning, will now be more tender of a Soul
that is like Him[,] in its Deordination.†

26

He thought that men were more to be Beloved now then before.
And which is a strange Paradox, the Worse they are the more they
were to be beloved. The Worse they are the more they were to be
Pittied and Tendered and Desired, becaus they had more need,
5 and were more Miserable · tho the Better they are, they are more to
be Delighted in. But his true Meaning in that saying was this,
Comparing them with what they were before they were faln, they
are more to be Beloved. They are now Worse yet more to be
Beloved. For Jesus Christ hath been Crucified for them. God loved
10 them more, and he gave his Son to die for them, and for me also ·
which are Strong Obligations, leading us to Greater Charity. So
that Mens unworthiness and our vertu are alike increased.

27

He conceived it his Duty and much Delighted in the Obligation;
. That he was to treat evry Man in the whole World as the Repre-
sentativ of Mankind, And that he was to meet in him, and to Pay
unto Him all the Lov of God Angels and Men.

28 ·

He thought that he was to treat evry man in the Person of Christ.
That is both as if Himself were Christ in the Greatnes of his Lov,
and also as if the Man were Christ he was to use him · having
respect to all others · for the Lov of Christ is to Dwell within Him,
5 and evry Man is the Object of it. God and he are to becom one

Spirit, that is one in Will, and one in desire. Christ must liv within him. He must be filled with the Holy Ghost which is the God of Lov, He must be of the same Mind with Christ Jesus, and led by His Spirit · for on the other side he was well acquainted with this Mystery, That evry man being the Object of our Saviors Lov, was to be treated as our Savior. Who hath said, Inasmuch as ye hav don it to the least of these my Brethren ye hav don it unto me. And thus he is to liv upon Earth among Sinners.

29

He had another saying, He lives most like an Angel that lives upon least Himself, and doth most Good to others. For the Angels neither eat nor Drink, and yet do Good to the whole World. Now a Man is an Incarnat Angel. And He that lives in the midst of Riches as a poor man Himself, Enjoying God and Paradice, or Christendom which is Better, conversing with the Poor, and seeing the valu of their Souls through their Bodies, and prizing all things cleerly with a due esteem, is arrived here to the Estate of Immortality. He cares little for the Delicacies either of food or Raiment himself: and Delighteth in others. God Angels and Men are his Treasures. He seeth through all the Mists and Vails of Invention, and possesseth here beneath the true Riches. And he that doth this always, is a rare Phœnix: But he confessed that he had often caus to bewail his Infirmities.

30

I speak not His Practices but His Principles. I should too much Prais your friend did I speak his Practices, but it is no shame for any man to declare his Principles, tho they are the most Glorious in the world. Rather they are to be Shamed that have no Glorious Principles: or that are ashamed of them. This he desired me to tell you becaus of Modesty. But with all, that indeed his Practices are so short of these Glorious Principles, that to relate them would be to his Shame; and that therfore you would never look upon him but as clothed in the Righteousness of Jesus Christ. Nevertheless I hav heard him often say, That he never allowd himself in Swerving from any of these. And that he repented deeply of evry Miscarriage:† and moreover firmly resolved as much as was possible never to erre or wander from them again.

31

I heard him often say that Holiness and Happiness were the same
and he quoted[1] a mighty Place of Scripture, All her ways are
pleasantness and her Paths are Peace. But he delighted in giving
the Reason of Scripture, and therfore said, That Holiness and
5 Wisdom in Effect were one · for no man could be Wise that Knew
Excellent Things, without doing them. Now to do them is Holiness,
and to do them Wisdom. No man therfore can be further Miserable
then he swerveth from the Ways of Holiness and Wisdom.

32

If he might hav had but one Request of GOD Almighty it should
hav been abov all other, that he might be a Blessing to Mankind.
That was his Daily Prayer abov all his Petitions. He wisely knew
that it included all Petitions · for He that is a Blessing to Mankind
5 must be Blessed, that he may be so, and must inherit all their
Affections and in that their Treasures. He could not Help it. But
he so desired to lov them, and to be a Joy unto them, that he pro-
tested often, that He could n   Himself, but as He was
enjoyed of others, and that a   Worlds, he
10 desired to be a Joy and Blessi
to be commended, for he di
had implanted in all that In

The desire of Riches was
often Protested, If he h
Delights, besides that he
worth of Benefit that h
5 away · but for others h
perceiving that Root c
grow as long as it was
quite up with this Pr
contemn the World in
10 *as first to get it with s*
ticular Charities.

Phocion

34

After this he could say with Luther, that Covetousness could never fasten the least hold upon Him. And concerning his friends even to the very Desire of seeing them rich, he could say as Phocion the Poor Athenian did of his children. Either they will be like me or not, if they are like me they will not need Riches, if they are not 5 they will be but needless and Hurtfull Superfluities.

35

He desired no other Riches for his friends, but those which cannot be Abused: to wit the True Treasures, God and Heaven and Earth and Angels and Men, &c. with the Riches of Wisdom and Grace to enjoy them. And it was his Principle That all the Treasures in the whole World would not make a Miser Happy. A Miser is not 5 only a Covetous Man but a fool. Any Needy Man, that wanteth the World, is Miserable. He wanteth God and all Things.

36

He thought also that no Poverty could befall him that enjoyd Paradice · for when all the Things are gone which Men can giv, A Man is still as Rich as Adam was in Eden: who was Naked there. A Naked Man is the Richest Creature in all Worlds: and can never be Happy; till he sees the Riches of his Nakedness. He is very 5 Poor in Knowledg that thinks Adam poor in Eden. See here how one Principle helps another. All our Disadvantages contracted by the fall are made up and recompensed by the Lov of God.

37

Tis not Change of Place, but Glorious Principles well Practiced that establish Heaven in the Life and Soul. An Angel will be Happy any where; and a Divel Miserable. Becaus the Principles of the one are always Good, of the other Bad · from the Centre to the utmost Bounds of the Everlasting Hills, all is Heaven before God, and full 5 of Treasure. And he that walks like God in the midst of them, Blessed.

34. 4. MS has an unneeded comma after *like*.

38

Lov God Angels and Men, Triumph in Gods Works, delight in
Gods Laws, Take Pleasure in Gods Ways in all Ages, Correct
Sins, bring good out of evil, subdue your Lusts order your sences,
Conquer the Customs and Opinions of men, and render Good
5 for evil, you are in Heaven evry where. Abov the Stars earthly
Things will be celestial Joys, and here beneath will things delight
you that are above the Heavens. All Things being infinitly Beautifull
in their Places: and wholy yours in all their Places. Your Riches
will be as infinit in value and Excellency, as they are in Beauty and
10 Glory, and that is, as they are in Extent.

39

Thus He was Possessor of the whole World, and held it his Treasure,
not only as the Gift of GOD, but as the Theatre of Virtues. Esteem-
ing it principaly his, becaus it upheld and ministered to Many
objects of his Lov and Goodness. Towards whom, before whom,
5 among whom he might do the work of fidelity and wisdom, exer-
cise his Courage and Prudence, shew his Temp(er)ance and Bring
forth the fruits of faith and Repentance. For all those are the
Objects of our Joy that are the Objects of our Care, They are our
true Treasures about whom we are wisely Employed.

40

He had one Maxime of notable concernment, and that was, That
GOD having reservd all other Things in his own Disposal, had
left his Heart to Him. Those things that were in GODs Care he
would commit to GOD, those things that were committed to his,
5 he would take care about. He said therfore, that he had but one
thing to do, and that was to order and keep his Heart · which alone
being well guided, would order all other things Blessedly and
Successfully. The Things about him were innumerable and out
of his Power, but they were in Gods Power. And if he pleased
10 God [within] in that which was committed to Him, God would be
sure to pleas Him in things without committed unto God · for He
was faithfull that had promised, in all that belonged unto him God
was perfect, all the Danger being, lest we should be imperfect in
ours, and unfaithfull in those Things that pertain unto us.

40. 10. *within* is deleted.

41

Having these Principles nothing was more easy then to enjoy the world · which being enjoyed, he had nothing more to do, then to spend his Life in Praises and Thanksgivings. All his Care being to be sensible of Gods Mercies, and to behave himself as the Friend of God in the Univers. If any thing were amiss, he still would have 5 recours to his own heart, and found nothing but that out of frame · by restoring which al things were rectified, and made Delightfull. As much as that had swerved from the Rule of Justice Equity and Right, so far was he miserable, and no more · so that by Experience he found the Words of the Wise Man True, and worthy of all 10 Acceptation; *In all thy Keeping Keep thy Heart, for out of it are the Issues of Life and Death.*

42

One thing he saw, which is not commonly discerned; and that is, that God made Man a free Agent for his own Advantage; and left him in the hand of his own Counsel, that he might be the more Glorious. It is hard to conceiv how much this tended to his Satisfaction · for all the things in Heaven and Earth being so Beautifull, 5 and made as it were on purpose for his own Enjoyment, he infinitly admired Gods Wisdom · in that it salved his and all Mens Exigencies, in which it fully answerd his Desires · for his Desire was that all Men should be happy as well as he. And he admired his Goodness, which had enjoyned no other Duty, than what pertained to the 10 more convenient fruition of the World which he had given: and at the Marvellous Excellency of his Lov, in committing that Duty to the Sons of Men, to be performed freely. For therby he adventured such a Power into the Hands of his Creatures, which Angels and Cherubims wonder at, and which when it is understood all 15 Eternity will admire the Bounty of Giving. For he therby committed to their hands a Power to do that which he infinitly hated · which nothing certainly could mov him to Entrust them with, but some infinit Benefit which might be attained therby. What that was if you desire to Know, it was the Excellency Dignity and Exaltation 20 of his Creature.

43

O Adorable and Eternal GOD! hast thou made me a free Agent!
And enabled me if I pleas to offend Thee infinitly! What other
End couldst Thou intend by this, but that I might pleas Thee
infinitly! That having the Power of Pleasing or displeasing I might
5 be the friend of God! Of all Exaltations in all Worlds this is the
Greatest. To make a World for me was much, to command Angels
and Men to lov me was much, to prepare Eternall Joys for me was
more. But to giv me a Power to displeas thee, or to set a Sin before
thy face, which Thou infinitly hatest, to profane Eternity, or to
10 defile thy Works, is more stupendious then all these. What other
couldst thou intend by it, but that I might infinitly please Thee?
And having the Power of Pleasing or Displeasing, might pleas thee
and my self infinitly, in being Pleasing! Hereby Thou hast pre-
pared a new fountain and Torrent of Joys, Greater then all that
15 went before, seated us in the Throne of God, made us thy Com-
panions, endued us with a Power most Dreadfull to ourselvs, that
we might liv in Sublime and Incomprehensible Blessednes for
evermore. For the Satisfaction of our Goodness, is the most
Soveraign Delight of which we are capable. And that by our own
20 Actions we should be wel pleasing to Thee, is the Greatest Felicity
Nature can contain. O Thou who art infinitly Delightfull to the
Sons of Men, make me, and the Sons of Men, infinitly Delightfull
unto Thee. Replenish our Actions with Amiableness and Beauty,
that they may be answerable to thine, and like unto Thine in
25 sweetness and value. That as Thou in all thy Works art pleasing
to us, we in all our Works may be so to Thee; our own Actions as
they are pleasing to Thee being an Offspring of Pleasures sweeter
then all.

44

This he thought a Principle at the Bottom of Nature, That what-
soever satisfied the Goodness of Nature, was the Greatest Treasure.
Certainly men therfore Erre becaus they Know not this Principle ·
for all Inclinations and Desires in the Soul flow from, and tend to the
5 Satisfaction of Goodness. Tis strange that an Excess of Goodness
should be the fountain of all Evil. An Ambition to pleas, a Desire to
Gratifie, a great Desire to Delight others being the Greatest Snare
in the world. Hence is it that all Hypocrisies and Honors arise, I

mean Esteem of Honors. Hence all Imitations of human customs, hence all compliances and submissions to the Vanities and Errors 10 of this World. For Men being mistaken in the Nature of Felicity, and we by a strong inclination prone to pleas them, follow a Multitud to do evil. We naturaly desire to approve our selvs to them, and abov all other things covet to be Excellent, to be Greatly Beloved, to be Esteemed, and Magnified, and therfore endeavor what they 15 endeavor, prize what they prize, Magnifie what they desire, desire what they Magnify: ever doing that which will render us accepted to them; and coveting that which they admire and prais: that so we might be delightfull. And the more there are that delight in us the more Great and Happy we account our selvs.   20

45

This Principle of Nature, when you remov the Rust it hath contracted by Corruption, is pure Gold; and the most Orient Jewel that shines in Man. Few consider it either in it self, or in the Design of the Implanter. No man doubts but it is Blessed to receiv. To be made a Glorious Creature, and to hav Worlds given to one is Excel- 5 lent. But to be a Glorious Creature and to Giv, is a Blessedness unknown. It is a Kind of Paradox in our Savior, and not (as we read of) revealed upon earth, but to S. Paul from heaven, *It is more Blessed to Giv then to receiv*. It is a Blessedness too high to be understood. To Giv is the Happiness of GOD; to Receiv, of Man. But O 10 the Mystery of His Loving Kindness, even that also hath He imparted to us. Will you that I ascend higher? In giving us him self, in giving us the World, in giving us our Souls and Bodies he hath don much, but all this had been Nothing, unless he had given us a Power to hav given him our selvs · in which is contained the Greatest 15 Pleasure and Honor that is. We lov our selvs earnestly, and therfore rejoyce to have Palaces and Kingdoms · but when we have these, yea Heaven and Earth, unless we can be Delightfull and Joyous to others they will be of no value. One soul to whom we may be pleasing is of Greater Worth then all Dead Things. Som unsearchable Good lieth 20 in this, without which the other is but a vile and desolate Estate. So that to hav all Worlds, with a certain sence that they are infinitly Beautiful and Rich and Glorious is miserable vanity, and leavs us forlorn, if all things are Dead, or if our selvs are not Divine and Illustrious Creatures.   25

Z.

46

O the Superlative Bounty of GOD! Where all Power seemeth to
ceas, he proceedeth in Goodness: and is wholy infinit Unsearch-
able and Endless. He seemeth to hav made as many things depend
upon Mans Liberty, as his own. When all that could be wrought
5 by the Use of His own Liberty were attained, by Mans Liberty
he attained more. This is Incredible, but Experience will make it
Plain. By his own Liberty he could but Creat Worlds and giv
himself to creatures Make Images and endow them with faculties,
or seat them in Glory. But to see them Obedient, or to enjoy the
10 Pleasure of their Amity and Praises, to make them Fountains of
Actions like his own, (without which indeed they could not be
Glorious:) or to enjoy the Beauty of their free Imitation, this could
by no means be, without the Liberty of his Creatures intervening.
Nor indeed could the World be Glorious, or they Blessed without
15 this Attainment. For can the World be Glorious unless it be Use-
full? And to what Use could the World serv Him, if it served not
those, that in this were supremely Glorious, that they could Obey
and Admire and Lov and Prais, and Imitat their Creator? Would
it not be wholy useless without such Creatures? In Creating
20 Liberty therfore and giving it to his Creatures he Glorified All
Things: Himself, his Works, and the Subjects of His Kingdom.

47

You may feel in your self how Conduciv this is to your Highest
Happiness. For that you should be Exalted to the fruition of
Worlds, and in the midst of innumerable most Glorious Creatures
be vile and Ingratfull, Injurious and Dishonorable, Hatefull and
5 evill, is the Greatest Misery and Dissatisfaction imaginable. But
to be the Joy and Delight of innumerable Thousands, to be admired
as the Similitud of God, to be Amiable and Honorable, to be an
Illustrious and Beautifull Creature, to be a Blessing. O the Good
we perceiv in this! O the Suavity! O the Contentation! O the
10 infinit and unspeakable Pleasure! Then indeed we Reign and
Triumph when we are Delighted in. Then are we Blessed when
we are a Blessing. When all the World is at Peace with us and takes
Pleasure in us, when our Actions are Delightfull, and our Persons
lovly, when our Spirits Amiable, and our Affections inestimable,
15 then are we Exalted to the Throne of Glory · for things when they

are usefull are most Glorious, and it is impossible for you or me to
be usefull, but as we are Delightfull to GOD and his Attendants.
And that the Head of the World, or the End for which all Worlds
were made should be useles, as it is improportiond to the Glory of
the Means, and Methods of his Exaltation, so is it the Reproach of 20
his Nature, and the utter undoing of all his Glory. It is improportionable to the Beauty of his Ways who made the World, and to the
Expectation of his Creatures.

48

By this you may see, that the Works or Actions flowing from your
own Liberty are of Greater Concernment to you then all that could
possibly happen besides. And that it is more to your Happiness
what you are, then what you enjoy. Should God giv him self and all
Worlds to you, and you refuse them, it would be to no purpose · 5
should he lov you and magnify you, should he giv his Son to Dy for
you and command all Angels and Men to lov you, should he
Exalt you in his Throne, and giv you Dominion over all his Works
and you neglect them it would be to no purpose. Should he make you
in his Image, and employ all his Wisdom and Power to fill Eternity 10
with Treasures, and you despise them it would be in vain. In all
these Things you hav to do; and therfore your Actions are great
and Magnificent, being of infinit Importance in all Eys. While all
Creatures stand in Expectation what will be the result of your
Liberty. Your Exterior Works are little in Comparison of these. 15
And God infinitly desires you should demean your self Wisely in
these Affairs: that is Rightly. Esteeming and receiving what he gives,
with Veneration and Joy and infinit Thanksgiving. Many other
Works there are, but this is the Great Work of all Works to be
performed. Consider Whether more depends upon Gods Lov to 20
you, or your Lov to Him. From His Lov all the Things in Heaven
and Earth flow unto you; but if you lov neither Him nor them,
you bereav your self of all, and make them infinitly evil and Hurtfull to you and your self abominable. So that upon your Lov
naturaly depends your own Excellency and the Enjoyment of His. 25
It is by your Lov that you enjoy all His Delights, and are Delightfull
to Him.

49

It is very observable by what small Principles infusing them in the
Beginning GOD attaineth infinit Ends. By infusing the Principle
of Self lov he hath made a Creature Capable of Enjoying all Worlds:
to whom, did he not lov him self, nothing could be given. By
5 infusing Gratefull Principles, and inclinations to Thanksgiving
He hath made that Creature Capable of more then all Worlds,
yea of more then Enjoying the Dietie in a Simple Way: tho we
should suppose it to be infinit. For to Enjoy God as the fountain
of infinit Treasures, and as the Giver of all, is infinit Pleasure:
10 But He by his Wisdom infusing Gratefull Principles, hath made
us upon the very Account of Self Lov to lov him more then our
selvs. And us, who without self Lov could not be pleased at all,
even as we lov our selvs he hath so infinitly pleased, that we are
able to rejoyce in him and to lov him more then our selvs. And by
15 loving him more then our selvs, in very Gratitud and Honor, to
take more Pleasure in his Felicity then in our own, By which way
we best Enjoy Him. To see his Wisdom Goodness and Power
Employed in Creating all Worlds for our Enjoyment, and infinitly
Magnified in Beautifying them for us, and Governing them for us;
20 satisfies our self lov; but withall it so obligeth us, that in Lov to
Him, which it createth in us, it maketh us more to Delight in those
Attributs as they are his, then as they are our own. And the truth
is, without this we could not fully Delight in them · for the most
Excellent and Glorious Effect of all had been unatchieved. But now
25 there is an infinit Union between Him and us, He being infinitly
Delightfull to us and we to Him. For he infinitly Delighteth to see
Creatures Act upon such Illustrious and Eternal Principles, in a
maner so Divine Heroick, and most truly Blessed · and we delight
in seeing Him giving us the Power.

50

That I am to receiv all the Things in Heaven and Earth is a Prin-
ciple not to be Sleighted. That in receiving I am to behav my self
in a Divine and Illustrious Maner, is equaly Glorious. That
GOD and all Eternity are mine is surely Considerable: That I
5 am His, is more. How ought I to Adorn my self, who am made
for his Enjoyment? If Mans heart be a Rock of Stone, these things
ought to be Engraven in it with a pen of a Diamond: and evry

letter to be filled up with Gold that it might Eternaly Shine in Him
and before him: Wherever we are living, whatever we are doing
these things ought always to be felt within him. Abov all Trades, 10
abov all Occupations this is most Sublime · this is the Greatest of
all Affairs. Whatever els we do, it is only in order to this End that
we may live Conveniently to Enjoy the World, and GOD within
it; which is the Soveraign Employment including and crowning all ·
the celestial Life of a Glorious Creature, without which all other 15
Estates are Servile and Impertinent.†

51

Man being to liv in the Image of GOD, and thus of Necessity to
becom productiv of Glorious Actions, was made Good, that he
might rejoyce in the fruits, which himself did yeeld. That Goodness
which by Error and Corruption becomes a Snare, being in the clear
and pure Estate of Innocency, the fountain and the chanell of all 5
His Joys.

52

Thus you see how GOD has perfectly pleased me: It ought also
to be my care perfectly to pleas Him. He has given me freedom,
and adventured the Power of Sinning into my Hands: it ought to
be a Principle engraven in me, to use it Nobly · to be Illustrious
and Faithfull, To please him in the Use of it, to consult his Honor, 5
and having all the Creatures in all Worlds by His Gift Ministering
unto Me, to behav my self as a faithfull Friend to so Great a Majesty,
so Bountifull a Lord, so Divine a Benefactor. Nothing is so Easy as
to yeeld ones Assent to Glorious Principles, nothing so Clear in
upright Nature, nothing so Obscure to find in perverted, nothing 10
so Difficult to practice at all. In the Rubbish of Depraved Nature
they are lost, tho when they are found by any one, and shewn, like
Jewels they shine by their Nativ Splendor.

53

If you ask, what is becom of us since the Fall? becaus all these
things now lately named seem to pertain to the Estate of Innocency;
Truly Now we hav superadded Treasures: Jesus Christ. And are
restored to the Exercise of the same Principles, upon higher

50. 11. *Occupations* deleted; above it, *Affairs* also deleted.

5 Obligations: I will not say with More Advantage. Tho perhaps
Obligations them selvs are to us Advantage. For what enabled
Adam to lov God? Was it not that God loved him? What con-
strained him to be avers from God? Was it not that God was
avers from Him? When he was faln he thought GOD would
10 hate him, and be his Enemy Eternaly. And this was the Miserable
Bondage that Enslaved him. But when he was restored; O the
infinit and Eternal Change! His very lov to Himself made him
to prize His Eternal Lov. I mean his Redeemers. Do we not all
lov our selvs? Self lov maketh us to lov those that lov us, and to
15 hate all those that hate us. So that Obligations themselvs are to us
Advantage. How we com to lose those Advantages I will not stand
here to relate. In a Clear Light it is certain no Man can perish.
For GOD is more Delightfull then He was in Eden. Then he was
as Delightfull as was possible but he had not that occasion, as by
20 Sin was offered, to superad many more Delights then before.
Being more Delightfull and more Amiable, He is more Desirable,
and may now be more Easily yea Strongly Beloved · for the Amiable-
ness of the Object Enables us to lov it.

54

It was your friends Delight to Meditat the Principles of Upright
Nature: and to see how things stood in Paradice before they were
Muddied and Blended and Confounded · for now they are lost
and buried in Ruines. Nothing appearing but fragments, that are
5 worthless Shreds and Parcels of them. To see the Intire Piece
ravisheth the Angels. It was his Desire to recover them and to
Exhibit them again to the Eys of Men. Abov all things he desired
to see those Principles which a Stranger in this World would covet
to behold upon his first appearance. And that is what Principles
10 those were, by which the Inhabitants of this World, are to liv
Blessedly and to Enjoy the same. He found them very Easy, and
infinitly Noble: very Noble, and productiv of unspeakable Good,
were they well persued. We hav named them, and they are such as
these, A Man should Know the Blessings he enjoyeth. A Man
15 should prize the Blessings which he Knoweth. A Man should be
Thankfull for the Benefits which he prizeth. A Man should rejoyce
in that for which He is Thankfull. These are easy things, and so
are those also which are drowned in a Deluge of Errors and Customs,

That Blessings the more they are, are the sweeter; the longer they
continue the more to be Esteemed; the more they serv, if Lovers and 20
Friends, the more Delightfull, yet these are the hard lessons, in a
pervers and Retrograde World to be practiced: and almost the only
Lessons necessary to its Enjoyment.

55

He was a Strict and Severe Applier of all Things to Himself. And
would first hav his Self Lov satisfied, and then his Lov of all others.
It is true that Self Lov is Dishonorable, but then it is when it is alone.
And Self endedness is Mercinary, but then it is when it endeth in
oneself. It is more Glorious to lov others, and more desirable, but 5
by Natural Means to be attained. That Pool must first be filled, that
shall be made to overflow. He was ten yeers studying before he could
satisfy his Self Lov. And now finds nothing more easy then to lov
others better than oneself. And that to love Mankind so is the com-
prehensiv Method to all felicity. For it makes a Man Delightfull 10
to GOD and Men, to Himself and Spectators, and God and Men
Delightfull to Him, and all creatures infinitly in them. But as not
to lov oneself at all is Bruitish: or rather Absurd and Stonish: (for
Beasts do lov themselvs) so hath GOD by rational Methods enabled
us to lov others better then our selvs, and therby made us the 15
most Glorious Creatures. Had we not loved our selvs at all we
could never hav been obliged to lov any thing. So that self Lov is
the Basis of all Lov. But when we do lov our selvs, and self Lov
is satisfied infinitly in all its Desires and possible Demands, then
it is easily led to regard the Benefactor more then it self, and for his 20
sake overflows abundantly to all others. So that God by satis-
fying my self Lov, hath enabled, and engaged me to love
others.

56

No man loves, but he loves another more then Himself. In mean In-
stances this is apparent. If you com into an Orchard with a person
you lov, and there be but one ripe cherry you prefer it to the other.
If two lovers Delight in the same piece of Meat, either takes pleasure
in the other, and more esteems the Beloveds Satisfaction. What 5
ailes men, that they do not see it? In greater Cases this is Evident.
A mother runs upon a sword to save her Beloved. A Father leaps

into the fire to fetch out his Beloved. Lov brought Christ from
Heaven to Die for his Beloved. It is in the Nature of Lov to Des-
10 pise it self: and to think only of its Beloveds Welfare. Look to it,
it is not right Lov, that is otherwise. Moses and S. Paul were no
fools. God make me one of their Number. I am sure Nothing is
more Acceptable to him, then to lov others so as to be willing to
impart even ones own Soul for their Benefit and welfare.

57

Nevertheless it is infinitly rewarded: tho it seemeth Difficult · for
by this Lov do we becom Heirs of all Mens Joys, and Coheirs
with Christ. For, what is the reason of your own Joys, when you
are Blessed with Benefits? Is it not self Lov? Did you lov others
5 as you lov your self, you would be as much affected with their
Joys. Did you lov them more, more · for according to the Measure
of your Lov to others will you be Happy in them · for according
therto you will be Delightfull to them, and Delighted in your
felicity. The more you lov men, the more Delightfull you will be
10 to God, and the more Delight you will take in God, and the more
you will enjoy Him. So that the more like you are to Him in Good-
ness, the more abundantly you will enjoy his Goodness. By loving
others you liv in others to receiv it.

58

Shall I not lov him infinitly for whom GOD made the World
and gav his Son? Shall I not lov him infinitly who loveth me
infinitly? Examin your self Well, and you will find it a difficult
matter to lov God so as to Die for him, and not to lov your Brother
5 so as to die for Him in like maner. Shall I not lov Him infinitly
whom God loveth infinitly, and commendeth to my Lov, as the
Representativ of Himself, with such a Saying, What ye do to Him
is don unto me? And if I lov him so can I forbear to Help him?
Verily had I but one Crown in the World, being in an open field,
10 where both he and I were ready to perish, and twere necessary
that one of us must hav it all, or be Destroyed, tho I knew not where
to hav relief, he should hav it, and I would die with Comfort.
I will not say, How small a comfort so small a succor is did I keep it:
but how Great a Joy, to be the occasion of anothers Life! Lov

56. 14. *Soul*: 'Souls' in MS, because the possessive was originally 'our'.

Knows not how to be Timerous, becaus it receives what it gives 15
away. And is unavoidably the End of its own Afflictions and
anothers Happiness. Let him that pleases Keep his mony. I am more
rich in this Noble Charity to all the World, and more enjoy my self
in it, then he can be in both the Indies.

59

Is it unnatural to do what Jesus Christ hath don? He that would
not in the same Cases do the same things can never be saved · for
unless we are led by the Spirit of Christ we are none of His. Lov
in him that in the same Cases would do the same Things, will be
an Oracle allways inspiring and teaching him what to doe: how 5
far to adventure upon all occasions. And certainly he, Whose Lov
is like his Saviors, will be far greater then any that is now alive, in
Goodness and Lov to GOD and Men. This is a sure Rule. Lov
studies not to be scanty in its Measures, but how to abound and over-
flow with Benefits. He that Pincheth and Studieth to Spare is a pitti- 10
full Lover: unless it be for others sakes. Lov studieth to be Pleasing
Magnificent and Noble, and would in all Things be Glorious and
Divine unto its Object. Its whole Being is to its Object, and its whole
felicity in its Object. And it hath no other thing to take care for.
It doth Good to its own Soul while it doth Good to another. 15

60

Here upon Earth, it is under many Disadvantages, and Impedi-
ments that maim it in its Exercise. But in Heaven it is most Glorious.
And it is my Happiness that I can see it on both sides the Vail or
Skreen. There it appeareth in all its Advantages for evry Soul being
full, and fully satisfied, at Eas, in rest, and Wanting nothing, easily 5
overflows and shines upon all. It is its perfect Interest so to do, and
nothing Hinders it. Self Love there being swallowed up and made
perfect in the Lov of others. But here it is pinched and straitned by
wants: here it is awakend and put in mind of it self: here it is
divided and Distracted between two. It has a Body to provide for, 10
necessities to reliev and a person to supply. Therfore is it in this
world the more Glorious, if in the midst of these Disadvantages it
exert it self in its Operations. In the other World it swimmeth down
the stream and acteth with its interest. Here therfore is the Place of
its Trial where its Operations and its Interest are Divided. And If 15
our Lord Jesus Christ as som think, Knew the Glory to which he

should ascend, by Dying for others, and that all was safe which he undertook, becaus in humbling Himself to the Death of the Cross he did not forsake but attain his Glory: The like Fate shall follow
20 us · only let us expect it after Death as he did. And remember that this and the other life are made of a Piece: but this is the time of Trial, that of Rewards. The Greatest Disadvantages of Lov are its Highest Advantages · in the Greatest Hazzards it atchieveth to it self the Greatest Glory. It is seldom considered; but a Lov to
25 others Stronger then what we bear to our selvs, is the Mother of all the Heroick Actions that hav made Histories pleasant and Beautified the World.

61

Since Lov will thrust in it self as the Greatest of all Principles, let us at last willingly allow it Room. I was once a Stranger to it, now I am familiar with it as a Daily acquaintance. Tis the only Heir and Benefactor of the World. It seems it will break in evry where,
5 as that without which the World could not be Enjoyed. Nay as that without which it would not be Worthy to be Enjoyed · for it was Beautified by Lov, and commandeth the Lov of a Donor to us. Lov is a Phœnix that will revive in its own Ashes, inherit Death, and smell sweetly in the Grave.

62

These two properties are in it · that it can attempt all, and suffer all. And the more it suffers the more it is Delighted, and the more it attempteth the more it is enriched · for it seems that all Lov is so Mysterious, that there is som thing in it which needs Expression, and
5 can never be understood by any Manifestation, (of it self, in it self:) but only by Mighty Doings and Sufferings. This moved GOD the Father to Creat the World and GOD, the Son to die for it. Nor is this all. There are many other ways wherby it manifests it self as well as these · there being still somthing infinit in it behind. In its Laws in
10 its Tenderness, in its Provisions, in its Caresses, in its Joys as well as in its Hazzards, in its Honors as well as in its Cares, nor does it ever ceas till it has poured out it self in all its Communications. In all which it ever rights and satisfies it self. For abov all Things in all Worlds it desires to be Magnified, and taketh pleasure in being
15 Glorified before its Object · for which caus also it does all those Things, which magnify its Object and increase its Happiness.

63

Whether Lov principaly intends its own Glory, or its Objects Happiness is a Great Question: and of the more importance, becaus the right ordering of our own Affections depends much upon the Solution of it · for on the one side, to be Self Ended is Mercenary, and Base and Slavish, and to do all things for ones own 5 Glory, is servile, and vain Glory. On the other GOD doth all things for Himself, and seeketh his Glory as his last End, and is himself the End whom he seeks and attains in all His Ways. How shall we reconcile this Riddle? or untie this Knot? for som Men hav taken occasion herby seeing this in Lov, to affirm that there is no true Lov in the 10 World. But it is all self Lov whatsoever a Man doth. Implying also that it was self lov in our Savior, that made Him to undertake for us. Wherupon we might justly Question, whether it were more for his own Ends, or more for ours? As also whether it were for his own End that God created the World or more for ours? for Extraordinary 15 much of our Duty and felicity hangeth upon this Point: and whatsoever sword untieth this Gordian Knot, will open a World of Benefit and Instruction to us.

64

GOD doth desire Glory as his Soveraign End, but True Glory. From whence it followeth that he doth soveraignly and supremely desire both his own Glory and Mans Happiness. Tho that be Miraculous, yet its very Plain · for True Glory is to lov another for his own sake, and to prefer his Welfare and to seek His Happiness. 5 Which God doth becaus it is true Glory. So that he seeks the Happiness of Angels and Men as his Last End, and in that his Glory: to wit His Tru Glory · fals and vain Glory is inconsistent with His Nature, but True Glory is the very Essence of his Being. Which is Lov unto His Beloved, Lov unto Himself, Lov unto His Creatures. 10

65

How can God be Lov unto Him self, without the Imputation of Self Lov? Did He lov Him self under any other Notion then as He is the Lover of his Beloved: there might be som Danger. But the reason why He loves Himself being becaus He is Lov: nothing is more Glorious then his Self Lov. For he loves himself becaus 5 he is infinit and Eternal Lov to others. Becaus he loves himself

He cannot endure that His Lov should be Displeased. And loving others vehemently and infinitly, all the Lov he bears to himself is Tenderness towards them. All that wherin he pleaseth Himself is Delightfull to them: He magnifieth Himself in Magnifying them. And in fine, His Lov unto Himself is his Lov unto them. And His Lov unto them is Lov unto Him self. They are individualy one· which it is very Amiable and Beautifull to Behold. Becaus therin the Simplicity of God doth evidently appear. The more he loveth them the Greater he is and the more Glorious. The more he loveth them the more precious and Dear they are to Him. The more he loveth them the more Joys and Treasures He possesseth. The more He loveth them the more he Delighteth in their Felicity. The more he loveth them, the more he delighteth in himself for being their felicity. The more he loveth them, the more he rejoyceth in all his Works for serving them: and in all his Kingdom for Delighting them. And being Lov to them the more he loveth Himself and the more jealous he is least himself should be Displeased, the more he loveth them and tendereth them and secureth their Welfare. And the more he desires his own Glory the more Good he doth for them, in the more Divine and genuine maner. You must lov after his similitude.

66

He from whom I derived these things delighted always that I should be acquainted with Principles, that would make me fit for all Ages. And truly in Lov there are enough of them. For since Nature never Created anything in vain, and Lov of all other is the most Glorious there is not any Relick or Parcel of that that shall be unused. It is not like Gold made to be Buried and Concealed in Darkness. But like the Sun to Communicat it self wholy in its Beams unto all. It is more Excellent and more Communicativ. It is hid in a Centre, and no where at all, if we respect its Body. But if you regard its Soul, it is an interminable Sphere, which as som say of the Sun, is infinities infinita, in the Extention of its Beams, being equaly vigorous in all Places, equaly near to all Objects, Equaly Acceptable to all Persons, and equaly abundant in all its Overflowings. Infinitly evry where. This of Naked and Divested Lov in its true Perfection. Its own Age is too little to Contain it, Its Greatness is Spiritual, like the Dieties. It filleth the World, and exceeds what it filleth. It is present with all Objects, and Tasts

all Excellencies, and meeteth the Infinitness of GOD in evry Thing.
So that in Length it is infinit as well as in Bredth, being equaly
vigorous at the utmost Bound to which it can extend as here, and 20
as wholy there as here and wholy evry where. Thence also it can see
into further Spaces, Things present and Things to come Hight and
Depth being open before it, and all things in Heaven Eternity and
Time equaly near.

67

Were not lov the Darling of GOD, this would be a Rash and a bold
Salley. But since it is His Image, and the Lov of GOD, I may almost
say the GOD of GOD, becaus His Beloved: all this Happeneth
unto Lov. And this Lov is your tru Self when you are in Act what
you are in Power · the Great Dæmon of the World, the End of all 5
Things · the Desire of Angels and of all Nations. A creature so
Glorious, that having seen it, it puts an End to all Curiosity and
Swallows up all Admiration. Holy, Wise, and Just towards all
Things, Blessed in all Things, the Bride of GOD, Glorious before
all, His Offspring and first Born, and so like Him that being de- 10
scribed, one would think it He. I should be afraid to say all this of it,
but that I know Him, How He delighteth to hav it magnified. And
how He hath magnified it infinitly before becaus it is his Bride and
first Born. I will speak only a little of its Violence and Vigor afar
off. It can lov an Act of Virtu in the utmost Indies, and hate a 15
Vice in the Highest Heavens, It can see into Hell and Adore
the Justice of GOD among the Damned, it can behold and Ad-
mire his Lov from Everlasting. It can be present with his infinit
and Eternal Lov, it can rejoyce in the Joys which it foreseeth ·
can Lov Adam in Eden, Moses in the Wilderness, Aaron in the 20
Tabernacle, David before the Ark, S. Paul among the Nations,
and Jesus either in the Manger or on the crosse. All these it can
lov with violence. And when it is restored from all that is Ter-
rene and Sensual, to its tru Spiritual Being, it can lov these
and any of these as violently as any Person in the Living 25
Age.

68

Shall it not lov violently what God loveth, what Jesus Christ
loveth, what all Saints and Angels lov? Moses Glorified GOD
in a Wonderfull Maner, he prophesied of Christ he Plagued the

Egyptians, he Brought the Israelites out of the Land of Egypt,
5 he Guided them in the Wilderness he gav us the Law, He Loved
the People more then his own life: yea then his own self and all the
possible Glory that might have accrued to Him. Shall not He be
Beloved? And what shall we think of Christ Himself? Shall not all
our Lov be where his is? Shall it not wholy follow and Attend Him?
10 Yet shall it not forsake other Objects· but lov them all in Him, and
Him in them, and them the more becaus of Him, and Him the more
becaus of them· for by Him it is redeemed to them. So that as God is
omnipresent our Lov shall be at once with all: that is We: having
these Strengths to Animat and Quicken our Affection.

69

To lov one Person with a Private Lov, is poor and miserable: To
lov all is Glorious. To lov all Persons in all Ages, All Angels, all
Worlds is Divine and Heavenly. To lov all Cities and all King-
doms, all Kings and all Peasants, and evry Person in all Worlds
5 with a natural intimat familiar Lov, as if Him alone, is Blessed.
This makes a Man Effectualy Blessed in all Worlds, a Delightfull
Lord of all Things, a Glorious friend to all Persons, a concerned
Person in all Transactions, and ever present with all Affairs. So
that he must ever be filled with Company, ever in the midst of all
10 Nations, ever joyfull, and ever Blessed. The Greatness of this Mans
Lov no Man can measure, it is stable like the Sun, it endureth for
ever as the Moon, it is a faithfull Witness in Heaven. It is stronger
and more Great than all Privat Affections. It representeth evry
person in the Light of Eternity, and loveth him with the Lov of
15 all Worlds. With a Lov conformable to Gods, Guided to the same
Ends and founded upon the same causes. Which however Lofty
and Divine it is, is ready to humble it self into the Dust to serv the
Person Beloved. And by how much the more Glorious and Sublime
it is, is so much the more Sweet and Truly Delightfull · Majesty
20 and Pleasure concurring together.

70

Now you may see what it is to be a Son of God more clearly. Lov
in its Glory is the friend of the Most High. It was begotten of
Him and is to sit in his Throne, and to reign in Communion with
Him. It is to Pleas him, and to be pleased by Him, in all his Works

Ways and Operations. It is ordained to hold an Eternal Correspon- 5
dence with Him in the Highest Heavens. It is here in its Infancy,
there in its Manhood and perfect Stature. He wills and commands
that it should be reverenced of all, and takes Pleasure to see it
Admired in its Excellencies. If Lov thus displayed be so Glorious
a Being, how much more Glorious and Great is He that is Soveraign 10
Lord of all Lords, and the Heavenly King of all these? So many
Monarchs under one Supreme, mightily set forth the Glory of
his Kingdom. If you ask by what Certainty, or by what Rules we
discover this? As by the Seed we conjecture what Plant will arise,
and know by the Acorn what Tree will Grow forth, or by the 15
Eagles Egge what Kind of Bird; so do we by the Powers of the Soul
upon Earth, Know what kind of Being, Person, and Glory it will
be in the Heavens. Its Blind and latent Powers shall be turned
into Act, its Inclinations shall be completed, and its Capacities
filled, for by this Means is it made Perfect. A Spiritual King is 20
an Eternal Spirit. Lov in the Abstract is a Soul Exerted. Neither
do you esteem yourself to be any other then LOV alone. GOD is
Lov. And you are never like Him, till you are so: Lov unto all
Objects in like maner.

71

To sit in the Throne of GOD is the most Supreme Estate that
can befall a Creature. It is Promised in the Revelations. But few
understand what is promised there, and but few believ it.

72

To sit in the Throne of God is to inhabit Eternity. To Reign
there is to be pleased with all Things in Heaven and Earth from
Everlasting to everlasting, as if we had the Soveraign Disposal of
them. For He is to Dwell in us, and We in Him, becaus He liveth
in our Knowledg and we in His. His Will is to be in our Will, and 5
our Will is to be in His Will, so that both being joyned and be-
coming one, We are pleased in all his Works as He is; and herin
the Image of God perfectly consisteth. No Artist maketh a Throne
too Wide for the Person. GOD is the Greatest and Divinest
Artist. Thrones proper and fit for the Persons, are always prepared 10
by the Wisest Kings · for little Bodies Bodily Thrones: for Spirits
invisible. GODs Throne is His Omnipresence, and that is infinit ·

who Dwelleth in Himself, or in that Light which is inaccessible.
The Omnipresence therfore and the Eternity of GOD are our
15 Throne · wherin we are to reign for ever more. His infinit and
Eternal Lov are the Borders of it, which evry where we are to meet,
and evry where to see for ever more. In this Throne our savior
sitteth, who is the Alpha and Omega, the first and the last, the
Amen, and the faithfull Witness, who said, The Glory which Thou
20 hast given me, I hav given them, That they may be one as we are
one. In Him the fulness of the Godhead dwelleth Bodily. If that
bee too Great to be applied to Men, remember what follows, His
Church is the fullness of Him that filleth all in all. The fulness of
the Godhead Dwelleth in Him for our sakes. And if yet it seemeth
25 too Great to be Enjoyed: by the surpassing Excellency of His
Eternal Power, it is made more then ours · for in Him we shall
more Enjoy it, then if it were infinitly, and wholy, all in our
selvs.

73

If any thing yet remaineth that is Dreadfull, or Terrible or Doubt-
full, that seemeth to Startle us, there is more behind that will more
amaze us · for God is infinit in the Expression of his Lov, as we shall
all find to our Eternal Comfort. Objects are so far from Diminish-
5 ing, that they magnify the faculties of the Soul beholding them.
A sand in your conception conformeth your soul, and reduceth
it to the Cize and Similitud of a sand. A Tree apprehended is a Tree
in your Mind, the whole Hemisphere and the Heavens magnifie
your soul to the Wideness of the Heavens. All the Spaces abov
10 the Heavens enlarg it Wider to their own Dimensions. And what
is without Limit maketh your Conception illimited and Endless.
The infinity of GOD is infinitly Profitable as well as Great: as
Glorious as Incomprehensible: so far from streightening that it
magnifieth all Things. And must be seen in you, or GOD will be
15 Absent. Nothing less then infinit is GOD, and as finit he cannot be
Enjoyed.

74

But what is there more that will more Amaze us? Can any thing
be behind such Glorious Mysteries? Is GOD more Soveraign in
other Excellencies? Hath He shewed Himself Glorious in any

thing besides? Verily there is no End of all His Greatness, his understanding is infinit, and His Ways innumerable. How Precious, saith the Psalmist, are thy Thoughts to me O God, when I would count them they are more then can be numbered. There is no man that reckoneth them up in order unto Thee. O my Lord I will endeavor it: and I will Glorify Thee for ever more. The most Perfect Laws are agreeable only to the most Perfect Creatures. Since therfore thy Laws are the most perfect of all that are Possible, so are thy Creatures. And if infinit Power be wholy exprest, O Lord what Creatures! what Creatures shall we becom! What Divine, what Illustrious Beings! Souls worthy of so Great a Lov, Blessed for ever. Made Worthy, tho not found · for Lov either findeth, or maketh an Object Worthy of it self · for which caus Picus Mirandula admirably saith, in his Tract De Dignitate Hominis, I hav read in the Monuments of Arabia, that Abdala the Saracen being Asked, Quid in hâc quasi mundanâ Scenâ admirandum maxime Spectaretur? What in this World was most Admirable?, Answerd, MAN · then whom he saw nothing more to be Admired. Which Sentence of his is seconded by that of Mercurius Trismegistus, Magnum, O Asclepî, Miraculum, Homo. Man is a Great and Wonderfull Miracle. Ruminating upon the Reason of these Sayings, those things did not satisfy me, which many hav spoken concerning the Excellency of Human Nature. As that Man was Creaturarum Internuncius; Superis familiaris, Inferiorum Rex; sensuum perspicaciâ, Rationis Indagine, Intelligentiæ Lumine, Naturæ Interpres · Stabilis Ævi et fluxi Temporis Interstitium, et (qd Persæ dicunt) Mundi Copula immo Hymenæus. A Messenger between the Creatures, Lord of Inferior things, and familiar to those abov; by the Keen[n]ess of his Sences, the Peircing of his Reason, and the Light of Knowledg, the Interpreter of Nature, A seeming Intervall between Time and Eternity and the Inhabitant of both, the Golden link or Tie of the World, yea the Hymenæus Marrying the Creator and his Creatures together; made as David witnesseth a little lower then the Angels. All these things are Great, but they are not the Principal: that is, They are not those which rightly chalenge the name and title of *most Admirable*. And so he goeth on, Admiring and Exceeding all that had been spoken before concerning the Excellency of Man. Why do we not rather Admire the Angels and the Quires abov the Heavens? At length I seemed to understand,

Why Man was the most Happy, and therfore the most Worthy
45 to be Admired of all the Creatures: and to Know that Estate,
which in the order of Things he doth enjoy, not only abov the
Beasts but abov the Stars, and that might be envied even of the
Supra Celestial Spirits, which he stileth, Ultra-Mundanis Menti-
bus invidiosam.

75

The Supreme Architect and our Everlasting father, having made
the World, this most Glorious Hous, and Magnificent Temple of
his Divinity, by the Secret Laws of his Hidden Wisdom; He
adorned the Regions above the Heavens with most Glorious
5 Spirits, the Spheres he Enlivened with Eternal Souls, the Dreggy
Parts of the Inferior World he filled with all Kind of Herds of
Living Creatures. Sed Opere Consummato, but His Work being
Compleated, He desired som one, that might Weigh and reason,
lov the Beauty, and admire the Vastness of so Great a Work.
10 All things therfore being, (as Moses and Tymæus Witness) already
finished, at last he thought of Creating Man. But there was not
in all the Platforms before conceived any Being after whom He
might form this New Offspring: Nor in all his Treasures what
He might giv this New Son by way of Inheritance: nor yet a
15 Place in all the Regions of the World, wherin this Contemplator
of the Univers might be Seated. All Things were already full,
all things were already distributed into their various Orders of
Supreme Middle and Inferior. But it was not the Part of infinit
Power, to fail as Defectiv in the last Production; it was not the Part
20 of infinit Wisdom, for want of Counsel to fluctuat in so Necessary
an Affair · it was not the part of infinit Goodness, or Soveraign
Lov, that He, who should be raised up to Prais the Divine Bounty
in other Things, should condemn it in himself. Statuit tandem
Opt. Opifex, ut cui dari nihil proprium poterat Commune esset,
25 quod privatum singulis fuit. The Wisest and Best of Workmen
appointed therfore, that he to whom nothing proper to himself
could be added, should have som thing of all that was peculiar to
evry thing. And therfore he took Man, the Image of all his Work,
and placing him in the Middle of the World, spake thus unto him.

76

O Adam, we hav given Thee neither a certain seat, nor a Private
face, nor a Peculiar office, that whatsoever seat or face or office
thou dost desire, thou mayst Enjoy. All other things hav a Nature
bounded within certain Laws, Thou only art loos from all, and
according to thy own Counsel in the hand of which I hav put 5
Thee, mayst chuse and prescribe what Nature thou wilt to thy
self. I hav placed Thee in the Middle of the World, that from
thence thou mayst behold on evry side more commodiously evry
thing in the whole World. We hav made Thee neither heavenly
nor Earthly Neither Mortal nor Immortal, that being the Honored 10
Former and Framer of thy self, thou mayst shape thy self into
what Nature thy self pleaseth.

77

O Infinit Liberality of God the father! O Admirable and supreme
felicity of Man! to whom it is given to hav what he desires and
to be what he Wisheth. The Bruits when they are brought forth
bring into the world with them what they are to possess con-
tinualy. The Spirits that are abov were, either from the begin- 5
ning or a little after, that which they are about to be to all Eternities.
Nascenti Homini omnigena vitæ Germina indidit Pater, God in-
fused the Seeds of evry Kind of Life into Man, Whatever seeds
evry one chuseth those spring up with him, and the fruits of those
shall he bear and enjoy. If sensual Things are chosen by Him 10
he shall becom a Beast, if Reasonable a Celestial Creature; if •
Intellectual an Angel and a Son of God; And if being content with
the lot of no Creatures, he withdraws Himself into the Centre of
His own Unitie, he shall be one Spirit with GOD, and Dwell
abov all in the Solitary Darkness of his Eternal Father.   15

78

This Picus Mirandula spake in an Oration made before a most
learned Assembly in a famous university. Any man may perceiv,
that He permitteth his fancy to wander a little Wantonly after the
maner of a Poet: but most deep and serious things are secretly
hidden under his free and luxuriant Language. The Changeable 5
Power he Ascribeth to Man is not to be referred to his Body · for as
he wisely saith, Neither doth the Bark make a Plant, but its stupid

and nothing-perceiving nature: neither doth the Skin make a Beast,
but his bruitish and sensual Nature, Neither doth Seperation from
10 a Body make an Angel but his Spiritual Intelligence. So neither
doth his Rinde or Coat or Skin or Body make a Man; to be this or
that, but the Interior Stupidness, or Sensuality, or Angelical
Intelligence of his Soul, make him accordingly a Plant, a Beast,
or an Angel. The Deformity, or Excellency is within.

79

Neither is it to be believed, that God filled all the World with
Creatures before he thought of man: but by that little Fable he
teacheth us the Excellency of Man. Man is the End, and therfore
the Perfection of all the Creatures · but as Eusebius Pamphilus
5 saith (in the Nicene Council) He was first in the Intention, tho
last in the Execution. All Angels were Spectators as well as He,
all Angels were free Agents as well as He: as we see by their Trial,
and the fall of Som; All Angels were seated in as convenient a
Place as he. But this is true, that He was the End of all, and the
10 last of all. And the Comprehensiv Head and the Bond of all, and
in that more Excellent then all the Angels: As for whom the visible
and Invisible Worlds were made, and to Whom all Creatures
ministered: as one also, that contained more Species in his Nature
then the Angels, which is not as som hav thought Derogatory,
15 but perfectiv to His Being. It is true also that GOD hath prevented
Him, and satisfied all Wishes, in giving Him such a Being as he
now enjoyeth. And that for infinit Reasons it was best that He
should be in a Changeable Estate, and hav power to chuse what
himself listed · for he may so chuse as to becom One Spirit with
20 GOD Almighty.

80

By chusing a Man may be turned and Converted into Lov. Which
as it is an Universal Sun filling and shining in the Eternity of
GOD, so is it infinitly more Glorious then the Sun is, not only
shedding abroad more Amiable and Delightfull Beams, Illumi-
5 nating and Comforting all Objects: yea Glorifying them in the
Supreme and Soveraign Maner, but is of all sensibles the most
Quick and Tender; being able to feel like the longlegged Spider,
at the utmost End of its Divaricated feet: and to be wholy present

in every place where any Beam of it self extends. The Sweetness
of its Healing Influences is Inexpressible. And of all Beings such 10
a Being would I chuse to be for ever. One that might inherit all
in the most Exquisit Maner, and be the Joy of all in the most
Perfect Measure.

81

Nazianzen professed him self to be a Lover of right reason · and
by it did undertake even to speak Oracles. Even so may we by
Right Reason discover all the Mysteries of heaven. And what our
Author here observeth, is very considerable, that Man by retiring
from all Externals and withdrawing into Him self, in the centre 5
of his own Unity becometh most like unto GOD. What Mercurius
said in the Dialogue is most true, Man is of all other the Greatest
Miracle. Yea verily. Should all the Miracles that ever were don
be drawn together, Man is a Miracle greater then they. And as
much may be written of Him alone as of the whole World. The 10
Dividing of the Sea, the commanding of the Sun, the making of the
World is nothing to the Single Creation of one Soul · there is so
much Wisdom and Power expressed in its faculties and Inclinations.
Yet is this Greatest of all Miracles unknown becaus Men are
addicted only to Sensible and Visible Things. So Great a World 15
in the Explication of its Parts is easy: but here the Dimensions of
Innumerable Worlds are shut up in a Centre. Where it should
lodg such innumerable Objects, as it doth by knowing whence it
should derive such infinit Streams, as flow from it by Loving,
how it should be a Mirror of all Eternity, being made of Nothing, 20
how it should be a fountain or a sun of Eternity out of which such
abundant Rivers of Affection flow, it is impossible to declare · but
abov all, how having no Material or Bodily Existence, its Substance
tho invisible should be so Rich and Precious. The Considera-
tion of one Soul is sufficient to convince all the Atheists in the 25
whole World.

82

The Abundance of its Beams, the Reality of its Beams, the free-
dom of its Beams, the Excellency and valu of its Beams are all
Transcendent. They shine upon all the Things in Heaven and
Earth and cover them all with Celestial Waters: Waters of Refresh-
ment, Beams of Comfort. They flow freely from a Mind desiring 5

to be Obedient Pleasing and Good. The Soul communicates it
self wholy by them: and is Richer in its Communications then
all Odors and Spices whatsoever. It containeth in its Nature
the Influences of the stars by way of Eminence, the Splendor of
10 the Sun, the verdure of Trees, the valu of Gold, the Lustre of·
precious stones, the sence of Beasts and the Life of Angels: the
fatness of feasts, the Magnificence of Palaces, the Melody of
Musick, the Sweetness of Wine, the Beauty of the Excellent, the
Excellency of Vertue and the Glory of cherubims. The Harmony
15 and the Joys of Heaven appear in Lov · for all these were made for
her, and all these are to be enjoyed in her.

83

Whether it be the Soul it self, or God in the Soul, that shines by
Lov, or both it is difficult to tell: but certainly the Lov of the Soul
is the sweetest Thing in the world. I have often admired what
should make it so Excellent. If it be God that lovs it is the Shining
5 of his Essence, if it be the Soul it is His Image: If it be both, it is
a double Benefit.

84

That GOD should lov in the Soul is most easy to believ, becaus
it is most easy to conceiv. But it is a Greater Mystery that the Soul
should lov in it self. If God loveth in the Soul it is the more precious,
if the Soul Loveth it is the more Marvellous. If you ask how a Soul
5 that was made of Nothing can return so many flames of Lov? Where
it should hav them or out of what Ocean it should communicat
them, it is impossible to declare · (for it can return those flames
upon all Eternity, and upon all the Creatures and Objects in it.)
Unless we say, as a Mirror returneth the very self-same Beams
10 it receiveth from the Sun, so the Soul returneth those Beams of
Lov that shine upon it from God. For as a Looking Glass is nothing
in Comparison of the World, yet containeth all the World in it,
and seems a real fountain of those Beams which flow from it, so
the Soul is Nothing in respect of God, yet all Eternity is con-
15 tained in it, and it is the real fountain of that Lov that proceedeth
from it. They are the Sun Beams which the Glass returneth: yet
they flow from the Glass and from the Sun within it. The Mirror
is the Well-Spring of them, becaus they Shine from the Sun within

the Mirror. Which is as deep within the Glass as it is high within
the Heavens. And this sheweth the Exceeding Richness and 20
preciousness of Lov, It is the Lov of God shining upon, and Dwell-
ing in the Soul· for the Beams that Shine upon it reflect upon
others and shine from it.

85

That the Soul shineth of it self is equaly manifest· for it can lov
with a lov distinct from GODs. It can lov irregularly. And no
irregular Lov is the Lov of GOD. It can forbear to lov while God
loveth. It can lov while GOD forbeareth. It can lov a Wicked
Man, Wickedly, and in his Wickedness. This shews plainly that 5
it can lov regularly, with a Lov that is not meerly the Reflexion of
Gods· for which caus it is not called a Mirror, but esteemed more,
a real fountain. Cant. . . . My Lov is a Spring shut up a Fountain
sealed. That is, Shut up like a letter, and concealed yet: but in the
Kingdom of Heaven, her Contents and Secrets shall be Known, 10
and her Beauty read of all Men. Her own Waters whence she
should receiv them it is most admirable.† Considering the Reality
and Beauty of them. But in this God hath magnified his infinit
Power, that He hath made them. Made them freely, made them her
own, out of her self to flow from her: Creatures as it were to which 15
her self givs their Existence. For indeed she could not lov, were not
her Beams of Lov, her own. Before She loves they are not, when she
lovs they are. And so she givs them their Being. Being Good her self,
becaus she can lov. Who els would be a Drie and Withered Stick,
having neither Life, nor value. But now she can Exalt a Creature 20
abov all the Things in Heaven and Earth, in her self: Esteem it
most Dear, Admire it, Honor it, Tender it, Desire it Delight in
it, be united to it, prefer it, forsake all things for it, giv all things
to it, Die for it. It can languish after it, when absent; take Pleasure
in it, when present; rejoyce in its happiness, liv only to it, study 25
to please it, Delight in suffering for it, feed it with Pleasures Honors
and Caresses, Do all things for its sake, Esteem Gold and Pearl
but Dross in Comparison, lay Crowns and Scepters at its feet,
Make it a Lord of Palaces, Delight in its own Beauties Riches and
pleasures, as they feed only and satisfy its Beloved; be ravished 30

8. *Cant*: 'Song of Solomon', 4¹².   17. *of*: MS 'or'.

with it. It can desire infinitly that Good things should be added to it. And all this shall we enjoy in evry Soul in the Kingdom of Heaven. All there being like so many Suns Shining upon one. All this Goodness is so like Gods, that Nothing can be more. And yet that it is
35 Distinct from his, is manifest becaus it is the Return or Recompence of it. The only thing which for and abov all Worlds he infinitly Desires.

86

Here upon Earth Souls lov what GOD hates, and hate what GOD loves. Did they keep their Ey Open always upon what He lovs, and see His Lov to them, and to all, they could not chuse but lov as He does. And were they Mirrors only that return his Lov, one
5 would think it impossible, while he shines upon them, to forbear to shine · but they are like the Ey, Mirrors with Lids, and the Lid of Ignorance or Inconsideration interposing, they are often times Ecclypsed, or shine only through som Cranies; so that here upon Earth having free Power to hold open or shut their Lids; to send,
10 or turn away their Beams; they may lov me, or forbear. The loss of their Lov is an Evil past Imagination · for it is a Removal of the End of Heaven and Earth, the Extinction of a Sun infinitly more Glorious then that in the Heavens. The Sun was made to serv this more Divine and Glorious Creature. The Lov of this Creature
15 is the End of Heaven and Earth, becaus the End for which Heaven and Earth were made for it. And in Recompence for all that God hath don for it it is to lov me. So that GOD hath Glorified me, by giving me a Communion with Himself in the End for which the World was made. And hath made that Creature to lov me, and
20 given me so Great a Certainty of its Lov and Title to it, that first it must ceas to lov it self, or to lov God, before it bereav me. It must ceas to be Wise, and forfeit all its Interest in Heaven and Earth, before it can ceas to lov me. In doing it it ruines it self and apostatizeth from all its Happiness.

87

In the Estate of Innocency the Lov of Man, seemed nothing but the Beams of Lov reverted upon another · for he loved no person but of whom he was beloved. All that he loved was Good, and nothing evil. His Lov seemed the Goodness of a Being expressed

87. 2. *he*: 'they' in M, but the *t* and *y* are deleted in MS.

in the Soul, or apprehended in the Lover, and returned upon it 5
self. But in the Estate of Misery, (or rather Grace;) a Soul lovs
freely and purely of its own self, with Gods Lov, things that seem
uncapable of Lov, Naught and evil. For as GOD shewed his
Eternity and Omnipotency, in that he could Shine upon Nothing,
and lov an Object when it was Nought, or Evil; As he did Adam 10
when he raisd him out of Nothing, and Mankind when He re-
deemd them from Evil: so now we can lov sinners, and them that
Deserv nothing at our Hands. Which as it is a Diviner Lov, and
more Glorious then the other, so were we redeemed to this Power,
and it was purchased for us with a Greater Price. 15

88

It is a Generous and Heavenly Principle, that where a Benefit is
fairly intended, we are equaly obliged for the Intention, or Success.
He is an Ungratefull Debtor, that measureth a Benefactor by the
Success of His Kindness. A clear Soul and a generous Mind is
as much obliged for the Intent of his freind, as the Prosperity of it: 5
And far more, if we seperat the Prosperity from the Intent · for
the Goodness lies principaly in the Intention. Since therfore God
intended me all the Joys in Heaven and Earth, I am as much
Obliged for them as if I received them. Whatever intervening
Accident bereaved me of them, He realy intended them. And in 10
that I contemplat the Riches of His Goodness. Whether Mens
Wickedness in the present Age, or my own perversness, or the fall
of Adam; he intended me all the Joys of Paradice, and all the Honors
in the World, whatever hinders me. In the Glass of His Intention
therfore I enjoy them all: And I do confess my Obligation. It is 15
as Great as if nothing had intervened, and I had wholy received
them. Seeing and Knowing Him to be infinitly Wise and Great and
Glorious, I rejoyce that he loved me, and confide in his Lov. His
Goodness is my Soveraign and Supreme Delight. That God is of
such a Nature in himself is my infinit Treasure. Being He is my 20
Friend, and delighteth in my Honor, tho I rob my self of all my
Happiness, he is justified. That He intended it, is His Grace and
Glory. But it animates me, as well as comforts me, to see the Per-
fection of His Lov towards me. As Things stood, He used Power
enough before the Fall to make me Happy. If he refuseth to use 25
any more since the Fall: I am obliged. But He hath used more. New
Occasions begot New Abilities. He redeemed me by His Son.

If He refuseth to use any more I cannot complain. If He refuseth
to curb my perverseness unless I consent, His Lov was infinitly
30 shewed. He desireth that I should by Prayers and Endeavors
clothe my self with Grace. If in Default of mine, he doth it Him-
self freely giving His Holy Spirit to me; it is an infinit Mercy,
but infinitly new, and superadded. If he refuseth to overrule the
Rebellion of other men, and to bring me to Honor, notwithstand-
35 ing their Malice; or refuseth to make them lov me, whether they
will or no · I cannot repine. By other Signes, he hath plainly shewd,
that He loveth me infinitly, which is enough for me, and that He
desireth my Obedience.

89

This Estate wherin I am placed is the Best for me: tho Encom-
passed with Difficulties. It is my Duty to think so, and I cannot
do otherwise. I cannot do otherwise, without reproaching my
Maker: that is, without suspecting, and in that offending His
5 Goodness and Wisdom. Riches are but Tarnish and Gilded
Vanities, Honors are but Aery and Empty Bubles, Affections are
but Winds, perhaps too Great, for such a ship as mine; of too light
a Ballast: Pleasures, yea all these, are but Witches that draw and
steal us away from GOD; Dangerous Allurements, interposing
10 Skreens, unseasonable Companions, Counterfeit Realities, Honied
poyson, Combersom Distractions. I hav found them so. At least
they lull us into Lethargies. And we need to be Quickened. Som
times they Puff us up with vain Glory and we need to be humbled.
Always they delude us if we place any Confidence in them, and
15 therfore it is as Good always to be without them. But it is as Good
also, were it not for our Weakness, somtimes to hav them. Becaus
a good use may be made of them. And therfore they are not to be
contemned when God doth offer them. But He is to be Admired
that maketh it Good on both sides, to hav them, and to be without
20 them. Riches are not to be Hated, nor Coveted. But I am to Bless
God in all Estates · Who hath given me the World, my Soul, and
Himself: and ever to be Great in the true Treasures. Riches
are Good, and therfore is it Good somtimes to Want them: that
we might shew our Obedience and Resignation to God, even in
25 being without those things that are Good, at his Appointment:
and that also we might cloth our selves with Patience and Faith

and Courage, which are Greater Ornaments then Gold and
Silver, and of Greater Price: And that shall stand us in stead of
all the Splendor of Alms Deeds. Assure your self, till you prize
one Vertu, abov a Trunk of Mony, you can never be Happy. One 30
Vertu before the face of God, is better then all the Gold in the
whole World.

90

Knowing the Greatness and Sweetness of Lov, I can never be
poor in any Estate. How Sweet a Thing is it as we go or ride or eat
or drink or convers abroad to remember, that one is the Heir of the
Whole World, and the Friend of GOD! That one has so Great a
Friend as God is: and that one is exalted infinitly by all His Laws! 5
That all the Riches and Honors in the World are ours in the Divine
Image to be Enjoyed. That a Man is tenderly Belovd of God and
always walking in his fathers Kingdom, under his Wing, and as
the Apple of his Ey! Verily that God hath don so much for one in
His Works and Laws, and Expresd so much Lov in His Word and 10
Ways, being as He is Divine and Infinit, it should make a man
to walk abov the stars, and seat Him in the Bosom of Men and
Angels. It should always fill Him with Joy, and Triumph, and lift
Him up abov Crowns and Empires.

91

That a Man is Beloved of God, should melt him all into Esteem
and Holy Veneration. It should make Him so Couragious as an
Angel of God. It should make him Delight in Calamities and
Distresses for Gods sake. By giving me all things els, he hath made
even Afflictions them selvs my Treasures. The Sharpest Trials, 5
are the finest furbishing. The most Tempestious Weather is the
Best Seed Time. A Christian is an Oak flourishing in Winter.
GOD hath so magnified and Glorified His Servant, and Exalted
him so highly in his Eternal Bosom, that no other Joy should be
able to mov us but that alone. All Sorrows should appear but 10
Shadows, besides that of his Absence. And all the Greatness of
Riches and Estates swallowed up in the Light of his favor. In-
credible Goodness lies in his Lov. And it should be Joy enough
to us to contemplat and possess it. He is Poor whom GOD hates.
Tis a tru Proverb. And besides that, we should so lov Him, that 15

the Joy alone of approving our selvs to Him, and making our selvs Amiable and Beautifull before Him should be a continual Feast, were we starving. A Beloved cannot feel Hunger in the Presence of His Beloved. Where Martyrdom is pleasant, what can 20 be Distastefull. To fight, to famish, to Die for ones Beloved, especialy with ones beloved, and in his Excellent Company, unless it be for his trouble, is truly Delightfull. God is always present, and always seeth us.

92

Knowing my self Beloved and so Glorified of God Almighty in another World, I ought to Honor Him in this always, and to Aspire to it. At Midnight will I rise to Giv Thanks unto Thee becaus of thy Righteous Judgements. Seven times a Day will I 5 prais Thee, for thy Glorious Mercy. Early in the Morning will I Bless Thee, I will Triumph in thy Works, I will Delight in thy Law Day and Night, At Evening will I prais Thee. I will ever be speaking of thy Marvellous Acts, I will tell out of thy Greatness, and talk of the Glorious Majesty of thy Excellent Kingdom; these 10 Things ought ever to breath in our souls. We ought to covet to liv in Privat, and in privat ever to overflow in Praises. I will Boast in Thee all the Day Long, and be Glad in the Lord. My Exceeding Joy, my Life, my Glory, what shall I render to Thee, for all His Benefits? I will sing and be Glad. Let all Nations sing unto Him: 15 for he covereth the Earth as it were with a Sheild. My Lips shall be fain when I sing unto Thee and my Soul O Lord which Thou hast redeemed. God is unseen till He be so Known: and Davids Spirit an inscrutable Mysterie, till this Experienced.

93

Our Friendship with God ought to be so Pure and so Clear, that Nakedly and Simply for his Divine Lov, for his Glorious Works and Blessed Laws, the Wisdom of His Counsels, his Ancient Ways and Attributs towards us, we should ever in Publick en- 5 deavor to Honor Him. Always taking care to Glorify Him before Men: to Speak of His Goodness, to Sanctify His Name, and do those Things that will stir up others, and occasion others to Glorify Him. Doing this so Zealously, that we would not forbear the least Act wherin we might serv Him for all Worlds. It ought to be a firm

Principle rooted in us, that this Life is the most precious Season 10
in all Eternity, becaus all Eternity dependeth on it. Now we may do
those Actions which herafter we shall never hav occasion to do.
And now we are to do them in another maner, which in its place is
the most Acceptable in all Worlds · namely by Faith and Hope, in
which God infinitly Delighteth. With Difficulty and Danger, 15
which God infinitly commiserats, and Greatly esteems. So piecing
this Life with the life of Heaven, and seeing it as one with all
Eternity · a Part of it, a Life within it. Strangely and Stupendiously
Blessed in its Place and Season.

94

Having once studied these Principles you are Eternaly to Practice
them. You are to warm your self at these fires, and to hav recours to
them evry Day. When you think not of these Things you are in the
Dark. And if you would walk in the Light of them, you must fre-
quently Meditat. These Principles are like Seed in the Ground, they 5
must continualy be visited with Heavenly Influences, or els your
Life will be a Barren feild. Perhaps they might be cast into Better
frame, and more Curiously Exprest; but if well Cultivated they will
be as fruitfull, as if every Husk were a Golden Rinde. It is the Sub-
stance that is in them that is productive of Joy, and Good to all. 10

95

It is an Indelible Principle of Eternal Truth · that Practice and
Exercise is the Life of all. Should God giv you Worlds, and Laws,
and Treasures, and Worlds upon Worlds and Himself also in the
Divinest Maner, If you will be lazy, and not Meditat, you lose all.
The Soul is made for Action, and cannot rest, till it be employd. 5
Idlenes is its Rust. Unless it will up and Think and Taste and See,
all is in vain. Worlds of Beauty and Treasure and Felicity may be
round about it, and it self Desolat. If therfore you would be Happy,
your Life must be as full of Operation, as God of Treasure. Your
Operation shall be Treasure to Him, as His Operation is Delightfull 10
to you.

96

To be Acquainted with celestial Things is not only to know them,
but by frequent Meditation to be familiar with them. The Effects
of which are Admirable · for by this those things that at first seemed

uncertain becom Evident, those things which seemed Remote
5 becom near, those things which appeared like shady clouds becom
Solid Realities; finaly those Things which seemed impertinent to
us, and of little concernment, appear to be our own, according to
the strictest Rules of Propriety and of infinit Moment.

97

General and Publick concernments seem at first unmanageable,
by reason of their Greatness: but in the soul there is such a Secret
Sufficiency, that it is able upon Trial, to manage all Objects with
Equal Ease; things infinit in Greatness as well as the smallest sand.
5 But this Secret Strength is not found in it, but meerly upon Ex-
perience, nor discerned but by Exercise. The Eternity of God
himself is manageable to the understanding, and may be used
innumerable Ways for its Benefit, so may his Almighty Power and
infinit Goodness: His Omnipresence and Immensity, the Wideness
10 of the world, and the multitude of Kingdoms. Which argueth a
Peculiar Excellency in the Soul; becaus it is a Creature that can
never be Exceeded · for Bodily Strength by this is perceived to be
finite, that Bulk is unweildy and by the Greatness of its Object may
easyly be overcom: but the Soul through God that Strengtheneth
15 her is able to do all Things. Nothing is too Great, nothing too
Heavy, nothing unweildly; it can rule and manage any thing with
infinit Advantage.

98

Becaus the Strength of the Soul is Spiritual it is generaly despised.
But if ever you would be Divine, you must admit this Principle:
That Spiritual Things are the Greatest, and that Spiritual Strength
is the most Excellent, Usefull and Delightfull · for which caus it
5 is made as Easy, as it is Endless and Invincible. Infinity is but one
Object, Almighty Power is another, Eternal Wisdom is another
which it can contemplat; from Infinity it can go to Power, from
Power to Wisdom, from Wisdom, to Goodnes, from Goodness,
to Glory, and so to Blessedness; and from these to any Object, or
10 all, whatsoever, Contemplating them as freely as if it had never
seen an Object before. If any one say, that tho it can proceed thus
from one Object to another, Yet it cannot comprehend any one
of them: All I shall answer is this, it can comprehend any one of
them as much as a Creature can possibly do: and the Possibility

of a Creature dependeth Purely upon the Power of GOD: for a creature may be made able to do all that, which its Creator is able to make it to doe. So that if there be any Defect in his Power there must of necessity a Limit follow in the Power of his Creature, which even God himself cannot make a Creature to Exceed. But this you will say, is an Argument only of what may be, not of what is · tho considering GODs infinit Lov, it is sufficient to shew what is Possible; becaus his Lov will do all it can for the Glory of it self and its Object: yet further to discover what is, we may Adde this, that when a Soul hath contemplated the Infinity of GOD, and passeth from that to another Object, all that it is able to contemplat on any other, it might have added to its first contemplation. So that its Liberty to Contemplat all shews its Illimitedness† to any one. And truly I think it Pious to believ that God hath without a Metaphore infinitly Obliged us.

99

The reason why learned Men have not Exactly measured the faculties of the Soul, is becaus they Knew not to what their Endless Extent should serv · for till we Know the Universal Beauty of GODs Kingdom, and that all Objects in His Omnipresence are the Treasures of the Soul; to enquire into the Sufficiency and Extent of its Power is impertinent. But when we know this, nothing is more Expedient then to consider whether a Soul be able to Enjoy them. Which if it be its Powers must extend as far as its Objects · for no Object without the Sphere of its Power, can be enjoyed by it. It cannot be so much as perceived, much lesse Enjoyed. From whence it will proceed, that the Soul will to all Eternity be Silent about it: A Limitation of Praises, and a Parsimony in Love following therupon, to the Endangering of the Perfection of Gods Kingdom.

100

Upon the Infinit Extent of the Understanding and Affection of the Soul, strange and Wonderfull Things will follow. 1. A manifestation of GODs infinit Lov. 2. The Possession of infinit Treasures. 3. a Return of infinit Thanksgivings. 4. A Fulnes of Joy which nothing can exceed. 5. an infinit Beauty and Greatness in the Soul. 6. An infinit Beauty in GODs Kingdom. 7. an Infinit Union

between GOD and the soul, (as well in Extent, as fervor.) 8. An Exact fitness between the Powers of the Soul and its Objects. Neither being Desolat, becaus neither Exceedeth the other. 9. An
10 Infinit Glory in the Communion of Saints, Every one being a Treasure to all the Residue and Enjoying the Residue, and in the Residue all the Glory of all Worlds. 10. A Perfect Indwelling of the Soul in GOD, and GOD in the Soul. So that as the fulness of the GODHEAD dwelleth in our Savior, it shall dwell in us;
15 and the Church shall be the fulness of Him that filleth all in all: GOD being manifested therby to be a King infinitly Greater, becaus Reigning over infinit Subjects. To Whom be all Glory and Dominion, for ever and ever. Amen.

THE FIFTH CENTURIE

1

The objects of Felicitie, and the Way of enjoying them, are two Material Themes; wherin to be instructed is infinitly desirable, becaus as Necessary, as Profitable. Whether of the Two, the Object, or the Way be more Glorious; it is difficult to determine. God is the Object, and God is the Way of Enjoying. God in all his 5 Excellencies, Laws and Works, in all his Ways and Counsels is the Sovereign Object of all Felicitie. Eternity and Time, Heaven and Earth, Kingdoms and Ages, Angels and Men, are in him to be enjoyed. In him, the fountain, in him the End; in him the Light, the Life, the Way, in him the Glory and Crown of all. Yet for 10 Distinction sake, we will speak of several eminent Particulars. Beginning with his Attributes.

2

The Infinity of God is our Enjoyment, because it is the Region and Extent of his Dominion. Barely† as it comprehends infinit Space, it is infinitly Delightfull; becaus it is the Room and the Place of our Treasures, the Repositorie of our Joys, and the Dwelling Place, yea the Sea and Throne, and Kingdom of our Souls. 5 But as it is the Light wherin we see, the Life that inspires us, the Violence of his Love, and the Strength of our Enjoyments, the Greatness and Perfection of evry Creature, the Amplitude that enlargeth us, and the field wherin our Thoughts expaciate without Limit or Restraint, the Ground and Foundation of all our Satis- 10 factions, the Operative Energie and Power of the Deitie, the Measure of our Delights, and the Grandure of our Souls, it is more our Treasure, and ought more abundantly to be delighted in. It surroundeth us continualy on evry side, it filles us, and inspires us. It is so Mysterious, that it is wholy within us, and even then it wholy 15 seems, and is without us. It is more inevitably and constantly, more neerly and immediately our Dwelling Place, then our Cities and Kingdoms and houses. Our Bodies them selvs are not so much ours, or within us as that is. The Immensitie of God is an Eternal

20 Tabernacle. Why then we should not be sensible of that as much as of our Dwellings, I cannot tell, unless our Corruption and Sensuality destroy us. We ought always to feel, admire, and walk in it. It is more clearly objected to the Ey of the Soul, then our Castles and Palaces to the Ey of the Body. Those Accidental Build-
25 ings may be thrown down, or we may be taken from them, but this can never be removed, it abideth for ever. It is impossible not to [be] within it, nay to be so surrounded as evermore to be in the centre and midst of it, wherever we can possibly remov, is inevitably fatal† to evry Being.

3

Creatures that are able to dart their Thoughts into all Spaces, can brook no Limit or Restraint, they are infinitly endebted to this illimited Extent, becaus were there no such Infinitie, there would be no Room for their Imaginations; their Desires and Affections
5 would be coopd up, and their Souls imprisoned. We see the Heavens with our Eys, and Know the World with our Sences. But had we no Eys, nor Sences, we should see Infinitie like the Holy Angels. The Place wherin the World standeth, were it all annihilated would still remain, the Endless Extent of which we
10 feel so realy and palpably, that we do not more certainly know the Distinctions and figures, and Bounds and Distances of what we see, then the Everlasting Expansion of what we feel and behold within us. It is an Object infinitly Great and Ravishing: as full of Treasures as full of Room, and as fraught with Joy as Capacitie.
15 To Blind men it seemeth dark, but is all Glorious within, as infinit in Light and Beauty, as Extent and Treasure. Nothing is in vain, much less Infinity. Evry Man is alone the Centre and Circumference of it. It is all his own, and so Glorious, that it is the Eternal and Incomprehensible Essence of the Deitie. A Cabinet of infinit
20 Value equal in Beauty Lustre and Perfection to all its Treasures. It is the Bosom of God, the Soul and Securitie of every Creature.

4

Were it not for this Infinitie, Gods Bountie would of Necessitie be limited. His Goodness would want a Receptacle for its Effu-sions. His Gifts would be confined into Narrow Room, and his Almighty Power for lack of a Theatre Magnificent enough, a

Storehouse large enough be Straitned. But Almighty Power in- 5
cludes Infinitie in its own Existence. For becaus God is infinitly
able to do all Things, there must of Necessity be an infinit Capacitie
to answer that Power, becaus Nothing it self is an Obedient Subject
to work upon: and the Eternal Privation of infinit Perfections is to
almighty Power a Being Capable of all. As sure as there is a Space 10
infinit, there is a Power, a Bounty, a Goodness, a Wisdom infinit,
a Treasure, a Blessedness, a Glory.

<h2 style="text-align:center">5</h2>

Infinity of Space is like a Painters Table,† prepared for the Ground
and feild of those Colors that are to be laid theron. Look how
great he intends the Picture, so Great doth he make the Table.
It would be an Absurditie to leav it unfinished, or not to fill it.
To leav any part of it Naked and bare, and void of Beauty, would 5
render the whole ungratefull to the Ey, and argue a Defect of Time,
or Materials, or Wit in the Limner. As the Table is infinit so are
the Pictures. Gods Wisdom is the Art, his Goodness the Will, his
Word the Penicill,† his Beauty and Power the Colors, his Pictures
are all his Works and Creatures · infinitly more Real, and more 10
Glorious, as well as more Great and Manifold then the Shadows of
a Landscape. But the Life of all is, they are the Spectators own.
He is in them as in his Territories, and in all these, views his own
Possessions.

<h2 style="text-align:center">6</h2>

One would think that besides infinit Space there could be no
more Room for any Treasure. Yet to shew that God is infinitly
infinit, there is Infinit Room besides, and perhaps a more Wonder-
full Region making this to be infinitly infinit. No man will believ
that besides the Space from the Centre of the Earth to the utmost 5
bounds of the Everlasting Hills, there should be any more. Beyond
those Bounds perhaps there may, but besides all that Space that
is illimited and present before us, and absolutly endles evry Way,
where can there be any Room for more? This is the Space that is
at this Moment only present before our Ey, the only Space that was, 10
or that will be, from Everlasting to Everlasting. This Moment
Exhibits infinit Space, but there is a Space also wherin all Moments

6. 5. *that*: not in M, but a very faint 'yt' is visible in MS.

are infinitly Exhibited, and the Everlasting Duration of infinit
Space is another Region and Room of Joys. Wherin all Ages appear
15 together, all Occurrences stand up at once, and the innumerable
and Endless Myriads of yeers that were before the Creation, and
will be after the World is ended are Objected† as a Clear and
Stable Object, whose several Parts extended out at length, giv an
inward Infinity to this Moment, and compose an Eternitie that is
20 seen by all Comprehensors and Enjoyers.

7

Eternity is a Mysterious Absence of Times and Ages: an Endless
Length of Ages always present, and for ever Perfect. For as there
is an immovable Space wherin all finit Spaces are enclosed, and
all Motions carried on, and performed: so is there an Immovable
5 Duration, that contains and measures all moving Durations.
Without which first the last could not be; no more then finit Places,
and Bodies moving without infinit Space. All Ages being but
successions correspondent to those Parts of that Eternitie wherin
they abide, and filling no more of it, then Ages can do. Whether
10 they are commensurat with it or no, is difficult to determine. But
the infinit immovable Duration is Eternitie, the Place and Duration
of all Things, even of Infinit Space it self: the Cause and End, the
Author and Beautifier, the Life and Perfection of all.

8

Eternitie magnifies our Joys exceedingly · for wheras things in them
selvs began, and quickly end · Before they came, were never in
Being; do service but for few Moments; and after they are gone,
pass away and leav us for ever · Eternity retains the Moments of
5 their Beginning and Ending within it self: and from Everlasting
to Everlasting those Things were in their Times and Places before
God, and in all their Circumstances Eternaly will be, serving him
in those Moments wherin they existed, to those Intents and Pur-
poses for which they were Created. The Swiftest Thought is
10 present with him Eternaly: the Creation and the Day of Judge-
ment, his first Consultation Choise and Determination, the Result
and End of all just now in full Perfection, ever Beginning, ever
Passing, ever Ending: with all the Intervalles of Space between
things and Things. As if those Objects that arise many thousand

yeers one after the other were all together. We also were our selvs 15
before God Eternaly: And hav the Joy of seeing our selvs Eternaly
beloved, and Eternaly Blessed, and infinitly Enjoying all the Parts
of our Blessedness, in all the Durations of Eternity appearing at
once before our selvs, when perfectly Consummat in the King-
dom of Light and Glory. The Smallest Thing by the Influence of 20
Eternity, is made infinit and Eternal. We pass thorow a standing
Continent or Region of Ages, that are already before us, Glorious
and perfect while we com to them. Like men in a ship we pass for-
ward, the shores and Marks seeming to go backward, tho we move,
and they stand still. We are not with them in our Progressive 25
Motion, but prevent† the Swiftness of our Course, and are present
with them in our Understandings. Like the Sun we dart our Rayes
before us, and occupy those Spaces with Light and Contempla-
tion, which we move towards, but possess not with our Bodies.
And seeing all Things in the Light of Divine Knowledg eternaly 30
serving God, rejoyce unspeakably in that service, and enjoy it all.

9

His Omnipresence is an ample Territory or Field of Joys, a Trans-
parent Temple of infinit Lustre, a Strong Tower of Defence, a
Castle of Repose, a Bulwark of Security, a Palace of Delights,
an Immediat Help, and a present Refuge in the needfull time of
Trouble, a Broad and a vast Extent of fame and Glory · a Theatre 5
of infinit Excellency, an infinit Ocean by means wherof evry
Action, Word and Thought, is immediatly diffused like a Drop
of Wine in a Pail of Water, and evry where present evry where seen
and Known, infinitly delighted in, as well as filling infinit Spaces.
It is the Spirit that pervades all his Works, the Life and Soul of 10
the Univers, that in evry point of Space from the Centre to the
Heavens, in evry Kingdom in the world in evry City in evry
Wilderness in evry house, evry Soul evry Creature, in all the Parts
of his infinity and Eternitie sees our Persons loves our virtues,
inspires us with it self, and crowns our Actions with Praise and 15
Glory. It makes our Honor infinit in Extent, our Glory immense,
and our Happiness Eternal. The Rayes of our Light are by this
Means darted from Everlasting to Everlasting. This Spiritual
Region makes us infinitly present with God, Angels and Men in
all Places from the utmost Bounds of the Everlasting hills, 20

throughout all the unwearied Durations of his Endless Infinitie, and gives us the sence and feeling of all the Delights and Praises we occasion, as well as of all the Beauties and Powers, and Pleasures and Glories which God enjoyeth or createth.

10

Our Bridegroom and our King being evry where, our Lover and Defender watchfully governing all Worlds, no Danger or Enemie can arise to hurt us, but is immediatly prevented and supprest, in all the Spaces beyond the utmost Borders of those unknown 5 Habitations which he possesseth. Delights of inestimable valu are there preparing. For evry thing is present by its own Existence. The Essence of God therfore being all Light and Knowledg, Lov and Goodness, Care and Providence, felicity and Glory, a pure and simple Act; it is present in its Operations, and by those Acts which 10 it eternaly exerteth, is wholly Busied in all Parts and places of his Dominion, perfecting and compleating our Bliss and Happiness.

Here T wrote the number 11, but wrote no more.

THREE THANKSGIVINGS

THREE of the nine *Thanksgivings* are printed here, from the 1699 edition (see Introduction, pp. xiii note and xvii). T quotes freely from the Authorized Version of the Psalms, though not always verbatim: some of the references were given in 1699; M supplied the rest. I have only noted direct quotations from the Bible, not allusions or paraphrases.

Thanksgivings for the Body

Bless the Lord, O my Soul: and all that is within me bless his holy name.

Bless the Lord, O my Soul: and forget not all his benefits.

Who forgiveth all thine Iniquities: who healeth all thy Diseases:

5

Who redeemeth thy life from destruction. Who crowneth thee with loving kindness and tender mercies.

Who satisfieth thy mouth with good things, so that thy youth is renewed as the Eagles.

O Lord who art clothed with Majesty,

10

    My desire is, to praise thee.
        With the holy Angels and Archangels
            To glorifie thee.

And with all thy Saints in the Church triumphant.

    For the eternal brightness

15

        Of thine infinite bounty,
    The freedom of thy love

Wherein thou excellest the beams of the Sun

        To celebrate thee.

I will praise thee, for I am fearfully and wonderfully made, 20 marvellous are thy works; and that my Soul knoweth right well.

My substance was not hid from thee when I was made in secret, and curiously wrought in the lowest parts of the earth.

Thine eyes did see my substance yet being unperfect; and in thy book all my members were written; which in continuance were 25 fashioned when as yet there was none of them.

How precious are thy thoughts also unto me, O God! How great is the sum of them!

If I should count them, they are more in number than the sand: When I awake I am still with thee.

30

    Blessed be thy holy Name,
        O Lord, my God!

For ever blessed be thy holy Name,
    For that I am made

Lines 1–9 from Ps. 103$^{1-5}$; lines 20–30 from Ps. 139$^{14-18}$.

35   The work of thy hands,
       Curiously wrought
              By thy divine Wisdom,
       Enriched
              By thy Goodness,
40   Being more thine
              Than I am mine own.
              O Lord!
       Thou hast given me a Body,
       Wherein the glory of thy Power shineth,
45   Wonderfully composed above the Beasts,
       Within distinguished into useful parts,
       Beautified without with many Ornaments.
       Limbs rarely poised,
              And made for Heaven:
50   Arteries filled
              With celestial Spirits:
       Veins, wherein Blood floweth,
              Refreshing all my flesh,
              Like Rivers.
55   Sinews fraught with the mystery
              Of wonderful Strength,
              Stability,
              Feeling.
       O blessed be thy glorious Name!
60   That thou hast made it,
              A Treasury of Wonders,
              Fit for its several Ages;
              For Dissections,
              For Sculptures in Brass,
65   For Draughts in Anatomy,
       For the Contemplation of the Sages.
       Whose inward parts,
     *Ps. 139. 16.   *Enshrined in thy Libraries,
              ⎧ The Amazement of the Learned,
70   ⎪ The Admiration of Kings and Queens,
       Are ⎨ The Joy of Angels;
              ⎪ The Organs of my Soul,
              ⎩ The Wonder of Cherubims.

              68. 'in thy book all my members were written'.

Those blinder parts of refined Earth,
      Beneath my Skin;   75
   Are full of thy Depths,
       (Many thousand Uses,
  For { Hidden Operations,
       (Unsearchable Offices.
But for the diviner Treasures wherewith thou hast endowed   80
   My Brains,   Mine Eyes,
   My Heart,   Mine Ears,
   My Tongue,   My Hands,
O what Praises are due unto thee,
   Who hast made me   85
      A living Inhabitant
         Of the great World.
      And the Centre of it!
   A sphere of Sense,
         And a mine of Riches,   90
Which when Bodies are dissected fly away.
   The spacious Room
      Which thou hast hidden in mine Eye,
   The Chambers for Sounds
      Which thou hast prepar'd in mine Ear,   95
   The Receptacles for Smells
      Concealed in my Nose;
   The feeling of my Hands,
      The taste of my Tongue.
But above all, O Lord, the Glory of Speech, whereby thy 100
Servant is enabled with Praise to celebrate thee.
             For
All the Beauties in Heaven and Earth,
The melody of Sounds,
The sweet Odours   105
      Of thy Dwelling-place.
The delectable pleasures that gratifie my Sense,
   That gratify the feeling of Mankind.
The Light of History,
      Admitted by the Ear.   110
The Light of Heaven,
      Brought in by the Eye.
The Volubility† and Liberty

Of my Hands and Members.
115   Fitted by thee for all Operations;
Which the Fancy can imagine,
Or Soul desire:
From the framing of a Needle's Eye,
To the building of a Tower:
120   From the squaring of Trees,
To the polishing of Kings Crowns.
For all the Mysteries, Engines, Instruments, wherewith the
World is filled, which we are able to frame and use to thy Glory.
For all the Trades, variety of Operations, Cities, Temples,
125 Streets, Bridges, Mariners Compass, admirable Picture, Sculpture,
Writing, Printing, Songs and Musick; wherewith the World is
beautified and adorned.
Much more for the Regent Life,
And Power of Perception,
130   Which rules within.
That secret depth of fathomless Consideration
That receives the information
Of all our senses,
That makes our centre equal to the Heavens,
135   And comprehendeth in it self the magnitude of the World;
The involved mysteries
Of our common sense;
The inaccessible secret
Of perceptive fancy;
140   The repository and treasury
Of things that are past;
The presentation of things to come;
Thy Name be glorified
For evermore.
145   For all the art which thou hast hidden
In this little piece
Of red clay.
For the workmanship of thy hand,
Who didst thy self form man
150   Of the dust of the ground,
And breath into his Nostrils
The breath of Life.

147. *red clay*: Adam = red. M.

For the high Exaltation whereby thou hast glorified every
body,
                    Especially mine,   155
        As thou didst thy Servant
        Adam's in *Eden*.
Thy Works themselves speaking to me the same thing that was
said unto him in the beginning,
                    WE ARE ALL THINE.   160
And why, O Lord, wouldst thou so delight
To magnify the dust taken from the ground?
From the dark obscurity of a silent Grave
Thou raisest it, O Lord!
                    Herein indeed   ᵛ   165
    Thou raisest the poor out of the dust, and liftest the needy out of
the dunghil,
    That thou mayst set him with Princes; even with the Princes of
thy people.
    But why would the Lord take pleasure in creating an earthly 170
Body? why at all in making a visible World? Couldst thou not have
made us immortal Souls, and seated us immediately in the throne
of Glory?
        O Lord, thou lover of Righteousness,
            Whose Kingdom is everlasting;   175
    Who lovest to govern thy Subjects by Laws, and takest delight
to distribute Rewards and Punishments according to right.
    Thou hast hidden thy self
            By an infinite miracle,
    And made this World the Chamber of thy presence; the ground 180
and theatre of thy righteous Kingdom.
    That putting us at a distance
            A little from thee,
    Thou mayest satisfie the Capacities
            Of thy righteous Nature.   185
Thou wast always fit to reign like a King,
    Able to rule by the best of Laws,
To distribute the greatest Rewards and Punishments.
    That therefore thou might'st raise up
            Objects for these,   190
Thou hast seated us at a little distance from thee,

        166. Adapted from Ps. 113⁷·⁸.

      Not in respect of thy Ubiquity, but degree of Knowledge.
In Heaven thou dwellest
   As a Bridegroom with thy Bride,
195   A Father with thy Children,
     A King with Kings, Governours and Peers,
   Shewing and manifesting all thy Glory.
  Unto which thou wouldst have us first to come,
As humble and obedient Servants:
200   That in us thou mightst see

Ingenuity,†	Thanksgiving,
Fidelity,	Wisdom,

          Love,
    Even to an absent Benefactor.
205 There is the Kingdom of eternal Glory,
Beyond which can be no Rewards,
   The highest of all being there attained.
In which can be no trial,
   Blessedness being seen with open face.
210 Beneath which it was necessary that we should be made:
   To the intent we might be governed
     In a righteous Kingdom.
  But couldst thou not have remitted† our Knowledge, and established to thy self a righteous Kingdom, without composing our
215 Bodies, or the World?
  By the Fall of some, we know, O Lord,
   That the Angels were tried,
   Which are invisible Spirits,
    Needing not the World,
220   Nor clothed in Bodies,
     Nor endued with Senses.
  For our Bodies therefore, O Lord, for our earthly Bodies, hast thou made the World: Which thou so lovest, that thou hast supremely magnified them by the works of thy hands:
225 And made them Lords of the whole Creation.
   Higher than the Heavens,
    Because served by them:
   More glorious than the Sun,
    Because it ministreth to them:
230   Greater in Dignity than the material World.
    Because the end of its Creation.

                Revived by the Air,
                Served by the Seas,
            Fed by the Beasts, and Fowls, and Fishes,
                        Our pleasure.   235
        Which fall as Sacrifices to
                        Thy glory.
        Being made to minister and attend upon us.
                O Miracle
                    Of divine Goodness!   240
        O Fire! O flame of Zeal, and Love, and Joy!
        Even for our earthly bodies, hast thou created all things.
                    ⎧ Visible.
            All things ⎨ Material.
                    ⎩ Sensible.   245
                    Animals,
                    Vegetables,
                    Minerals,
                Bodies celestial,
                Bodies terrestrial,   250
                The four Elements,
                Volatile Spirits,
            Trees, Herbs, and Flowers,
                The Influences of Heaven,
            Clouds, Vapors, Wind,   255
                Dew, Rain, Hail, and Snow,
            Light and Darkness, Night and Day,
                The Seasons of the Year.
        Springs, Rivers, Fountains, Oceans,
            Gold, Silver, and precious Stones.   260
                Corn, Wine, and Oyl,
            The Sun, Moon, and Stars,
                Cities, Nations, Kingdoms.
        And the Bodies of Men, the greatest Treasures of all,
                For each other.   265
            What then, O Lord, hast thou intended for our Souls, who
        givest to our Bodies such glorious things!
                Every thing in thy Kingdom, O Lord,
            Conspireth to mine Exaltation.
                In every thing I see thy Wisdom and Goodness.   270
                And I praise the Power by which I see it.

My Body is but the Cabinet, or Case of my Soul:
   What then, O Lord, shall the Jewel be!
   Thou makest it the heir of all the profitable trades and occupa-
275 tions in the World.
            And the Heavens and the Earth
                More freely mine,
                More profitably,
                More gloriously,
280   More comfortably
   Than if no man were alive but I alone.
        Yea though I am a Sinner, thou lovest me more than if thou
hadst given all things to me alone.
   The sons of men thou hast made my treasures,
285   Those Lords,
           Incarnate Cherubims,
           Angels of the World,
           The Cream of all things,
           And the sons of God,
290 Hast thou given to me, and made them mine,
   For endless Causes ever to be enjoyed.
          Were I alone,
   Briars and thorns would devour me;
   Wild beasts annoy me;
295   My Guilt terrifie me;
   The World it self be a Desart to me;
   The Skies a Dungeon,
          But mine Ignorance more.
   The Earth a Wilderness;
300   All things desolate:
          And I in solitude,
          Naked and hungry,
          Blind and brutish,
          Without house or harbour;
305   Subject unto storms;
          Lying upon the ground;
          Feeding upon roots;
             But more upon melancholy,
             Because void of thee.

272-3. cf. *Hexameron*, p. 80: 'But if the Case be so rich, how glorious must the Jewel be?'
which gives yet another proof of T's authorship of that work.

Therefore thou providest for me, and for me they build, and ₃₁₀
get and provide for me

     My Bread,   Drink,
        Clothes,   Bed,

     My Household stuff, { Books,
                        Utensils,   315
                        Furniture.

The use of Meats, Fire, Fuel, &c.
They teach unto me, provide for me.

While I, O Lord, exalted by thy hand,
Above the Skies in Glory seem to stand: 320
The Skies being made to serve me, as they do,
While I thy Glories in thy Goodness view.
To be in Glory higher than the Skies,
Is greater bliss, than 'tis in place to rise
Above the Stars: More blessed and divine,   325
To liv and see, than like the Sun to shine.
O what Profoundness in my Body lies,
For whom the Earth was made, the Sea, the Skies!
So greatly high our humane Bodies are,
That Angels scarcely may with these compare.   330
In all the heights of Glory seated, they,
Above the Sun in thine eternal day,
Are seen to shine; with greater gifts adorn'd
Than Gold with Light, or Flesh with Life suborn'd†
Suns are but Servants! Skies beneath their feet;   335
The Stars but Stones; Moons but to serve them meet.
Beyond all heights above the World they reign,
In thy great Throne ordained to remain.
    All Tropes are Clouds; Truth doth it self excel,
    Whatever Heights, Hyperboles can tell.   340

O that I were as *David*, the sweet Singer of *Israel!*
    In meeter Psalms to set forth thy Praises.
Thy Raptures ravish me, and turn my soul all into melody.
    Whose Kingdom is so glorious, that nothing in it shall at all be
unprofitable, mean, or idle.   345
        So constituted!
That every one's Glory is beneficial unto all; and every one
magnified in his place by Service.

What is man, O Lord, that thou art mindful of him! or the son
350 of man, that thou visitest him!

Kings in all their Glory minister to us, while we repose in peace
and safety.

Priests and Bishops serve at thine Altar, guiding our Bodies to
eternal Glory.

355 Physicians heal us.

Courts of Judicature stand open for our preservation.

The Outgoings of the morning and evening rejoyce to do us
service.

The holy Angels minister unto us.

360 Architects and Masons build us Temples.

The Sons of Harmony fill thy Quires.

Where even our sensible bodies are entertained by thee with
great magnificence; and solaced with Joys.

Jesus Christ hath washed our feet.

365 He ministred to us by dying for us.

And now in our humane body, sitteth at thy right hand, in
the throne of Glory.

As our Head,
For our Sakes,

370 Being there adored by Angels and Cherubims.

What is it Lord
That thou so esteemest us!
Thou passed'st by the Angels,
Pure Spirits;

375 And didst send thy Son to die for us
That are made of both
Soul and Body.

Are we drawn unto thee?
O why dost thou make us

380 So thy treasures?

Are Eyes and Hands such Jewels unto thee?
What, O Lord, are Tongues and Sounds,
And Nostrils unto thee?

Strange Materials are visible bodies!

385 Things strange even compared to thy Nature,
Which is wholly spiritual.

For our sakes do the Angels enjoy the visible Heavens.

349–50. Ps. 84.

The Sun and Stars,
   Thy terrestrial Glories,
And all thy Wisdom   390
In the { Ordinances of Heaven.
        { Seasons of the Year.
Wondering to see thee by another way,
So highly exalting dust and ashes.
   Thou makest us treasures   395
      And joys unto them;
Objects of Delight, and spiritual Lamps,
   Whereby they discern visible things.
They see thy Paradise among the sons of men.
   Thy Wine and Oyl, thy Gold and Silver,   400
      By our Eyes.
   They smell thy Perfumes,
And taste thy Honey, Milk, and Butter,
      By our Senses.
   Thy Angels have neither ears nor eyes,   ~   405
      Nor tongues nor hands,
   Yet feel the Delights of all the World,
And hear the Harmonies, not only which Earth but Heaven
      maketh.
   The melody of Kingdoms,   410
   The joys of Ages,
      Are Objects of their joy.
They sing thy Praises for our sakes;
   While we upon Earth are highly exalted
      By being made thy Gifts,   415
      And Blessings unto them:
   Never their contempt;
      More their amazement;
And did they not love us
      Their Envy hereafter,   420
      But now their Joy.
   When our Glory being understood,
We shall shine as the Sun
   In thy heavenly Kingdom.
From whence also we look for the Saviour, the Lord Jesus 425
Christ.

425–9. Philippians 3$^{20-21}$.

Who shall change our vile body, that it may be fashioned like
unto his glorious body; according to the working whereby he is
able to subdue all things to himself.

430   *Then shall each Limb a spring of Joy be found,*
      And ev'ry Member with its Glory crown'd:
      While all the Senses, fill'd with all the Good
      That ever Ages in them understood,
      Transported are: Containing Worlds of Treasure,
435   *At one Delight with all their Joy and Pleasure.*
      From whence, like Rivers, Joy shall overflow,
      Affect the Soul, though in the Body grow.
      Return again, and make the Body shine
      Like Jesus Christ, while both in one combine,
440   *Mysterious Contacts are between the Soul,*
      Which touch the Spirits, and by those its Bowl:
      The Marrow, Bowels, Spirits, melt and move,
      Dissolving ravish, teach them how to love.
      He that could bring the Heavens thro the Eye,
445   *And make the World within the Fancy lie,*
      By beams of Light that closing meet in one,
      From all the Parts of his celestial Throne,
      Far more than this in framing Bliss can do,
      Inflame the Body and the Spirit too:
450   *Can make the Soul by Sense to feel and see,*
      And with her Joy the Senses wrap'd to be.
      Yea while the Flesh or Body subject lies
      To those Affections which in Souls arise;
      All holy Glories from the Soul redound,
455   *And in the Body by the Soul abound,*
      Are felt within, and ravish ev'ry Sense,
      With all the Godheads glorious Excellence:
      Who found the way himself to dwell within,
      As if even Flesh were nigh to him of kin.
460   *His Goodness, Wisdom, Power, Love divine,*
      Make, by the Soul convey'd, the Body shine.
      Not like the Sun (that earthly Darkness is)
      But in the strengths and heights of all this bliss.
      For God designs thy Body, for his sake,
465   A Temple of the Deity *to make.*

440. *Contacts*: emended by M from 'Conrtacts' 1699, as fitting the sense better than
'contracts'.

But now, O Lord, how highly great have my Transgressions been, who have abused this thy glorious Creature, by Surfeiting and Excess, by Lust and Wantonness, by Drunkenness, by Passion, by immoderate Cares, excessive Desires, and earthly Fears?   470

Yea, had I been guilty of none of those, had no Lies and Oaths polluted my Tongue, no vain Imaginations defiled my Heart, no stealing my Hands, nor idle Speeches profaned mine Ears,

Yet have I been wholly estranged from thee, by the sinful 475 Courses of this World, by the Delusions of vain Conversation.†

Being unsensible of these things, I have been blind and dead, profane and stupid, seared† and ingrateful; and for living beneath such a glorious Estate, may justly be excluded thine everlasting 480 Kingdom.

Enable me to keep thy Temple sacred!
   Which thou hast prepared for thy self.
Turn away mine Eyes
   From beholding Vanity.   485
Enable me to wash my hands in Innocency.
That I may compass thine altar about,
   And lift up my Hands
      To thy Holy Oracle.
Put a Watch over the Door of my Lips,   490
That I speak not unadvisedly with my Tongue.
Let my Glory awake early in the morning,
   To bring praises unto thee.
Enter, O Lord, the Gates of my Heart.
   Bow down the Heavens, O Lord,   495
And break open those Everlasting Doors,
   That the King of Glory may enter in.
Let the Ark of thy Presence rest within me.
Let not Sin reign in our mortal Bodies, that we should obey it in the Lusts thereof.   500

Neither let us yield our Members as instruments of Unrighteousness unto Sin, but let us yield our selves to God, as those that are alive from the Dead: and our Members as Instruments of Righteousness to God. *Rom.* 6.

496-7. Ps. 24⁹.

505 My Beloved put in his Hand by the Hole of the Door, and my
Bowels were moved for him.

I rose up to open to my beloved, and my Hands dropped with
Myrrh, and my fingers with sweet smelling Myrrh, upon the
Handles of the Lock.

510 O my beloved be not as a Wayfaring Man, that turneth aside
to tarry but for a Night.

Thou hast ravished mine Heart with one of thine Eyes.

How fair is thy Love my Sister, my Spouse! How much better
is thy Love than Wine! and the smell of thine Oyntments than
515 all Spices!

Thy Lips, O my Spouse, drop as an Hony Comb; Hony and
Milk are under thy Tongue, and the smell of thy Garments is as
the smell of *Lebanon.*

Or ever I was aware my Soul made me like the Chariots of
520 *Aminadab.*

Return O my Love!

I would lead thee, and bring thee
Into my Mothers House.

I would kiss thee, yet should I not be despised.

525   O let me live in thy Bosom for ever.

O Infinite God, Center of my Soul, Convert me powerfully unto thee,
that in thee I may take Rest, for thou didst make me for thee, and my
heart's unquiet till it be united to thee. And seeing, O Eternal Father,
thou didst create me that I might love thee as a Son, give me Grace that
530 *I may love thee as my Father. O only begotten Son of God, Redeemer*
of the World, seeing thou didst Create and Redeem me that I might Obey
and Imitate thee, make me to Obey and Imitate thee in all thy imitable
Perfection. O Holy Ghost, seeing thou didst create me to Sanctify me,
do it, O do it for thine own Glory; that I may acceptably praise and serve
535 *the holy and undivided Trinity in Unity, and Unity in Trinity. Amen.*

Let all thy Creatures bless thee O Lord, and my Soul praise and
bless thee for them all. I give thee Thanks for the Being thou givest unto
the Heavens, Sun, Moon, Stars, and Elements; to Beasts, Plants, and
all other Bodies of the Earth; to the Fowls of the Air, the Fishes of the
540 *Sea. I give thee thanks for the beauty of Colours, for the harmony of*
Sounds, for the pleasantness of Odours, for the sweetness of Meats, for

505-24. From the Song of Solomon, except 510-11 which are from Jeremiah 14[8].

the warmth and softness of our Raiment, and for all my five Senses, and all the Pores of my Body, so curiously made as before recited, and for the Preservation as well as Use of all my Limbs and Senses, in keeping me from Precipices,† Fractures, and Dislocations in my Body, from a dis- 545 *tracted, discomposed, confused, discontented Spirit. Above all, I praise thee for manifesting thy self unto me, whereby I am made capable to praise and magnify thy name for evermore.*

Thanksgivings for the Soul

I will sing of the mercies of the Lord for ever: with my mouth will I make known thy faithfulness to all Generations.

And the Heavens shall praise thy Wonders O Lord: thy faithfulness also in the Congregation of the Saints.

5   The Heavens shall praise thy Wonders:
        But more the Powers of my immortal Soul.

Which thou hast made more excellent than the Clouds, and greater than the Heavens!

O Lord I rejoyce, and am exceeding glad;

10   Because of thy Goodness,

In $\begin{cases}\text{Creating the World.}\\\text{Giving Brightness to the Sun.}\\\text{Ruling the Sea.}\\\text{Framing the Limbs and Members of my Body.}\end{cases}$

15   But much more abundantly,
          For the Glory of my Soul:

Which out of Nothing thou hast builded,
          To be a Temple unto God.

A living Temple of thine Omnipresence.

20   An understanding Eye.

A Temple of Eternity.
          A Temple of thy Wisdom, Blessedness, and Glory.

O ye Powers of mine immortal Soul, bless ye the Lord, praise him, and magnifie him for ever.

25   He hath made you greater,
          More glorious,   Brighter,
          Better than the Heavens.

A meeter dwelling place for his eternal Godhead
          Than the Heaven of Heavens.

30   The Heaven of Heavens,
          And all the Spaces above the Heavens,
    Are not able to contain him.

Being but dead and silent Place,
          They feel not themselves.

1-4. Ps. 89$^{1-5}$.   '23-24. The *Benedicite*.

They know nothing.   35
      See no immensity nor wideness at all.
But in thee, my Soul, there is a perceptive Power
        ⎧ Comprehend the Heavens.
To ⎨ Feel thy self.
        ⎪ Measure all the Spaces beyond the Heavens.   40
        ⎩ Receive the Deity of the eternal God,
      And those Spaces,
        By him into thee.
To feel and see the Heaven of Heavens,
      All things contained in them,   45
        And his Presence in thee.
Nor canst thou only feel his Omnipresence in thee,
      But adore his Goodness,
        Dread his Power,
        Reverence his Majesty,   50
        See his Wisdom,
        Rejoyce in his Bounty,
        Conceive his Eternity,
        Praise his Glory.
Which being things transcendent unto place,   55
Cannot by the Heavens at all be apprehended.
    With Reverence, O God, and Dread mixed with Joy, I come
before thee.
    To consider thy Glory in the perfection of my Soul,
      The Workmanship of the Lord,   60
        In so great a Creature.
From ⎰ East to West
      ⎱ Earth to Heaven,
    In the twinkling of an eye
      My Sight removeth,   65
Throughout all the Spaces beyond the Heavens:
My Thoughts in an instant like the holy Angels.
    Nor Bounds nor Limits doth my Soul discern,
      But an infinite Liberty beyond the World.
Mine Understanding being present   70
      With whatsoever it knoweth.
An infinite Bulk excludeth all things.
      Being void of Life, is next to nothing.
        Feeleth not it self,

75   Is a dead Material,
            Vain,   Useless.   But
    I admire, O Lord, thine infinite Wisdom; ⎰ *O give me*
        In advancing me to the similitude   ⎱ *Grace to*
            Of thine eternal Greatness.   *understand*
80   A Greatness like thine   *its Excellency.*
            Hast thou given unto me.
        A living Greatness:
            A Soul within:
            That receiveth all things.

85   ⎰ Spiritual.   *That doth not fill,*
            | Heavenly.   *but feeleth all*
    A Greatness ⎨ Divine.   *Things. Receiveth,*
            | Intelligent.   *seeth, discerneth,*
            ⎱ Profitable.   *enjoyeth them.*

90   Blessed be the Lord,
            Whose Understanding is infinite,
        For giving me a Soul
            Able to comprehend with all Saints the length, and breadth,
    and depth, and heighth of the Love of God, which passeth
95 Knowledge, that I might be filled with all the fullness of God.
    Eph. 3.
            And if the fullness of God,
        Then not only his Immensity
                Beyond the Heavens:
100   But his fullness in the Ages:
        His Absent-Presence in all Generations,
        He whose Greatness is the only useful Greatness,
        Hath made my Soul the Image of his own:
    Whose Wisdom and Greatness both are one.
105   A Simple Life;
    An eternal sphere of infinite Knowledge,
        In every Centre:
            Expanded every where,
                Yet indivisible.
110 The similitude of thine Infiniteness
            I see printed in it:
    But that of thine Eternity is supremely wonderful.
            In both I adore!
        So strangely glorious

     Hast thou made my Soul: 115
That even Yesterday is present
     To mine inward eye,
$$\text{The days of my} \left\{ \begin{array}{l} \text{Infancy,} \\ \text{Childhood,} \\ \text{Old Age.} \end{array} \right.$$
                       120
     We have
     An endless Liberty.
     Being able to see, walk, be present there,
Where neither the Eagles eye, nor the Lions thought can at all
  approach.   125
         The deeds of our Progenitors,
           Their Lives and Persons;
       Thy ways among the Ancients,
The services of the Sun in all Generations,
The Sun of Righteousness in his Rising and Eclipse;   130
     The Creation of the World,
     And the Government of Kingdoms,
       Can we behold;
     The day of Judgment,
     The Delights of Ages,   135
     The Sphere of time.
Nor will that contain us.
An infinite liberty we find beyond them;
     Can walk in thine Eternity,
       All at large;   140
     In every moment see it wholly,
       Know every where,
That from everlasting to everlasting thou art God:
Whose everlasting Glory is the Treasure of my Soul,
And thine eternal continuance a permanent   145
       NOW;
     With all its Contents
     For ever enjoyed.
       What, O Lord, hath thy Hand created!
       Who! how! what is thy Creature!   150
         O my King,
     Thou hast made me like thee,
       To measure Heaven with a span,
       Comprehend a thousand Ages as one day,

155　　　　See an Infinity before and after.
　　Thine Infinity is abused
　　　　　By the ignorance of men:
　　　　It restraineth nothing,
　　　　　But magnifieth all.
160　Thou hast made the World
　　　　　Most wide and glorious
　　　　　　　　　　⎧ Age,
　　In respect of its ⎨ Immensity,
　　　　　　　　　　⎩ Contents.
165　　　　　　　　　⎧ The drop of a Bucket,
　　To me nevertheless but ⎨ The dust of a ballance,
　　　　　　　　　　　⎩ A very little thing.
　　　　　　　　　　　　⎧ The Omnipresent ⎫
　　And in comparison of thee ⎨　　Eternal　　⎬ God,
170　　　　　　　　　　　　⎩ My Beloved　　⎭
　　　　A very Nothing.
　　Unsatiable is my Soul,
　　　　Because nothing can fill it.
　　A living Centre, wider than the Heavens.
175　　　　An infinite Abyss,
　　So made by the perfection of thy Presence,
　　　Who art an infinite *KNOWLEDGE* in ev'ry Centre;
　　　Not corporeal, but simple Life;
　　　Wonderfully sufficient in all its Powers,
180　　　　　　　⎧ Objects ⎧ Material,
　　　　　　　　⎪　　　　⎩ Immaterial.
　　　For all ⎨　　　　　⎧ Earthly,
　　　　　　　⎪ Operations ⎨ Heavenly,
　　　　　　　⎪　　　　　⎪ Temporal,
185　　　　　　⎩　　　　　⎩ Eternal;
　　　A work worthy of Immortality!
　　To create an endless unsensible Body,
　　　Is not the way to Celestial Greatness.
　　A Body endless, though endued with Sense,
190　　　Can see
　　　　　Only visible things,
　　　Taste
　　　　　The Qualities in Meat and Drink,
　　　Feel

Gross or tangible Bodies,   195
Hear
The harshness or melody of Sounds,
Smell
The things that have Odours in them.
But those things which neither Sight, nor Smell, nor Taste, 200
can discern, nor Feeling try, nor Ear apprehend,
The Cream and Crown and Flower of all,

Thoughts,	Counsels,
Kingdoms,	Ages,
Angels,	Cherubims, 205

The Souls of Men,

Wisdom,	Holiness,
Dominion,	Soveraignty,
Honour,	Glory,
Goodness,	Blessedness, 210

Heroick Love,
yea
GOD HIMSELF,
Come not within the sphere of Sense:
Are all Nullities to such a Creature.   215
Only Souls, immortal Souls, are denied nothing.
All things are penetrable to the Soul of Man.
All things open and naked to it.
The Understanding seeth

Natures,   220
Uses,
Extents,
Their { Relations,
Ends,
Properties,   225
Services,

Even all their Excellencies.
And thee my God is she able to behold,
Who dwellest in her,
In all the Spaces of thy great Immensity;   230
To accompany thy Goodness, and see whatsoever thy hand is
doing.
That in the Joy of all,

195. *Gross*: misprinted 'Cross'.

She might abide in Communion
235   With thee for ever,
Whose works are her Treasures,
Whose ways her Delights,
Whose joys thy Counsels.
She is fit indeed to be the Bride of God!
240   By this I see that thy hand hath made me
                The End of all things.
I know thou hast pleased me
In every Being which I am able to behold,
Since thou hast made me thy Image.
245   There is not a Sand
                    In the utmost *Indies*
            Which I cannot apprehend;
    Nor a Thought
                    In any part of all Eternity
250   But I am fit to know.
O the bounty of an eternal God!
        The $\left\{\begin{array}{l}\text{Swiftest Thought,}\\\text{Smallest Sand,}\end{array}\right.$
Are infinitely enriched by thy disposal of them.
255   And every thing contained in the
                Womb of Eternity,
Made a Gift transcendent to my Soul,
    Equally near to mine Understanding,
    By thine infinite Goodness, Wisdom, Power,
260   Expressed in them,
                    Fraught with Treasure
    Eternally to be seen,
                In Heaven to be enjoyed.
        Atheists,   Physicians,
265   Divines,   Philosophers,
            All agree and consent to this,
                    That
Nature never gave to any thing a power in vain.
    To what end therefore am I endued with these eternal Powers,
270   The similitude of thy $\left\{\begin{array}{l}\text{Greatness}\\\text{Infinity}\\\text{Eternity}\end{array}\right\}$ in my Soul?
        Is it not that I might live,

In the similitude of thy $\begin{cases} \text{Wisdom} \\ \text{Goodness} \\ \text{Holiness} \end{cases}$ towards all thy Creatures? 275

For to nothing that is without the reach of my Comprehension
   Can my Thoughts extend.
 To nothing without the sphere of my Knowledge,

Can I behave my self $\begin{cases} \text{Amiably,} \\ \text{Beautifully,} \\ \text{Wisely.} \end{cases}$ 280

To the intent therefore that being wise like thee,
I might be just and good to all thy Creatures,

And be holy towards them in all my $\begin{cases} \text{Ways,} \\ \text{Thoughts,} \\ \text{Affections,} \end{cases}$ 285

 Hast thou made me thus in thy great similitude;
 That being wise and holy towards thee and all things, as I
ought to be, 290
 I might evermore be gloriously blessed,
In thy diviner Likeness:
   To which I am created.
  O my God!
   In the contemplation of my Soul 295
   I see the Truth of all Religion,
   Behold all the Mysteries of Blessedness,
   Admire thy Greatness,
   Rejoyce in thy Goodness,
   Praise thy Power, 300
   Adore thy Love,
   Am ravished with thy Wisdom,
   Transported,
   Pleased with the beauty of thy Holiness,
 Who hast made me the best and greatest 305
   Like thee,

Thine $\begin{cases} \text{Image,} \\ \text{Son,} \end{cases}$ Friend,
      Bride,

  More than thy Throne,
  Thy peculiar Treasure! 310
Such wonderful Power hast thou created in me,
 That I am able to do more than my Soul durst once attempt
to imagine.
 A greater Power have I received of thee

315 Than that of creating Worlds.
    Could I create Worlds, and not enjoy them,
      It would be to no purpose.
  Could I create millions of Worlds, and enjoy them all,
    I could only enjoy created things.
320 In receiving a Power, *To enjoy all things*,
    I am made able to enjoy even thee,
      Who art infinitely greater;
      Thee in every thing,
      Every thing in thee,
325   My self in all things for evermore.
I have received a Power infinitely greater
    Than that both of Creating and Enjoying Worlds;

                  Blessed,
    Infinitely more { Profitable,
330   Divine,
                  Glorious.

  O Lord, I am contented with my Being.
    I rejoyce in thine infinite Bounty,
      And praise thy Goodness.
335   I see plainly that thy love is infinite.
And having made me such a Creature,
    I will put my Trust in Thee.
  Could I have chosen what power soever I pleased
    I would have chosen this;
340   A Power to { Please thee.
                { Enjoy thee.
  In all the Varieties of { Works and
                    { Creatures.
  Compared unto these
345   A Power
      To Divide the Sea,
      Turn Mountains into Gold,
      Command the Sun,
      Trample upon Divels,
350   Raise up the Dead,
With whatsoever all the fancy of man can imagine or desire,
          { Very feebleness
      Is { Unprofitable Vanity,
          { Foolish Childishness.

Blessed be thy Name, that thou hast given me   355
      Power to Praise thee;
A Power not only to Comprehend,
      The Magnitude,   Being,
       Nature,   Order,
      Place of Things: 360
But to love their Goodness,
Prize their value,
Delight in their Beauty,
Rejoyce in the Benefits which I receive from them.
      Which is Wholly to enjoy them.   365
  These things thou commandest my Soul to do
    That I might be Wise and Holy;
      Yet givest me Liberty
        To do what I please,
Not that thou art careless or indifferent what I chuse,   370
    But because thou wouldest make me
      Blessed and Glorious.
  An Object of Delight to thine Eternal Godhead,
And like unto thee, the Joy and Blessing of all thy Creatures:
      Who by Loving them freely   375
        As Thou dost,
    Delighting in their Beauty,
    And prizing their Goodness,
Shall my self be Beautiful in all their eyes;
    Thine *IMAGE*, O Lord;   380
To thee and them a peculiar Treasure.
The Works thou commandest thou infinitely desirest; and tellest us
  plainly,
      They are better than Wine,
      More precious than Fruits.   385
    More pleasant than Spices.
      Living Waters
      Even to thee our God,
Which satisfy the fire of thine eternal Love,
Being desired of thee, because they are necessary   390
    To our happiness.
  [My soul, O Lord, doth magnify thee;
Because out of nothing thou hast exalted thy Servant,

392–405. Enclosed in square brackets in 1699.

D d

Requiring that I should do the works which thy soul com-
395   mandeth,
          And not another;
That the glory of such Deeds might shine in me,
    And the pleasure of the goodness whereby I do them;
That being honoured in the eyes of Angels and Men,
400   I might be enlarged by them,
          Acknowledged,
          Received into their bosoms,
          Delighted in,
          Embraced,
405   Crowned.]
Thou makest thy Bride *All Glorious* within;
    And her own Works
          Shall praise her in the Gates,
    While she is chiefly beautiful
410   To thee her God,
          Shineth in thine Image,
          Reigneth in thy Throne,
          Most in thy bosom.
They all delight to look upon her.
415   And in every work thou requirest of her
          Rivers of Oyl and Wine are hidden,
      Yea living Streams of Divine Affection,
Which thou more prizest then Thousands of Rams and tens of
    thousands of Rivers of Oyl,
420   Then Worlds though Millions, of Gold and Silver.
      The Work of Love
          Is the Soveraign Delight
          Of all the Angels.
    The Cream and Crown of all Operations,
425   The Cause efficient and the end of all Things,
          The Navil
Which conveys all the Joys of Heaven and Earth,
          Into the Soul of Man.
      The Oyl ⎫ wherewith ⎧ We anoint,
430   The Gold ⎭   ⎩ We Crown,
          Thy Holy Angels,
          Thy Saints,
          Thy Son,

Our selves in them,
And thee in all.   435
A Power in this have we received O Lord,
To please thee more
And to enrich thy Kingdom with Greater
Treasure
Than if Creating Worlds   440
We presented them at thy feet,
At the feet of thy Saints,
Of every Angel.
They all like Thee
More Desire our Good Works,   445
Than Crowns and Scepters.
Which are Holy Treasures,
In communion with Thee,
For ever to be enjoyed.
By doing them our selves we are made thine Image. 450
That we should have the Glory,
Of being Crowned with the Beauty,
Of our own Works;
Is not less but more thy Glory.
Infinitely more thy Glory and Joy, Most Holy Lord! 455
How infinite is thy Thirst,
That we should perform the thing thou desirest!
O Lord!
Thou so loved'st us,
That for our perfect Glory,   460
Thou didst adventure into our hands
A Power of displeasing thee.
Which very confidence of thine ought more to oblige me,
than all the things in Heaven and Earth, faithfully to love thee.
But wo is me, I have sinned against thee.   465
I have sinned, O Lord,
And put an Object before thee
Which thou infinitely hatest.
An ugly Object,
Of infinite Deformity;   470
From which it is impossible
Thou should'st turn away thine eyes.
And hadst thou not loved me

With a greater Love
475   Than all this,
I must, like *Lucifer*,
Have sunk into the Pit
Of eternal Perdition.
But thou hast redeemed me.
480   And therefore with Hallelujahs
Do I praise thy Name.
Recounting the ancient Glories
Which thou createdst in my Soul:
And confessing,
485   That infinitely more is left unsaid.
O my God,
Sanctify me by thy Spirit.
Make me a Temple of the Holy Ghost,
A willing Person in the day of thy Power.
490 Let my Saviour's Incarnation be my Exaltation;
His Death, my Life, Liberty, and Glory;
His Love, my Strength,
And the incentive of mine;
His Resurrection, my Release;
495   His Ascension, my Triumph;
His Gospel, my Joy;
The Light of his Countenance,
(And of thine in him)
500   My $\left\{\begin{array}{l}\text{Reviving,}\\\text{Healing,}\\\text{Comforting}\end{array}\right\}$ Sun.
In the day of thy Grace, let me work for thy Glory;
Rejoyce in thy Goodness;
And according to the wideness of mine Understanding,
505   The Greatness of my Soul,
The Liberty of my Thoughts,
Walk at large
In all the Regions of $\left\{\begin{array}{l}\text{Heaven and Earth,}\\\text{Time and Eternity;}\end{array}\right.$
510   Living in thine Image
Towards all thy Creatures;
On Angels wings,
Holy Meditations.

According to the transcendent Presence of my Spirit every-
where,　　　　　　　　　　　　　　　　　　　　　　515
　　　Let me see thy Beauties,
　　　　Thy Love to me,
　　　　　To all thy Creatures.

　　　　　⎧ First Creation,
In the ⎨ Government of Ages,　　　　　　　　　　· 520
　　　　　⎩ Day of Judgment,
　　　　　　Work of Redemption,

　　　　⎧ My Conception and Nativity,
In ⎨ All my Deliverances,
　　　⎩ The Peace of my Country,　　　　　　　525
　　　　　Noah's Ark.
　　　　　With *Moses* and *David*,
　　　　Let me behold thy ways,
　　　Delight in thy Mercies,
　　　　Be praising thee.　　　　　　　　　　　530
O shew me the excellency of all thy works!
In the Eternity that is before the World began, let me behold the
beauty of thine everlasting Counsels.
And in the Eternity which appeareth when the World is ended,
let me see thy Glory.　　　　　　　　　　　　　　535

*O God of infinite Majesty, now I confess that the Knowledge I have of
thee is admirable, by that which I discover in my self: for if in a thing
so gross as is my Body, there be a Spirit so noble as is my Soul, which
giveth it Being and Life, governeth it, and in it and by it worketh such
stupendious things; how much more necessary is it that thou be in the* 540
*midst of this extended World, who art that supream Spirit, by whom we
all are, live, move, and have our being. Since therefore thou art my Being
and my Life, thou art my Soul too, and I rejoice to have thee for my God,
loving thee infinitely more than my self. O that all did know thee, and
love thee more than their Life and their own Soul, since thou art the* 545
*true Life and Soul of all: To whom be Glory, Honour, and Praise, for
evermore.* Amen.

Thanksgivings for the Beauty of his Providence

Thy Mercy, O Lord, is in the Heavens, and thy Faithfulness reacheth unto the Clouds.

Thy Righteousness is like the great Mountains, thy Judgments are a great Deep: O Lord, thou preservest Man and Beast.

5   How excellent is thy loving Kindness, O God; therefor the Children of Men put their trust under the shadow of thy Wings.

They shall abundantly be satisfied with the fatness of thy House; and thou shalt make them drink of the River of thy Pleasures.

10   For with thee is the Fountain of Life; and in thy Light shall we see Light.

O continue thy loving Kindness to them that know thee, and thy Righteousness, to the upright in heart.

Let not the foot of Pride come against me, and let not the 15 hand of the Wicked remove me.

There are the workers of Iniquity faln; they are cast down, and shall not be able to arise. *Ps. 36.*

Let us with all the Saints in the Church Triumphant;
> Sing
20   The Song of *Moses* the servant of God,
> And
> The Song of the Lamb,
> Saying,

Great and Marvelous are thy Works, Lord God Almighty; Just 25 *and true are thy Ways, thou King of Saints.*

Let their
- Beauty ravish us,
- Fatness delight us,
- Goodness enrich us,
- Wisdom please us,
30 - Abundance transport us.

Let them ever be such in our Eyes, as they are in thine;

Whose Delights have been in the habitable Parts of the Earth, among the Children of Men.

O Lord, I delight in thee,

1–17. Ps. 36$^{5-12}$.

For making my Soul so wholly Active,   35
    So prone to Imployment,
    So apt to Love,
That it can never rest, nor cease from thinking.
      I praise thee with Joy,
For making it so wide, that it can measure Ages,   40
    See thine Eternity,
And walk with thee in all thy Ways.
It must be busie: And it is happy for me
Thou hast made it a *LIFE* like thine, O God
      All Activity.   45
Its Rest is Imployment, and its Ease is Business.
    Teach me the best and fairest Business.
    Teach my Soul to walk with thee,
    By thinking Wisely
      Upon all thy Doings.   50
Let me never rust in Idleness or Sloth,
    Nor sleep in Death,
Nor delude my self with Vanity,
Nor pierce my self thorow with needless Fears or Sorrows.
We are always Desolate, while our Souls are Idle,   55
But when our Thoughts are employed far and near upon their
glorious Objects, then are we encompassed with Festivals of Joy,
Solemnities, and Sabbaths.
    Blessed be thou, O Lord,
And for ever Blessed be thy glorious Name,   60
For preparing for us, in all Ages,
    Perfect Treasures.
THE WORKS OF THY RIGHTEOUSNESS,
    Are more pleasant to Angels
Than apples of Gold in Pictures of Silver,   65
O Lord, let me be in all my Solitudes,
      Jeweller among thy Jewels,
As a   Perfumer among thy Odors,
      Servant among thy Treasures,
      Son among thy Servants,   70
    Thine Image and thine Heir,
Among all thy Works, in all Kingdoms and Nations.
    In the dead time of the Night,
    In my greatest Retirements,

75   Let all thy Works be neer unto me;
All thy Ways,   Thy Wonders,
      Thy Revelations from Heaven,
Thy *MERCIES*,   Thy *JUDGMENTS*,
      My familiar Joys.
80 Let them fill me with Company when I am most alone,
      Fill me with Delights,
            Surround me with Beauty,
            Turn my Retirements into Songs,   ·
      My Days into Sabbaths,
85   My Darkness into Day,
      Or into a Night of Joy, as in the solemn Assemblies.
      For enflaming my Soul with the Thirst of Happiness;
      For shewing me its Objects, and the manner of Enjoying
them;
90   For causing me to prefer Wisdom above hidden Treasure; and
to search for her as for Gold and Silver,
            I Bless and Praise thy Holy Name.
      The Desire satisfied, is a Tree of Life.
      Had I never thirsted, I should never have valued, nor enjoy'd,
95   *WISDOM.*
      I know by experience, that she is better than Rubies,
And all the things I can desire, are not to be
            Compared with her;
      She putteth on my head an ornament
100   Of Grace;
      A crown of Glory she giveth to me; *Prov.* 4. 9.
      Maketh me a possessor of all thy Joys;
Bringeth me to the Store-house of thine everlasting Riches;
            Seateth me in Paradice,
105   Surroundeth me with Flowers,
      Yea with all the Delights in the Garden of God.
      May Lillies compare with the Souls of Men?
Perfumes with Virtues? Gold with Affections?
            Crowns with Ages?
110   Temples, Cities, Kingdoms, are in my ways!
Coronations, Triumphs, Victories, surround my Feet!
      No ways strewed with Lillies, Pearls, and Diamonds can equal
these.

I

These sweeter far than Lillies are,
No Roses may with these compare! 115
How these excel,
No Tongue can tell!
Which he that well and truly knows,
With praise and joy he goes.
How great and happy's he, that knows his Ways, 120
To be divine and heavenly Joys!
To whom each City is more brave,
Than Walls of Pearl, and Streets which Gold doth pave:
Whose open Eyes,
Behold the Skies; 125
Who loves their Wealth and Beauty more,
Than Kings love golden Ore.

II

Who sees the heavenly antient Ways,
Of GOD the Lord, with Joy and Praise;
More than the Skies, 130
With open Eyes,
Doth prize them all; yea more than Gems
And Regal Diadems.
That more esteemeth Mountains as they are,
Than if they Gold and Silver were: 135
To whom the *SUN* more pleasure brings,
Than Crowns and Thrones, and Palaces, to Kings.
That knows his Ways,
To be the Joys,
And Way of God. These things who knows, 140
With Joy and Praise he goes.

The Souls of Men, and Holy Angels, are my delights.
How endless are thy Treasuries,
How wide thy Mansions,
How delectable my Joys! 145
Many millions of Miles from hence
The Sun doth serve me!
The Stars, many thousand Leagues beyond the Sun,
The morning Stars, and Sons of God,

150   Abundantly beyond them all.
Nor is there any Bounds of my Habitation.
The inestimable Presence of Almighty God
    Endlessly extendeth, protracting my Joys,
    And, with an Eye from Infinity,
155   Beholdeth my Soul.
The Sun of Righteousness is my perfect Joy,
Mine Understanding seeth him
        In the highest Heavens;
    In every moment I see Eternity,
160   Conceived in its Womb;
In every moment an infinity of Joys.
Thy Ways, O my God, are infinitely Delicious,
    From the beginning until now!

165 Blessed be thy Name, whose infinite $\begin{cases} \text{Wisdom,} \\ \text{Goodness,} \\ \text{Power,} \end{cases}$

    Are in every thing $\begin{cases} \text{Magnified,} \\ \text{Perfectly exalted,} \end{cases}$

        Towards all thy Creatures.
170 Thy Condescention in creating the Heavens
        And the Earth,
    Is wholly Wonderful!
Thy Bounty to *Adam*, To me in him,
    Most Great and Infinite!
175 Blessed be thy Name for the Employment thou gavest him,
        More Glorious than the World;
To see thy Goodness,
        Contemplate thy Glory,
Rejoyce in thy Love,
180   Be Ravish'd with thy Riches,
Sing thy Praises,
        Enjoy thy Works,
Delight in thy Highness,
        Possess thy Treasures,
185   And much more Blessed be thy Holy Name,
    For Restoring me by the Blood of Jesus,

To $\begin{cases} \text{Thy glorious Works,} \\ \text{Those blessed Employments.} \end{cases}$

156. Malachi 4².

It is my Joy, O Lord, to see the Perfection of thy Love towards
us in that Estate.   190

The $\begin{cases} \text{Glory of thy Laws,} \\ \text{Blessedness of thy Works,} \\ \text{Highness of thine Image,} \\ \text{Beauty of the Life, that there was to be led} \end{cases}$
                   In Communion with Thee.   195
        Those intended Joys are mine, O Lord,
In thee, my God,   In Jesus Christ,
In every Saint,   In every Angel.
But the glorious Covenant, so graciously renewed!
        O the Floods, the Seas, the Oceans,   200
        Of Honey and Butter contained in it!
So many thousand Years since, my standing Treasure.

O teach me to $\begin{cases} \text{Esteem it,} \\ \text{Reposite it in my Family;} \end{cases}$

        As that, which by its Value, is made sacred,   205
Infinitely Sacred, because infinitely Blessed.
How ought our first Fathers
        To have esteemed that Covenant!
        To have laid it up for their Childrens Children,
        As the choicest Treasure,   210
        The *Magna Charta* of Heaven and Earth,
        By which they held their Blessedness;
        The Evidence of their Nobility;
        The antient Instrument of their League with God;
        Their pledge & claim to eternal Glory;   215
        The sacred Mystery of all their Peace!
But they Apostatized and provoked thy Displeasure,
        Sixteen hundred and fifty six Years,
        Till thou did'st send a Flood that swept them away:
        Yet did'st thou give them   220
                The Rite of Sacrificing
                The Lamb of God.
        To betoken his Death,
                From the beginning of the World;
Shewedst them thy Glory; And that of Immortality   225
        By *Enochs* Translation:
        (Of which me also hast thou made the heir!)
In the midst of Judgments thou hadst mercy on *Noah*,

And saved'st us both
230   In an *ARK* by Water.
That Ark is mine,
          Thy Goodness gave it me;
By preserving my Being and Felicity in it.
It more serveth me there where it is,
235   Than if all its Materials were now in my Fold.
In that Act did'st thou reveal thy Glory,
As much as by the Creation of the World it self;
          Reveal thy Glory to me; and, by many such,
          Dispel the foggs of Ignorance and Atheism,
240   That else would have benighted,
          And drowned my Soul.
The Rainbow is a Seal,
          Of thy renewed Covenant,
          For which, to day, I praise thy Name.
245   As for the wicked
They revolted back from the Life of God,
          But the holy Sages brightly shined:
Whom thy Goodness prepared,
          To be the Light of the World,
250   *Melchisedec*, *Noah*, *Abraham* himself,
          In whom thy Goodness Blessed $\begin{cases} \text{Me thy Servant,} \\ \text{And all Nations.} \end{cases}$
Whom thy Goodness chiefly Blessed, by making a Bless-
ing.
255   When the World would have extinguished Knowledge,
          And have lost thy Covenant,
Thou heldest the Clew, and maintained'st my Lot,
          and sufferedst not all to perish for ever.
Out of the Loins of thy beloved,
260   Thy Glory form'd a Kingdom for thy self,
                Govern'd by Laws,
                Made famous by Miracles,
                Exalted by Mercys,
                Taught from Heaven.
265 In the Tabernacle of Witness, thou dwelledst among them.
Thy Servant *David*, in most Solemn Assemblies, sang
                Thy Praises.
Thy Glory appeared in *Solomon's* Temple,

But more in his Wisdom;
      And the Prosperity of thy People.   270
Thy Prophets, in their order, ministred to us.
The concealed Beauty of thy Ceremonies,
      Is wholly mine.
To me they exhibit in the best of Hieroglyphicks,
      JESUS CHRIST.   275
The Glory of their Ministery Service, and Expectation,
      For two thousand Years, is my Enjoyment.
      For my sake, and for thy Promise sake,
          Did thy goodness forbear,
      When their Sins had provoked Thee,   280
          To destroy them wholly.
      How did thy Goodness in the time of Distress,
          Watch over them for Good!
      When like a Spark in the Sea,
They were almost wholly Extinguished,   285
          In the Babilonish Waves.
How, Lord, did'st thou Work, in that Night of Darkness!
Making thy Glory, and the Glory of Love,
          More to appear:
Then was our Welfare turning upon the hinge,   290
      Our Hope gasping for a little Life,
Our Glory brought to the pits brink,
      And beyond the possibility of human remedy,
Endangered in the Extinction of that Nation.
      How then did thy Power shine!   295
In making *Nehemiah* the King's Cupbearer;
      Hester Queen;
      Mordecai a Prince;
The three Children cold in the furnace;
Daniel Lord chief President of 127 Provinces.   300
Zorobbabel and *Ezra* especial favorites;
And in sending thy people home,
          Without any Ransom,
      That the influence of thy promise
          Might surely descend;   305
And our Saviour arise, out of *Davids* Loins,
          Be born at *Bethlehem*,
          Crucified at *Jerusalem*,

According to the Prophesies,

310   That went before concerning him.

Blessed Lord, I magnifie thy holy Name,

For his Incarnation;

For the

     Joy of the Angels that sang his praises;

     Star of his Birth;

315   Wise men's Offerings that came from the East;

     Salutation of thy handmaid *Mary*;

     Ravishing Song of the blessed Virgin;

     Rapture and Inspiration of *Zacharias* thy Servant;

     Birth of *John* our Saviours forerunner.

320 O Lord,

Who would have believed, that such a worm as I, should have had such Treasures,

In thy celestial Kingdom!

In the Land of *Jury*, 3000 miles from hence

325   So great a Friend! such a Temple!

Such a Brest-plate! Glittering with Stones of endless price!

Such Ephod! Mytre! Altar! Court! Priest! and Sacrifices!

All to shew me my Lord and Saviour.

330 By the

     Shining Light of nearer Ages,

     Universal consent of many Nations,

     Most powerful Light of thy blessed Gospel,

see that remoter in the Land of *Jury*,

More clearly to shine.

The universal Good which redounded to all,

335   Is poured upon me.

The root being beautified by all its branches,

The fountain enriched, and made famous by its streams;

Their Temple, Sacrifices, Oracles, Scriptures,

Ceremonies, Monuments of Antiquity

340   Miracles, Transactions, Hopes,

Have received credit, and magnificence;

by successes.

345 By the

     Lustre, Authority and Glory,

     Conviction of Ages,

     Acknowledgment of Sages,

     Conversion of Philosophers,

Of Flourishing Cities, Empires,

Potentates, and mighty States.

All which enamel the Book of God,
And enrich it more for mine exaltation. 350
The very Trees and Fruits, and Fields, and Flowers, that did
service unto them,
Flourished for me!
And here I live,
Praising thy Name! 355
For the silencing of Oracles,
And the flight of Idolatry;
For demolishing the Temple,
When its Service ended.
For permitting the Jews { In severity to them, 360
{ In mercy to me,
To kill my Saviour.
For breaking their Covenant,
Casting them off,
Dispersing them throughly, 365
Punishing them with Destruction,
In revenge of the Murder of Jesus Christ.
Now if the Fall of them be the Riches of the World, and the
Demolishing of them, the enriching of the Gentiles, how much
more their fulness? *Rom.* 11. 12. 370
What shall the receiving of them be, but life from the dead?
Rom. 11. 15.
Restore them, O Lord!
That as we have obtained Mercy
Through their unbelief, 375
So they by our Mercy (and our Faith prevailing) may obtain
Mercy.
The death of Jesus, that universal Benefit,
Spreads from a Centre,
Through all the World, 380
And is wholly the Joy of all People.
The Patience of *Job* was once obscure,
Which is now the Publick Right
Of Mankind.
The Cross of Christ exceeding vile, 385
Yet now in my Closet, my perfect Treasure.
Pregnant Signes,

372. 15, misprinted 14.

What infinite Depths may lie concealed,
In the rude appearance of the smallest Actions.
390   A world of Joys hid in a Manger,
           For me, for every one.
       His Cross, a prospect of eternal Glory,
           Sheweth, that
       All things are treasures infinitely Diffusive;
395   Earthly Occurrences, celestial Joys.
For the Learning of the Fathers,
           I glorifie Thee;
       More for the Labors of the holy Apostles,
           My crown and my joy:
400   ⎧ Persecutions are my Glory;
           ⎪ Doctrine my Foundations;
   Their ⎨ Sweat my Dew;
           ⎪ Tears my Pearl;
           ⎩ Blood my Rubies.
405 For giving of the Holy Ghost
           Upon the day of *Pentecost*,
           I supremely praise Thee.
           O let me be filled with it!
           ⎧ I may clearly see the Powers of my Soul;
410   ⎪ As a Temple of thy Presence,
   That ⎨ I may inherit all things;
           ⎪ In the Light of my Knowledge,
           ⎩ All Ages may abide;
       And I in them, walking with thee,
415   In the Light of Glory.
   What shall I render to the Lord for all his benefits toward me?
   I will take the cup of Salvation, and call upon the Name of the
Lord. *Ps.* 116. 12, 13.
       With reverence I will learn
420   The riches of our Saviour,
           At the time of his Ascension;
       And see what a Paradise
           The Glory of his Resurrection
           Made the World.
425   Who, when he ascended up on high, led captivity captive, and
gave gifts unto men.
       And he gave some Apostles, some Prophets, some Evange-
lists, some Pastors and Teachers. *Eph.* 4. 8. and 11.

O let me see into the deeper Value of such glorious Treasures!
    Nearer to our Saviour,   430
    Greater than the Angels,
    Images of God,
    Labouring to death
        For our sakes.
  Of all the benefits   435
    Which they did to all,
  My bosom is the recipient,
    I the Heir.
How beautiful upon the mountains, are the feet of them that
bring the glad tidings of good things. *Rom.* 10   440
O blessed be thy glorious Name,
  For the Conversion of this Island
    Wherein I live:
  The Day-spring from on high,
    That visited us;   445
  The Light of the Gospel;
  The Conversion of our Kings;
  The professed Subjection
    Of our Lords and Senators,
    Our Ministers, Bishops, Pastors, Churches, Sacra- 450
ments, Liturgy, Sabbaths, Bibles, Laws Ecclesiastical, Establish-
ment of Tythes, Universities, Colledges, liberal Maintenance of
our Saviours Clergy, Christian Schools, Cathedrals and Quires,
where they sing his praises.
  That Pillars are erected in our Land   455
    To his Name;
  That his Cross is exalted to the top of Crowns;
    Seated on high;
    On more than kingly Palaces;
      His Temple in our Borders;   460
  That his Gospel is owned and fully received;
  His Kingdom established by Laws
    In our Land,

                 (a Wilderness,
Which might have been { a Golgotha,   465
                 (a very Tophet,
A blind corner of brutish Americans;

467-71. Red Indians were called Americans in the seventeenth century, but 'Negroe . . .
horrid Island' presumably refers to imported slaves—in the West Indies? Peter Carder in
Purchas's *Pilgrimes* speaks of being 'overseer of my friend's Negros and Savages'.

And I a torn desolate confessor,
Or far worse,
470   A Negroe like them,
In the horrid Island.
For all this I glorify thy Name;
Humbly confessing, and acknowledging
With Joy,
475 Thy Mercy in this to have been greater
Towards us,
Than in delivering *Israel* from the *Egyptian*
Bondage:
Earnestly beseeching thee, to forgive the Ingratitude and
480 Stupidity of thy People.
Open their Eyes; Cause every one to see,
That he is the Heir and Possessor
Of all thy Joys.
In their Peace and Prosperity,
485   Let me thy Servant inherit Peace:
And in thy Light, let me see Light.
Make them more my Treasures,

By making { Them better,
            { Me wiser,

490   Increasing both our love.
What hast thou done for me thy Servant?

In giving me { The Beauty of the World,
             { The Land in which I live,
             { The Records of all Ages,
495   { Thy self in all for evermore.

Being done for thousands, for all, O Lord,
It is more my Joy.
I bless thy Name for the Perfection of thy Goodness, so wholly
communicable to many Thousands;
500   So endlesly communicated from all Generations, Coasts, and
Regions, to every Soul.
By enriching whom, thou magnifiest me;

Because they are My { Friends,
                     { Temples,
505   { Treasures;

And I am theirs,
Delighted by my love in all their happiness.

Tho War should arise, in this will I be confident.
One thing have I desired of the Lord, that will I seek after,
that I may dwell in the house of the Lord all the days of my life, 510
to behold the beauty of the Lord, and to enquire in his Temple.
Ps. 27. 3, 4.
He hath chained Ages & Kingdoms together.
    Nor can they without us,
        Nor we without them,   515
            Be made perfect. *Heb.* 11. 40.
    The Lord is King throughout all Generations,
        Magnifying his eternal Wisdom
In making every true Christian possessor
            Of his Joys: 520
    The multitude of Possessors enrichers of Enjoyment:
    Every one the end of all his Ways.
    Me! even me!
Hath thy Glory exalted in all these things:
    I am possessor, and they my treasures,   525
I am delighted abundantly, by being possessed,
    That thou, O Lord, art supreme possessor;
And, every one of thine, possessor
           In thy Likeness;
Pleaseth me supremely, pleaseth me wholy;   530
        Furthereth my Joys,
        Addeth to them,
        Maketh them Infinite,
      Yea, infinitely Infinite,
        The very manner of Enjoying.   535
    O Lord!
Let all the Greatness whereby thou advancest thy Servant,
Make me not more proud, but more humble:
        Obedient to the King,
        Diligent in my Calling,   540
        Subservient to my Spiritual Fathers, Pastors and Teachers;
        Meek to mine Inferiours,
More   Humble to all;
        Compassionate on the ignorant;
        Sensible of my Sins;   545
        Lowly to the poor,
        Charitable to the needy;

550 More {
Loving to mine Enemies;
Tender to the erroneous,
    Thirsting their return;
Industrious in serving thee,
    In calling them,
    In saving all.

Teach me by Wisdom to see the Excellency of all thy Doings;
555 And by goodness, to rejoyce in all thy mercys.

To delight in the Praises which they offer unto thee,
And in the Blessings which descend upon all thy Creatures.

O make my life here, upon Earth, beautiful, O Lord! that my
Soul may be pleasing to thy Saints and Angels.

560   To be well pleasing to whom, is an unspeakable delight; because
thy love is infinite to them.

APPENDIX

SOME of the poems in *Christian Ethicks* gain from being read in their context, and some brief prose extracts are given here. (There is some duplication of page numbers in the volume, but the numbers given are all from the signature Z.) The poem 'For Man to Act . . .' (p. 140) is introduced thus:

> Take it in Verse made long ago upon this occasion.

After it Traherne continues:

The beatific Vision is so sweet and strong a Light, that it is impossible for any thing that Loves it self, (and sees the face of God) to turn away to any vanity from so Divine and Strong a Blessedness. To Love God in the clear and perfect Light is a cheap and Easie Thing: The Love that is shewed in a more weak Estate to an absent Object, is more remiss perhaps, and Black in appearance; but far Deeper, if in the Lovers Weakness, and its Objects absence; it be Faithful to the Death; constantly Solicitous, and careful to please, Laborious and Industrious, Wakeful and Circumspect, even and immutable, and freely springing from its own Desire, not out of bare pleasure; but humble Obedience to the Laws of its Benefactor. All the Courage which it shews in such occasions is more full of Mystery and Divinity then is imaginable; far more Moving and full of Vertue, while it struggles with Impediment, Disadvantages, and Difficulties, then if without any such Occasion of shewing its Vertue, it did smoothly and Peaceably proceed in the Highest Rapture. (pp. 345–6.)

In the same chapter, two pages further on:

When the Angels fell, the Devil was let loose upon man, for the increase of his Honour and Dominion: Yet like a Dog in his Chain so far, and no further. He had but one Way, and that was to perswade our first Parents to do what was forbidden: Perswade he might, and try his Skill to deceive, but could not compell, nor otherwise afflict, or hurt him in the least. He had not power so much as to diminish the least Hair of his Head: yet so Gracious was Almighty God, that upon this Trial of his Prudence and Courage, the Exercise of these Vertues had been infinitely pleasing to his Eternal Love because he infinitely delighted in the Welfare and Preservation of what was so precious to himself, as a Soul is, that is infinitely Beloved. In that Complacency *Adam* had found little less then infinite Glory. It did not become the tenderness of GODS Love to expose him to any Severer Trial.

> For there are certain Periods and fit Bounds,
> Which he that passeth, all his Work confounds.

But when *Adam* fell, and brought more hazards and difficulties on himself (,) God might justly leave him to them, for his greater Trial and more perfect Glory.

Now we are more blind and Weak by Nature, yet infinitely Beloved and more Precious: For the price of the Blood of the Eternal Son of GOD is laid upon the Soul as an Addition to its interior Value. (pp. 348–50.)

From chapter xxii, 'Of Temperance in Art':

In matters of Art, the force of *Temperance* is undeniable. It relateth not only to our Meats and Drinks, but to all our Behaviours, Passions, and Desires.

All Musick, Sawces, Feasts, Delights and Pleasures,
Games, Dancing, Arts consist in govern'd Measures;
Much more do Words, and Passions of the Mind
In Temperance their sacred Beauty find.

A Musician might rash his finger over all his strings in a moment, but *Melody* is an effect of *Judgment* and *Order*: it springs from a variety of *Notes* to which Skill giveth *Time* and *Place* in their Union. A Painter may daub his Table† all over in an instant, but a Picture is made by a regulated Hand, and by variety of Colours. A Cook may put a Tun† of Sugar, or Pepper, or Salt in his Dishes: but Delicates are made by mixture and Proportion. There is a Temperance also in the Gesture of the Body, the Air of the face, the carriage of the Eye, the Smile, the Motion of the Feet and Hands, and by the Harmony of these is the best Beauty in the World either much commended, or disgraced. (pp. 326–7.)

After the poem 'Were all the world . . .' from chapter xxv, 'Of Meekness', Traherne continues:

No man but He that came down from Heaven, and gave his Apostles power to handle Vipers, and drink any deadly thing without harm, was able to reveal the way of Peace and Felicity to Sinners. He, and only he that made them able to trample Satan under feet, and taught them how to vanquish all the Powers of darkness, was worthy to make known this glorious mystery of Patience and Meekness, by which in despite of all the Corruptions and Violences in the World, the holy Soul of a quiet Man is armed and prepared for all Assaults, and so invironed with its own repose, that in the midst of provocations it is undisturbed, and dwells as it were in a Sanctuary of Peace within it self, in a Paradice of Bliss, while it is surrounded with the howlings of a terrible Wilderness. Nothing else can make us live happily in this World, for among so many Causes of Anger and Distaste, no man can live well, but he that carries about him perpetual *Antidotes* and *Victories*.

There are two things absolutely necessary to Felicity, outward *Security*, and inward *Contentment*. Meekness is as it were the *Bulwark* of *Security*, which though it be as soft as *Wool*, is able with more success to repel the violence of a Cannon-Bullet, than the rough temper of a *Stone-Wall*. *Contentment* springs from the satisfaction of Desire in the sight and fruition of all Treasures and Glories: And as the Sun is surrounded with its own Light, the felicity of the Enjoyment becomes its own fortress and security. For he that is throughly Happy, has so much work to do in Contemplation and Thanksgiving, that he cannot have while to be concerned with other men's disorders, he loves his Employment too well to be disturbed, and will not allow himself the thoughts of Revenge or Anger. (pp. 383–5.)

Later in the chapter he writes:

To do good to an innocent Person is Humane, but to be kind and bountiful to a man, after he has been injurious, is Divine. . . . The very nature of the Work encourageth us to its exercise, because it is GOD-like, and truly Blessed. But there are many other Considerations moving us unto it.

The poem 'Mankind is sick . . .' follows, and Traherne continues:

When we understand the perfection of the Love of GOD, the excellency of immortal Souls, the prize and value of our Saviours Blood, the misery of Sin, and the malady of distempered Nature, the danger of Hell, and the Joyes of which our sorest Enemies are capable, the Obligations that lie on our selves, and the peace and blessedness of so sweet a Duty. Compassion it self will melt us into Meekness, and the wisdom of knowing these great things will make it as natural to us as Enjoyment itself, as sweet and easie, as it is to live and breath(e). It will seem the harshest and most unnatural thing in the World to forbear so fair, so just, so reasonable, so divine a Duty. (p. 398.)

GLOSSARY OF UNFAMILIAR WORDS
AND MEANINGS

Abridgment (60). Epitome.
Abus'd (116). Deceived.
Adaequate (246). Equal.
Admiration (172 etc.). Wonder. (*so*
Admirable. To be wondered at.)
Annihilate (130). Consider valueless.
Antedate (140). Anticipate.
Antepast (12). Foretaste.

Barely (367). Merely.
Brave (65 etc.). Fine.

Case (16). Outer covering.
Complacency (71 etc.). Delight.
Concoct (125). Mature by heat.
Conforming (28). Shaping.
Contingents (14). Inessential things.
Conversation (387). Way of life.
Creek (96). Out-of-the-way corner.
Cross (114). Contrary.

Deordination (328). Disorder.
Derive (3, 125). Channel off.
Devis'd (8, 179). Bequeathed, con-
trived.

End (52 etc.). Purpose, final cause.
Exerted (30). Thrust forth.
Extensions (70). Expanses.

Fatal (368). Destined.
Formal (114). Precise. ('He is precisely
a hypocrite'.)
Fountain (16 etc.). Source.

Ideas (45). Forms or patterns.
Illimitedness (365). Freedom from
being confined.
Illustrate (85). Illumine.
Impertinent (339 etc.). Irrelevant.

Inconvenient (233). Inappropriate.
Ingenuity (380). Nobility.
Intending true (116). With a true
meaning.

Miscarriage (322, 329). Misbehaviour.

Objected (370). Projected.
Orient (65, 264). Red ('like the dawn'),
shining.

Parile (68). Equal.
Penicill (369). Paintbrush.
Precipice (389). Fall.
Presently (154). Immediately.
Preternatural (268). Unnatural.
Prevent (24 etc.). Go before.
Price (82). Value.
Proprieties (8 etc.). Properties, pos-
sessions.

Recollect (18). Rearrange.
Remit (380). Forgo, dispense with.
Resentments (205 etc.). Feelings.

Suborn'd (383). Equipped, adorned.
Seared (387). Dried up, incapable of
feeling.
Shops (94 etc.). Workshops.

Table (369, 420). Canvas.
Transeunt (29). Passing outward, opp.
to immanent.
Tun (420). Cask.

Virtualy (20, 246). In essentials.
Visiv (77, 121). Visible.
Voluble (28, 68). Protean.
Volubility (377). Versatility.

INDEX OF FIRST LINES OF POEMS

(including rhymed passages in the *Thanksgivings*)